PRACTICAL ADVIC

NICEIC

EC

Representing the best
engineering and buildi

CW01647575

Inspection, Testing and Certification

including Periodic Reporting

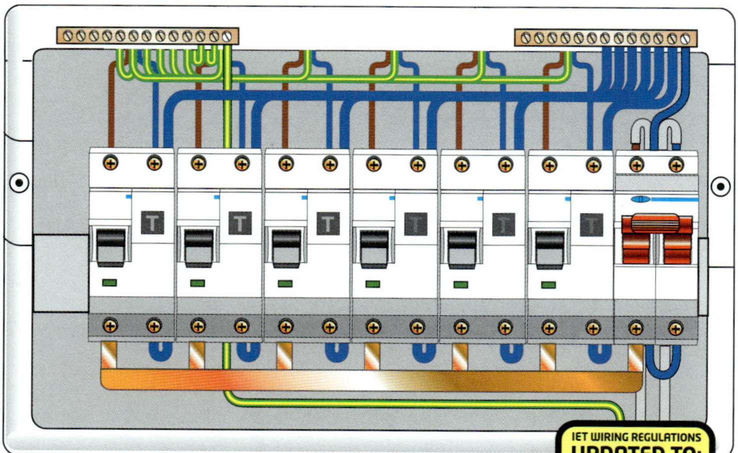

7th Edition

IET WIRING REGULATIONS
UPDATED TO:
17TH EDITION
BS 7671:2008
Amd 3: 2015

Certsure

Certsure LLP is a limited liability partnership between the Electrical Safety First and the Electrical Contractors' Association (ECA) registered in England and Wales. Its brands include NICEIC the UK's leading voluntary regulatory body for the electrical contracting industry, which has been assessing the electrical competence of electricians for over fifty years and currently maintains a roll of over 26,000 registered contractors. It also includes ELECSA, who provide inspection, assessment and certification services to contractors working with electrical and renewable technology installations in private dwellings.

Certsure products are delivered through the NICEIC and ELECSA brands. The products include, amongst others:

- The NICEIC Approved Contractor Scheme, a scheme for electrical contractors undertaking design, installation, commissioning and maintenance of electrical installations to BS 7671.
- The ELECSA and NICEIC Part P Domestic Installer Schemes, which register installers to Full Scope or Defined Competence for domestic electrical installation work in accordance with Part P of the Building Regulations in England and Wales.
- The Microgeneration Certification Scheme (MCS), developed to assess businesses installing microgeneration technology and is designed to protect the consumer.
- The Green Deal Scheme, for energy saving improvements to dwellings and other buildings.

Electrical Safety First

Electrical Safety First (formerly the Electrical Safety Council) is an independent charity committed to reducing deaths and injuries through electrical accidents at home and at work.

Electrical Safety First is supported by all sectors of the electrical industry, approvals and research bodies, consumer interest organisations, the electricity distribution industry, professional institutes and institutions, regulatory bodies, trade and industry associations and federations, trade unions and local and central government.

The Electrical Contractors' Association

The Electrical Contractors' Association (ECA) is the leading trade association for contractors involved in electrical engineering projects in England, Northern Ireland and Wales.

Published by:

Certsure LLP, Warwick House, Houghton Hall Park, Houghton Regis, Dunstable, Bedfordshire LU5 5ZX

Tel: 0870 013 0458 Fax: 01582 556024 Website: www.certsure.com

ISBN: 978-1-906091-59-0 EAN: 9781906091590 Sap code: 5598

Contents

Chapter 1

Chapter 2

Contents

Chapter 2 Continued

Chapter 3

THE DOMESTIC ELECTRICAL INSTALLATION CERTIFICATE

Contents

Chapter 3 Continued

Chapter 4

THE MINOR ELECTRICAL INSTALLATION WORKS CERTIFICATE

Chapter 5

THE ELECTRICAL INSTALLATION CONDITION REPORT

Contents

Chapter 5 Continued

Chapter 6

THE SCHEDULE OF CIRCUIT DETAILS AND THE SCHEDULE OF TEST RESULTS FOR NEW INSTALLATION WORK AND CONDITION REPORTING

Contents

Chapter 7

Contents

Chapter 7 Continued

Contents

Chapter 7 Continued

Chapter 8

Contents

Chapter 9

This book, the NICEIC and ELECSA Inspection, Testing and Certification book aligns with the requirements of BS 7671: 2008 (as amended), Requirements for Electrical Installations. The regulations listed in BS 7671 represent the principal legal requirements from the statutory regulations which include the Electricity Safety, Quality and Continuity Regulations 2002 as amended. Refer to item (i) of Appendix 2 of BS 7671: 2008 (as amended), Statutory Regulations and Associated Memoranda.

This seventh edition of the NICEIC and ELECSA book on inspection, testing, certification and reporting has been fully revised. It takes into account, amongst other things, the changes introduced by Amendment No. 3, which comes into effect on the 1st July 2015.

January 2015

Chapter

1

Introduction

AIMS AND OBJECTIVES

SCOPE

ARRANGEMENT OF THE BOOK

THE PURPOSE OF INSPECTION, TESTING AND CERTIFICATION OR REPORTING

NICEIC AND ELECSA CERTIFICATES AND REPORTS

COMPUTER-ASSISTED PREPARATION OF CERTIFICATES AND REPORTS

ASSESSMENT OF INSPECTION AND TEST RESULTS

LEGAL ASPECTS

THE INSPECTOR

SAFE WORKING PROCEDURE

TEST EQUIPMENT

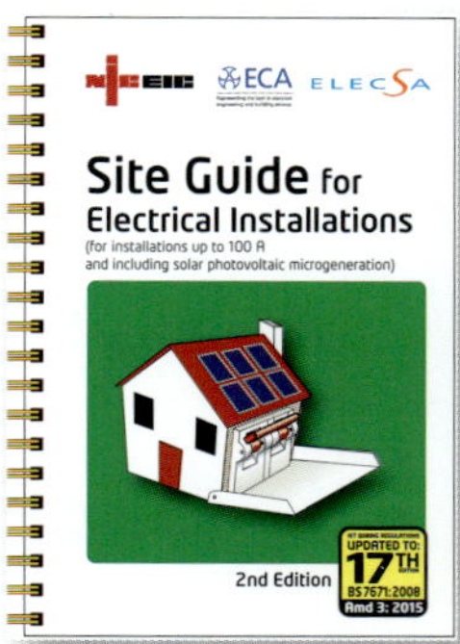

NICEIC and ELECSA Site Guide for Electrical Installations (including solar photovoltaic microgeneration)
This contains detailed advice and guidance relating to the application of the requirements of *BS 7671: 2008 Amendment 3: 2015.*

Chapter 1

1 INTRODUCTION

AIMS AND OBJECTIVES

Even the most experienced electrical engineers and electricians can be expected to make the occasional mistake when carrying out electrical installation work. This is one of the main reasons why every new electrical installation, and every alteration and addition to an existing installation, must be thoroughly inspected and tested, and any defects or omissions found made good, before the installation, or the alteration or addition, is put into service. The other key reason for inspection and testing is to provide a record of the condition of a new installation when it is first put into service, or when an altered or extended installation is restored to service.

All electrical equipment deteriorates with age, as well as with wear and tear from use. Every electrical installation therefore needs to be inspected and tested at appropriate intervals during its lifetime to establish that its condition is such that, subject to the completion of any necessary remedial work, the installation is safe to remain in service at least until the next inspection is due.

Correctly compiled Electrical Installation Certificates, Domestic Electrical Installation Certificates, Minor Electrical Installation Works Certificates and Electrical Installation Condition Reports provide the persons responsible for the safety of electrical installations (including contractors, owners and users) with an important record of the condition of those installations at the time they were inspected and tested. Such certificates and reports also provide an essential basis for subsequent inspection and testing, without which a degree of costly exploratory work might be necessary on each occasion. In the event of injury or fire alleged to have been caused by an electrical installation, certificates and reports will provide documentary evidence to help demonstrate that, in the opinion of skilled persons, competent in such work, the installation had been installed and subsequently maintained to a satisfactory standard of safety.

Every electrical contractor should employ at least one experienced person who has responsibility for inspecting and testing electrical installation work in accordance with the requirements of the national standard for electrical safety, *BS 7671: 2008 (as amended) Requirements for Electrical Installations* (otherwise known as the *IET Wiring Regulations Seventeenth Edition*). This includes the preparation, to a satisfactory standard, of the forms of certification and reporting associated with inspection and testing, in order to accurately record the results for the benefit of both the contractor and the users.

The aim of this book is to promote good practice by providing Approved Contractors, Registered Domestic Installers and others with practical advice and guidance which answers many of the questions commonly arising during the inspection and testing of electrical installation work, or during the preparation of the associated certificates and reports.

This seventh edition of the book updates the guidance given and takes into account changes to the regulatory requirements arising from the publication of Amendment 3 to *BS 7671: 2008*.

BS 7671: 2008, incorporating Amendment No. 3, 2015
Requirements for Electrical Installations

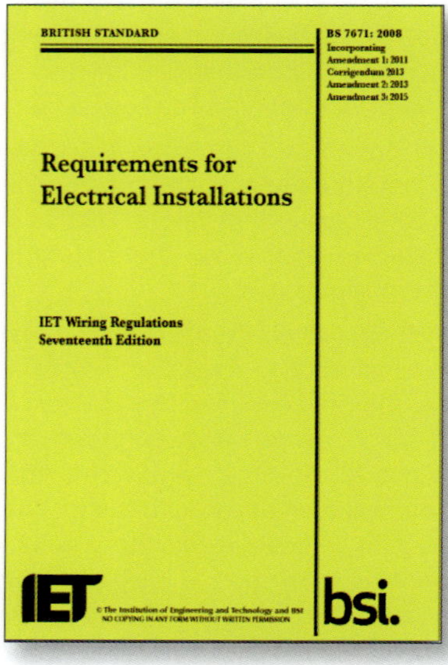

The purpose of inspecting and testing electrical installation work is to check whether it:

- meets the requirements of *BS 7671* and any other applicable standards
- is properly constructed
- only incorporates equipment which has been correctly selected for its intended purpose.

It is in the best interests of both the contractor and the user that inspection, testing, certification and reporting is carried out correctly.

Chapter 1

SCOPE

This book is intended to complement Part 6 of *BS 7671* and covers the general requirements relating to the inspection and testing of electrical installations forming part of TN-C-S, TN-S and TT systems. It does not cover the particular requirements relating to TN-C and IT systems, which are not common in the UK.

The book does not cover the particular requirements relating to the inspection, testing and certification of specialised electrical installations such as fire alarm and emergency lighting systems, or installations in hazardous areas. Nor does it cover in detail the particular requirements relating to non-conducting locations, and earth-free equipotential zones.

The book is not intended to instruct untrained and inexperienced persons to undertake the inspection and testing of electrical installations. It assumes that all persons proposing to undertake such work have already acquired the necessary knowledge, understanding and skill, and are properly equipped to undertake such work without putting themselves and others at risk.

Persons who consider that they are not fully skilled (electrically) to undertake the inspection and testing of electrical installations without direct supervision should, as a first step, complete an appropriate course and assessment provided by a reputable training organisation.

Extracts from *Rules and Regulations for the Prevention of Fire Risks Arising from Electric Lighting* published by the Society of Telegraph Engineers and of Electricians, 11 May, 1882.

"The difficulties that beset the electrical engineer are chiefly internal and invisible, and they can only be guarded against by 'testing,' or probing with electric currents." (Introduction)

" .... It is an operation, skill in which is easily acquired and applied. The escape of electricity cannot be detected by the sense of smell, as can gas, but it can be detected by apparatus far more certain and delicate. Leakage not only means waste, but in the presence of moisture it means destruction of the conductor and its insulating covering, by electric action." (Note to Rule 17)

Inspection, Testing, Certification and Reporting

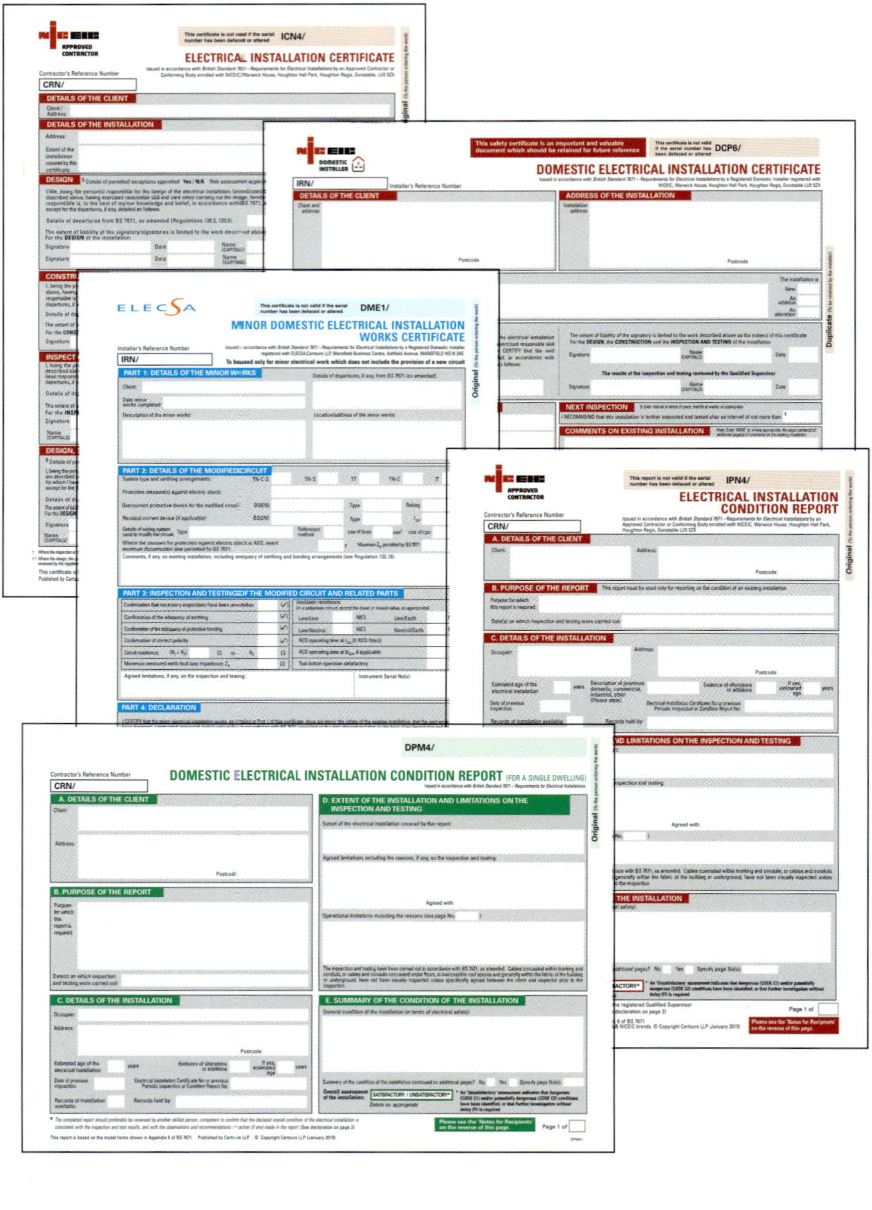

ARRANGEMENT OF THE BOOK

This book uses as its main theme the preparation of NICEIC, ELECSA and the related uncontrolled (green) versions of the principal forms of certification and reporting used in the electrical industry. All the relevant details and declarations relating to the safety of an electrical installation are intended to be recorded on these forms, which consist of:

- The **Electrical Installation Certificate** - intended for new installation work, including alterations and additions to existing installations.
- The **Domestic Electrical Installation Certificate** - intended for new installation work, including alterations and additions to existing installations, in a single dwelling (house or individual flat).
- The **Minor Electrical Installation Works Certificate** - intended for minor installation work that does not include the provision of a new circuit.
- The **Electrical Installation Condition Report** - intended for reporting on the condition of an existing installation.
- The **Domestic Electrical Installation Condition Report** - intended for reporting on the condition of an existing installation in a single dwelling (house or individual flat).

The particular versions of the forms on which this book is based are those published by NICEIC for use by Approved Contractors and Registered Domestic Installers and those published by ELECSA for Registered Domestic Installers.

However, the guidance is equally applicable to other forms of certification and reporting based on the model forms given in *BS 7671*, especially the green versions for use by non-approved contractors. (See page 11).

Some of the inspection and testing procedures required for periodic inspection reporting are common to those required to verify new installation work. To avoid duplication, such procedures are covered in the book only once, the reader being referred to another chapter where appropriate.

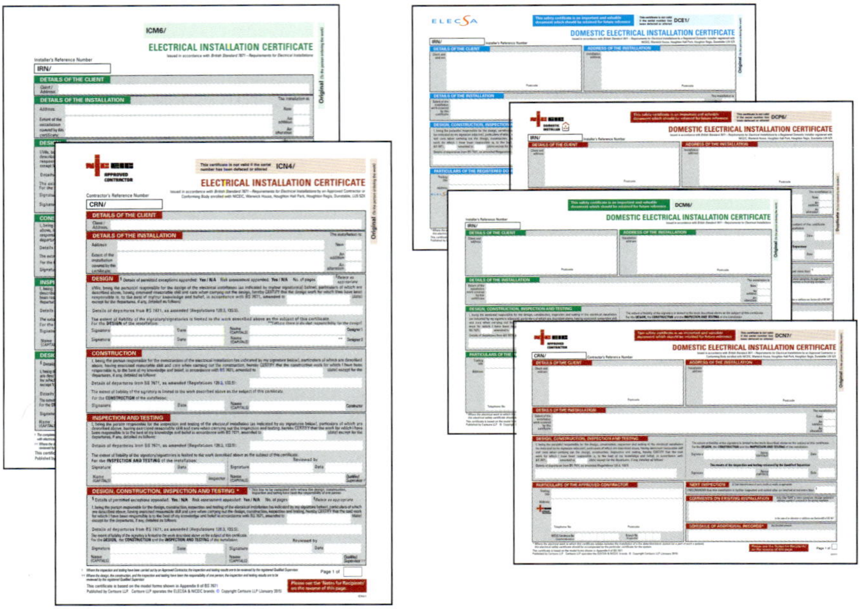
ICM6/
ELECTRICAL INSTALLATION CERTIFICATE

ICN4/
ELECTRICAL INSTALLATION CERTIFICATE

DCE1/
DOMESTIC ELECTRICAL INSTALLATION CERTIFICATE

DCP6/
DOMESTIC ELECTRICAL INSTALLATION CERTIFICATE

DCM6/
DOMESTIC ELECTRICAL INSTALLATION CERTIFICATE

DCN7/
DOMESTIC ELECTRICAL INSTALLATION CERTIFICATE

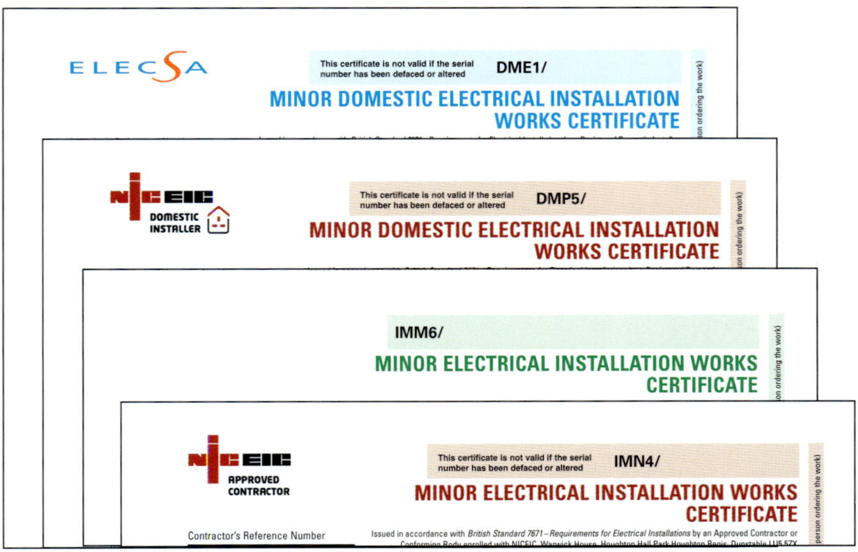
This certificate is not valid if the serial number has been defaced or altered DME1/
MINOR DOMESTIC ELECTRICAL INSTALLATION WORKS CERTIFICATE

DOMESTIC INSTALLER
This certificate is not valid if the serial number has been defaced or altered DMP5/
MINOR DOMESTIC ELECTRICAL INSTALLATION WORKS CERTIFICATE

IMM6/
MINOR ELECTRICAL INSTALLATION WORKS CERTIFICATE

APPROVED CONTRACTOR
This certificate is not valid if the serial number has been defaced or altered IMN4/
MINOR ELECTRICAL INSTALLATION WORKS CERTIFICATE
Contractor's Reference Number
Issued in accordance with *British Standard 7671 – Requirements for Electrical Installations* by an Approved Contractor or

THE PURPOSE OF INSPECTION, TESTING AND CERTIFICATION OR REPORTING

The Wiring Regulations date back to 1882. The first edition, called the *Rules and Regulations for the Prevention of Fire Risks Arising from Electric Lighting*, was published by the Society of Telegraph Engineers and of Electricians, the predecessor of the current Institution of Engineering and Technology (IET). The importance of testing was recognised even in the earliest days, as can be seen from the extracts shown on page 5.

The sentiments expressed in those early rules and regulations are as significant today as they were in 1882.

The fundamental reason for inspecting and testing an electrical installation is to determine whether new installation work is safe to be put into service, or whether an existing installation is safe to remain in service until the next inspection is due.

If it is verified that new installation work fully complies with the current requirements of *BS 7671*, it will have been correctly designed and constructed, all equipment will be suitable for its intended purpose and, consequently, the installation will be safe to be put into service. Verification includes inspection and testing during construction and on completion, and comparison of the results with the requirements of *BS 7671* and with any particular electrical safety requirements detailed in the design information. The process of verification is intended to ensure that the electrical installation is safe to put into service, and that it is likely to remain in such a condition at least until the first periodic inspection is due.

Confirmation that a new installation is safe for use is provided by the issue of a correctly compiled Electrical Installation Certificate or Domestic Electrical Installation Certificate to the person who ordered the work. For an alteration or addition to a circuit and not extending to the provision of a new circuit, a Minor Electrical Installation Works Certificate may be used instead of an Electrical Installation Certificate or a Domestic Electrical Installation Certificate. Any defects or omissions found during the process of verification must be corrected (and inspection and tests repeated as necessary) before the certificate is issued.

Having been certificated and put into service, all electrical installations need to be inspected and tested at appropriate intervals throughout their lifetime. On each occasion, details of the condition of the installation should be recorded in an Electrical Installation Condition Report for the benefit of the person ordering the inspection, and of the persons subsequently involved in remedial or alteration work, or further inspections.

Certificates and reports provide an important and valuable record of the condition of an electrical installation at the time of the inspecting and testing, together with details of any extension or alteration work which may have been carried out since the installation was first put into service.

NICEIC and ELECSA certificates and reports used for inspection and testing

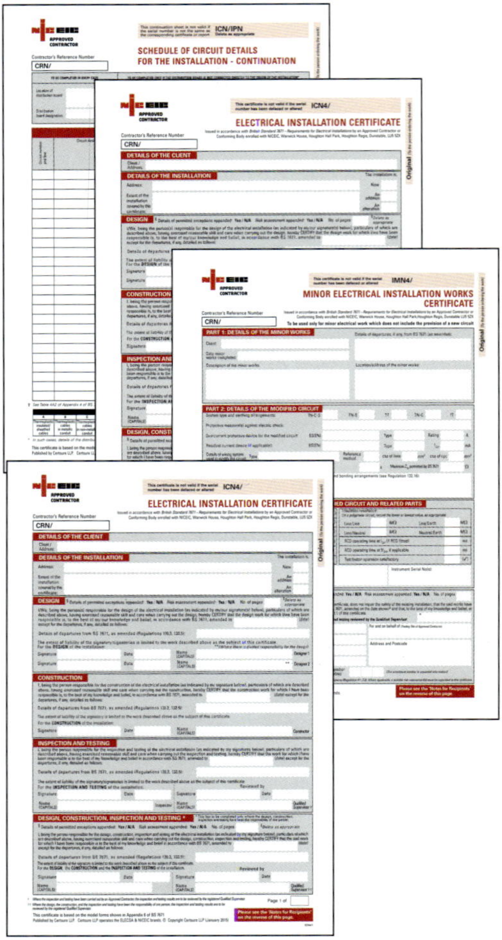

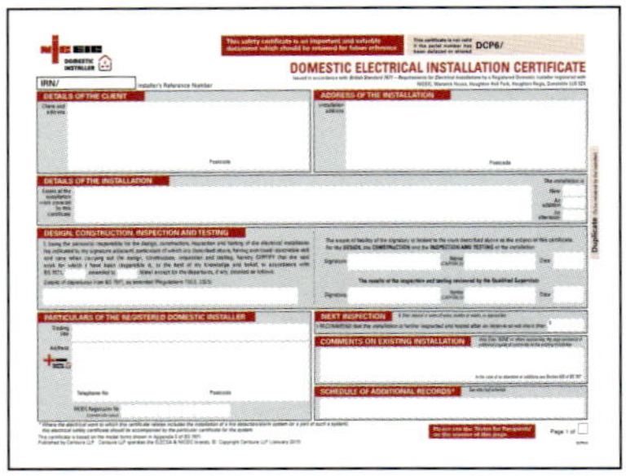

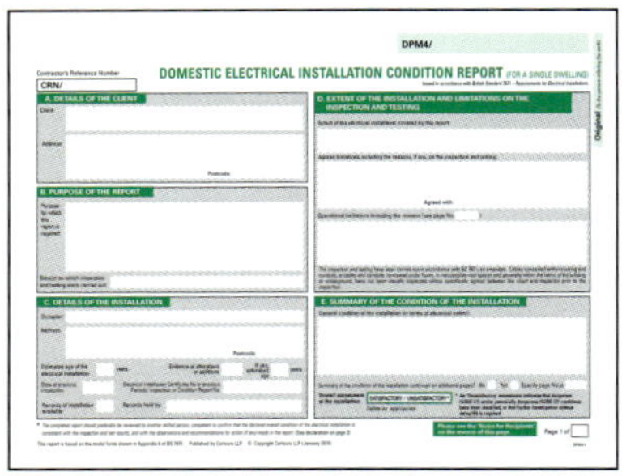

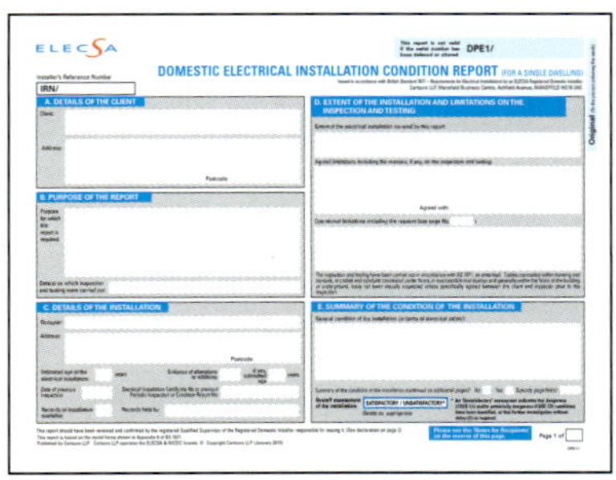

NICEIC AND ELECSA CERTIFICATES AND REPORTS

NICEIC Red certificates and report forms for use by NICEIC Approved Contractors and Registered Domestic Installers and Blue certificates and report forms for use by ELECSA Registered Domestic Installers are accountable documents.

Unused copies should be kept secure by the Qualified Supervisor and records of each certificate or report issued should be made on the record sheet provided. Unused sets of obsolete forms must be destroyed to prevent their misuse.

Such certificates and report forms must not be used for electrical installations in potentially explosive atmospheres (hazardous areas) unless the registered or enrolled contractor holds an appropriate extension to enrolment for such work.

A unique serial number (including prefix) is printed on the original and duplicate of each certificate and report form published for use by contractors enrolled or registered with NICEIC or ELECSA. The number allows the origin of the certificate or report to be traced by the respective registration body in the event of a query as to its authenticity.

For this reason, only the organisation supplied with a certificate or report from NICEIC or ELECSA is authorised to issue the form. If the serial number has been erased or altered in any way, the certificate or report is deemed invalid.

NICEIC and ELECSA strongly prefer their registered contractors to issue certificates and report forms supplied by their registration body as this provides a measure of safety assurance and confidence to the recipients.

- **NICEIC Approved Contractor Scheme**

  RED (badged) certificates and reports are available for use by Approved Contractors

- **NICEIC Domestic Installer Scheme**

  RED (badged) certificates are available for use by Registered Domestic Installers

- **ELECSA Domestic Installer Scheme**

  BLUE (badged) certificates and reports are available for use by Registered Domestic Installers

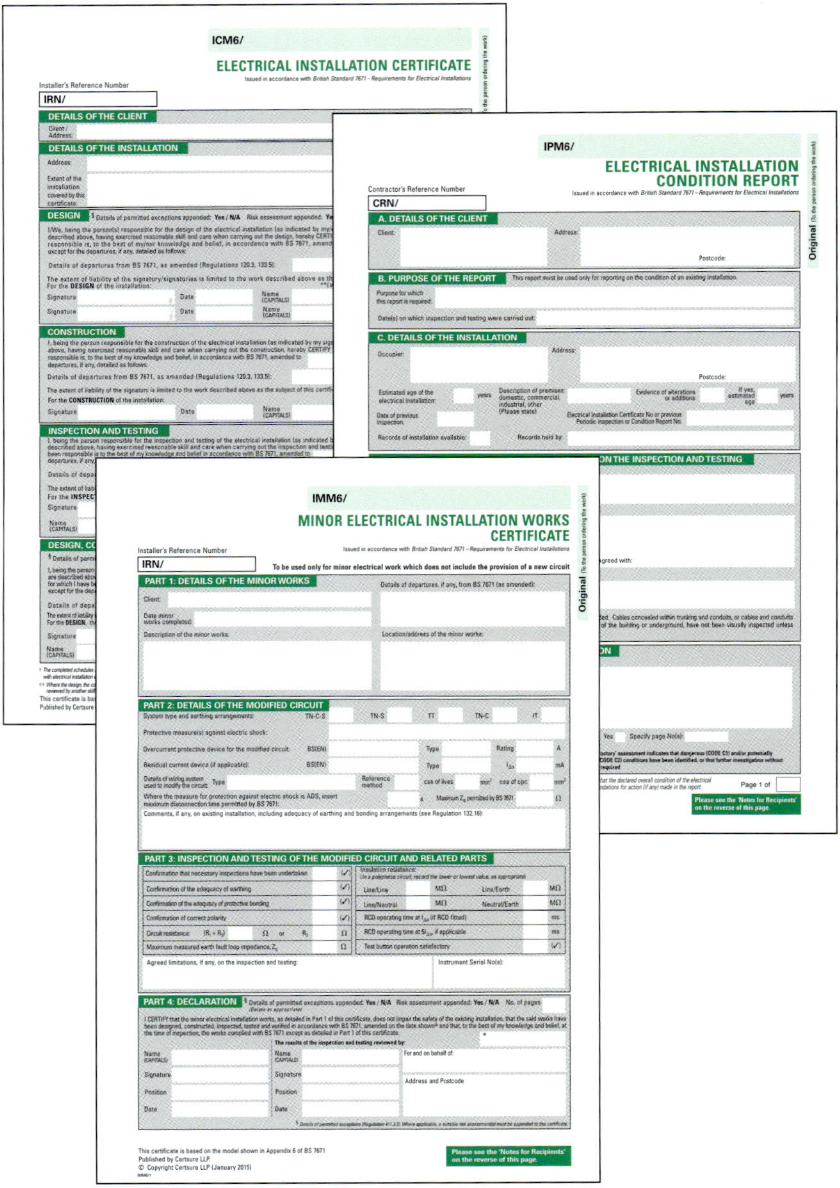
ICM6/

ELECTRICAL INSTALLATION CERTIFICATE

Issued in accordance with British Standard 7671 – Requirements for Electrical Installations

Installer's Reference Number IRN/

DETAILS OF THE CLIENT

DETAILS OF THE INSTALLATION

DESIGN

CONSTRUCTION

INSPECTION AND TESTING

IPM6/

ELECTRICAL INSTALLATION CONDITION REPORT

Issued in accordance with British Standard 7671 – Requirements for Electrical Installations

Contractor's Reference Number CRN/

Original (To the person ordering the work)

A. DETAILS OF THE CLIENT

Client: Address: Postcode:

B. PURPOSE OF THE REPORT This report must be used only for reporting on the condition of an existing installation.

Purpose for which this report is required:

Date(s) on which inspection and testing were carried out:

C. DETAILS OF THE INSTALLATION

Occupier: Address: Postcode:

Estimated age of the electrical installation: years Description of premises: domestic, commercial, industrial, other (Please state) Evidence of alterations or additions If yes, estimated age years

Date of previous inspection: Electrical Installation Certificate No or previous Periodic Inspection or Condition Report No:

Records of installation available: Records held by:

Page 1 of

Please see the 'Notes for Recipients' on the reverse of this page.

IMM6/

MINOR ELECTRICAL INSTALLATION WORKS CERTIFICATE

Issued in accordance with British Standard 7671 – Requirements for Electrical Installations

Installer's Reference Number IRN/

To be used only for minor electrical work which does not include the provision of a new circuit

Original (To the person ordering the work)

PART 1: DETAILS OF THE MINOR WORKS

Client: Date minor works completed: Description of the minor works:

Details of departures, if any, from BS 7671 (as amended): Location/address of the minor works:

PART 2: DETAILS OF THE MODIFIED CIRCUIT

System type and earthing arrangements: TN-C-S TN-S TT TN-C IT

Protective measure(s) against electric shock:

Overcurrent protective device for the modified circuit: BS(EN) Type Rating A

Residual current device (if applicable): BS(EN) Type $I_{\Delta n}$ mA

Details of wiring system used to modify the circuit: Type Reference method csa of lives mm² csa of cpc mm²

Where the measure for protection against electric shock is ADS, insert maximum disconnection time permitted by BS 7671: s Maximum Z_s permitted by BS 7671 Ω

Comments, if any, on existing installation, including adequacy of earthing and bonding arrangements (see Regulation 132.16):

PART 3: INSPECTION AND TESTING OF THE MODIFIED CIRCUIT AND RELATED PARTS

Confirmation that necessary inspections have been undertaken	(✓)	Insulation resistance: (in a polyphase circuit, record the lower or lowest value, as appropriate)	
Confirmation of the adequacy of earthing	(✓)	Line/Line MΩ Line/Earth	MΩ
Confirmation of the adequacy of protective bonding	(✓)	Line/Neutral MΩ Neutral/Earth	MΩ
Confirmation of correct polarity	(✓)	RCD operating time at $I_{\Delta n}$ (if RCD fitted)	ms
Circuit resistance: $(R_1 + R_2)$ Ω or R_2	Ω	RCD operating time at $5I_{\Delta n}$ if applicable	ms
Maximum measured earth fault loop impedance, Z_s	Ω	Test button operation satisfactory	(✓)

Agreed limitations, if any, on the inspection and testing: Instrument Serial No(s):

PART 4: DECLARATION § Details of permitted exceptions appended: Yes / N/A Risk assessment appended: Yes / N/A No. of pages (Delete as appropriate)

I CERTIFY that the minor electrical installation works, as detailed in Part 1 of this certificate, does not impair the safety of the existing installation, that the said works have been designed, constructed, inspected, tested and verified in accordance with BS 7671, amended on the date shown* and that, to the best of my knowledge and belief, at the time of inspection, the works complied with BS 7671 except as detailed in Part 1 of this certificate.

The results of the inspection and testing reviewed by:

Name (CAPITALS) Signature Position Date

Name (CAPITALS) Signature Position Date

For and on behalf of: Address and Postcode

This certificate is based on the model shown in Appendix 6 of BS 7671

Published by Certsure LLP

© Copyright Certsure LLP (January 2015)

Please see the 'Notes for Recipients' on the reverse of this page.

For contractors that are not authorised to issue NICEIC or ELECSA certificates and reports similar green forms conforming to the national standard are available for use.

- **GREEN (unbadged) certificates and reports**

  Uncontrolled versions of the four main NICEIC and ELECSA certificates and reports, coloured green and not serially-numbered, are available for use by electrical contractors not enrolled or registered with NICEIC or ELECSA, and are particularly useful to those preparing for enrolment. These green coloured certificates have no serial numbers and are not covered by the 'Platinum Promise'.

  The uncontrolled (green) versions are also intended for use by contractors undertaking work outside the scope of their enrolment.

COMPUTER-ASSISTED PREPARATION OF CERTIFICATES AND REPORTS

Whilst the use of personal computers to assist with the compilation of certificates and reports, perhaps in conjunction with data-logging test instruments, is not a substitute for a skilled person competent to verify that the requirements of the standard have been met, such use may improve the clarity and presentation of the completed certificates and reports.

Some software packages also provide an element of validation or checking of the inspection and test results, identifying obvious errors, omissions and other problems in the data for consideration by a skilled person, before the details are printed on to the certificate or report. Such software packages, correctly used, can be expected to help ensure the completeness and accuracy of certificates and reports.

The principal certificate and report forms published by NICEIC and ELECSA are designed to be completed by hand, computer printer or using the respective NICEIC or ELECSA online certifcation system.

NICEIC and ELECSA Online Certification System

In addition, to printed pads and computer print-outs of certificates and forms NICEIC and ELECSA have recently launched new online certification services known as the 'Cloud'.

This service allows certificates and forms to be issued and notified on-site, in the office or at home using a PC, Tablet or Smartphone, and securely stores and archives records in the Cloud. For information about online certification refer to the appropriate website address. (**www.niceiconline.com**) (**www.elecsaonline.com**)

Irrespective of the method used to compile an Electrical Installation Condition Report, it remains the responsibility of the compiler of the report to ensure that the information provided therein is factual and accurately records the condition of the electrical installation to which the report relates, having regard to the stated extent and the reasons for the limitations of the report clearly explained.

HSE Memorandum of guidance on the Electricity at Work Regulations 1989 (2nd Edition)

Correctly compiled certificates and reports:

- are a record of your involvement and responsibility
- demonstrate that you have carried out the necessary inspection and testing
- can be significant in providing you, if necessary, with a defence under Regulation 29 of the *Electricity at Work Regulations*.

NOTE: In Northern Ireland, the *Electricity at Work Regulations (Northern Ireland) 1991* apply, and there is a corresponding Memorandum of Guidance issued by the Health and Safety Agency for Northern Ireland. The Regulations and the Memorandum of Guidance are similar to those applicable in other parts of the UK.

ASSESSMENT OF INSPECTION AND TEST RESULTS

It is not sufficient for the inspector simply to record the results of inspection and testing on a certificate or report. The inspector should consider and assess the results and compare them with the relevant criteria to determine whether they are as expected for the particular type of installation, and that they are consistent with installation work complying with all the relevant requirements of *BS 7671*.

For example, it would not be acceptable for the inspector to issue an Electrical Installation Certificate or a Domestic Electrical Installation Certificate recording a measured earth fault loop impedance value for a circuit in a new installation which exceeded the limiting value permitted by Chapter 41 (taking account of the appropriate correction factors, for example, the conductor operating temperature at the time of the measurement) for disconnection of the protective device within the appropriate time limit to provide protection. Such an excessive impedance would need to be investigated, appropriate remedial action taken, and the test repeated before the Electrical Installation Certificate or Domestic Electrical Installation Certificate was issued and the installation put into service.

If an excessive earth fault loop impedance is discovered during the course of a periodic inspection of an existing installation, the measured (excessive) value should be recorded, together with an appropriate observation and recommendation for remedial action, on the Electrical Installation Condition Report or Domestic Electrical Installation Condition Report.

LEGAL ASPECTS

Whilst the *Electricity at Work Regulations 1989 (EWR)* do not specifically require electrical installation certificates or reports to be issued and retained, such documents may provide the only effective evidence for the contractor or the person(s) responsible for the safety of an electrical installation should either or both be prosecuted under the provisions of those statutory regulations.

All persons carrying out inspection and testing of electrical installations, whether as an employee or self-employed person, must comply with the relevant requirements of the *EWR*. They apply to all persons carrying out any work activity falling within the scope of the Regulations. They therefore apply to inspection and testing (as well as to other aspects of electrical work) even when being carried out in locations not normally considered to be places of work, such as domestic premises.

Persons undertaking inspection and testing should pay particular attention to Regulation 14, 'working on or near live conductors', and to the associated guidance provided in the *Memorandum of guidance on the Electricity at Work Regulations* published by the Health and Safety Executive (HSE).

Electrical contractors that issue inaccurate or misleading certificates or reports are liable to criminal prosecution by Trading Standards Officers under the Trade

The importance of competence and safe working procedure

Everyone may occasionally be tempted to cut corners to save time or money, but the personal, legal and financial consequences of taking such risks can be severe, especially where inspection and testing is concerned. The following is based on an article that appeared in the technical press in 1997:

An enquiry into an electrical accident in which a man was temporarily blinded revealed that unqualified workers were being used by an electrical contractor to carry out electrical testing work.

The injured electrician, who was carrying out a continuity test on a sub-main cable, failed to check that two phase (line) conductor terminals were dead before he began work. In fact the terminals were live, with 400 V between them. A flash of electric current which engulfed his body causing electrical burns to his hands and face, and temporarily blinding him, occurred when he attempted to put a length of copper wire across the terminals.

On interviewing the injured electrician, Local Authority Inspectors found that he had no formal qualifications relating to electrical work, and that all his knowledge was gained from working with other electricians. He had little experience of testing work, and did not fully understand the tests being carried out.

The electrical contractor was charged with three breaches of Section 2 of the Health and Safety at Work etc Act 1974, for each of which they were fined £12,000. The company was also fined £3,000 for a breach of the Electricity at Work Regulations 1989.

Based on an article published in the August 1997 issue of The Safety and Health Practitioner.

Descriptions Act 1968 or other relevant legislation. There have also been successful claims for damages in the civil courts by persons who have relied upon the content of an electrical installation certificate or report, when considering whether (or not) to buy a property.

Such prosecutions can be avoided by employing only skilled persons competent in that aspect of the work to perform the construction and inspection and testing of electrical installations and to produce the certificates and reports, and by agreeing the exact scope of work with the client before commencing.

THE INSPECTOR

Throughout this book, the term 'inspector' is used to describe a person responsible for inspecting and testing an electrical installation. All persons carrying out the inspection and testing of electrical installations must be skilled (electrically) or Instructed (electrically).

NICEIC and ELECSA considers that, to undertake the inspection and testing of an electrical installation, persons must as a minimum:

- Have sufficient knowledge and experience of electrical installation matters to avoid danger to themselves and to others.
- Be familiar with, and understand, the requirements of *BS 7671*, including those relating to inspection, testing, certification and reporting.
- Have a sound knowledge of the particular type of installation to be inspected and tested.
- Have sufficient information about the function and construction of the installation to allow them to proceed in safety.

If the inspector is a skilled person competent in such work and takes all the necessary safety precautions, including following the correct procedure, the process of inspection and testing should not create danger to persons or livestock, or cause damage to property.

Generally persons undertaking periodic inspection, testing and reporting need to have above-average knowledge and experience of electrical installation matters to enable them to safely and accurately assess the condition of an existing electrical installation, especially when they do not have access to the design information relating to that installation.

Safe working procedure

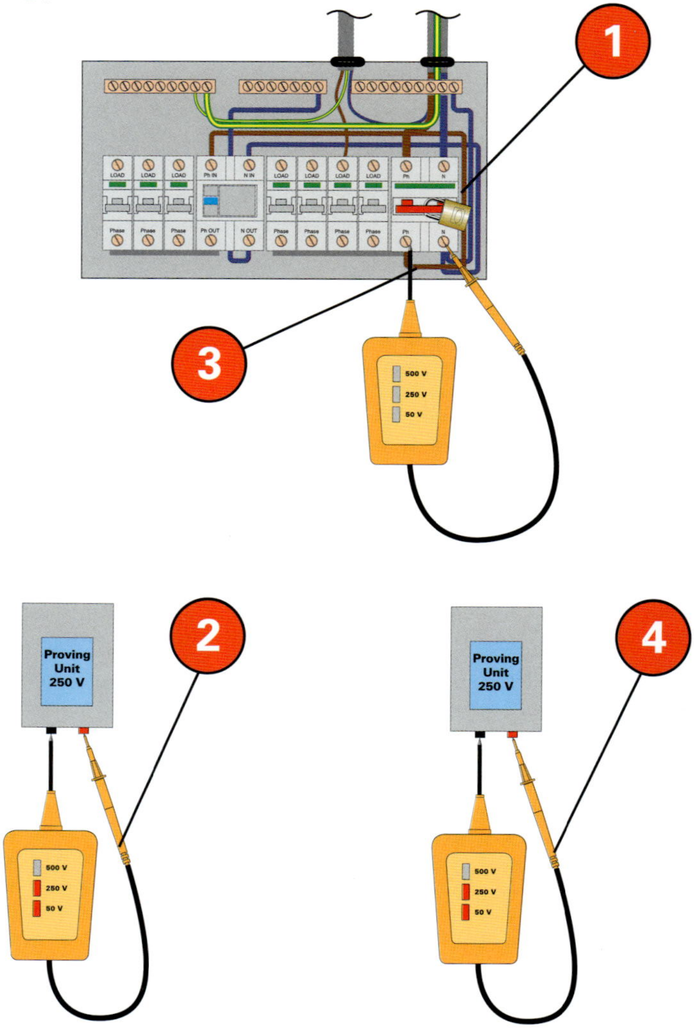

SAFE WORKING PROCEDURE

Isolation

Regulation 12 of the *Electricity at Work Regulations 1989* deals with means of cutting off the supply and with isolation. The Regulation requires that where necessary to prevent danger, suitable means (including, where appropriate, methods of identifying circuits) are made available:

- for cutting off the supply of electrical energy to any electrical equipment, and
- for the isolation of electrical equipment.

Regulation 611.1 of *BS 7671* states that 'Inspection shall precede testing and shall normally be done with that part of the installation under inspection disconnected from the supply'. The appropriate form of disconnection is isolation.

Isolation is not simply the operation of an isolating device. It is a procedure, the objective of which is to ensure that the supply is cut off and remains cut off for reasons of safety. The process of isolation can be broken down into a number of steps as necessary for the particular circumstances. As a minimum[†], and with reference to the illustration on the opposite page, the following safe working procedure should be adopted before commencing inspection:

✔ **Step 1**

Open the means of isolation for the circuit(s) to be inspected (having first removed the load, if the isolator is an off-load device), and secure the isolating device in the open position with a lock or other suitable means.

✔ **Step 2**

Prove the correct operation of a suitable voltage test instrument against a known source.

✔ **Step 3**

Test, with the voltage test instrument, all conductors* of the circuit(s) to be worked on to verify that no dangerous voltage is present.

✔ **Step 4**

Prove the voltage test instrument again against the known source to check that it was functioning correctly when the circuit(s) were tested for the presence of voltage.

† HSG85 *Electricity at Work safe working practices* gives detailed guidance on devising safe working practices for people who carry out work on or near electrical equipment.

* It should be confirmed that protective conductors are not live due to, for example, a wiring fault.

HSE Guidance Note GS 38 - *Electrical test equipment for use by electricians* and HSG85 *Electricity at Work, safe working practices*

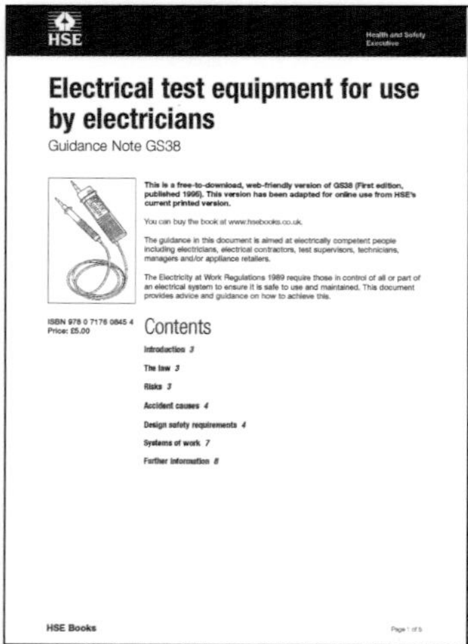
HSE

Health and Safety Executive

Electrical test equipment for use by electricians

Guidance Note GS38

This is a free-to-download, web-friendly version of GS38 (First edition, published 1995). This version has been adapted for online use from HSE's current printed version.

You can buy the book at www.hsebooks.co.uk

The guidance in this document is aimed at electrically competent people including electricians, electrical contractors, test supervisors, technicians, managers and/or appliance retailers.

The Electricity at Work Regulations 1989 require those in control of all or part of an electrical system to ensure it is safe to use and maintained. This document provides advice and guidance on how to achieve this.

ISBN 978 0 7176 0845 4
Price: £5.00

Contents

Introduction 3
The law 3
Risks 3
Accident causes 4
Design safety requirements 4
Systems of work 7
Further information 8

HSE Books

HSE Guidance Note GS 38

This HSE publication gives guidance on the safe use of electrical test equipment.

HSG85 *Electricity at Work safe working practices*

This second edition of HSG85 gives guidance on the key elements that need to be considered when devising safe working practices for people who carry out work on or near electrical equipment.

Measurement of voltage and current

Particular care should be taken when measuring voltage, prospective fault current and earth fault loop impedance, as the tests have to be conducted when the installation is energised. Take appropriate precautions to prevent accidents, such as ensuring that test instruments and test leads are suitable and properly used, that the equipment to be worked upon is safe for the intended tests, and that the working environment does not present additional dangers (see HSE Guidance Note GS 38).

TEST EQUIPMENT

HSE Guidance Note GS 38: *Electrical test equipment for use by electricians* gives advice to competent persons on the selection and use of test equipment for circuits with rated voltages not exceeding 650 V. Those involved in electrical inspection and testing should familiarise themselves with the guidance given in this publication.

Aspects that should be checked with regard to test equipment include the following (refer to the HSE Guidance Note for full information):

- Test instruments and their associated test leads must be suitably constructed and fit for the purpose for which they are to be used. Such equipment should preferably meet the safety requirements set out in *BS EN 61010* and the performance standards detailed in the appropriate Part(s) of *BS EN 61557*.
- Test equipment should be checked for suitable rating for the anticipated voltage prior to testing any circuit which is, or may be, energised.
- Test instruments and their associated test leads should be checked before each use for signs of damage and deterioration, and be maintained such that they remain safe for use in the intended manner.
- Test instruments and test leads should be used only in the environment(s) for which they have been designed.
- In the case of voltage test lamps, the leads (and therefore the person using the instrument) should be protected by either:
    - a high breaking capacity (HBC) fuse of rating not exceeding 500 mA, or
    - a current limiting resistor and a fuse
- In the case of voltage detectors, the current that may pass through the instrument is limited by the internal circuit design, protective impedance and current limiting resistors built into the probes
- Probes should have no more than 4 mm of exposed metal tip. (It is strongly recommended that the exposed metal tip does not exceed 2 mm).

Test probes and leads

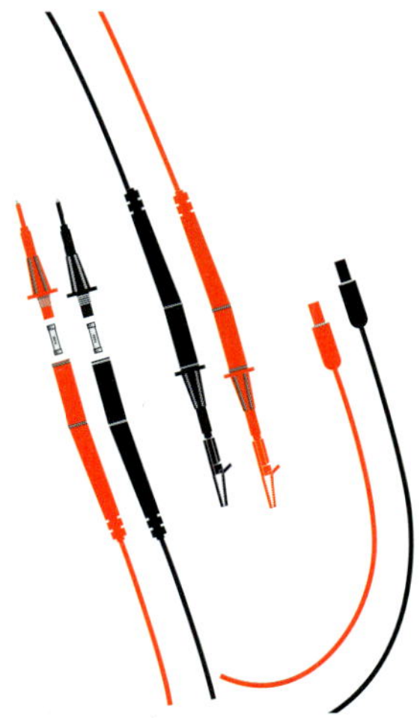

Test probes and leads must be selected to avoid danger.

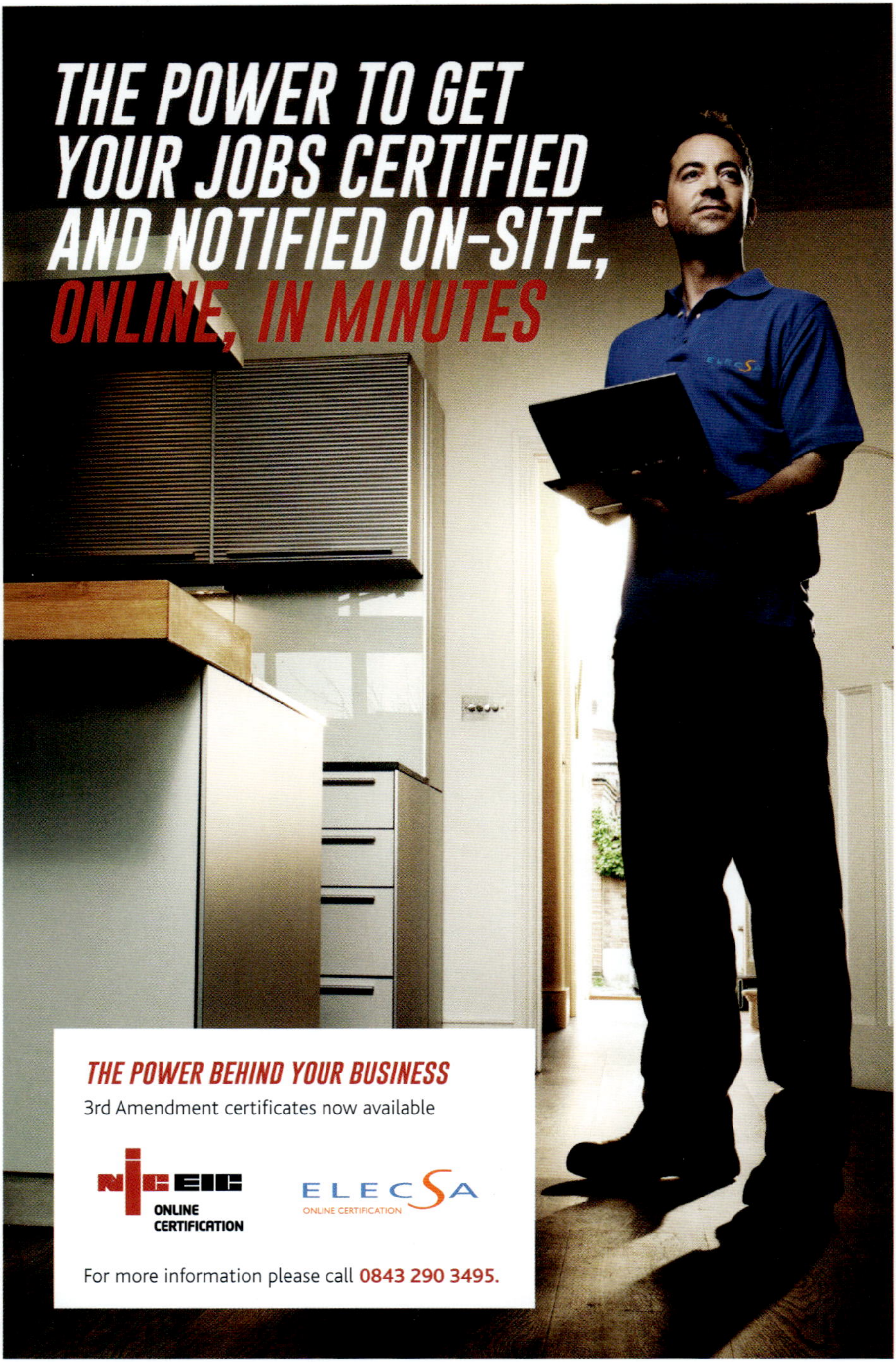
THE POWER TO GET YOUR JOBS CERTIFIED AND NOTIFIED ON-SITE, ONLINE, IN MINUTES
THE POWER BEHIND YOUR BUSINESS
3rd Amendment certificates now available
NICEIC ONLINE CERTIFICATION
ELECSA ONLINE CERTIFICATION
For more information please call 0843 290 3495.

Chapter

2

The Electrical Installation Certificate

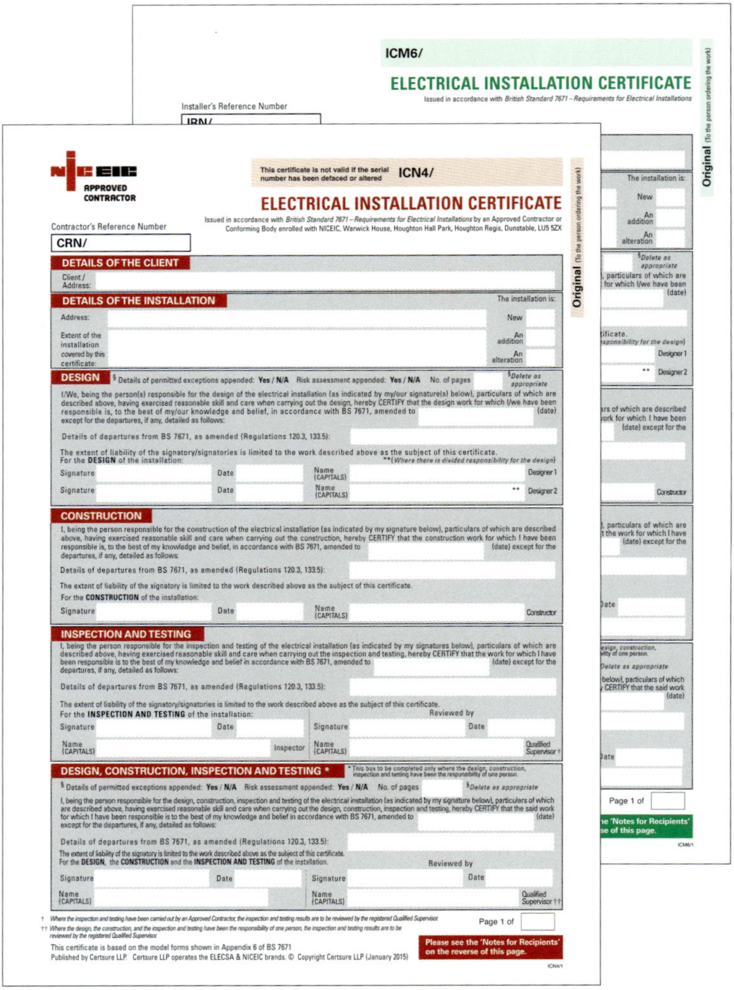

ICM6/

ELECTRICAL INSTALLATION CERTIFICATE

Issued in accordance with *British Standard 7671 – Requirements for Electrical Installations*

Installer's Reference Number IRN/

Original (To the person ordering the work)

NICEIC APPROVED CONTRACTOR

This certificate is not valid if the serial number has been defaced or altered ICN4/

ELECTRICAL INSTALLATION CERTIFICATE

Issued in accordance with *British Standard 7671 – Requirements for Electrical Installations* by an Approved Contractor or Conforming Body enrolled with NICEIC, Warwick House, Houghton Hall Park, Houghton Regis, Dunstable, LU5 5ZX

Contractor's Reference Number CRN/

Original (To the person ordering the work)

DETAILS OF THE CLIENT

Client / Address:

DETAILS OF THE INSTALLATION

The installation is:

Address: New

Extent of the installation covered by this certificate: An addition / An alteration

DESIGN § Details of permitted exceptions appended: **Yes / N/A** Risk assessment appended: **Yes / N/A** No. of pages §*Delete as appropriate*

I/We, being the person(s) responsible for the design of the electrical installation (as indicated by my/our signature(s) below), particulars of which are described above, having exercised reasonable skill and care when carrying out the design, hereby CERTIFY that the design work for which I/we have been responsible is, to the best of my/our knowledge and belief, in accordance with BS 7671, amended to (date) except for the departures, if any, detailed as follows:

Details of departures from BS 7671, as amended (Regulations 120.3, 133.5):

The extent of liability of the signatory/signatories is limited to the work described above as the subject of this certificate.
For the **DESIGN** of the installation: **(*Where there is divided responsibility for the design*)

Signature Date Name (CAPITALS) Designer 1

Signature Date Name (CAPITALS) ** Designer 2

CONSTRUCTION

I, being the person responsible for the construction of the electrical installation (as indicated by my signature below), particulars of which are described above, having exercised reasonable skill and care when carrying out the construction, hereby CERTIFY that the construction work for which I have been responsible is, to the best of my knowledge and belief, in accordance with BS 7671, amended to (date) except for the departures, if any, detailed as follows:

Details of departures from BS 7671, as amended (Regulations 120.3, 133.5):

The extent of liability of the signatory is limited to the work described above as the subject of this certificate.

For the **CONSTRUCTION** of the installation:

Signature Date Name (CAPITALS) Constructor

INSPECTION AND TESTING

I, being the person responsible for the inspection and testing of the electrical installation (as indicated by my signatures below), particulars of which are described above, having exercised reasonable skill and care when carrying out the inspection and testing, hereby CERTIFY that the work for which I have been responsible is to the best of my knowledge and belief in accordance with BS 7671, amended to (date) except for the departures, if any, detailed as follows:

Details of departures from BS 7671, as amended (Regulations 120.3, 133.5):

The extent of liability of the signatory/signatories is limited to the work described above as the subject of this certificate.

For the **INSPECTION AND TESTING** of the installation: Reviewed by

Signature Date Signature Date

Name (CAPITALS) Inspector Name (CAPITALS) Qualified Supervisor †

DESIGN, CONSTRUCTION, INSPECTION AND TESTING * * This box to be completed only where the design, construction, inspection and testing have been the responsibility of one person.

§ Details of permitted exceptions appended: **Yes / N/A** Risk assessment appended: **Yes / N/A** No. of pages §*Delete as appropriate*

I, being the person responsible for the design, construction, inspection and testing of the electrical installation (as indicated by my signature below), particulars of which are described above, having exercised reasonable skill and care when carrying out the design, construction, inspection and testing, hereby CERTIFY that the said work for which I have been responsible is to the best of my knowledge and belief in accordance with BS 7671, amended to (date) except for the departures, if any, detailed as follows:

Details of departures from BS 7671, as amended (Regulations 120.3, 133.5):

The extent of liability of the signatory is limited to the work described above as the subject of this certificate.
For the **DESIGN**, the **CONSTRUCTION** and the **INSPECTION AND TESTING** of the installation. Reviewed by

Signature Date Signature Date

Name (CAPITALS) Name (CAPITALS) Qualified Supervisor ††

† *Where the inspection and testing have been carried out by an Approved Contractor, the inspection and testing results are to be reviewed by the registered Qualified Supervisor.*

†† *Where the design, the construction, and the inspection and testing have been the responsibility of one person, the inspection and testing results are to be reviewed by the registered Qualified Supervisor.*

Page 1 of

This certificate is based on the model forms shown in Appendix 6 of BS 7671
Published by Certsure LLP. Certsure LLP operates the ELECSA & NICEIC brands. © Copyright Certsure LLP (January 2015)

Please see the 'Notes for Recipients' on the reverse of this page.

ICN4/1

The front page of the NICEIC Electrical Installation Certificate and the green Electrical Installation Certificate. Green certificates are available for use by:

- electrical contractors not enrolled with NICEIC or ELECSA, in particular those preparing for enrolment, and
- NICEIC or ELECSA contractors working outside the scope of their enrolment or registration.

2 THE ELECTRICAL INSTALLATION CERTIFICATE

REQUIREMENTS

BS 7671 requires a standard form of Electrical Installation Certificate (including a record of the inspection and the results of testing) to be issued for all new installation work, and for all alterations and additions to existing installations. A separate certificate must be issued for each distinct electrical installation. The certificate provides a formal assurance from those responsible for the design, construction, and inspection and testing of the installation that it complies with the requirements of the national standard for electrical safety.

A certificate (based on the model form given in *BS 7671*) must be issued to the person who ordered the work, whether or not the contractor is registered with NICEIC, and whether or not a certificate has been specifically requested by the client. Only an NICEIC Approved Contractor is authorised to issue the Red NICEIC Electrical Installation Certificate, but for those not authorised to issue the Red Electrical Installation Certificate similar (green) certificates based on the model form given in *BS 7671* are available from NICEIC.

If the contractor responsible for the construction of the installation is not also responsible for its design and/or inspection and testing, it will be necessary for the contractor to liaise with the other parties responsible for those aspects in order to complete all the details required on the certificate.

It should be noted that the Electrical Installation Certificate is not intended to be issued to confirm the completion of a contract. The certificate is a declaration of electrical safety which should be issued before an installation is put into service. The certificate should not be withheld for contractual reasons, especially if the electrical installation is available for use.

The Electrical Installation Certificate is to be used only for the initial certification of a new installation, or for new work associated with an alteration or addition to an existing installation, carried out in accordance with *BS 7671* as amended. Alternatively, where the electrical installation work relates to a single dwelling (house or individual flat), a Domestic Electrical Installation Certificate may be used, provided the installation falls within the scope of that certificate (see Chapter 3). Neither certificate is to be used for a periodic inspection of an existing installation, for which either an Electrical Installation Condition Report or Domestic Electrical Installation Condition Report should be used (see Chapter 5).

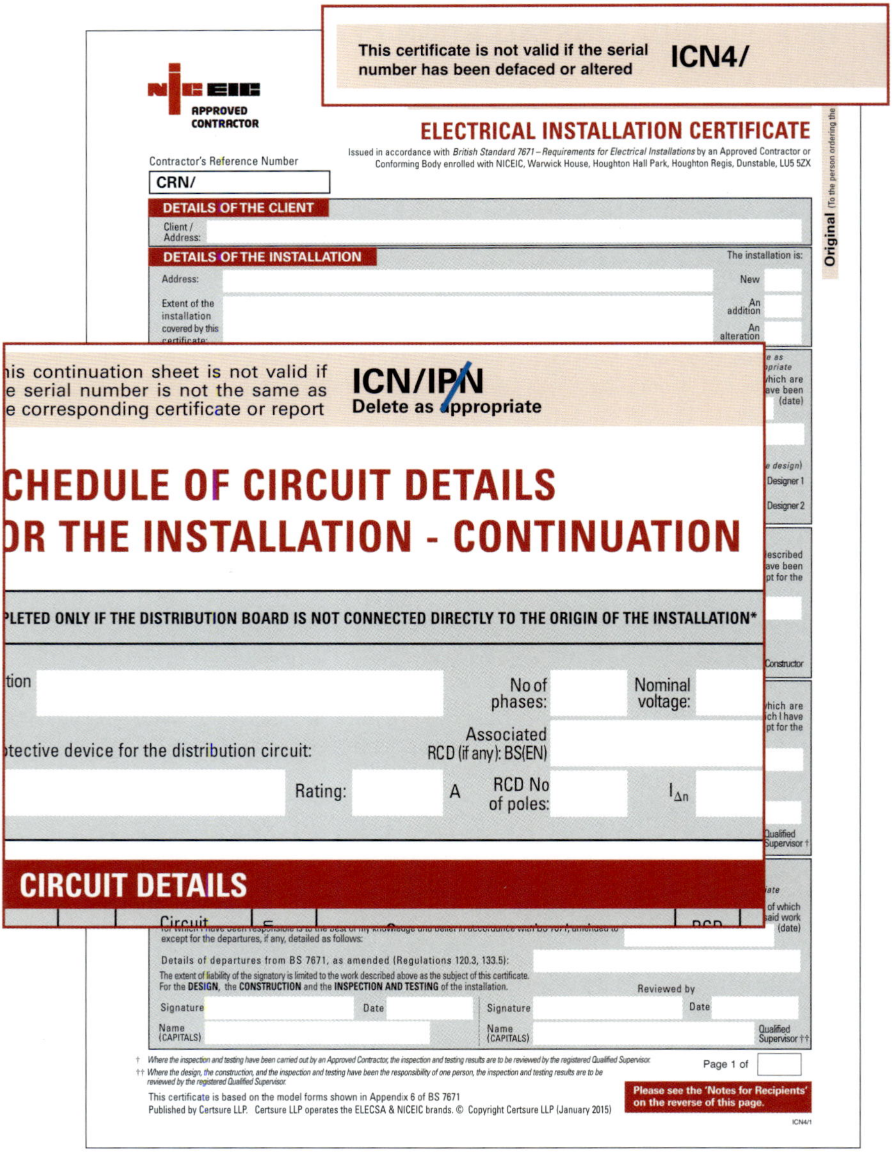

This certificate is not valid if the serial number has been defaced or altered ICN4/

NICEIC APPROVED CONTRACTOR

Contractor's Reference Number CRN/

ELECTRICAL INSTALLATION CERTIFICATE

Issued in accordance with *British Standard 7671 – Requirements for Electrical Installations* by an Approved Contractor or Conforming Body enrolled with NICEIC, Warwick House, Houghton Hall Park, Houghton Regis, Dunstable, LU5 5ZX

Original (To the person ordering the

DETAILS OF THE CLIENT

Client / Address:

DETAILS OF THE INSTALLATION

The installation is:

Address: New

Extent of the installation covered by this certificate: An addition An alteration

his continuation sheet is not valid if e serial number is not the same as e corresponding certificate or report

ICN/IPN Delete as appropriate

CHEDULE OF CIRCUIT DETAILS OR THE INSTALLATION - CONTINUATION

PLETED ONLY IF THE DISTRIBUTION BOARD IS NOT CONNECTED DIRECTLY TO THE ORIGIN OF THE INSTALLATION*

tion No of phases: Nominal voltage:

tective device for the distribution circuit: Associated RCD (if any): BS(EN)

Rating: A RCD No of poles: $I_{\Delta n}$

CIRCUIT DETAILS

except for the departures, if any, detailed as follows:

Details of departures from BS 7671, as amended (Regulations 120.3, 133.5):

The extent of liability of the signatory is limited to the work described above as the subject of this certificate.
For the **DESIGN**, the **CONSTRUCTION** and the **INSPECTION AND TESTING** of the installation.

Reviewed by

Signature Date Signature Date

Name (CAPITALS) Name (CAPITALS) Qualified Supervisor ††

† *Where the inspection and testing have been carried out by an Approved Contractor, the inspection and testing results are to be reviewed by the registered Qualified Supervisor.*

†† *Where the design, the construction, and the inspection and testing have been the responsibility of one person, the inspection and testing results are to be reviewed by the registered Qualified Supervisor.*

Page 1 of

This certificate is based on the model forms shown in Appendix 6 of BS 7671

Published by Certsure LLP. Certsure LLP operates the ELECSA & NICEIC brands. © Copyright Certsure LLP (January 2015)

Please see the 'Notes for Recipients' on the reverse of this page.

ICN4/1

Each NICEIC certificate has a unique serial number to provide traceability.

Where a certificate is to be issued for an alteration or addition to an existing installation, the designer is required to ascertain that the rating and condition of any existing equipment, including that of the distributor will be adequate for the altered circumstances, and that the earthing and protective bonding arrangements, if necessary for the protective measure applied for the safety of the addition or alteration are also adequate (see Regulation 132.16).

Where an Approved Contractor discovers the existence of a dangerous or potentially dangerous situation in the existing installation (such as the absence of earthing or protective bonding where the protective measure for fault protection is Automatic Disconnection of Supply (ADS), the new work should not proceed and the client should be advised immediately, preferably in writing, to satisfy the duties imposed on competent persons by the *Electricity at Work Regulations 1989.*

An NICEIC Electrical Installation Certificate may be issued only by the Approved Contractor responsible for the installation work. A certificate must never be issued to cover another contractor's installation work.

An NICEIC Electrical Installation Certificate which has pages missing is considered invalid. The NICEIC certificate has at least six pages, depending on the number and type of circuits in the installation. For installations having more than one distribution board or more circuits than can be recorded on pages 5 and 6, one or more additional pages of the Schedule of Circuit Details for the Installation and Schedule of Test Results for the Installation will be required.

Continuation schedules are available separately from NICEIC. The additional pages should be given the same unique serial number as the other pages of the certificate, by first striking out 'IPN' and then adding the remainder of the unique serial number in the space allocated. Superseded versions of the continuation schedules must not be used in conjunction with these certificates. The page number for each additional schedule should be inserted, together with the total number of pages comprising the certificate (e.g. page 7 of 8).

Generally, irrespective of the method of compilation of the form, all unshaded data-entry boxes should be completed by inserting the necessary text, or a '✔' to indicate that the task has been completed and the result was satisfactory, or a numeric value of the measured parameter, or by entering 'N/A' meaning 'Not Applicable', where appropriate.

Regardless of the method of compilation of the certificate (by hand, software-assisted or using the NICEIC's online certification system), it remains the responsibility of the compiler of the certificate to ensure that the information provided on the certificate is factual, and that the electrical installation work to which the certificate relates is safe to be put into service.

NICEIC APPROVED CONTRACTOR

This certificate is not valid if the serial number has been defaced or altered **ICN4/**

ELECTRICAL INSTALLATION CERTIFICATE

Original (To the person ordering the work)

Contractor's Reference Number

CRN/

Issued in accordance with *British Standard 7671 – Requirements for Electrical Installations* by an Approved Contractor or Conforming Body enrolled with NICEIC, Warwick House, Houghton Hall Park, Houghton Regis, Dunstable, LU5 5ZX

DETAILS OF THE CLIENT

Client / Address:

DETAILS OF THE INSTALLATION

The installation is:

Address: New

Extent of the installation covered by this certificate: An addition / An alteration

I/We, being the person(s) responsible for the design of the electrical installation (as indicated by my/our signature(s) below), particulars of which are described above, having exercised reasonable skill and care when carrying out the design, hereby CERTIFY that the design work for which I/we have been responsible is, to the best of my/our knowledge and belief, in accordance with BS 7671, amended to (date) except for the departures, if any, detailed as follows:

Details of departures from BS 7671, as amended (Regulations 120.3, 133.5):

The extent of liability of the signatory/signatories is limited to the work described above as the subject of this certificate.

For the **DESIGN** of the installation: **(*Where there is divided responsibility for the design*)

Signature | Date | Name (CAPITALS) | Designer 1

Signature | Date | Name (CAPITALS) | ** Designer 2

CONSTRUCTION

I, being the person responsible for the construction of the electrical installation (as indicated by my signature below), particulars of which are described above, having exercised reasonable skill and care when carrying out the construction, hereby CERTIFY that the construction work for which I have been responsible is, to the best of my knowledge and belief, in accordance with BS 7671, amended to (date) except for the departures, if any, detailed as follows:

Details of departures from BS 7671, as amended (Regulations 120.3, 133.5):

The extent of liability of the signatory is limited to the work described above as the subject of this certificate.

For the **CONSTRUCTION** of the installation:

Signature | Date | Name (CAPITALS) | Constructor

INSPECTION AND TESTING

I, being the person responsible for the inspection and testing of the electrical installation (as indicated by my signatures below), particulars of which are described above, having exercised reasonable skill and care when carrying out the inspection and testing, hereby CERTIFY that the work for which I have been responsible is to the best of my knowledge and belief in accordance with BS 7671, amended to (date) except for the departures, if any, detailed as follows:

Details of departures from BS 7671, as amended (Regulations 120.3, 133.5):

The extent of liability of the signatory/signatories is limited to the work described above as the subject of this certificate.

For the **INSPECTION AND TESTING** of the installation: Reviewed by

Signature | Date | Signature | Date

Name (CAPITALS) | Inspector | Name (CAPITALS) | Qualified Supervisor †

DESIGN, CONSTRUCTION, INSPECTION AND TESTING *

* This box to be completed only where the design, construction, inspection and testing have been the responsibility of one person.

§ Details of permitted exceptions appended: **Yes / N/A** Risk assessment appended: **Yes / N/A** No. of pages §*Delete as appropriate*

I, being the person responsible for the design, construction, inspection and testing of the electrical installation (as indicated by my signature below), particulars of which are described above, having exercised reasonable skill and care when carrying out the design, construction, inspection and testing, hereby CERTIFY that the said work for which I have been responsible is to the best of my knowledge and belief in accordance with BS 7671, amended to (date) except for the departures, if any, detailed as follows:

Details of departures from BS 7671, as amended (Regulations 120.3, 133.5):

The extent of liability of the signatory is limited to the work described above as the subject of this certificate.

For the **DESIGN**, the **CONSTRUCTION** and the **INSPECTION AND TESTING** of the installation. Reviewed by

Signature | Date | Signature | Date

Name (CAPITALS) | Name (CAPITALS) | Qualified Supervisor ††

† *Where the inspection and testing have been carried out by an Approved Contractor, the inspection and testing results are to be reviewed by the registered Qualified Supervisor.*

†† *Where the design, the construction, and the inspection and testing have been the responsibility of one person, the inspection and testing results are to be reviewed by the registered Qualified Supervisor.*

Page 1 of

This certificate is based on the model forms shown in Appendix 6 of BS 7671

Published by Certsure LLP. Certsure LLP operates the ELECSA & NICEIC brands. © Copyright Certsure LLP (January 2015)

Please see the 'Notes for Recipients' on the reverse of this page.

ICN4/1

Where the electrical work to which the certificate relates includes the installation of a fire alarm system and/or an emergency lighting system (or a part of such systems) in accordance with British Standards *BS 5839* and *BS 5266* respectively, the Electrical Installation Certificate must be accompanied by a separate certificate or certificates as prescribed by those Standards.

COMPILATION OF THE CERTIFICATE

The remainder of this chapter provides guidance on completing each part of the certificate.

CONTRACTOR'S REFERENCE NUMBER

At the top of page 1 a box - CRN, is provided to record a reference number for the particular contract or client, as appropriate. In cases where no contract reference has been allocated, 'None' should be recorded in the box.

DETAILS OF THE CLIENT

The details to be provided are the name and address of the person or organisation that engaged the contractor to carry out the installation work. Where, for example, the electrical contractor is engaged by a builder, the details entered should be those of the builder. In the case of lengthy name and address details, suitable abbreviations may be used if acceptable to the client.

DETAILS OF THE INSTALLATION

Address

The address to be provided is the complete postal address of the installation, including the postcode.

Extent of the installation covered by this certificate

For a new installation, the certificate may be intended to apply to the whole of the electrical installation at the address given. If not, it is essential to clearly define the extent of the installation to which the certificate applies in terms of areas or services; for example, 'whole electrical installation second floor' or 'whole electrical installation except fire detection and alarm system'.

The description will depend on the particular circumstances, and must be tailored to identify explicitly the extent of the installation work covered by the certificate. In the case of additions or alterations, particular care must be taken to define exactly what work the certificate covers.

NICEIC APPROVED CONTRACTOR

This certificate is not valid if the serial number has been defaced or altered **ICN4/**

dering the work)

ELECTRICAL INSTALLATION CERTIFICATE

Issued in accordance with *British Standard 7671 – Requirements for Electrical Insta*
Conforming Body enrolled with NICEIC, Warwick House, Houghton Hall Park,

Contractor's Reference Number

CRN/

Origina

DETAILS OF THE CLIENT

Client / Address:

DETAILS OF THE INSTALLATION

Address:

Extent of the installation covered by this certificate:

The installation is:

New

An addition

An alteration

An alteration

DESIGN § Details of permitted exceptions appended: **Yes / N/A** Risk assessment appended: **Yes / N/A** No. of pages §*Delete as appropriate*

I/We, being the person(s) responsible for the design of the electrical installation (as indicated by my/our signature(s) below), particulars of which are described above, having exercised reasonable skill and care when carrying out the design, hereby CERTIFY that the design work for which I/we have been responsible is, to the best of my/our knowledge and belief, in accordance with BS 7671, amended to (date) except for the departures, if any, detailed as follows:

Details of departures from BS 7671, as amended (Regulations 120.3, 133.5):

The extent of liability of the signatory/signatories is limited to the work described above as the subject of this certificate.
For the **DESIGN** of the installation: **(*Where there is divided responsibility for the design*)

Signature Date Name (CAPITALS) Designer 1

Signature Date Name (CAPITALS) ** Designer 2

CONSTRUCTION

I, being the person responsible for the construction of the electrical installation (as indicated by my signature below), particulars of which are described above, having exercised reasonable skill and care when carrying out the construction, hereby CERTIFY that the construction work for which I have been responsible is, to the best of my knowledge and belief, in accordance with BS 7671, amended to (date) except for the departures, if any, detailed as follows:

Details of departures from BS 7671, as amended (Regulations 120.3, 133.5):

The extent of liability of the signatory is limited to the work described above as the subject of this certificate.
For the **CONSTRUCTION** of the installation:

Signature Date Name (CAPITALS) Constructor

INSPECTION AND TESTING

I, being the person responsible for the inspection and testing of the electrical installation (as indicated by my signatures below), particulars of which are described above, having exercised reasonable skill and care when carrying out the inspection and testing, hereby CERTIFY that the work for which I have been responsible is to the best of my knowledge and belief in accordance with BS 7671, amended to (date) except for the departures, if any, detailed as follows:

Details of departures from BS 7671, as amended (Regulations 120.3, 133.5):

The extent of liability of the signatory/signatories is limited to the work described above as the subject of this certificate.
For the **INSPECTION AND TESTING** of the installation: Reviewed by

Signature Date Signature Date

Name (CAPITALS) Inspector Name (CAPITALS) Qualified Supervisor †

DESIGN, CONSTRUCTION, INSPECTION AND TESTING * * This box to be completed only where the design, construction, inspection and testing have been the responsibility of one person.

§ Details of permitted exceptions appended: **Yes / N/A** Risk assessment appended: **Yes / N/A** No. of pages §*Delete as appropriate*

I, being the person responsible for the design, construction, inspection and testing of the electrical installation (as indicated by my signature below), particulars of which are described above, having exercised reasonable skill and care when carrying out the design, construction, inspection and testing, hereby CERTIFY that the said work for which I have been responsible is to the best of my knowledge and belief in accordance with BS 7671, amended to (date) except for the departures, if any, detailed as follows:

Details of departures from BS 7671, as amended (Regulations 120.3, 133.5):

The extent of liability of the signatory is limited to the work described above as the subject of this certificate.
For the **DESIGN**, the **CONSTRUCTION** and the **INSPECTION AND TESTING** of the installation. Reviewed by

The box should be used to identify and clarify any particular exclusions agreed with the client. Any other exclusions which may not be readily apparent to the client or the installation user should also be recorded here.

If there is insufficient space in the box to give a clear description of the work done and/or any exclusions, then an additional record should be included in the certificate by attaching a separate sheet. Reference to this additional page should be included in the box.

It should be appreciated that failure to clearly describe the extent of the work covered by the certificate could involve the contractor in unforeseen liabilities at a later date.

Nature of installation work

Three boxes are provided to enable the contractor to identify the nature of the installation work:

- **'New'** - This box should be ticked only if the whole installation has been installed as new, or if a complete rewire has been carried out.
- **'An addition'** (to an existing installation) - This box should be ticked if an existing installation has been modified by the addition of one or more new circuits.
- **'An alteration'** (to an existing installation) - This box should be ticked where one or more existing circuits have been modified or extended, or items such as distribution boards and switchgear have been replaced.

Where appropriate, both the 'addition' and the 'alteration' boxes may be ticked.

THE SIGNATORIES

Two options are available for certification of the installation. Where the design, the construction and the inspection and testing are all the responsibility of one person, these three elements may be collectively certified in the section headed 'Design, Construction, Inspection and Testing'. Alternatively, where the NICEIC Approved Contractor issuing the certificate has not been responsible for the design and/or the inspection and testing of the electrical work, certification of the three elements must be carried out separately using the three sections headed 'Design', 'Construction' and 'Inspection and Testing', respectively. Where one person is not responsible for all three elements, the division of responsibility should be established and agreed before commencement of the work.

NICEIC considers that the absence of certification for the construction or the inspection and testing elements of the work would render the certificate invalid. If the

NICEIC APPROVED CONTRACTOR

This certificate is not valid if the serial number has been defaced or altered **ICN4/**

ELECTRICAL INSTALLATION CERTIFICATE

Issued in accordance with *British Standard 7671 – Requirements for Electrical Installations* by an Approved Contractor or Conforming Body enrolled with NICEIC, Warwick House, Houghton Hall Park, Houghton Regis, Dunstable, LU5 5ZX

Contractor's Reference Number

CRN/

DESIGN

§ Details of permitted exceptions appended: **Yes / N/A** Risk assessment appended: **Yes / N/A** No. of pages §*Delete as appropriate*

I/We, being the person(s) responsible for the design of the electrical installation (as indicated by my/our signature(s) below), particulars of which are described above, having exercised reasonable skill and care when carrying out the design, hereby CERTIFY that the design work for which I/we have been responsible is, to the best of my/our knowledge and belief, in accordance with BS 7671, amended to (date) except for the departures, if any, detailed as follows:

Details of departures from BS 7671, as amended (Regulations 120.3, 133.5):

The extent of liability of the signatory/signatories is limited to the work described above as the subject of this certificate.
For the **DESIGN** of the installation: **(*Where there is divided responsibility for the design*)

Signature Date Name (CAPITALS) Designer 1

Signature Date Name (CAPITALS) ** Designer 2

CONSTRUCTION

I, being the person responsible for the construction of the electrical installation (as indicated by my signature below), particulars of which are described above, having exercised reasonable skill and care when carrying out the construction, hereby CERTIFY that the construction work for which I have been responsible is, to the best of my knowledge and belief, in accordance with BS 7671, amended to (date) except for the departures, if any, detailed as follows:

Details of departures from BS 7671, as amended (Regulations 120.3, 133.5):

The extent of liability of the signatory is limited to the work described above as the subject of this certificate.
For the **CONSTRUCTION** of the installation:

Signature Date Name (CAPITALS) Constructor

INSPECTION AND TESTING

I, being the person responsible for the inspection and testing of the electrical installation (as indicated by my signatures below), particulars of which are described above, having exercised reasonable skill and care when carrying out the inspection and testing, hereby CERTIFY that the work for which I have been responsible is to the best of my knowledge and belief in accordance with BS 7671, amended to (date) except for the departures, if any, detailed as follows:

Details of departures from BS 7671, as amended (Regulations 120.3, 133.5):

The extent of liability of the signatory/signatories is limited to the work described above as the subject of this certificate.
For the **INSPECTION AND TESTING** of the installation: Reviewed by

Signature Date | Signature Date

Name (CAPITALS) Inspector | Name (CAPITALS) Qualified Supervisor †

DESIGN, CONSTRUCTION, INSPECTION AND TESTING *

* This box to be completed only where the design, construction, inspection and testing have been the responsibility of one person.

§ Details of permitted exceptions appended: **Yes / N/A** Risk assessment appended: **Yes / N/A** No. of pages §*Delete as appropriate*

I, being the person responsible for the design, construction, inspection and testing of the electrical installation (as indicated by my signature below), particulars of which are described above, having exercised reasonable skill and care when carrying out the design, construction, inspection and testing, hereby CERTIFY that the said work for which I have been responsible is to the best of my knowledge and belief in accordance with BS 7671, amended to (date) except for the departures, if any, detailed as follows:

Details of departures from BS 7671, as amended (Regulations 120.3, 133.5):

The extent of liability of the signatory is limited to the work described above as the subject of this certificate.
For the **DESIGN,** the **CONSTRUCTION** and the **INSPECTION AND TESTING** of the installation. Reviewed by

Signature Date | Signature Date

Name (CAPITALS) | Name (CAPITALS) Qualified Supervisor ††

† *Where the inspection and testing have been carried out by an Approved Contractor, the inspection and testing results are to be reviewed by the registered Qualified Supervisor.*

†† *Where the design, the construction, and the inspection and testing have been the responsibility of one person, the inspection and testing results are to be reviewed by the registered Qualified Supervisor.*

Page 1 of

This certificate is based on the model forms shown in Appendix 6 of BS 7671
Published by Certsure LLP. Certsure LLP operates the ELECSA & NICEIC brands. © Copyright Certsure LLP (January 2015)

Please see the 'Notes for Recipients' on the reverse of this page.

ICN4/1

'Design' section of the certificate has not been completed, the notes on the reverse of the certificate advise the recipient to question why those responsible for the design have not certified that this important element of the work is in accordance with the national electrical safety standard.

Certification for inspection and testing provides an assurance to the recipient that the results of the inspection and testing have been compared with the relevant criteria (Regulation 612.1) and that the electrical installation work is in accordance with *BS 7671*, except for any departures sanctioned by the designer(s) and recorded in the appropriate box(es) of the certificate.

The date of the amendment to *BS 7671* current at the time the work was carried out should be stated in the relevant space in the text contained under the headings 'Design', 'Construction' and 'Inspection and Testing' or in the section headed 'Design, Construction, Inspection and Testing', as appropriate.

Where the inspection and testing has been carried out by an Approved Contractor, the inspection and testing results should be reviewed by the registered Qualified Supervisor who should confirm such review by signing in the appropriate one of the two boxes provided. Only a registered Qualified Supervisor employed by the Approved Contractor is recognised by NICEIC as eligible to sign the certificate to take responsibility for both the inspection and testing, and for reviewing the results.

For the uncontrolled (green) version of the certificate, the completed schedules of inspection and testing should preferably be reviewed by another skilled person, competent to verify that the recorded results are consistent with electrical installation work conforming to the requirements of *BS 7671*. The review should be confirmed by signing in the appropriate box.

DESIGN, CONSTRUCTION, INSPECTION AND TESTING

This section may be completed only where all the three elements of the installation work, namely, the design, the construction and the inspection and testing, are the responsibility of one person. Where this is not the case, the three elements should be certified separately, as indicated.

The person signing this section of the certificate bears the same responsibility as if that person had signed the separate design, construction and inspection and testing sections of the certificate.

Where this section is utilised for collective certification of the three elements, it is not necessary to complete the three separate sections for the design, the construction, and the inspection and testing.

NICEIC APPROVED CONTRACTOR

This certificate is not valid if the serial number has been defaced or altered **ICN4/**

Original (To the person ordering the work)

ELECTRICAL INSTALLATION CERTIFICATE

Issued in accordance with *British Standard 7671 – Requirements for Electrical Installations* by an Approved Contractor or Conforming Body enrolled with NICEIC, Warwick House, Houghton Hall Park, Houghton Regis, Dunstable, LU5 5ZX

Contractor's Reference Number

CRN/

DETAILS OF THE CLIENT

Client / Address:

DETAILS OF THE INSTALLATION

The installation is:

Address: New

Extent of the installation covered by this certificate: An addition / An ...

DESIGN § Details of permitted exceptions appended: **Yes / N/A** Risk assessment appended: **Yes / N/A** No. of pages §*Delete as appropriate*

I/We, being the person(s) responsible for the design of the electrical installation (as indicated by my/our signature(s) below), particulars of which are described above, having exercised reasonable skill and care when carrying out the design, hereby CERTIFY that the design work for which I/we have been responsible is, to the best of my/our knowledge and belief, in accordance with BS 7671, amended to (date) except for the departures, if any, detailed as follows:

Details of departures from BS 7671, as amended (Regulations 120.3, 133.5):

The extent of liability of the signatory/signatories is limited to the work described above as the subject of this certificate.
For the **DESIGN** of the installation: **(*Where there is divided responsibility for the design*)

Signature Date Name (CAPITALS) Designer 1

Signature Date Name (CAPITALS) ** Designer 2

responsible is, to the best of my knowledge and belief, in accordance with BS 7671, amended to (date) except for the departures, if any, detailed as follows:

Details of departures from BS 7671, as amended (Regulations 120.3, 133.5):

The extent of liability of the signatory is limited to the work described above as the subject of this certificate.
For the **CONSTRUCTION** of the installation:

Signature Date Name (CAPITALS) Constructor

INSPECTION AND TESTING

I, being the person responsible for the inspection and testing of the electrical installation (as indicated by my signatures below), particulars of which are described above, having exercised reasonable skill and care when carrying out the inspection and testing, hereby CERTIFY that the work for which I have been responsible is to the best of my knowledge and belief in accordance with BS 7671, amended to (date) except for the departures, if any, detailed as follows:

Details of departures from BS 7671, as amended (Regulations 120.3, 133.5):

The extent of liability of the signatory/signatories is limited to the work described above as the subject of this certificate.
For the **INSPECTION AND TESTING** of the installation: Reviewed by

Signature Date | Signature Date

Name (CAPITALS) Inspector | Name (CAPITALS) Qualified Supervisor †

DESIGN, CONSTRUCTION, INSPECTION AND TESTING * * This box to be completed only where the design, construction, inspection and testing have been the responsibility of one person.

§ Details of permitted exceptions appended: **Yes / N/A** Risk assessment appended: **Yes / N/A** No. of pages §*Delete as appropriate*

I, being the person responsible for the design, construction, inspection and testing of the electrical installation (as indicated by my signature below), particulars of which are described above, having exercised reasonable skill and care when carrying out the design, construction, inspection and testing, hereby CERTIFY that the said work for which I have been responsible is to the best of my knowledge and belief in accordance with BS 7671, amended to (date) except for the departures, if any, detailed as follows:

Details of departures from BS 7671, as amended (Regulations 120.3, 133.5):

The extent of liability of the signatory is limited to the work described above as the subject of this certificate.
For the **DESIGN**, the **CONSTRUCTION** and the **INSPECTION AND TESTING** of the installation. Reviewed by

Signature Date | Signature Date

Name (CAPITALS) | Name (CAPITALS) Qualified Supervisor ††

† *Where the inspection and testing have been carried out by an Approved Contractor, the inspection and testing results are to be reviewed by the registered Qualified Supervisor.*

†† *Where the design, the construction, and the inspection and testing have been the responsibility of one person, the inspection and testing results are to be reviewed by the registered Qualified Supervisor.*

Page 1 of

This certificate is based on the model forms shown in Appendix 6 of BS 7671

Please see the 'Notes for Recipients' on the reverse of this page.

ICN4/1

Design

Unless certification of the installation work has been undertaken by means of the section headed 'Design, Construction, Inspection and Testing', the design section should be completed and signed by the person who has taken responsibility for the design work. A signature for this element of the certification should preferably be obtained before installation work commences, at the time the design is handed over to the installing contractor.

Where responsibility for the design is divided between the Approved Contractor and one or more other bodies, the division of responsibility should be established and agreed before commencement of the installation work. The names and signatures of the designers should be inserted in the appropriate spaces provided.

The designer is the person or organisation responsible for all aspects of the installation design, such as the selection of protective devices, sizing of cables, method of installation, selection of suitable equipment, and precautions for special locations. The positioning of socket-outlets, lights etc are considered to be layout details and not electrical design, though the electrical designer will need to know the proposed positions of the equipment before completing the design calculations and determining that such positions will allow compliance with the requirements of *BS 7671*. In simple terms, the client or installation user may be able to decide where they require such items to be positioned, but the sizing and method of installing the cables and the selection of suitable equipment are matters for the designer.

Contractors that normally undertake installation work in domestic or small commercial premises only, may consider that they are not involved in installation design. However, if no other person or organisation is specifically responsible for the installation design, then the contractor will inevitably assume the role of the designer. This is the case even if the design work only involves the application of industry standards, such as for ring final circuits. In such cases the contractor will be responsible for the correct application of the industry standards and, consequently, for the whole installation design.

Where a designer applies a permitted exception in accordance with Regulation 411.3.3, the designer should confirm in the appropriate section of the certificate that details of the particular exception applied are appended to the certificate.

For an installation other than a dwelling, the designer may apply a permitted exception so that an RCD in accordance with Regulation 415.1.1 is not required for socket-outlets having a rating not exceeding 20 A. However, where such an exception is applied (as agreed with the client) it must be based on the clients documented risk assessment, and the designer should confirm that the risk assessment, or copy of it, is appended to the certificate.

Details of any intended departures from *BS 7671* should be stated, but exceptionally it may be necessary to attach a separate page to the certificate rather than to attempt to give an adequate description in the box provided. In such cases, write in the box

NICEIC APPROVED CONTRACTOR

This certificate is not valid if the serial number has been defaced or altered **ICN4/**

Original (To the person ordering the work)

ELECTRICAL INSTALLATION CERTIFICATE

Issued in accordance with *British Standard 7671 – Requirements for Electrical Installations* by an Approved Contractor or Conforming Body enrolled with NICEIC, Warwick House, Houghton Hall Park, Houghton Regis, Dunstable, LU5 5ZX

Contractor's Reference Number

CRN/

DETAILS OF THE CLIENT

Client / Address:

DETAILS OF THE INSTALLATION

The installation is:

Address: New

Extent of the installation covered by this certificate: An addition / An alteration

DESIGN

§ Details of permitted exceptions appended: **Yes / N/A** Risk assessment appended: **Yes / N/A** No. of pages §*Delete as appropriate*

I/We, being the person(s) responsible for the design of the electrical installation (as indicated by my/our signature(s) below), particulars of which are described above, having exercised reasonable skill and care when carrying out the design, hereby CERTIFY that the design work for which I/we have been responsible is, to the best of my/our knowledge and belief, in accordance with BS 7671, amended to (date) except for the departures, if any, detailed as follows:

Details of departures from BS 7671, as amended (Regulations 120.3, 133.5):

CONSTRUCTION

I, being the person responsible for the construction of the electrical installation (as indicated by my signature below), particulars of which are described above, having exercised reasonable skill and care when carrying out the construction, hereby CERTIFY that the construction work for which I have been responsible is, to the best of my knowledge and belief, in accordance with BS 7671, amended to (date) except for the departures, if any, detailed as follows:

Details of departures from BS 7671, as amended (Regulations 120.3, 133.5):

The extent of liability of the signatory is limited to the work described above as the subject of this certificate.

For the **CONSTRUCTION** of the installation:

Signature Date Name (CAPITALS) Constructor

INSPECTION AND TESTING

I, being the person responsible for the inspection and testing of the electrical installation (as indicated by my signatures below), particulars of which are described above, having exercised reasonable skill and care when carrying out the inspection and testing, hereby CERTIFY that the work for which I have been responsible is to the best of my knowledge and belief in accordance with BS 7671, amended to (date) except for the departures, if any, detailed as follows:

Details of departures from BS 7671, as amended (Regulations 120.3, 133.5):

The extent of liability of the signatory/signatories is limited to the work described above as the subject of this certificate.

For the **INSPECTION AND TESTING** of the installation: Reviewed by

Signature Date Signature Date

Name (CAPITALS) Inspector Name (CAPITALS) Qualified Supervisor †

DESIGN, CONSTRUCTION, INSPECTION AND TESTING *

* This box to be completed only where the design, construction, inspection and testing have been the responsibility of one person.

§ Details of permitted exceptions appended: **Yes / N/A** Risk assessment appended: **Yes / N/A** No. of pages §*Delete as appropriate*

I, being the person responsible for the design, construction, inspection and testing of the electrical installation (as indicated by my signature below), particulars of which are described above, having exercised reasonable skill and care when carrying out the design, construction, inspection and testing, hereby CERTIFY that the said work for which I have been responsible is to the best of my knowledge and belief in accordance with BS 7671, amended to (date) except for the departures, if any, detailed as follows:

Details of departures from BS 7671, as amended (Regulations 120.3, 133.5):

The extent of liability of the signatory is limited to the work described above as the subject of this certificate.

For the **DESIGN**, the **CONSTRUCTION** and the **INSPECTION AND TESTING** of the installation. Reviewed by

Signature Date Signature Date

Name (CAPITALS) Name (CAPITALS) Qualified Supervisor ††

† *Where the inspection and testing have been carried out by an Approved Contractor, the inspection and testing results are to be reviewed by the registered Qualified Supervisor.*

†† *Where the design, the construction, and the inspection and testing have been the responsibility of one person, the inspection and testing results are to be reviewed by the registered Qualified Supervisor.*

Page 1 of

This certificate is based on the model forms shown in Appendix 6 of BS 7671

Please see the 'Notes for Recipients' on the reverse of this page.

ICN4/1

'See details of departures on page X of this certificate'. The page number of the additional page will vary, depending on the number of schedules required.

Where the use of new materials or inventions leads to departures from *BS 7671*, details of the departures, which must not reduce the degree of safety, are to be recorded in the data-entry box provided in the Design section of the certificate (Regulation 133.5), and repeated in the data-entry boxes provided in the Construction and the Inspection and Testing sections to confirm the intent of the designer(s). Where no departures have been sanctioned by the designer(s), the data-entry boxes should be completed by entering 'None'.

The signatory or signatories to the design section are certifying that, with the exception of any stated departures, the design fully meets the requirements of the current issue of *BS 7671*. In signing this section, the signatory or signatories are accepting responsibility for the safety of the design.

Construction

Unless certification of the installation work has been undertaken by means of the section headed 'Design, Construction, Inspection and Testing', the construction section should be completed by the person who has taken responsibility for the construction work.

Certification of the construction is usually straightforward since the certificate should be issued by the installing contractor. **(In the case of an NICEIC certificate, it must be the installing Approved Contractor).**

In signing this section, the signatory is certifying that the construction, except for any intended departure(s) sanctioned by the designer, satisfies the requirements of *BS 7671*. Such certification can only be given if the signatory has a detailed knowledge of the construction of the particular installation.

If the signatory personally carried out the installation work, this presents little difficulty. If, however, the signatory is the Qualified Supervisor or other person involved in a supervisory capacity only, the level of supervision of the installation work must have been sufficient to enable the certification to be provided with confidence.

Inspection and testing

Unless certification of the installation work has been undertaken by means of the section headed 'Design, Construction, Inspection and Testing', the inspection and testing section should be completed and signed by the person who has taken responsibility for the inspection and testing work.

The person responsible for the inspection and testing of the new installation work should certify that the inspection and testing process has been carried out in accordance with *BS 7671*. If the signatory is the person who actually conducted the whole of the inspection and testing, this should be straightforward. However, if the

CONTRACTOR

PARTICULARS OF THE ORGANISATION(S) RESPONSIBLE FOR THE ELECTRICAL INSTALLATION

Original (To the person ordering

DESIGN (1)	Organisation †		
Address:	Postcode	NICEIC Enrolment No (where appropriate)	
		Branch number: (if applicable)	
DESIGN (2)	Organisation †		
Address:	Postcode	NICEIC Enrolment No (where appropriate)	
		Branch number: (if applicable)	
† CONSTRUCTION	Organisation		
Address: NICEIC APPROVED CONTRACTOR	Postcode	NICEIC Enrolment No (Essential information)	
		Branch number: (if applicable)	
INSPECTION AND TESTING	Organisation †		
Address:	Postcode	NICEIC Enrolment No (where appropriate)	
		Branch number: (if applicable)	

SUPPLY CHARACTERISTICS AND EARTHING ARRANGEMENTS *Tick boxes and enter details, as appropriate*

❖ System Type(s)	❖ Number and Type of Live Conductors			Nature of Supply Parameters		❖ Characteristics of Primary Supply Overcurrent Protective Device(s)	
TN-S	a.c.		d.c.	Nominal voltage(s): $U^{(1)}$ V	$U_0^{(1)}$ V	BS(EN)	
TN-C-S	1-phase (2-wire)	1-phase (3-wire)	2-pole	Nominal frequency, $f^{(1)}$ Hz	*Notes:* *(1) by enquiry*	Type	
TN-C	2-phase (3-wire)		3-pole	Prospective fault current, $I_{pf}^{(2)(3)}$ kA	*(2) by enquiry or by measurement*	Rated current	A
TT	3-phase (3-wire)	3-phase (4-wire)	other	External earth fault loop impedance, $Z_e^{(2)(3)}$ Ω	*(3) where more than one supply, record the higher or highest values*	Short-circuit capacity	kA
IT	Other	Please state		Number of sources		Confirmation of supply polarity	(✓)

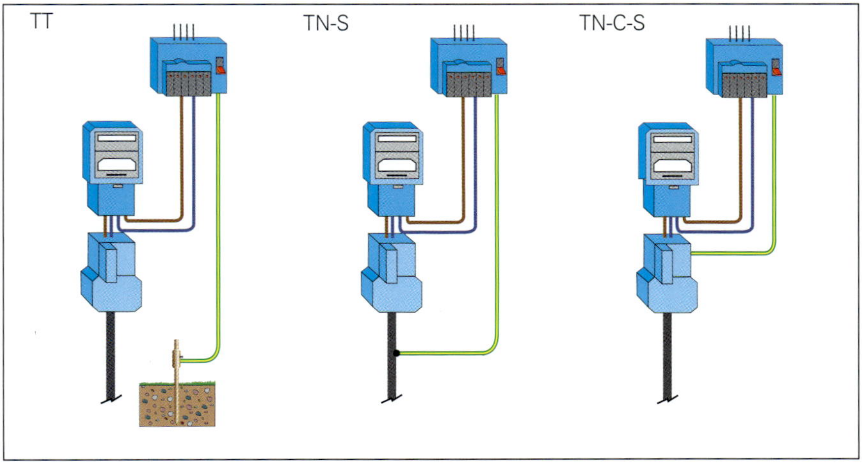

process was conducted by more than one person, or if a Qualified Supervisor or someone in a similar supervisory capacity certifies the inspection and testing work on behalf of the Approved Contractor, that person must be entirely satisfied that the process was carried out thoroughly and in accordance with Part 6 of *BS 7671*, and that the results are consistent with installation work complying with all the relevant requirements of that standard.

The body responsible for the inspection and testing of the electrical work is also responsible for comparing the results with the relevant criteria (Regulation 612.1).

PARTICULARS OF THE ORGANISATION(S) RESPONSIBLE FOR THE ELECTRICAL INSTALLATION

Completion of the 'Particulars of the Organisation(s) Responsible for the Electrical Installation' on page 2 of the certificate will identify to the recipient the organisation(s) responsible for the work certified by their representative(s) on page 1. The organisation(s), address(es) and postcode(s) must be given, together with their NICEIC Enrolment Number and Branch Number, where appropriate. Where an Approved Contractor has been responsible for elements of the work in addition to construction, repetition of the 'Particulars of the Organisation(s) Responsible for the Electrical Installation' section is unnecessary and, in such cases, the words 'Details as given for Construction' may be inserted, where appropriate.

SUPPLY CHARACTERISTICS AND EARTHING ARRANGEMENTS

System type(s)

In the United Kingdom, it is likely that the type of system will be either TT, TN-S or TN-C-S. TN-C and IT systems are not common in the UK, and are therefore not covered in this book.

The common types of system can be briefly described by means of their particular earthing arrangements (assuming that the supply is derived from an electricity distributor at low voltage):

- TT - Earthing provided by the consumer's own installation earth electrode - no earthing facility is made available to the consumer by the distributor, or if such a facility is made available, it is not used.
- TN-S - Earthing facility provided by the distributor for the consumer's use - provision usually by means of a connection to the supply cable sheath or a separate protective conductor in the form of a split-concentric cable or overhead conductor.
- TN-C-S - Earthing facility provided by the distributor, connected to the incoming supply neutral to give a Protective Multiple Earth (PME) supply, where the supply neutral and protective conductors are in the form of a Combined Neutral and Earth (CNE) conductor.

APPROVED CONTRACTOR

This certificate is not valid if the serial number has been defaced or altered **ICN4/**

Original (To the person ordering the work)

PARTICULARS OF THE ORGANISATION(S) RESPONSIBLE FOR THE ELECTRICAL INSTALLATION

DESIGN (1) Organisation †
Address:
Postcode
NICEIC Enrolment No (where appropriate)
Branch number: (if applicable)

DESIGN (2) Organisation †
Address:
Postcode
NICEIC Enrolment No (where appropriate)
Branch number: (if applicable)

† CONSTRUCTION Organisation
Address:
Postcode
NICEIC Enrolment No (Essential information)
Branch number: (if applicable)

INSPECTION AND TESTING Organisation †
Address:
NICEIC Enrolment No (where appropriate)
Branch number:

SUPPLY CHARACTERISTICS AND EARTHING ARRANGEMENTS

Tick boxes and enter details, as appropriate

✣ System Type(s)	✣ Number and Type of Live Conductors			Nature of Supply Parameters		✣ Characteristics of Primary Supply Overcurrent Protective Device(s)	
TN-S	a.c.		d.c.	Nominal voltage(s): $U^{(1)}$ V	$U_0^{(1)}$ V	BS(EN)	
TN-C-S	1-phase (2-wire)	1-phase (3-wire)	2-pole	Nominal frequency, $f^{(1)}$ Hz	*Notes:*	Type	
TN-C	2-phase (3-wire)		3-pole	Prospective fault current, $I_{pf}^{(2)(3)}$ kA	*(1) by enquiry*	Rated current	A
TT	3-phase (3-wire)	3-phase (4-wire)	other	External earth fault loop impedance, $Z_e^{(2)(3)}$ Ω	*(2) by enquiry or by measurement*	Short-circuit capacity	kA
IT	Other	Please state		Number of sources	*(3) where more than one supply, record the higher or highest values*	Confirmation of supply polarity	(✓)

✣ Means of Earthing	Details of Installation Earth Electrode (where applicable)	
Distributor's facility:	Type: (eg rod(s), tape etc)	Location:
Installation earth electrode:	Electrode resistance, R_A: (Ω)	Method of measurement:

✣ Main Switch/Switch-Fuse/ Circuit-Breaker/RCD

Type BS(EN)		Voltage rating	V
No of poles		Rated current, I_n	A
Supply conductors material		RCD operating current, $I_{\Delta n}$*	mA
Supply conductors csa	mm²	RCD operating time (at $I_{\Delta n}$)*	ms
		Rated time delay*	ms

* (applicable only where an RCD is suitable and is used as a main circuit-breaker)

Maximum Demand (Load): kVA / Amps *Delete as appropriate

Protective measures against electric shock:

Earthing and Protective Bonding Conductors

Earthing conductor		Main protective bonding conductors		Bonding of extraneous-conductive-parts (✓)	
Conductor material		Conductor material		Water installation pipes	Lightning protection
Conductor csa	mm²	Conductor csa	mm²	Oil installation pipes	Structural steel
Continuity/ connection verified	(✓)	Continuity/ connection verified	(✓)	Gas installation pipes	Other

COMMENTS ON EXISTING INSTALLATION

In the case of an alteration or additions see Section 633

Note: Enter 'NONE' or, where appropriate, the page number(s) of additional page(s) of comments on the existing installation.

NEXT INSPECTION**

§ *Enter interval in terms of years, months or weeks, as appropriate* §

I/We, the designer(s), RECOMMEND that this installation is further inspected and tested after an interval of not more than

** *The proposed date for the next inspection should take into consideration the frequency and quality of maintenance that the installation can reasonably be expected to receive during its intended life, and the period should be agreed between the designer, installer and other relevant parties.*

† *Where the Approved Contractor responsible for the construction of the electrical installation has also been responsible for the design* ***and*** *the inspection and testing of that installation, the 'Particulars of the Organisation(s) responsible for the Electrical Installation' may be recorded only in the section entitled 'CONSTRUCTION'.*

✣ *Where a number of sources are available to supply the installation, and where the data given for the primary source may differ from other sources, a separate sheet must be provided which identifies the relevant information relating to each additional source.*

This certificate is based on the model forms shown in Appendix 6 of BS 7671

Page 2 of

Please see the 'Notes for Recipients' on the reverse of this page.

ICN4/3

Within certain types of building or site, more than one system earthing arrangement may have been employed by the designer. For example, an installation in a sports complex may as a whole form part of a TN-C-S system, with the majority of the installation earthed to the PME earthing facility. For electrical design reasons, however, particular parts of the installation, such as a swimming pool area, may form part of a TT system. Where an installation has more than one system earthing arrangement, each arrangement needs to be recorded on the certificate.

Number and type of live conductors

The details required to complete this section are straightforward, requiring an identification of the nature of supply current, in terms of a.c. or d.c., and the number of the supply live conductors (including the neutral). In most cases, the supply will be single-phase (two-wire) or three-phase (three-wire or four-wire). Facilities for recording other configurations are also provided.

Nature of supply parameters

Provision is made in this section to record the supply parameters which comprise:

- Nominal voltage(s), U (line-to-line), and U_0 (line-to-earth) (in volts). For public two-phase and three-phase supplies in the UK, U is 400 V and U_0 is 230 V, and for public single-phase supplies, U is not applicable (N/A) and U_0 is 230 V. Do not record measured values, however accurate.
- Nominal frequency, f (in Hz). This parameter can generally be determined only by enquiry, but in the UK the nominal frequency is almost invariably 50 Hz.
- Prospective fault current, I_{pf} (in kA). This is the maximum fault current likely to occur in the installation, on which value the design and selection of equipment have been based. The magnitude of the prospective fault current may be obtained by 'measurement', or 'by enquiry'. Detailed guidance on the measurement of prospective fault current is given in Chapter 9. Alternatively, the designer may obtain a value of prospective fault current by enquiring at the appropriate department of the electricity distributor. Usually, neither the designer nor the person responsible for inspection and testing will have sufficient information to enable a realistic value to be calculated.
- External earth fault loop impedance, Z_e (in Ω). As with the prospective fault current, guidance relating to the measurement of the external earth fault loop impedance (Z_e) is given in Chapter 9. The external earth fault loop impedance is measured in much the same way as the earth fault loop impedance at any other point in the installation. The alternative method, namely 'enquiry', is permitted

NICEIC APPROVED CONTRACTOR

This certificate is not valid if the serial number has been defaced or altered **ICN4/**

Original (To the person ordering the work)

PARTICULARS OF THE ORGANISATION(S) RESPONSIBLE FOR THE ELECTRICAL INSTALLATION

DESIGN (1) Organisation †
Address:
Postcode
NICEIC Enrolment No (where appropriate)
Branch number: (if applicable)

DESIGN (2) Organisation †
Address:
Postcode
NICEIC Enrolment No (where appropriate)
Branch number: (if applicable)

CONSTRUCTION † Organisation
Address:
NICEIC APPROVED CONTRACTOR
Postcode
NICEIC Enrolment No (Essential information)
Branch number: (if applicable)

INSPECTION AND TESTING Organisation †
Address:
Postcode
NICEIC Enrolment No (where appropriate)
Branch number (if applicable)

SUPPLY CHARACTERISTICS AND EARTHING ARRANGEMENTS

Tick boxes and enter details, as appropriate

❖ System Type(s): TN-S, TN-C-S, TN-C, TT, IT

❖ Number and Type of Live Conductors: a.c. | d.c.; 1-phase (2-wire); 1-phase (3-wire); 2-pole; 2-phase (3-wire); 3-pole; 3-phase (3-wire); 3-phase (4-wire); other; Other Please state

Nature of Supply Parameters:
Nominal voltage(s): U (1) V, U_0 (1)
Nominal frequency, f (1) Hz
Prospective fault current, I_{pf} (2)(3) kA
External earth fault loop impedance, Z_e (2)(3) Ω
Number of

Notes:
(1) by enquiry
(2) by enquiry or by measurement
(3) where more than one supply, record the higher or highest values

❖ Characteristics of Primary Supply Overcurrent Protective Device(s)
BS(EN)
Type
Rated current A
Short-circuit capacity kA
Confirmation of supply polarity (✓)

PARTICULARS OF INSTALLATION AT THE ORIGIN

Tick boxes and enter details, as appropriate

❖ **Means of Earthing**
Distributor's facility:
Installation earth electrode:

Details of Installation Earth Electrode (where applicable)
Type: (eg rod(s), tape etc)
Location:
Electrode resistance, R_A: (Ω)
Method of measurement:

❖ Main Switch/Switch-Fuse/Circuit-Breaker/RCD
Type BS(EN); Voltage rating V
No of poles; Rated current, I_n A
Supply conductors material; RCD operating current, $I_{\Delta n}$* mA
Supply conductors csa mm²; RCD operating time (at $I_{\Delta n}$)* ms
Rated time delay* ms
* (applicable only where an RCD is suitable and is used as a main circuit-breaker)

Maximum Demand (Load): kVA / Amps *Delete as appropriate
Protective measures against electric shock:

Earthing and Protective Bonding Conductors

Earthing conductor: Conductor material; Conductor csa mm²; Continuity/connection verified (✓)

Main protective bonding conductors: Conductor material; Conductor csa mm²; Continuity/connection verified (✓)

Bonding of extraneous-conductive-parts (✓): Water installation pipes; Lightning protection; Oil installation pipes; Structural steel; Gas installation pipes; Other

COMMENTS ON EXISTING INSTALLATION

In the case of an alteration or additions see Section 633

Note: Enter 'NONE' or, where appropriate, the page number(s) of additional page(s) of comments on the existing installation.

NEXT INSPECTION**

§ *Enter interval in terms of years, months or weeks, as appropriate* §

I/We, the designer(s), RECOMMEND that this installation is further inspected and tested after an interval of not more than

** *The proposed date for the next inspection should take into consideration the frequency and quality of maintenance that the installation can reasonably be expected to receive during its intended life, and the period should be agreed between the designer, installer and other relevant parties.*

† *Where the Approved Contractor responsible for the construction of the electrical installation has also been responsible for the design* ***and*** *the inspection and testing of that installation, the 'Particulars of the Organisation(s) responsible for the Electrical Installation' may be recorded only in the section entitled 'CONSTRUCTION'.*

❖ *Where a number of sources are available to supply the installation, and where the data given for the primary source may differ from other sources, a separate sheet must be provided which identifies the relevant information relating to each additional source.*

Page 2 of

Please see the 'Notes for Recipients' on the reverse of this page.

This certificate is based on the model forms shown in Appendix 6 of BS 7671

ICN4/3

for the determination of Z_e. If Z_e is determined by enquiry, it is normally necessary also to obtain a measured value to verify that the intended means of earthing is present and of the expected value.

- **Number of sources**. This detail is required even where there is only one source of supply, in which case the entry should be '1'. Where more than one source of supply is available, for example the public supply and a standby generator, the total number must be recorded (in this case '2').

Where the installation can be supplied by more than one source, such as the public supply and a standby generator, the higher or highest values of prospective fault current, I_{pf}, and external earth fault loop impedance, Z_e, must be recorded in the data-entry boxes provided for this purpose.

Characteristics of primary supply overcurrent protective device(s)

The information to be recorded here is the British Standard (or other appropriate Standard) product specification in terms of BS (EN) number, together with the type, the rated current (I_n), and the short-circuit capacity of the device. This information should be obtained from the installation designer at an early stage, or by reference to the Electrical Installation Certificate issued on completion of the original electrical installation. Where it has not been possible to determine the details of the supply fuse(s) by these means, confirmation of type and rating should be sought from the electricity distributor. In addition, polarity of the supply should be confirmed and indicated by ticking the box provided.

Where a number of sources are available to supply the installation, and where the data given for the primary source may differ from other supplies, an additional page should be included in the certificate giving the relevant information for each additional supply.

PARTICULARS OF INSTALLATION AT THE ORIGIN

Means of earthing

Where the protective measure for fault protection is provided by Automatic Disconnection of Supply (ADS), there is a need to provide a connection of all exposed-conductive-parts and extraneous-conductive-parts to a means of protective earthing via the main earthing terminal. The information required here is for the purpose of identifying the particular means of earthing used, in terms of a **distributor's facility** and/or an **installation earth electrode.**

Details of installation earth electrode

Every TT system must have an installation earth electrode. If the system is not TT and there is no earth electrode, write 'NONE' for the type and 'N/A' (Not Applicable) for the location. Do not leave any boxes empty.

NICEIC APPROVED CONTRACTOR

This certificate is not valid if the serial number has been defaced or altered **ICN4/**

Original (To the person ordering the work)

PARTICULARS OF THE ORGANISATION(S) RESPONSIBLE FOR THE ELECTRICAL INSTALLATION

DESIGN (1) Organisation †

Address:

Postcode

NICEIC Enrolment No (where appropriate)

Branch number: (if applicable)

DESIGN (2) Organisation †

Address:

Postcode

NICEIC Enrolment No (where appropriate)

Branch number: (if applicable)

CONSTRUCTION † Organisation

Address:

NICEIC APPROVED CONTRACTOR

Postcode

NICEIC Enrolment No (Essential information)

Branch number: (if applicable)

INSPECTION AND TESTING Organisation †

Address:

Postcode

NICEIC Enrolment No (where appropriate)

Branch number: (if applicable)

SUPPLY CHARACTERISTICS AND EARTHING ARRANGEMENTS

Tick boxes and enter details, as appropriate

❖ System Type(s): TN-S, TN-C-S, TN-C, TT, IT

❖ Number and Type of Live Conductors

a.c.: 1-phase (2-wire), 1-phase (3-wire), 2-phase (3-wire), 3-phase (3-wire), 3-phase (4-wire), Other (Please state)

d.c.: 2-pole, 3-pole, other

Nature of Supply Parameters

Nominal voltage(s): $U^{(1)}$ V $U_0^{(1)}$ V

Nominal frequency, $f^{(1)}$ Hz

Prospective fault current, $I_{pf}^{(2)(3)}$ kA

External earth fault loop impedance, $Z_e^{(2)(3)}$ Ω

Number of sources

Notes:
(1) by enquiry
(2) by enquiry or by measurement
(3) where more than one supply, record the higher or highest values

❖ Characteristics of Primary Supply Overcurrent Protective Device(s)

BS(EN)

Type

Rated current A

Short-circuit capacity kA

Confirmation of supply polarity (✓)

PARTICULARS OF INSTALLATION AT THE ORIGIN

Tick boxes and enter details, as appropriate

❖ Means of Earthing

Distributor's facility:

Installation

Details of Installation Earth Electrode (where applicable)

Type: (eg rod(s), tape etc)

Location:

Electrode (Ω)

Method of measurement:

❖ Main Switch/Switch-Fuse/ Circuit-Breaker/RCD

Type BS(EN)

No of poles

Supply conductors material

Supply conductors csa mm²

Voltage rating V

Rated current, I_n A

RCD operating current, $I_{\Delta n}$* mA

RCD operating time (at $I_{\Delta n}$)* ms

Rated time delay* ms

* (applicable only where an RCD is suitable and is used as a main circuit-breaker)

Maximum Demand (Load): kVA / Amps *Delete as appropriate

Protective measures against electric shock:

Earthing and Protective Bonding Conductors

Earthing conductor: Conductor material; Conductor csa mm²; Continuity/connection verified (✓)

Main protective bonding conductors: Conductor material; Conductor csa mm²; Continuity/connection verified (✓)

Bonding of extraneous-conductive-parts (✓): Water installation pipes; Oil installation pipes; Gas installation pipes; Lightning protection; Structural steel; Other

INSTALLATION

In the case of an alteration or additions see Section 633

Note: Enter 'NONE' or, where appropriate, the page number(s) of additional page(s) of comments on the existing installation.

NEXT INSPECTION**

§ *Enter interval in terms of years, months or weeks, as appropriate* §

I/We, the designer(s), RECOMMEND that this installation is further inspected and tested after an interval of not more than

** *The proposed date for the next inspection should take into consideration the frequency and quality of maintenance that the installation can reasonably be expected to receive during its intended life, and the period should be agreed between the designer, installer and other relevant parties.*

† *Where the Approved Contractor responsible for the construction of the electrical installation has also been responsible for the design **and** the inspection and testing of that installation, the 'Particulars of the Organisation(s) responsible for the Electrical Installation' may be recorded only in the section entitled 'CONSTRUCTION'.*

❖ *Where a number of sources are available to supply the installation, and where the data given for the primary source may differ from other sources, a separate sheet must be provided which identifies the relevant information relating to each additional source.*

Page 2 of

Please see the 'Notes for Recipients' on the reverse of this page.

This certificate is based on the model forms shown in Appendix 6 of BS 7671

ICN4/3

If the installation has an earth electrode, give a brief description of its type. The types of earth electrode recognised by *BS 7671* are listed in Regulation 542.2.3. Metal pipework forming part of a gas, flammable liquids, water or any other service network must not be used as an earth electrode (Regulation 542.2.6 refers).

Sufficient details must be given under 'location' so that skilled persons unfamiliar with the installation and building layout will be able to locate the electrode for periodic inspection and testing purposes.

The earth electrode resistance, R_A, must be measured and the ohmic value recorded in the space provided for the purpose.

The method used to measure the earth electrode resistance to earth must also be recorded. Guidance on the following test methods are provided in Chapter 9:

- Using a proprietary earth electrode test instrument.
- Using an earth fault loop impedance test instrument.

Where suitable and sufficient ground area is available for measurement purposes, a proprietary earth electrode test instrument may be used. Where hard surfaces or lack of space make the use of this method impracticable, the use of an earth fault loop impedance test instrument is appropriate.

Factors to be considered when choosing the method to use are given in Chapter 9.

Main Switch/Switch-Fuse/Circuit-Breaker/RCD

Type BS (EN)

This is normally a straightforward process of copying down the details from the installation design, having checked that the installed device conforms to that design. The types of main switch/switch-fuse/circuit-breaker and RCD commonly used should have the relevant British Standard or BS EN number clearly marked. If, after checking both the design information and the device, no BS number or any other meaningful identification of the type of the device can be found, the lack of this essential information should be referred to the designer for clarification. Do not leave the box blank.

Voltage rating

This is normally a straightforward process of copying down the relevant details from the installation design, having first checked that the device has been selected and installed in accordance with that design.

Number of poles

The number of poles is usually 2 for a single-phase device, and 3 or 4 for a three-phase device. The actual number of poles must be confirmed before writing the number in the box, as a variety of switching arrangements are available.

NICEIC APPROVED CONTRACTOR

This certificate is not valid if the serial number has been defaced or altered **ICN4/**

Original (To the person ordering the work)

PARTICULARS OF THE ORGANISATION(S) RESPONSIBLE FOR THE ELECTRICAL INSTALLATION

DESIGN (1) Organisation †

Address:

Postcode

NICEIC Enrolment No (where appropriate)

Branch number: (if applicable)

DESIGN (2) Organisation †

Address:

Postcode

NICEIC Enrolment No (where appropriate)

Branch number: (if applicable)

† CONSTRUCTION Organisation

Address:

NICEIC APPROVED CONTRACTOR

Postcode

NICEIC Enrolment No (Essential information)

Branch number: (if applicable)

INSPECTION AND TESTING Organisation †

Address:

Postcode

NICEIC Enrolment No (where appropriate)

Branch number: (if applicable)

SUPPLY CHARACTERISTICS AND EARTHING ARRANGEMENTS

Tick boxes and enter details, as appropriate

✣ System Type(s)	✣ Number and Type of Live Conductors			Nature of Supply Parameters		✣ Characteristics of Primary Supply Overcurrent Protective Device(s)
TN-S	a.c.		d.c.	Nominal voltage(s): $U^{(1)}$ V	$U_0^{(1)}$ V	BS(EN)
TN-C-S	1-phase (2-wire)	1-phase (3-wire)	2-pole	Nominal frequency, $f^{(1)}$ Hz	*Notes:* *(1) by enquiry*	Type
TN-C	2-phase (3-wire)		3-pole	Prospective fault current, $I_{pf}^{(2)(3)}$ kA	*(2) by enquiry or by measurement*	Rated current A
TT	3-phase (3-wire)	3-phase (4-wire)	other	External earth fault loop impedance, $Z_e^{(2)(3)}$ Ω	*(3) where more than one supply, record the higher or highest values*	Short-circuit capacity kA
IT	Other Please state			Number of sources		Confirmation of supply polarity (✓)

PARTICULARS OF INSTALLATION AT THE ORIGIN

Tick boxes and enter details, as appropriate

✣ Means of Earthing	Details of Installation Earth Electrode (where applicable)	
Distributor's facility:	Type: (eg rod(s), tape etc)	Location:
Installation	Electrode	Method of

✣ Main Switch/Switch-Fuse/ Circuit-Breaker/RCD

Type BS(EN)		Voltage rating	V
No of poles		Rated current, I_n	A
Supply conductors material		RCD operating current, $I_{\Delta n}$*	mA
Supply conductors csa	mm²	RCD operating time (at $I_{\Delta n}$)*	ms
		Rated time delay*	ms

* *(applicable only where an RCD is suitable and is used as a main circuit-breaker)*

Maximum Demand (Load): kVA / Amps *Delete as appropriate

Protective measures against electric shock:

Earthing and Protective Bonding Conductors

Earthing conductor		Main protective bonding conductors	
Conductor material		Conductor material	
Conductor csa	mm²	Conductor csa	mm²
Continuity/ connection verified	(✓)	Continuity/ connection verified	(✓)

Bonding of extraneous-conductive-parts (✓)

Water installation pipes		Lightning protection	
Oil installation pipes		Structural steel	
Gas installation pipes		Other	

In the case of an alteration or additions see Section 633 ... *of additional page(s) of comments on the existing installation.*

NEXT INSPECTION**

§ *Enter interval in terms of years, months or weeks, as appropriate* §

I/We, the designer(s), RECOMMEND that this installation is further inspected and tested after an interval of not more than

** *The proposed date for the next inspection should take into consideration the frequency and quality of maintenance that the installation can reasonably be expected to receive during its intended life, and the period should be agreed between the designer, installer and other relevant parties.*

† *Where the Approved Contractor responsible for the construction of the electrical installation has also been responsible for the design **and** the inspection and testing of that installation, the 'Particulars of the Organisation(s) responsible for the Electrical Installation' may be recorded only in the section entitled 'CONSTRUCTION'.*

✣ *Where a number of sources are available to supply the installation, and where the data given for the primary source may differ from other sources, a separate sheet must be provided which identifies the relevant information relating to each additional source.*

Page 2 of

Please see the 'Notes for Recipients' on the reverse of this page.

This certificate is based on the model forms shown in Appendix 6 of BS 7671

ICN4/3

Rated current (I_n)

The information required here is the rated current , which is normally clearly indicated on the device (or on the fuse, if provided). This should be checked against the design information.

Supply conductors: material

The supply conductor material is required to be identified here. This is generally the conductor material of the 'tails' from the electricity distributor's meter to the consumer's installation main switch, and is usually copper.

Supply conductors: csa

This is the cross-sectional area of the supply conductors (for example, 50 mm^2).

Where the main circuit-breaker is an RCD

The BS (EN) number, voltage rating, number of poles and rated current should be determined by examining both the design information and the installed device. The rating referred to in this case is the rated current, I_n, **not** the rated residual operating (tripping) current, $I_{\Delta n}$, of the device.

RCD residual operating current ($I_{\Delta n}$)

This should be determined from the design information and checked with the marking on the device. The rated residual operating (tripping) current will usually be given in units of mA (for example '300 mA'), but in some instances it may be stated in amperes (for example '0.3 A'). An RCD may operate (trip) at a current just a little more than half its rated residual operating current. Where an RCD is used as a main circuit-breaker, it should generally not have a low rated residual operating current (i.e. below 100 mA), in order to minimise the risk of unwanted tripping.

RCD operating time (at $I_{\Delta n}$)

Guidance on this test, which requires the use of an RCD test instrument, is given in Chapter 9. Record in the box the measured operating time in milliseconds when subjected to a test current equal to the rated residual operating current, $I_{\Delta n}$.

Rated time delay

Where an RCD is installed as the main circuit-breaker, to provide discrimination between that device and any RCD positioned downstream of it requires an RCD classified as 'type S' (for selectivity) which incorporates a time-delay. Where this is the case, the rated time-delay in milliseconds of the RCD should be recorded.

It should be noted that an RCDs used for additional protection are not permitted to have an operating time delay. Such devices must operate in accordance with Regulation 415.1.1.

NICEIC APPROVED CONTRACTOR

This certificate is not valid if the serial number has been defaced or altered **ICN4/**

Original (To the person ordering the work)

PARTICULARS OF THE ORGANISATION(S) RESPONSIBLE FOR THE ELECTRICAL INSTALLATION

DESIGN (1) Organisation †

Address:

Postcode

NICEIC Enrolment No (where appropriate)

Branch number: (if applicable)

DESIGN (2) Organisation †

Address:

Postcode

NICEIC Enrolment No (where appropriate)

Branch number: (if applicable)

† CONSTRUCTION Organisation

Address:

NICEIC APPROVED CONTRACTOR

Postcode

NICEIC Enrolment No (Essential information)

Branch number: (if applicable)

INSPECTION AND TESTING Organisation †

Address:

Postcode

NICEIC Enrolment No (where appropriate)

Branch number: (if applicable)

SUPPLY CHARACTERISTICS AND EARTHING ARRANGEMENTS

Tick boxes and enter details, as appropriate

✣ System Type(s)

TN-S · TN-C-S · TN-C · TT · IT

✣ Number and Type of Live Conductors

a.c. · d.c.

1-phase (2-wire) · 1-phase (3-wire) · 2-pole

2-phase (3-wire) · 3-pole

3-phase (3-wire) · 3-phase (4-wire) · other

Other — Please state

Nature of Supply Parameters

Nominal voltage(s): $U^{(1)}$ V $U_0^{(1)}$ V

Nominal frequency, $f^{(1)}$ Hz

Prospective fault current, $I_{pf}^{(2)(3)}$ kA

External earth fault loop impedance, $Z_e^{(2)(3)}$ Ω

Number of sources

Notes:

(1) by enquiry

(2) by enquiry or by measurement

(3) where more than one supply, record the higher or highest values

✣ Characteristics of Primary Supply Overcurrent Protective Device(s)

BS(EN)

Type

Rated current A

Short-circuit capacity kA

Confirmation of supply polarity (✓)

PARTICULARS OF INSTALLATION AT THE ORIGIN

Tick boxes and enter details, as appropriate

✣ Means of Earthing

Distributor's facility:

Installation earth electrode:

Details of Installation Earth Electrode (where applicable)

Type: (eg rod(s), tape etc)

Location:

Electrode resistance, R_A:

✣ Main Switch/Switch-Fuse/ Circuit-Breaker/R

Type BS(EN)

No of poles

Supply conductors material

Supply conductors csa mm²

Voltage rating V

Rated current, I_n A

RCD operating current, $I_{\Delta n}$* mA

RCD operating time (at $I_{\Delta n}$)* ms

Rated time delay* ms

* (applicable only where an RCD is suitable and is used as a main circuit-b...er)

Maximum Demand (Load): kVA / Amps *Delete as appropriate

Protective measures against electric shock:

Earthing and Protective Bonding Conductors

Earthing conductor

Conductor material

Conductor csa mm²

Continuity/ connection verified (✓)

Main protective bonding conductors

Conductor material

Conductor csa mm²

Continuity/ connection verified (✓)

Bonding of extraneous-conductive-parts (✓)

Water installation pipes · Lightning protection

Oil installation pipes · Structural steel

Gas installation pipes · Other

COMMENTS ON EXISTING INSTALLATION

In the case of an alteration or additions see Section 633

Note: Enter 'NONE' or, where appropriate, the page number(s) of additional page(s) of comments on the existing installation.

NEXT INSPECTION**

§ *Enter interval in terms of years, months or weeks, as appropriate* §

I/We, the designer(s), RECOMMEND that this installation is further inspected and tested after an interval of not more than

** *The proposed date for the next inspection should take into consideration the frequency and quality of maintenance that the installation can reasonably be expected to receive during its intended life, and the period should be agreed between the designer, installer and other relevant parties.*

† *Where the Approved Contractor responsible for the construction of the electrical installation has also been responsible for the design* ***and*** *the inspection and testing of that installation, the 'Particulars of the Organisation(s) responsible for the Electrical Installation' may be recorded only in the section entitled 'CONSTRUCTION'.*

✣ *Where a number of sources are available to supply the installation, and where the data given for the primary source may differ from other sources, a separate sheet must be provided which identifies the relevant information relating to each additional source.*

Page 2 of

Please see the 'Notes for Recipients' on the reverse of this page.

This certificate is based on the model forms shown in Appendix 6 of BS 7671

ICN4/3

Maximum demand (load)

This is not, as is sometimes assumed, the rating of the electricity distributor's cut-out fuse(s). The maximum demand is a value, expressed in amperes or kVA per phase, evaluated on the basis of the connected load (in amperes) with an allowance for diversity, and if required converted to kVA. The installation designer would normally be expected to provide the maximum demand value. For smaller installations, guidance on estimating the maximum demand is given in *IET Guidance Note 1: Selection and Erection*. There are, however, other methods by which the maximum demand current may be assessed, and these are not precluded provided they give realistic values.

In the case of alterations and additions, it is essential that an assessment of the maximum demand of the existing installation is made prior to carrying out modifications. To this assessment of the existing maximum demand must be added all additional loads resulting from the proposed new work, taking account of diversity as appropriate, so that the suitability of the incoming electricity service to supply the proposed increase in load can be ascertained.

Protective measure against electric shock

This refers to the principal protective measure for fault protection. In many, if not all, cases the method will be Automatic Disconnection of Supply (ADS). The particular method the designer has chosen to use from those listed in Chapter 41 must be fully described here.

Earthing and protective bonding conductors

Earthing conductor

The earthing conductor is the protective conductor that connects the main earthing terminal of the installation to the means of earthing. The conductor material and cross-sectional area of the earthing conductor must be stated here, followed by a tick to confirm that its continuity has been checked. This indication confirms that the inspector has tested the earthing conductor, and/or inspected it throughout its length and checked its connections, and that the result is satisfactory.

Main protective bonding conductors

The conductor material and cross-sectional area of the protective bonding conductors must be stated here, followed by a tick to confirm that their continuity has been checked. This indication confirms that the inspector has tested the continuity of the protective bonding conductors and/or inspected them throughout their length and checked their connections, and that the results are satisfactory.

NICEIC APPROVED CONTRACTOR

This certificate is not valid if the serial number has been defaced or altered **ICN4/**

Original (To the person ordering the work)

PARTICULARS OF THE ORGANISATION(S) RESPONSIBLE FOR THE ELECTRICAL INSTALLATION

DESIGN (1) Organisation †
Address: Postcode
NICEIC Enrolment No (where appropriate)
Branch number: (if applicable)

DESIGN (2) Organisation †
Address: Postcode
NICEIC Enrolment No (where appropriate)
Branch number: (if applicable)

† CONSTRUCTION Organisation
Address: Postcode
NICEIC Enrolment No (Essential information)
Branch number: (if applicable)

INSPECTION AND TESTING Organisation †
Address: Postcode
NICEIC Enrolment No (where appropriate)
Branch number: (if applicable)

SUPPLY CHARACTERISTICS AND EARTHING ARRANGEMENTS

Tick boxes and enter details, as appropriate

❖ System Type(s): TN-S, TN-C-S, TN-C, TT, IT

❖ Number and Type of Live Conductors: a.c. / d.c.; 1-phase (2-wire), 1-phase (3-wire), 2-pole; 2-phase (3-wire), 3-pole; 3-phase (3-wire), 3-phase (4-wire), other; Other (Please state)

Nature of Supply Parameters
Nominal voltage(s): $U^{(1)}$ V $U_0^{(1)}$ V
Nominal frequency, $f^{(1)}$ Hz
Prospective fault current, $I_{pf}^{(2)(3)}$ kA
External earth fault loop impedance, $Z_e^{(2)(3)}$ Ω
Number of sources

Notes:
(1) by enquiry
(2) by enquiry or by measurement
(3) where more than one supply, record the higher or highest values

❖ Characteristics of Primary Supply Overcurrent Protective Device(s)
BS(EN)
Type
Rated current A
Short-circuit capacity kA
Confirmation of supply polarity (✓)

PARTICULARS OF INSTALLATION AT THE ORIGIN

Tick boxes and enter details, as appropriate

❖ Means of Earthing: Distributor's facility; Installation earth electrode

Details of Installation Earth Electrode (where applicable)
Type: (eg rod(s), tape etc)
Location:
Electrode resistance, R_A: (Ω)
Method of measurement:

❖ Main Switch/Switch-Fuse/ Circuit-Breaker/RCD
Type BS(EN)
Voltage rating V
No of poles
Rated current, I_n A
Supply conductors material
RCD operating current, $I_{\Delta n}$* mA
Supply conductors csa mm²
RCD operating time (at $I_{\Delta n}$)* ms
Rated time ...

Maximum Demand (Load): kVA / Amps *Delete as appropriate

Protective measures against electric shock:

Earthing and Protective Bonding Conductors
Earthing conductor: Conductor material; Conductor csa mm²; Continuity/ connection (✓)
Main protective bonding conductors: Conductor material; Conductor csa mm²; Continuity/ connection (✓)
Bonding of extraneous-conductive-parts (✓): Water installation pipes; Lightning protection; Oil installation pipes; Structural steel; Gas installation ...; Other

COMMENTS ON EXISTING INSTALLATION

In the case of an alteration or additions see Section 633

Note: Enter 'NONE' or, where appropriate, the page number(s) of additional page(s) of comments on the existing installation.

NEXT INSPECTION**

§ *Enter interval in terms of years, months or weeks, as appropriate* §

I/We, the designer(s), RECOMMEND that this installation is further inspected and tested after an interval of not more than

** *The proposed date for the next inspection should take into consideration the frequency and quality of maintenance that the installation can reasonably be expected to receive during its intended life, and the period should be agreed between the designer, installer and other relevant parties.*

† *Where the Approved Contractor responsible for the construction of the electrical installation has also been responsible for the design **and** the inspection and testing of that installation, the 'Particulars of the Organisation(s) responsible for the Electrical Installation' may be recorded only in the section entitled 'CONSTRUCTION'.*

❖ *Where a number of sources are available to supply the installation, and where the data given for the primary source may differ from other sources, a separate sheet must be provided which identifies the relevant information relating to each additional source.*

Page 2 of

Please see the 'Notes for Recipients' on the reverse of this page.

This certificate is based on the model forms shown in Appendix 6 of BS 7671

ICN4/3

Bonding of extraneous-conductive-parts

Provision is made to record the extraneous-conductive-parts to which main protective bonding to the main earthing terminal of the installation has been effected, such as the incoming water, gas and oil services, the connection being made to the consumers metallic installation pipework (Regulation 544.1.2 refers). A tick in the appropriate box confirms that the inspector has tested the conductor and/or inspected it throughout its length and checked the connections, and that the results are satisfactory.

COMMENTS ON EXISTING INSTALLATION

This section of the certificate is applicable only where the work carried out is an addition or alteration to an existing installation, or where a complete rewire of an installation has been carried out and the installation is connected to an existing main incoming supply. Any deficiencies observed in the existing installation which do not affect the safety of the new work must be recorded here, by reference to an additional sheet of the certificate giving the detailed comments. Examples of such deficiencies are deterioration and minor defects. Where there are no comments to be made, the entry should read 'None'.

It is important to appreciate that any defects which would result in a reduced level of safety in the new work (that is a level of safety less than would be afforded by compliance with *BS 7671*), must be corrected before the new work is put into service. Consequently, no such defects should be recorded on the Electrical Installation Certificate.

In particular, by the time the installation work is ready to be certified and put into service, the contractor should have ensured that the rating and condition of any existing equipment (including that of the distributor), such as the main incoming supply, cables and switchgear, (which may have to carry any additional load as a result of the new work), are adequate to accommodate in safety the altered circumstances resulting from the modifications, and that the existing earthing and protective bonding arrangement if necessary for the protective measure applied for the safety of the work are also adequate.

Inadequacies identified on the distributor's equipment should be reported, by the client, to the appropriate authority.

NEXT INSPECTION

This section should be completed by the person responsible for the design of the installation work. A time interval, in terms of years, months or weeks, should be agreed between the designer, installer and other relevant parties and inserted to indicate when the next inspection will be due. The proposed date for the next inspection should take into consideration the frequency and quality of maintenance that the installation can reasonably be expected to receive during its intended life, any mandatory inspection requirements relating to the particular installation, and any other special circumstances that prevail. Under no circumstances should 'N/A' (or 'Not Applicable') be inserted.

SCHEDULES

The remainder of the Electrical Installation Certificate comprises various schedules. Guidance on how to complete these schedules is given in Chapter 6 (The schedule of circuit details and schedule of test results), Chapter 7 ('The schedule of inspection for new work') and Chapter 9 (Testing).

For installations having more than one distribution board or more circuits than can be recorded on pages 5 and 6, one or more additional *Schedule of Circuit Details for the Installation - Continuation* and *Schedule of Test Results for the Installation -* Continuation (pages 7 and 8 onwards) should form part of the certificate.

Where an installation includes one or more distribution boards that are not connected directly to the origin of the installation, details of the distribution (sub-main) circuit(s), together with the test results for the circuit(s), must be provided on continuation schedules.

Where required, continuation schedules are available from NICEIC.

The total number of pages comprising the certificate must be inserted in the box provided at the foot of each of the pages on the right-hand side.

Test instruments (serial numbers) used

On the top right-hand side of the page of *Schedule of Test Results for the Installation*, a panel is provided for recording information about the test instruments used. The serial number of each of the instruments used to obtain the test results should be recorded here. If any instrument does not have a serial number, a suitable number should be assigned and permanently marked on the instrument for traceability purposes. Where a combined instrument such as an insulation/continuity test instrument is used to carry out more than one type of test, the serial number of that instrument should be listed in the space corresponding to each of the relevant types of test.

Chapter 3

The Domestic Electrical Installation Certificate

The front page of the 'red' Domestic Electrical Installation Certificate for NICEIC Approved Contractors, the 'red' Domestic Electrical Installation Certificate for NICEIC Registered Domestic Installers, the 'blue' Domestic Electrical Installation Certificate for ELECSA Registered Domestic Installers and the uncontrolled 'green Domestic Electrical Installation Certificate.

Subject to certain limitations, the certificate is designed to be used for electrical installation work relating to a single dwelling (house or individual flat).

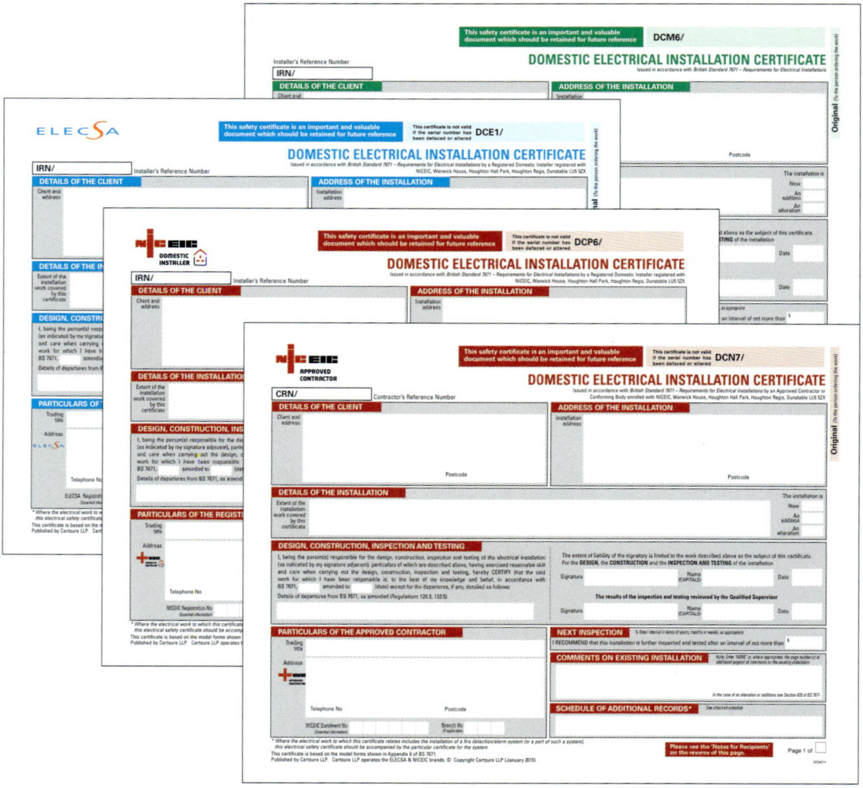

Green (uncontrolled) certificates are available for use by:

- NICEIC or ELECSA contractors working outside the scope of their enrolment or registration, and
- electrical contractors not enrolled or registered with either NICEIC or ELECSA.

3 THE DOMESTIC ELECTRICAL INSTALLATION CERTIFICATE

REQUIREMENTS AND LIMITATIONS

BS 7671 requires a standard form of Electrical Installation Certificate (including a record of the inspection and the results of testing) to be issued for all new installation work, and for all alterations and additions to existing installations. A separate certificate must be issued for each distinct electrical installation. The certificate provides a formal assurance that the installation complies with the requirements of the national standard for electrical safety.

A certificate (based on the model form given in *BS 7671*) must be issued to the person who ordered the work, whether or not the contractor is enrolled or registered and whether or not a certificate has been specifically requested by the client. NICEIC and ELECSA strongly prefer those registered or enrolled on to their schemes to issue the certificates supplied by their respective registering bodies, as this provides a measure of safety assurance and confidence to the recipients. Non-approved contractors are not authorised to issue NICEIC or ELECSA certificates, but similar (green) certificates based on the model form given in *BS 7671* are available from NICEIC.

It should be noted that the Domestic Electrical Installation Certificate is not intended to be issued to confirm the completion of a contract. The certificate is a declaration of electrical safety which should be issued before an installation is put into service. The certificate should not be withheld for contractual reasons, especially if the electrical installation is available for use.

The Domestic Electrical Installation Certificate is to be used only for the initial certification of a new installation, or for new work associated with an alteration or addition to an existing installation, carried out in accordance with *BS 7671* (as amended). The certificate may only be used where every one of the following conditions apply:

- The electrical installation work relates to a single dwelling (house or individual flat).
- The design, the construction, and the inspection and testing of the electrical installation work has been the responsibility of one Approved Contractor or Registered Domestic Installer.
- The installation forms part of a TT, TN-S or TN-C-S (PME) system.
- The protective measure for fault protection is provided primarily by Automatic Disconnection of Supply (ADS).

In the case of new installation work associated with an alteration or an addition to an existing installation, the installation when modified must meet all of the four conditions previously listed if the Domestic Electrical Installation Certificate is to be used. Otherwise, the Electrical Installation Certificate must be used.

For all other installation work in premises, including work in common areas of apartment blocks etc, and where the *Electricity at Work Regulations 1989* apply under normal circumstances (i.e. places where a work activity is undertaken), an Electrical Installation Certificate (see Chapter 2) should be used, unless the work falls within the limited scope of the Minor Electrical Installation Works Certificate (see Chapter 4).

Where a certificate is to be issued for an alteration or addition to an existing installation, the designer is required to ascertain that the rating and condition of any existing equipment, including that of the distributor (which may have to carry any additional load), are adequate to accommodate in safety the altered circumstances resulting from the modifications, and that the earthing and protective bonding arrangements if necessary for the protective measure applied for the safety of the addition or alteration are also adequate (see Regulation 132.16).

Electrical contractors that undertake installation work in domestic premises may consider that they are not involved in installation design. However, for installation work falling within the scope of the Domestic Electrical Installation Certificate, the contractor will invariably have assumed the role of the designer, even where the design work only involves the application of industry standards, such as for ring final circuits. In such cases, the contractor is responsible for the correct application of the industry standards and, consequently, for the design of the installation work.

The design of electrical installation work includes such aspects as the selection of protective devices, sizing of cables, methods of installation, selection of suitable equipment, and precautions for special locations such as bathrooms. The positioning of socket-outlets, lights etc are considered to be layout details and not electrical design, though the electrical designer will need to know the proposed positions of the equipment before completing the design calculations and determining that such positions will allow compliance with the requirements of *BS 7671*. In simple terms, the client or installation user may be able to decide where they require such items to be positioned, but the sizing and method of installing the cables and the selection of suitable equipment are matters for the designer of the installation work.

Where an electrical contractor discovers the existence of a dangerous or potentially dangerous situation in the existing installation (such as the absence of earthing or protective bonding where the protective measure for fault protection is ADS), the new work should not proceed and the client should be advised immediately, preferably in writing, to satisfy the duties imposed on competent persons by the *Electricity at Work Regulations 1989.*

An NICEIC or ELECSA Domestic Electrical Installation certificate may be issued only by the Approved Contractor or Registered Domestic Installer responsible for the installation work. A certificate must never be issued to cover another contractor's or installer's installation work.

The Domestic Electrical Installation Certificate consists of at least four pages, all of which must be fully completed and issued. Generally, all unshaded data-entry boxes should be completed by inserting the necessary text, or a 'tick' to indicate that the task has been completed and the results are satisfactory, or a numeric value of the measured parameter, or exceptionally by entering 'N/A' meaning 'Not Applicable', where appropriate.

Regardless of the method of compilation of the certificate (by hand, software assisted or using the NICEIC or ELECSA online certification system), it remains the responsibility of the person(s) signing the certificate to ensure that the information provided on the certificate is factual, and that the electrical installation work to which the certificate relates is safe to be put into service.

Where the electrical installation work to which the certificate relates includes the provision of a mains-powered fire detection and alarm system (such as one or more smoke alarms), the Domestic Electrical Installation Certificate must be accompanied by a separate certificate in accordance with British Standard *BS 5839-6: 2013 Code of practice for the design, installation, commissioning and maintenance of fire detection and fire alarm systems in domestic premises.*

COMPILATION OF THE CERTIFICATE

The remainder of this Chapter provides guidance on completing each section of the certificate.

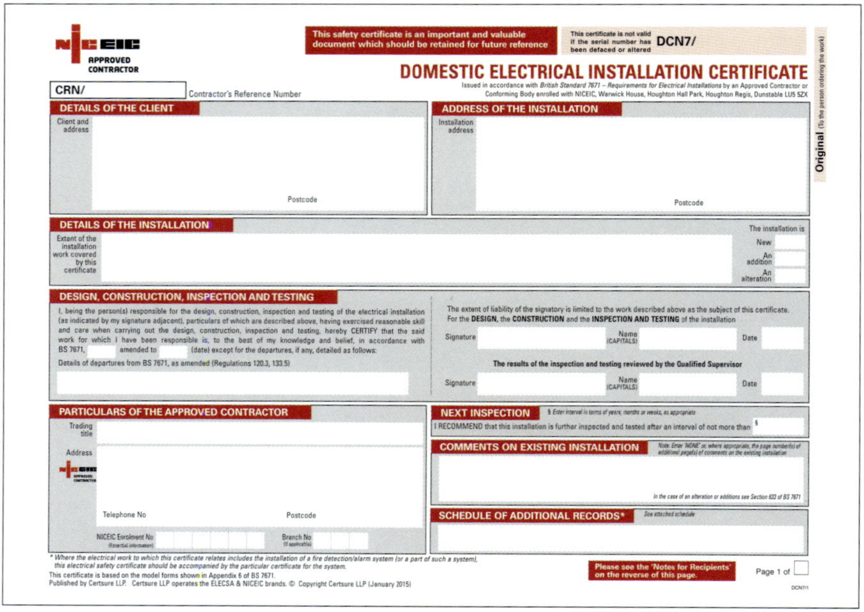

APPROVED CONTRACTOR

This safety certificate is an important and valuable document which should be retained for future reference

This certificate is not valid if the serial number has been defaced or altered DCN7/

Original (To the person ordering the work)

DOMESTIC ELECTRICAL INSTALLATION CERTIFICATE

Issued in accordance with *British Standard 7671 – Requirements for Electrical Installations* by an Approved Contractor or Conforming Body enrolled with NICEIC, Warwick House, Houghton Hall Park, Houghton Regis, Dunstable LU5 5ZX

CRN/ Contractor's Reference Number

DETAILS OF THE CLIENT
Client and address
Postcode

ADDRESS OF THE INSTALLATION
Installation address
Postcode

DETAILS OF THE INSTALLATION
Extent of the installation work covered by this certificate
The installation is: New / An addition / An alteration

DESIGN, CONSTRUCTION, INSPECTION AND TESTING
I, being the person(s) responsible for the design, construction, inspection and testing of the electrical installation (as indicated by my signature adjacent), particulars of which are described above, having exercised reasonable skill and care when carrying out the design, construction, inspection and testing, hereby CERTIFY that the said work for which I have been responsible is, to the best of my knowledge and belief, in accordance with BS 7671, ____ amended to ____ (date) except for the departures, if any, detailed as follows:
Details of departures from BS 7671, as amended (Regulations 120.3, 133.5)

The extent of liability of the signatory is limited to the work described above as the subject of this certificate.
For the **DESIGN**, the **CONSTRUCTION** and the **INSPECTION AND TESTING** of the installation
Signature / Name (CAPITALS) / Date

The results of the inspection and testing reviewed by the Qualified Supervisor
Signature / Name (CAPITALS) / Date

PARTICULARS OF THE APPROVED CONTRACTOR
Trading title
Address
Telephone No
Postcode
NICEIC Enrolment No (Essential information)
Branch No (If applicable)

NEXT INSPECTION § Enter interval in terms of years, months or weeks, as appropriate
I RECOMMEND that this installation is further inspected and tested after an interval of not more than §

COMMENTS ON EXISTING INSTALLATION
Note: Enter 'NONE' or, where appropriate, the page number(s) of additional page(s) of comments on the existing installation
In the case of an alteration or additions see Section 633 of BS 7671

SCHEDULE OF ADDITIONAL RECORDS* See attached schedule

* *Where the electrical work to which this certificate relates includes the installation of a fire detection/alarm system (or a part of such a system), this electrical safety certificate should be accompanied by the particular certificate for the system.*
This certificate is based on the model forms shown in Appendix 6 of BS 7671.
Published by Certsure LLP. Certsure LLP operates the ELECSA & NICEIC brands. © Copyright Certsure LLP (January 2015)

Please see the 'Notes for Recipients' on the reverse of this page.

Page 1 of

DCN7/1

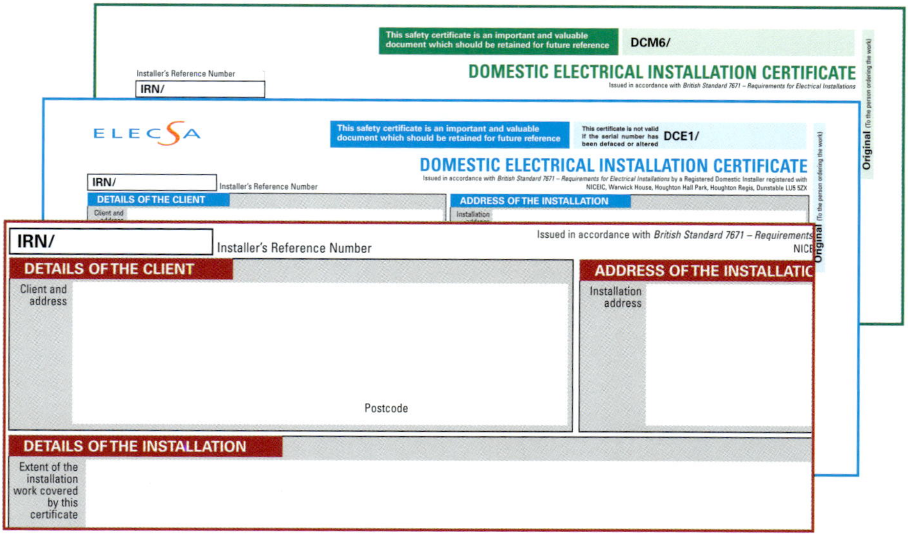

This safety certificate is an important and valuable document which should be retained for future reference DCM6/

Installer's Reference Number IRN/

DOMESTIC ELECTRICAL INSTALLATION CERTIFICATE

Issued in accordance with *British Standard 7671 – Requirements for Electrical Installations*

Original (To the person ordering the work)

ELECSA

This safety certificate is an important and valuable document which should be retained for future reference

This certificate is not valid if the serial number has been defaced or altered DCE1/

DOMESTIC ELECTRICAL INSTALLATION CERTIFICATE

Issued in accordance with *British Standard 7671 – Requirements for Electrical Installations* by a Registered Domestic Installer registered with NICEIC, Warwick House, Houghton Hall Park, Houghton Regis, Dunstable LU5 5ZX

IRN/ Installer's Reference Number

DETAILS OF THE CLIENT

ADDRESS OF THE INSTALLATION

IRN/ Installer's Reference Number

Issued in accordance with *British Standard 7671 – Requirements*

DETAILS OF THE CLIENT
Client and address
Postcode

ADDRESS OF THE INSTALLATIC
Installation address

DETAILS OF THE INSTALLATION
Extent of the installation work covered by this certificate

DETAILS OF THE CLIENT

The details to be provided are the name and address of the person or organisation that engaged the contractor to carry out the installation work. Where, for example, the electrical contractor is engaged by a builder, the details entered should be those of the builder. In the case of lengthy name and address details, suitable abbreviations may be used if acceptable to the client.

ADDRESS OF THE INSTALLATION

The address to be provided is the complete postal address of the installation, including the postcode, where known.

DETAILS OF THE INSTALLATION

Extent of the installation work covered by this certificate

For a new installation, the certificate may be intended to apply to the whole of the electrical installation at the address given. If not, it is essential to clearly define the extent of the installation to which the certificate applies in terms of areas or services; for example, 'whole electrical installation in refurbished kitchen'.

The description will depend on the particular circumstances, and must be tailored to identify explicitly the extent of the installation work covered by the certificate. In the case of additions or alterations, particular care must be taken to define exactly what work the certificate covers.

The box should be used to identify and clarify any particular exclusions agreed with the client. Any other exclusions that may not be readily apparent to the client or the installation user should also be recorded here.

It should be appreciated that failure to clearly describe the extent of the work covered by the certificate could involve the contractor in unforeseen liabilities at a later date.

Nature of the installation work. Three boxes are provided to enable the contractor to identify the nature of the installation work:

- **'New'** - This box should be ticked only if the whole installation has been installed as new, or if a complete rewire has been carried out.
- **'An addition'** (to an existing installation) - This box should be ticked if an existing installation has been modified by the addition of one or more new circuits.
- **'An alteration'** (to an existing installation) - This box should be ticked where one or more existing circuits have been modified or extended, or where, for example, the consumer unit has been replaced.

Where appropriate, both the 'addition' and the 'alteration' boxes may be ticked.

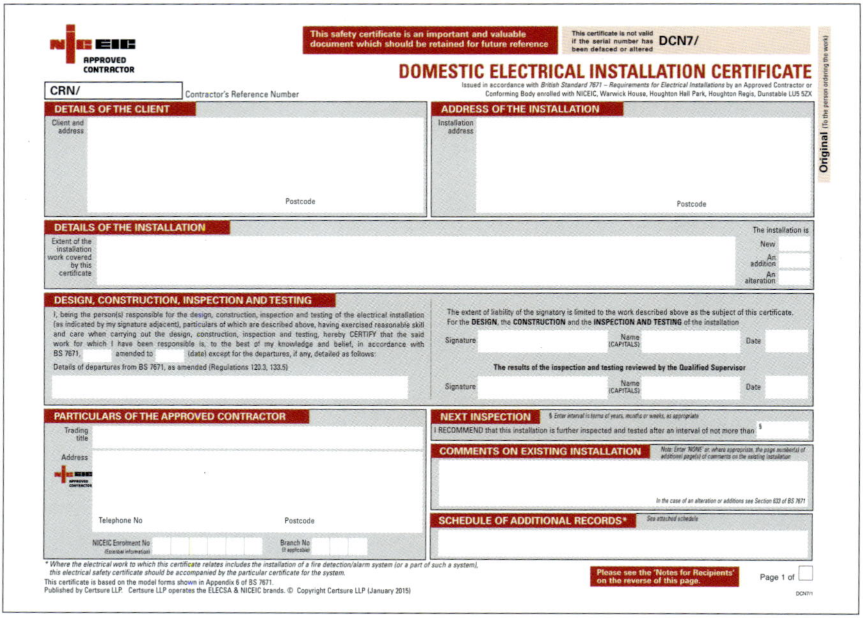

APPROVED CONTRACTOR

This safety certificate is an important and valuable document which should be retained for future reference

This certificate is not valid if the serial number has been defaced or altered DCN7/

Original (To the person ordering the work)

DOMESTIC ELECTRICAL INSTALLATION CERTIFICATE

Issued in accordance with *British Standard 7671 – Requirements for Electrical Installations* by an Approved Contractor or Conforming Body enrolled with NICEIC, Warwick House, Houghton Hall Park, Houghton Regis, Dunstable LU5 5ZX

CRN/ Contractor's Reference Number

DETAILS OF THE CLIENT

Client and address

Postcode

ADDRESS OF THE INSTALLATION

Installation address

Postcode

DETAILS OF THE INSTALLATION

Extent of the installation work covered by this certificate

The installation is: New / An addition / An alteration

DESIGN, CONSTRUCTION, INSPECTION AND TESTING

I, being the person(s) responsible for the design, construction, inspection and testing of the electrical installation (as indicated by my signature adjacent), particulars of which are described above, having exercised reasonable skill and care when carrying out the design, construction, inspection and testing, hereby CERTIFY that the said work for which I have been responsible is, to the best of my knowledge and belief, in accordance with BS 7671, amended to (date) except for the departures, if any, detailed as follows:

Details of departures from BS 7671, as amended (Regulations 120.3, 133.5)

The extent of liability of the signatory is limited to the work described above as the subject of this certificate.
For the **DESIGN**, the **CONSTRUCTION** and the **INSPECTION AND TESTING** of the installation

Signature | Name (CAPITALS) | Date

The results of the inspection and testing reviewed by the Qualified Supervisor

Signature | Name (CAPITALS) | Date

PARTICULARS OF THE APPROVED CONTRACTOR

Trading title

Address

Telephone No

Postcode

NICEIC Enrolment No (Essential information)

Branch No (If applicable)

NEXT INSPECTION *§ Enter interval in terms of years, months or weeks, as appropriate*

I RECOMMEND that this installation is further inspected and tested after an interval of not more than §

COMMENTS ON EXISTING INSTALLATION *Note: Enter 'NONE' or, where appropriate, the page number(s) of additional page(s) of comments on the existing installation*

In the case of an alteration or additions see Section 633 of BS 7671

SCHEDULE OF ADDITIONAL RECORDS* *See attached schedule*

* *Where the electrical work to which this certificate relates includes the installation of a fire detection/alarm system (or a part of such a system), this electrical safety certificate should be accompanied by the particular certificate for the system.*

This certificate is based on the model forms shown in Appendix 6 of BS 7671.
Published by Certsure LLP. Certsure LLP operates the ELECSA & NICEIC brands. © Copyright Certsure LLP (January 2015)

Please see the 'Notes for Recipients' on the reverse of this page.

Page 1 of

DCN7/1

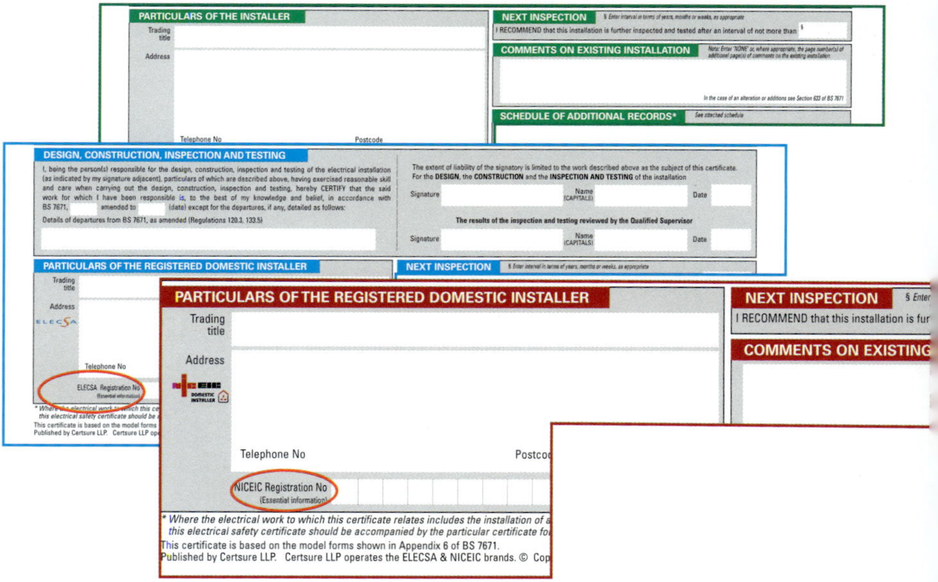

PARTICULARS OF THE INSTALLER

Trading title

Address

Telephone No

Postcode

NEXT INSPECTION *§ Enter interval in terms of years, months or weeks, as appropriate*

I RECOMMEND that this installation is further inspected and tested after an interval of not more than §

COMMENTS ON EXISTING INSTALLATION *Note: Enter 'NONE' or, where appropriate, the page number(s) of additional page(s) of comments on the existing installation*

In the case of an alteration or additions see Section 633 of BS 7671

SCHEDULE OF ADDITIONAL RECORDS* *See attached schedule*

DESIGN, CONSTRUCTION, INSPECTION AND TESTING

I, being the person(s) responsible for the design, construction, inspection and testing of the electrical installation (as indicated by my signature adjacent), particulars of which are described above, having exercised reasonable skill and care when carrying out the design, construction, inspection and testing, hereby CERTIFY that the said work for which I have been responsible is, to the best of my knowledge and belief, in accordance with BS 7671, amended to (date) except for the departures, if any, detailed as follows:

Details of departures from BS 7671, as amended (Regulations 120.3, 133.5)

The extent of liability of the signatory is limited to the work described above as the subject of this certificate.
For the **DESIGN**, the **CONSTRUCTION** and the **INSPECTION AND TESTING** of the installation

Signature | Name (CAPITALS) | Date

The results of the inspection and testing reviewed by the Qualified Supervisor

Signature | Name (CAPITALS) | Date

PARTICULARS OF THE REGISTERED DOMESTIC INSTALLER

Trading title

Address

ELECSA

Telephone No

ELECSA Registration No (Essential information)

NEXT INSPECTION *§ Enter interval in terms of years, months or weeks, as appropriate*

PARTICULARS OF THE REGISTERED DOMESTIC INSTALLER

Trading title

Address

DOMESTIC INSTALLER

Telephone No

Postco

NICEIC Registration No (Essential information)

NEXT INSPECTION § Enter

I RECOMMEND that this installation is fur

COMMENTS ON EXISTING

* *Where the electrical work to which this certificate relates includes the installation of a*
this electrical safety certificate should be accompanied by the particular certificate fo
This certificate is based on the model forms shown in Appendix 6 of BS 7671.
Published by Certsure LLP. Certsure LLP operates the ELECSA & NICEIC brands. © Cop

DESIGN, CONSTRUCTION, INSPECTION AND TESTING

Completion of this section is essential as it provides for certification of the three elements of the installation work; the design, the construction, and the inspection and testing. In signing this section, the signatory is accepting responsibility for the safety of the completed installation work, including its design and construction.

The signatory is also certifying that, with the exception of any departures recorded on the certificate, the design, the construction, and the inspection and testing fully meet the requirements of the current issue of *BS 7671*. The signatory must be entirely satisfied that the processes of inspection and testing and verification were carried out thoroughly and in accordance with Part 6 of *BS 7671*, and that the results obtained are consistent with installation work complying with all the relevant requirements of that standard.

The amendment number and the date of the amendment to *BS 7671* current at the time the electrical work was carried out should be stated in the relevant space in the text. Details of any departures from *BS 7671* should be entered in the space provided.

For NICEIC and ELECSA certificates, the inspection and testing results should be reviewed by the registered Qualified Supervisor who should confirm such review by signing in the appropriate space provided. By signing this section, the Qualified Supervisor is confirming that the certificate has been completed satisfactorily prior to issue.

Only a registered Qualified Supervisor employed by the Approved Contractor or the Registered Domestic Installer is eligible to sign the certificate to take responsibility for reviewing the results of the inspection and testing.

For the uncontrolled (green) version of the certificate, the completed schedules of inspection and testing should preferably be reviewed by a skilled person, competent to confirm whether the recorded results are consistent with electrical installation work conforming to the requirements of *BS 7671*. The review should be confirmed by signing in the appropriate box.

PARTICULARS OF THE CONTRACTOR

Completion of the 'Particulars of the Approved Contractor', 'Particulars of the Registered Domestic Installer' or 'Particulars of the Electrical Contractor' will identify to the recipient the contractor responsible for the work which is the subject of the certificate. The Contractor's trading title, address and postcode must be given, together with the NICEIC or ELECSA Enrolment Number or Registration Number as appropriate.

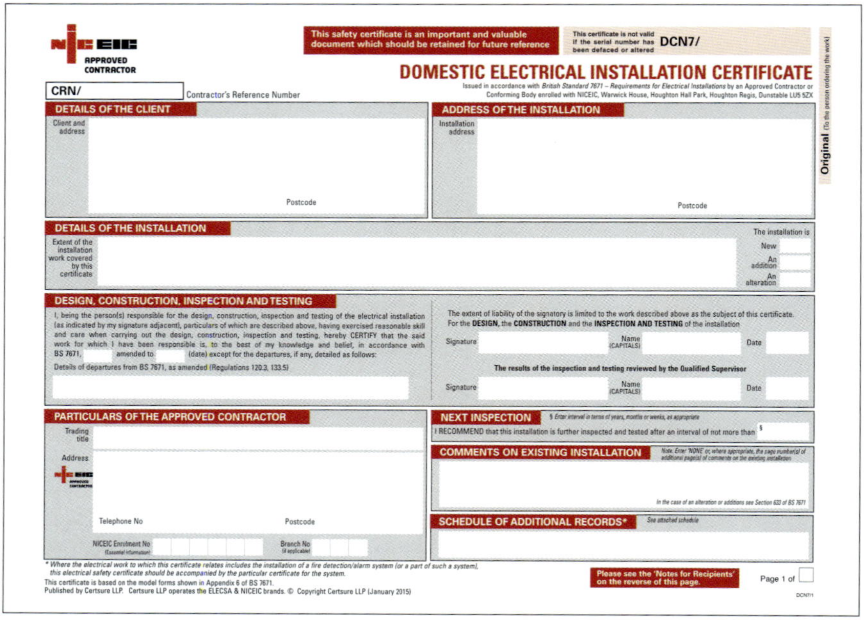

APPROVED CONTRACTOR

This safety certificate is an important and valuable document which should be retained for future reference

This certificate is not valid if the serial number has been defaced or altered DCN7/

Original (To the person ordering the work)

CRN/ Contractor's Reference Number

DOMESTIC ELECTRICAL INSTALLATION CERTIFICATE

Issued in accordance with *British Standard 7671 – Requirements for Electrical Installations* by an Approved Contractor or Conforming Body enrolled with NICEIC, Warwick House, Houghton Hall Park, Houghton Regis, Dunstable LU5 5ZX

DETAILS OF THE CLIENT

Client and address

Postcode

ADDRESS OF THE INSTALLATION

Installation address

Postcode

DETAILS OF THE INSTALLATION

Extent of the installation work covered by this certificate

The installation is: New / An addition / An alteration

DESIGN, CONSTRUCTION, INSPECTION AND TESTING

I, being the person(s) responsible for the design, construction, inspection and testing of the electrical installation (as indicated by my signature adjacent), particulars of which are described above, having exercised reasonable skill and care when carrying out the design, construction, inspection and testing, hereby CERTIFY that the said work for which I have been responsible is, to the best of my knowledge and belief, in accordance with BS 7671, amended to (date) except for the departures, if any, detailed as follows:

Details of departures from BS 7671, as amended (Regulations 120.3, 133.5)

The extent of liability of the signatory is limited to the work described above as the subject of this certificate.
For the **DESIGN**, the **CONSTRUCTION** and the **INSPECTION AND TESTING** of the installation

Signature Name (CAPITALS) Date

The results of the inspection and testing reviewed by the Qualified Supervisor

Signature Name (CAPITALS) Date

PARTICULARS OF THE APPROVED CONTRACTOR

Trading title

Address

Telephone No Postcode

NICEIC Enrolment No (Essential information) Branch No (if applicable)

NEXT INSPECTION *§ Enter interval in terms of years, months or weeks, as appropriate*

I RECOMMEND that this installation is further inspected and tested after an interval of not more than §

COMMENTS ON EXISTING INSTALLATION *Note: Enter 'NONE' or, where appropriate, the page number(s) of additional page(s) of comments on the existing installation*

In the case of an alteration or additions see Section 633 of BS 7671

SCHEDULE OF ADDITIONAL RECORDS* *See attached schedule*

** Where the electrical work to which this certificate relates includes the installation of a fire detection/alarm system (or a part of such a system), this electrical safety certificate should be accompanied by the particular certificate for the system.*

This certificate is based on the model forms shown in Appendix 6 of BS 7671.

Published by Certsure LLP. Certsure LLP operates the ELECSA & NICEIC brands. © Copyright Certsure LLP (January 2015)

Please see the 'Notes for Recipients' on the reverse of this page.

Page 1 of

DCN7/1

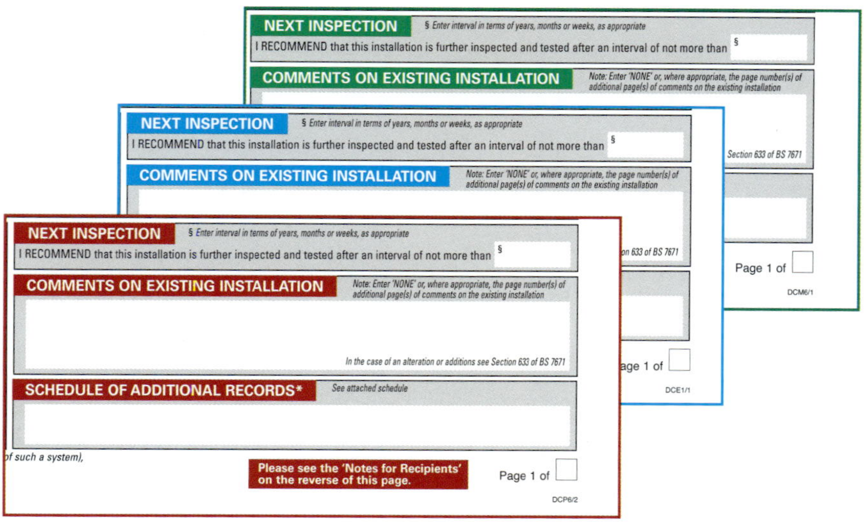

NEXT INSPECTION *§ Enter interval in terms of years, months or weeks, as appropriate*

I RECOMMEND that this installation is further inspected and tested after an interval of not more than §

COMMENTS ON EXISTING INSTALLATION *Note: Enter 'NONE' or, where appropriate, the page number(s) of additional page(s) of comments on the existing installation*

Section 633 of BS 7671

Page 1 of

DCM6/1

NEXT INSPECTION *§ Enter interval in terms of years, months or weeks, as appropriate*

I RECOMMEND that this installation is further inspected and tested after an interval of not more than §

COMMENTS ON EXISTING INSTALLATION *Note: Enter 'NONE' or, where appropriate, the page number(s) of additional page(s) of comments on the existing installation*

on 633 of BS 7671

age 1 of

DCE1/1

NEXT INSPECTION *§ Enter interval in terms of years, months or weeks, as appropriate*

I RECOMMEND that this installation is further inspected and tested after an interval of not more than §

COMMENTS ON EXISTING INSTALLATION *Note: Enter 'NONE' or, where appropriate, the page number(s) of additional page(s) of comments on the existing installation*

In the case of an alteration or additions see Section 633 of BS 7671

SCHEDULE OF ADDITIONAL RECORDS* *See attached schedule*

f such a system),

Please see the 'Notes for Recipients' on the reverse of this page.

Page 1 of

DCP6/2

NEXT INSPECTION

This section should be completed by the person responsible for the installation work. A time interval, generally in terms of years, should be inserted to indicate when the next inspection will be due. For domestic purposes, the maximum interval to the first periodic inspection is normally ten years. The interval recorded on the certificate should take account of the available guidance material and any other special circumstances relating to the particular installation. Under no circumstances should 'N/A' (or 'Not Applicable') be inserted.

COMMENTS ON EXISTING INSTALLATION

This section of the certificate is applicable only where the work carried out is an addition or alteration to an existing installation, or where a complete rewire of an installation has been carried out and the installation is connected to an existing incoming supply. Any deficiencies observed in the existing installation which do not affect the safety of the new work must be recorded here. Examples of such deficiencies are deterioration and minor defects. Where there are no comments to be made, the entry should read 'None'.

It is important to appreciate that any defects which would result in a reduced level of safety in the new work (that is a level of safety less than would be afforded by compliance with *BS 7671*), must be corrected before the new work is put into service. Consequently, no such defects should be recorded on the Domestic Electrical Installation Certificate.

In particular, by the time the installation work is ready to be certified and put into service, the contractor should have ensured that the rating and condition of any existing equipment (including that of the distributor), such as the incoming supply, cables and consumer unit, which will have to carry any additional load as a result of the new work, are adequate for the altered circumstances. The existing earthing and protective bonding arrangement, if necessary for the protective measure applied for the safety of the work, must also be adequate.

SCHEDULE OF ADDITIONAL RECORDS

Where the electrical work to which the certificate relates includes the installation of a fire alarm system and/or an emergency lighting system (or a part of such systems) the domestic electrical safety certificate should be accompanied by the particular certificate(s) for the systems and the serial numbers of the certificates recorded in this box.

Where an installation consists of more circuits than can be recorded on page 4 of the certificate, one or more continuation schedules should be employed and their page number(s) recorded in this section.

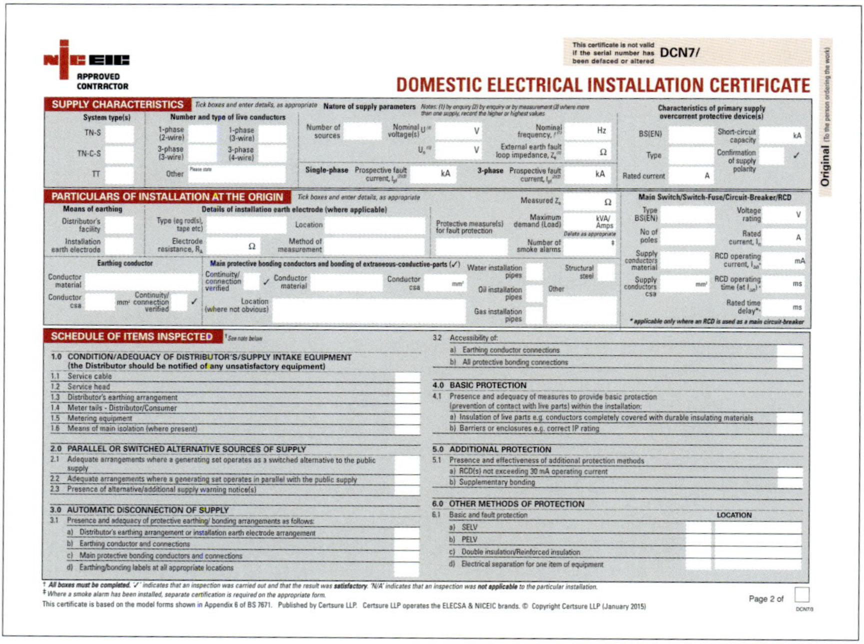

APPROVED CONTRACTOR

This certificate is not valid if the serial number has been defaced or altered DCN7/

Original (To the person ordering the work)

DOMESTIC ELECTRICAL INSTALLATION CERTIFICATE

SUPPLY CHARACTERISTICS *Tick boxes and enter details, as appropriate*

System type(s): TN-S / TN-C-S / TT

Number and type of live conductors: 1-phase (2-wire) / 1-phase (3-wire) / 3-phase (3-wire) / 3-phase (4-wire) / Other (Please state)

Nature of supply parameters *Notes: (1) by enquiry (2) by enquiry or by measurement (3) where more than one supply, record the higher or highest values*

Number of sources; Nominal voltage(s) $U^{(1)}$ V; $U_0^{(1)}$ V; Nominal frequency, $f^{(1)}$ Hz; External earth fault loop impedance, $Z_e^{(2)}$ Ω

Single-phase Prospective fault current, $I_{pf}^{(2)(3)}$ kA; 3-phase Prospective fault current, $I_{pf}^{(2)(3)}$ kA

Characteristics of primary supply overcurrent protective device(s): BS(EN); Type; Rated current A; Short-circuit capacity kA; Confirmation of supply polarity ✓

PARTICULARS OF INSTALLATION AT THE ORIGIN *Tick boxes and enter details, as appropriate*

Means of earthing: Distributor's facility; Installation earth electrode

Details of installation earth electrode (where applicable): Type (eg rod(s), tape etc); Location; Electrode resistance, R_A Ω; Method of measurement

Protective measure(s) for fault protection; Measured Z_e Ω; Maximum demand (Load) kVA/Amps *Delete as appropriate*; Number of smoke alarms ‡

Earthing conductor: Conductor material; Conductor csa mm²; Continuity/connection verified ✓

Main protective bonding conductors and bonding of extraneous-conductive-parts (✓): Continuity/connection verified ✓; Conductor material; Conductor csa mm²; Location (where not obvious); Water installation pipes; Oil installation pipes; Gas installation pipes; Structural steel; Other

Main Switch/Switch-Fuse/Circuit-Breaker/RCD: Type BS(EN); No of poles; Supply conductors material; Supply conductors csa mm²; Voltage rating V; Rated current, I_n A; RCD operating current, $I_{\Delta n}$* mA; RCD operating time (at $I_{\Delta n}$)* ms; Rated time delay* ms

** applicable only where an RCD is used as a main circuit-breaker*

SCHEDULE OF ITEMS INSPECTED † *See note below*

1.0 CONDITION/ADEQUACY OF DISTRIBUTOR'S/SUPPLY INTAKE EQUIPMENT (the Distributor should be notified of any unsatisfactory equipment)
1.1 Service cable
1.2 Service head
1.3 Distributor's earthing arrangement
1.4 Meter tails - Distributor/Consumer
1.5 Metering equipment
1.6 Means of main isolation (where present)

2.0 PARALLEL OR SWITCHED ALTERNATIVE SOURCES OF SUPPLY
2.1 Adequate arrangements where a generating set operates as a switched alternative to the public supply
2.2 Adequate arrangements where a generating set operates in parallel with the public supply
2.3 Presence of alternative/additional supply warning notice(s)

3.0 AUTOMATIC DISCONNECTION OF SUPPLY
3.1 Presence and adequacy of protective earthing/ bonding arrangements as follows:
a) Distributor's earthing arrangement or installation earth electrode arrangement
b) Earthing conductor and connections
c) Main protective bonding conductors and connections
d) Earthing/bonding labels at all appropriate locations
3.2 Accessibility of:
a) Earthing conductor connections
b) All protective bonding connections

4.0 BASIC PROTECTION
4.1 Presence and adequacy of measures to provide basic protection (prevention of contact with live parts) within the installation:
a) Insulation of live parts e.g. conductors completely covered with durable insulating materials
b) Barriers or enclosures e.g. correct IP rating

5.0 ADDITIONAL PROTECTION
5.1 Presence and effectiveness of additional protection methods
a) RCD(s) not exceeding 30 mA operating current
b) Supplementary bonding

6.0 OTHER METHODS OF PROTECTION
6.1 Basic and fault protection — LOCATION
a) SELV
b) PELV
c) Double insulation/Reinforced insulation
d) Electrical separation for one item of equipment

† *All boxes must be completed. '✓' indicates that an inspection was carried out and that the result was* ***satisfactory****. 'N/A' indicates that an inspection was* ***not applicable*** *to the particular installation.*
‡ *Where a smoke alarm has been installed, separate certification is required on the appropriate form.*

This certificate is based on the model forms shown in Appendix 6 of BS 7671. Published by Certsure LLP. Certsure LLP operates the ELECSA & NICEIC brands. © Copyright Certsure LLP (January 2015)

Page 2 of

DCN7/3

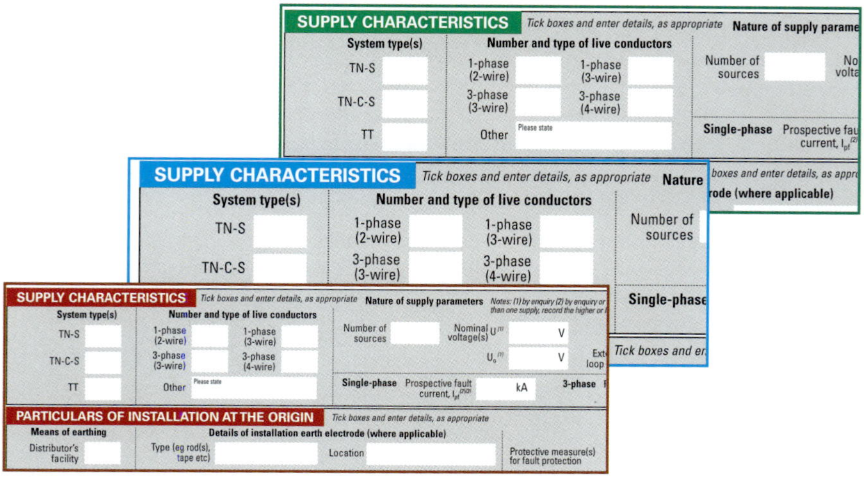

SUPPLY CHARACTERISTICS

System type(s)

In the United Kingdom, it is likely that, for domestic accommodation, the system type will be either TT, TN-S or TN-C-S, each of which falls within the scope of the Domestic Electrical Installation Certificate.

The types of system can be briefly described by means of their particular earthing arrangements:

- TN-S – Earthing facility provided by the distributor for the consumer's use – provision usually by means of a connection to the supply cable sheath or a separate protective conductor in the form of a split-concentric cable or overhead conductor.
- TN-C-S – Earthing facility provided by the distributor, connected to the incoming supply neutral to give a Protective Multiple Earth (PME) supply, where the supply neutral and protective conductors are in the form of a Combined Neutral and Earth (CNE) conductor.
- TT – Earthing provided by the consumer's own installation earth electrode – no earthing facility is made available to the consumer by the electricity distributor or, if such a facility is made available, it is not used.

For some dwellings, more than one system earthing arrangement may be used. For example, the installation within a dwelling may form part of a TN-C-S system, being earthed to the PME earthing facility. However, another part of the installation, such as a final circuit supplying a garage or shed, may form part of a TT system. Where an installation has two system earthing arrangements (one of which must essentially be a TT system), both types are required to be recorded on the certificate (i.e. TN-S or TN-C-S, and TT).

Number and type of live conductors

The details required to complete this section are straightforward, requiring identification of the number of the supply live conductors (including the neutral conductor). In most cases, the supply will be single-phase (two-wire) or three-phase (three-wire or four-wire). Facilities for recording other configurations are also provided.

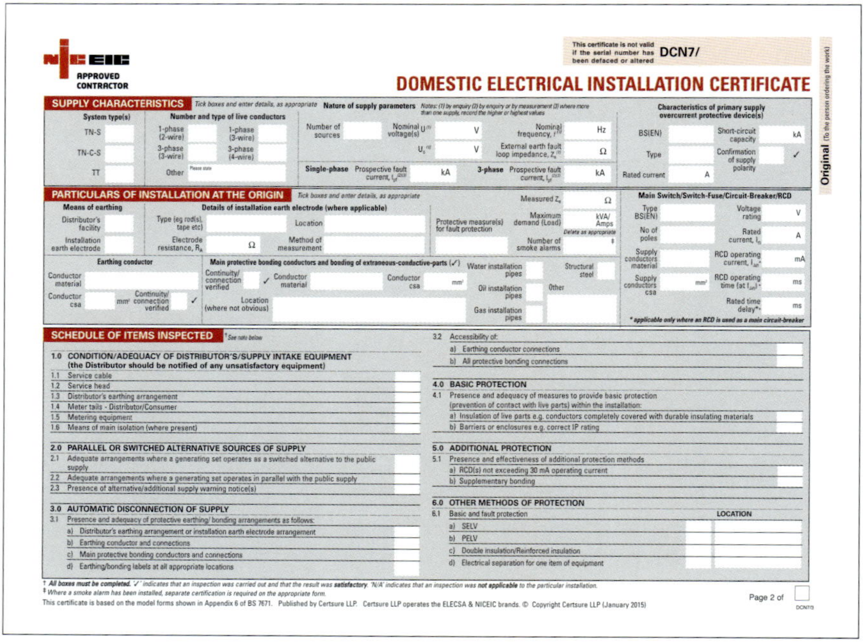

APPROVED CONTRACTOR

This certificate is not valid if the serial number has been defaced or altered **DCN7/**

Original (To the person ordering the work)

DOMESTIC ELECTRICAL INSTALLATION CERTIFICATE

SUPPLY CHARACTERISTICS

Tick boxes and enter details, as appropriate

System type(s): TN-S; TN-C-S; TT

Number and type of live conductors: 1-phase (2-wire); 1-phase (3-wire); 3-phase (3-wire); 3-phase (4-wire); Other (Please state)

Nature of supply parameters *Notes: (1) by enquiry (2) by enquiry or by measurement (3) where more than one supply, record the higher or highest values*

Number of sources; Nominal voltage(s) U [1] ___ V; U_0 [1] ___ V; Nominal frequency, f [1] ___ Hz; External earth fault loop impedance, Z_e [1] ___ Ω

Single-phase Prospective fault current, I_{pf} [2][3] ___ kA; 3-phase Prospective fault current, I_{pf} [2][3] ___ kA

Characteristics of primary supply overcurrent protective device(s): BS(EN); Type; Rated current ___ A; Short-circuit capacity ___ kA; Confirmation of supply polarity ✓

PARTICULARS OF INSTALLATION AT THE ORIGIN

Tick boxes and enter details, as appropriate

Means of earthing: Distributor's facility; Installation earth electrode

Details of installation earth electrode (where applicable): Type (eg rod(s), tape etc); Location; Electrode resistance, R_A ___ Ω; Method of measurement

Measured Z_e ___ Ω; Protective measure(s) for fault protection; Maximum demand (Load) ___ kVA/Amps *Delete as appropriate*; Number of smoke alarms ‡

Earthing conductor: Conductor material; Conductor csa ___ mm²; Continuity/connection verified ✓

Main protective bonding conductors and bonding of extraneous-conductive-parts (✓): Continuity/connection verified ✓; Conductor material; Conductor csa ___ mm²; Location (where not obvious); Water installation pipes; Oil installation pipes; Gas installation pipes; Structural steel; Other

Main Switch/Switch-Fuse/Circuit-Breaker/RCD: Type BS(EN); No of poles; Supply conductors material; Supply conductors csa ___ mm²; Voltage rating ___ V; Rated current, I_n ___ A; RCD operating current, $I_{\Delta n}$* ___ mA; RCD operating time (at $I_{\Delta n}$)* ___ ms; Rated time delay* ___ ms

** applicable only where an RCD is used as a main circuit-breaker*

SCHEDULE OF ITEMS INSPECTED

† *See note below*

1.0 CONDITION/ADEQUACY OF DISTRIBUTOR'S/SUPPLY INTAKE EQUIPMENT (the Distributor should be notified of any unsatisfactory equipment)

1.1 Service cable
1.2 Service head
1.3 Distributor's earthing arrangement
1.4 Meter tails - Distributor/Consumer
1.5 Metering equipment
1.6 Means of main isolation (where present)

2.0 PARALLEL OR SWITCHED ALTERNATIVE SOURCES OF SUPPLY

2.1 Adequate arrangements where a generating set operates as a switched alternative to the public supply
2.2 Adequate arrangements where a generating set operates in parallel with the public supply
2.3 Presence of alternative/additional supply warning notice(s)

3.0 AUTOMATIC DISCONNECTION OF SUPPLY

3.1 Presence and adequacy of protective earthing/ bonding arrangements as follows:
a) Distributor's earthing arrangement or installation earth electrode arrangement
b) Earthing conductor and connections
c) Main protective bonding conductors and connections
d) Earthing/bonding labels at all appropriate locations

3.2 Accessibility of:
a) Earthing conductor connections
b) All protective bonding connections

4.0 BASIC PROTECTION

4.1 Presence and adequacy of measures to provide basic protection (prevention of contact with live parts) within the installation:
a) Insulation of live parts e.g. conductors completely covered with durable insulating materials
b) Barriers or enclosures e.g. correct IP rating

5.0 ADDITIONAL PROTECTION

5.1 Presence and effectiveness of additional protection methods
a) RCD(s) not exceeding 30 mA operating current
b) Supplementary bonding

6.0 OTHER METHODS OF PROTECTION

6.1 Basic and fault protection — LOCATION
a) SELV
b) PELV
c) Double insulation/Reinforced insulation
d) Electrical separation for one item of equipment

† *All boxes must be completed. '✓' indicates that an inspection was carried out and that the result was* ***satisfactory****. 'N/A' indicates that an inspection was* ***not applicable*** *to the particular installation.*
‡ *Where a smoke alarm has been installed, separate certification is required on the appropriate form.*

This certificate is based on the model forms shown in Appendix 6 of BS 7671. Published by Certsure LLP. Certsure LLP operates the ELECSA & NICEIC brands. © Copyright Certsure LLP (January 2015)

Page 2 of

DCN7/3

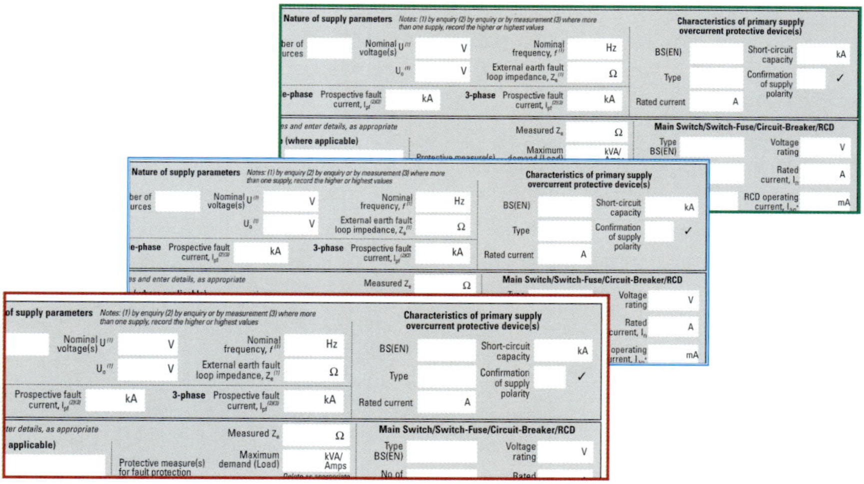

Nature of supply parameters

Provision is made in this section to record the supply parameters which comprise:

- **Number of sources,** should be entered here. Where a number of sources are available to supply the installation, and where the data given for the primary source may differ from other supplies, an additional page should be included in the certificate giving the relevant information for each additional supply.
- **Nominal voltage(s),** U (line-to-line), and U_0 (line-to-earth), in volts. For public two-phase and three-phase supplies in the UK, U is 400 V and U_0 is 230 V, and for public single-phase supplies, U is not applicable (N/A) and U_0 is 230 V. Do not record measured values, however accurate.
- **Nominal frequency,** f, in Hz. This parameter can generally be determined only by enquiry, but in the UK the nominal frequency is almost invariably 50 Hz.
- **External earth fault loop impedance,** (Z_e) in Ω (by enquiry). The method of 'enquiry' is permitted for the determination of Z_e. If Z_e is determined by enquiry, it is normally necessary also to obtain a measured value to verify that the intended means of earthing is present and of the expected value.
- **Prospective fault current,** Ipf, in kA. This is the maximum fault current likely to occur in the installation, on which value the design and selection of equipment have been based. The magnitude of the prospective fault current may be obtained by 'measurement', or 'by enquiry'. Detailed guidance on the measurement of prospective fault current is given in Chapter 9. Alternatively, the designer may obtain a value of prospective fault current by enquiring at the appropriate department of the electricity distributor. Usually, neither the designer nor person responsible for inspection and testing will have sufficient information to enable a realistic value to be calculated.

Characteristics of primary supply overcurrent protective device(s)

The information to be recorded here is the British Standard (or other appropriate Standard) product specification in terms of BS (EN) number, together with the type, the rated current (I_n), and the short-circuit capacity of the device. This information should be obtained from the installation designer at an early stage or by reference to the Electrical Installation Certificate issued on completion of the original electrical installation. Where it has not been possible to determine the details of the supply fuse(s) by these means, confirmation of its type and rating should be sought from the electricity distributor. Additionally, the polarity of the incoming supply should be confirmed and then indicated by ticking the appropriate box.

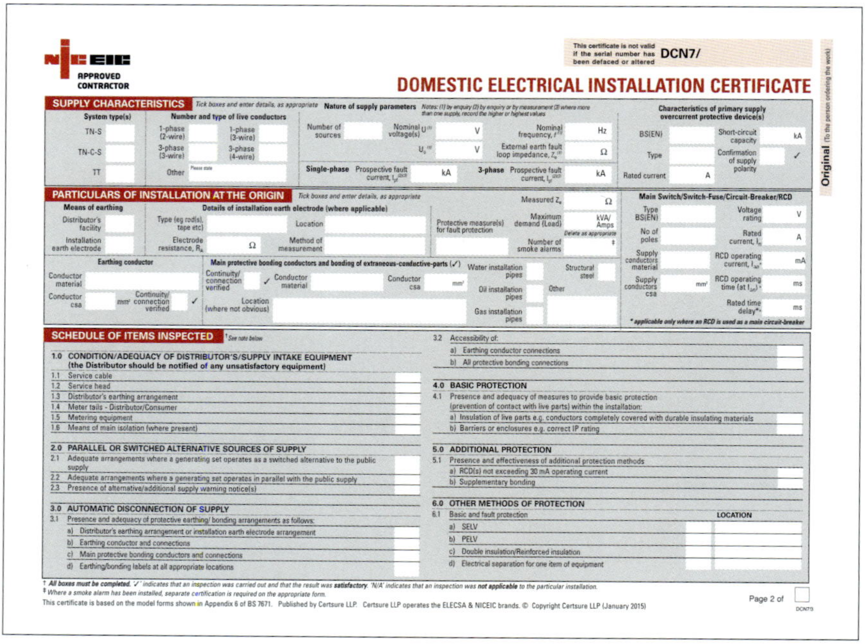

NICEIC APPROVED CONTRACTOR

This certificate is not valid if the serial number has been defaced or altered **DCN7/**

Original (To the person ordering the work)

DOMESTIC ELECTRICAL INSTALLATION CERTIFICATE

SUPPLY CHARACTERISTICS *Tick boxes and enter details, as appropriate*

System type(s): TN-S, TN-C-S, TT

Number and type of live conductors: 1-phase (2-wire), 1-phase (3-wire), 3-phase (3-wire), 3-phase (4-wire), Other (Please state)

Nature of supply parameters *Notes: (1) by enquiry (2) by enquiry or by measurement (3) where more than one supply, record the higher or highest values*

Number of sources; Nominal voltage(s) $U^{(1)}$ V; $U_0^{(1)}$ V; Nominal frequency, $f^{(1)}$ Hz; External earth fault loop impedance, $Z_e^{(2)}$ Ω

Single-phase Prospective fault current, $I_{pf}^{(2)(3)}$ kA; **3-phase** Prospective fault current, $I_{pf}^{(2)(3)}$ kA

Characteristics of primary supply overcurrent protective device(s): BS(EN); Type; Rated current A; Short-circuit capacity kA; Confirmation of supply polarity ✓

PARTICULARS OF INSTALLATION AT THE ORIGIN *Tick boxes and enter details, as appropriate*

Means of earthing: Distributor's facility; Installation earth electrode

Details of installation earth electrode (where applicable): Type (eg rod(s), tape etc); Location; Electrode resistance, R_A Ω; Method of measurement

Measured Z_e Ω; Protective measure(s) for fault protection; Maximum demand (Load) kVA/Amps *Delete as appropriate*; Number of smoke alarms ‡

Main Switch/Switch-Fuse/Circuit-Breaker/RCD: Type BS(EN); Voltage rating V; No of poles; Rated current, I_n A; Supply conductors material; RCD operating current, $I_{\Delta n}$* mA; Supply conductors csa mm²; RCD operating time (at $I_{\Delta n}$)* ms; Rated time delay* ms

** applicable only where an RCD is used as a main circuit-breaker*

Earthing conductor: Conductor material; Conductor csa mm²; Continuity/connection verified ✓

Main protective bonding conductors and bonding of extraneous-conductive-parts (✓): Continuity/connection verified ✓; Conductor material; Conductor csa mm²; Location (where not obvious); Water installation pipes; Oil installation pipes; Gas installation pipes; Structural steel; Other

SCHEDULE OF ITEMS INSPECTED †*See note below*

1.0 CONDITION/ADEQUACY OF DISTRIBUTOR'S/SUPPLY INTAKE EQUIPMENT (the Distributor should be notified of any unsatisfactory equipment)

1.1 Service cable
1.2 Service head
1.3 Distributor's earthing arrangement
1.4 Meter tails - Distributor/Consumer
1.5 Metering equipment
1.6 Means of main isolation (where present)

2.0 PARALLEL OR SWITCHED ALTERNATIVE SOURCES OF SUPPLY

2.1 Adequate arrangements where a generating set operates as a switched alternative to the public supply
2.2 Adequate arrangements where a generating set operates in parallel with the public supply
2.3 Presence of alternative/additional supply warning notice(s)

3.0 AUTOMATIC DISCONNECTION OF SUPPLY

3.1 Presence and adequacy of protective earthing/ bonding arrangements as follows:
a) Distributor's earthing arrangement or installation earth electrode arrangement
b) Earthing conductor and connections
c) Main protective bonding conductors and connections
d) Earthing/bonding labels at all appropriate locations

3.2 Accessibility of:
a) Earthing conductor connections
b) All protective bonding connections

4.0 BASIC PROTECTION

4.1 Presence and adequacy of measures to provide basic protection (prevention of contact with live parts) within the installation:
a) Insulation of live parts e.g. conductors completely covered with durable insulating materials
b) Barriers or enclosures e.g. correct IP rating

5.0 ADDITIONAL PROTECTION

5.1 Presence and effectiveness of additional protection methods
a) RCD(s) not exceeding 30 mA operating current
b) Supplementary bonding

6.0 OTHER METHODS OF PROTECTION

6.1 Basic and fault protection — LOCATION
a) SELV
b) PELV
c) Double insulation/Reinforced insulation
d) Electrical separation for one item of equipment

† *All boxes must be completed. '✓' indicates that an inspection was carried out and that the result was* ***satisfactory****. 'N/A' indicates that an inspection was* ***not applicable*** *to the particular installation.*
‡ *Where a smoke alarm has been installed, separate certification is required on the appropriate form.*

This certificate is based on the model forms shown in Appendix 6 of BS 7671. Published by Certsure LLP. Certsure LLP operates the ELECSA & NICEIC brands. © Copyright Certsure LLP (January 2015)

Page 2 of

DCN7/3

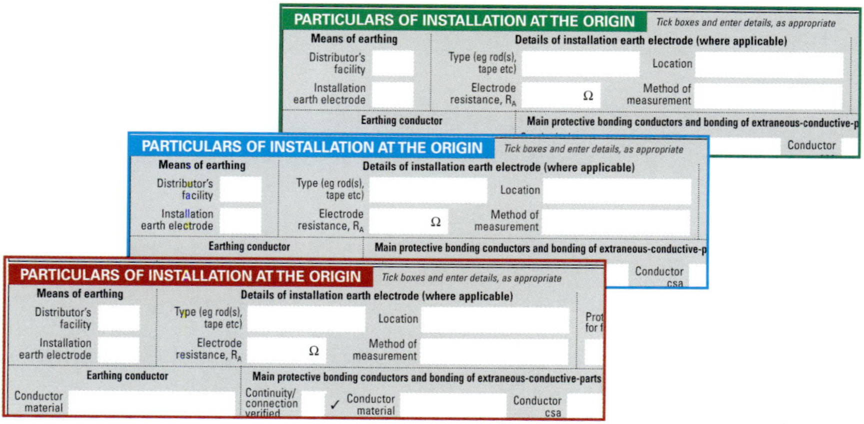

PARTICULARS OF INSTALLATION AT THE ORIGIN

As the use of the Domestic Electrical Installation Certificate is restricted to installation work where the design, the construction, and the inspection and testing of the electrical installation work has been the responsibility of one Approved contractor or Registered Domestic Installer, the following information should be readily available from that person's installation design:

Means of earthing

The protective measure Automatic Disconnection of Supply (ADS) incorporates the requirements for fault protection in the form of protective earthing, protective bonding and automatic disconnection in case of a fault. This requires all exposed-conductive-parts and extraneous-conductive-parts to be connected to a means of earthing via a main earthing terminal (MET). The information recorded here is to identify the particular means of earthing, in terms of a **distributor's facility** and/or an **installation earth electrode**.

Distributor's facility

Where the electricity distributor provides an earthing facility, and it has been used to earth the installation, this must be indicated in the space provided.

Details of installation earth electrode (where applicable)

Every TT system must have an installation earth electrode. If the system is not TT and there is no earth electrode, write 'NONE' for the type and 'N/A' (Not Applicable) for the location. Do not leave any boxes empty.

If the installation has an earth electrode, give a brief description of its type. The types of earth electrode recognised by *BS 7671* are listed in Regulation 542.2.3. Metal pipework forming part of a gas, flammable liquids, water or any other service network must not be used as an earth electrode (Regulation 542.2.6 refers).

Sufficient details must be given under 'location' so that persons unfamiliar with the installation and building layout will be able to locate the electrode for periodic inspection and testing purposes.

The earth electrode resistance, R_A, must be measured and the ohmic value recorded in the space provided for the purpose.

The method used to measure the earth electrode resistance to earth must also be recorded. Details of the following test methods are provided in Chapter 9:

- Using a proprietary earth electrode test instrument.
- Using an earth fault loop impedance test instrument.

APPROVED CONTRACTOR

This certificate is not valid if the serial number has been defaced or altered **DCN7/**

Original (To the person ordering the work)

DOMESTIC ELECTRICAL INSTALLATION CERTIFICATE

SUPPLY CHARACTERISTICS

Tick boxes and enter details, as appropriate

System type(s): TN-S; TN-C-S; TT

Number and type of live conductors: 1-phase (2-wire); 1-phase (3-wire); 3-phase (3-wire); 3-phase (4-wire); Other (Please state)

Nature of supply parameters *Notes: (1) by enquiry (2) by enquiry or by measurement (3) where more than one supply, record the higher or highest values*

Number of sources; Nominal voltage(s) $U^{(1)}$ V; $U_0^{(1)}$ V; Nominal frequency, $f^{(1)}$ Hz; External earth fault loop impedance, $Z_e^{(2)}$ Ω

Single-phase Prospective fault current, $I_{pf}^{(2)(3)}$ kA; **3-phase** Prospective fault current, $I_{pf}^{(2)(3)}$ kA

Characteristics of primary supply overcurrent protective device(s): BS(EN); Type; Rated current A; Short-circuit capacity kA; Confirmation of supply polarity ✓

PARTICULARS OF INSTALLATION AT THE ORIGIN

Tick boxes and enter details, as appropriate

Means of earthing: Distributor's facility; Installation earth electrode

Details of installation earth electrode (where applicable): Type (eg rod(s), tape etc); Location; Electrode resistance, R_A Ω; Method of measurement

Measured Z_e Ω; Protective measure(s) for fault protection; Maximum demand (Load) kVA/Amps *Delete as appropriate*; Number of smoke alarms ‡

Earthing conductor: Conductor material; Conductor csa mm²; Continuity/connection verified ✓

Main protective bonding conductors and bonding of extraneous-conductive-parts (✓): Continuity/connection verified ✓; Conductor material; Conductor csa mm²; Location (where not obvious); Water installation pipes; Oil installation pipes; Gas installation pipes; Structural steel; Other

Main Switch/Switch-Fuse/Circuit-Breaker/RCD: Type BS(EN); No of poles; Supply conductors material; Supply conductors csa mm²; Voltage rating V; Rated current, I_n A; RCD operating current, $I_{\Delta n}$* mA; RCD operating time (at $I_{\Delta n}$)* ms; Rated time delay* ms

** applicable only where an RCD is used as a main circuit-breaker*

SCHEDULE OF ITEMS INSPECTED

† *See note below*

1.0 CONDITION/ADEQUACY OF DISTRIBUTOR'S/SUPPLY INTAKE EQUIPMENT (the Distributor should be notified of any unsatisfactory equipment)

1.1 Service cable
1.2 Service head
1.3 Distributor's earthing arrangement
1.4 Meter tails - Distributor/Consumer
1.5 Metering equipment
1.6 Means of main isolation (where present)

2.0 PARALLEL OR SWITCHED ALTERNATIVE SOURCES OF SUPPLY

2.1 Adequate arrangements where a generating set operates as a switched alternative to the public supply
2.2 Adequate arrangements where a generating set operates in parallel with the public supply
2.3 Presence of alternative/additional supply warning notice(s)

3.0 AUTOMATIC DISCONNECTION OF SUPPLY

3.1 Presence and adequacy of protective earthing/ bonding arrangements as follows:
a) Distributor's earthing arrangement or installation earth electrode arrangement
b) Earthing conductor and connections
c) Main protective bonding conductors and connections
d) Earthing/bonding labels at all appropriate locations

3.2 Accessibility of:
a) Earthing conductor connections
b) All protective bonding connections

4.0 BASIC PROTECTION

4.1 Presence and adequacy of measures to provide basic protection (prevention of contact with live parts) within the installation:
a) Insulation of live parts e.g. conductors completely covered with durable insulating materials
b) Barriers or enclosures e.g. correct IP rating

5.0 ADDITIONAL PROTECTION

5.1 Presence and effectiveness of additional protection methods
a) RCD(s) not exceeding 30 mA operating current
b) Supplementary bonding

6.0 OTHER METHODS OF PROTECTION

6.1 Basic and fault protection — LOCATION
a) SELV
b) PELV
c) Double insulation/Reinforced insulation
d) Electrical separation for one item of equipment

† ***All boxes must be completed.*** *'✓' indicates that an inspection was carried out and that the result was* ***satisfactory****. 'N/A' indicates that an inspection was* ***not applicable*** *to the particular installation.*
‡ *Where a smoke alarm has been installed, separate certification is required on the appropriate form.*

This certificate is based on the model forms shown in Appendix 6 of BS 7671. Published by Certsure LLP. Certsure LLP operates the ELECSA & NICEIC brands. © Copyright Certsure LLP (January 2015)

Page 2 of

DCN7/3

PARTICULARS OF INSTALLATION AT THE ORIGIN *Tick boxes and enter details, as appr*
Means of earthing: Distributor's facility; Installation earth electrode
Details of installation earth electrode (where applicable): Type (eg rod(s), tape etc); Location; Electrode resistance, R_A Ω; Method of measurement
Earthing conductor; Main protective bonding conductors and bonding of extraneous-c

PARTICULARS OF INSTALLATION AT THE ORIGIN *Tick boxes and enter details, as appropriate*
Means of earthing: Distributor's facility; Installation earth electrode
Details of installation earth electrode (where applicable): Type (eg rod(s), tape etc); Location; Electrode resistance, R_A Ω; Method of measurement
Earthing conductor; Main protective bonding conductors and bonding of extraneous-conductive-p

PARTICULARS OF INSTALLATION AT THE ORIGIN *Tick boxes and enter details, as appropriate*
Measured Z_e Ω
Means of earthing: Distributor's facility; Installation earth electrode
Details of installation earth electrode (where applicable): Type (eg rod(s), tape etc); Location; Electrode resistance, R_A Ω; Method of measurement
Protective measure(s) for fault protection; Maximum demand (Load) kVA/Amps *Delete as appropriate*; Number of smoke alarms ‡
Earthing conductor: Conductor material
Main protective bonding conductors and bonding of extraneous-conductive-parts (✓): Continuity/connection verified ✓; Conductor material; Conductor csa mm²; Water installation pipes; Oil installation; Structural steel; Other

Where suitable and sufficient ground area is available for measurement purposes, a proprietary earth electrode test instrument may be used. Where hard surfaces or lack of space make the use of this method impracticable, the use of an earth fault loop impedance test instrument is appropriate.

Factors to be considered when choosing the test method to use are given in Chapter 9.

Measured Z_e.

Guidance relating to the measurement of the external earth fault loop impedance (Z_e) is given in Chapter 9.

Maximum demand (Load)

This is not, as is sometimes assumed, the rating of the electricity distributor's cut-out fuse(s). The maximum demand is a value, expressed in amperes or kVA per phase, evaluated on the basis of the connected load (in amperes) with an allowance for diversity, and if required converted to kVA. The installation designer would normally be expected to provide the maximum demand value. Guidance on estimating maximum demand is given in *IET Guidance Note 1: Selection and Erection*. There are, however, other methods by which the maximum demand current may be assessed, and these are not precluded provided they give realistic values.

In the case of alterations and additions, it is essential that an assessment of the maximum demand of the existing installation is made prior to carrying out modifications. To this assessment of the existing maximum demand must be added all additional loads, taking account of diversity as appropriate, resulting from the proposed new work so that the suitability of the incoming electricity service to supply the proposed increase in load can be ascertained.

Protective measure(s) for fault protection

This refers to the principal protective measure for fault protection. In many, if not most, cases the method will be Automatic Disconnection of Supply (ADS). The particular method the designer has chosen to use from those listed in Chapter 41 must be fully described here.

Number of smoke alarms

Where the electrical work involves the installation of one or more smoke alarms, record the number of smoke alarms that have been installed. It should be noted that the installation of smoke alarms must be separately certificated in accordance with *BS 5839-6: 2013 Code of practice for the design, installation, commissioning and maintenance of fire detection and fire alarm systems in domestic premises.*

NICEIC APPROVED CONTRACTOR

This certificate is not valid if the serial number has been defaced or altered **DCN7/**

Original (To the person ordering the work)

DOMESTIC ELECTRICAL INSTALLATION CERTIFICATE

SUPPLY CHARACTERISTICS
Tick boxes and enter details, as appropriate

System type(s): TN-S ☐ TN-C-S ☐ TT ☐

Number and type of live conductors: 1-phase (2-wire) ☐ 1-phase (3-wire) ☐ 3-phase (3-wire) ☐ 3-phase (4-wire) ☐ Other (Please state)

Nature of supply parameters *Notes: (1) by enquiry (2) by enquiry or by measurement (3) where more than one supply, record the higher or highest values*

Number of sources		Nominal voltage(s) U	V
		U_0	V
Nominal frequency, f	Hz	External earth fault loop impedance, Z_e	Ω
Single-phase Prospective fault current, I_{pf}	kA	3-phase Prospective fault current, I_{pf}	kA

Characteristics of primary supply overcurrent protective device(s)

BS(EN)		Short-circuit capacity	kA
Type		Confirmation of supply polarity	✓
Rated current	A		

PARTICULARS OF INSTALLATION AT THE ORIGIN
Tick boxes and enter details, as appropriate

Means of earthing: Distributor's facility ☐ Installation earth electrode ☐

Details of installation earth electrode (where applicable): Type (eg rod(s), tape etc) · Location · Electrode resistance, R_A Ω · Method of measurement

Measured Z_e Ω · Protective measure(s) for fault protection · Maximum demand (Load) kVA/Amps *Delete as appropriate* · Number of smoke alarms ‡

Earthing conductor: Conductor material · Conductor csa mm² · Continuity/connection verified ✓

Main protective bonding conductors and bonding of extraneous-conductive-parts (✓): Continuity/connection verified ✓ · Conductor material · Conductor csa mm² · Location (where not obvious) · Water installation pipes · Oil installation pipes · Gas installation pipes · Structural steel · Other

Main Switch/Switch-Fuse/Circuit-Breaker/RCD

Type BS(EN)		Voltage rating	V
No of poles		Rated current, I_n	A
Supply conductors material		RCD operating current, $I_{\Delta n}$*	mA
Supply conductors csa	mm²	RCD operating time (at $I_{\Delta n}$)*	ms
		Rated time delay*	ms

** applicable only where an RCD is used as a main circuit-breaker*

SCHEDULE OF ITEMS INSPECTED
† See note below

1.0 CONDITION/ADEQUACY OF DISTRIBUTOR'S/SUPPLY INTAKE EQUIPMENT (the Distributor should be notified of any unsatisfactory equipment)
- 1.1 Service cable
- 1.2 Service head
- 1.3 Distributor's earthing arrangement
- 1.4 Meter tails - Distributor/Consumer
- 1.5 Metering equipment
- 1.6 Means of main isolation (where present)

2.0 PARALLEL OR SWITCHED ALTERNATIVE SOURCES OF SUPPLY
- 2.1 Adequate arrangements where a generating set operates as a switched alternative to the public supply
- 2.2 Adequate arrangements where a generating set operates in parallel with the public supply
- 2.3 Presence of alternative/additional supply warning notice(s)

3.0 AUTOMATIC DISCONNECTION OF SUPPLY
- 3.1 Presence and adequacy of protective earthing/ bonding arrangements as follows:
  - a) Distributor's earthing arrangement or installation earth electrode arrangement
  - b) Earthing conductor and connections
  - c) Main protective bonding conductors and connections
  - d) Earthing/bonding labels at all appropriate locations
- 3.2 Accessibility of:
  - a) Earthing conductor connections
  - b) All protective bonding connections

4.0 BASIC PROTECTION
- 4.1 Presence and adequacy of measures to provide basic protection (prevention of contact with live parts) within the installation:
  - a) Insulation of live parts e.g. conductors completely covered with durable insulating materials
  - b) Barriers or enclosures e.g. correct IP rating

5.0 ADDITIONAL PROTECTION
- 5.1 Presence and effectiveness of additional protection methods
  - a) RCD(s) not exceeding 30 mA operating current
  - b) Supplementary bonding

6.0 OTHER METHODS OF PROTECTION — LOCATION
- 6.1 Basic and fault protection
  - a) SELV
  - b) PELV
  - c) Double insulation/Reinforced insulation
  - d) Electrical separation for one item of equipment

† *All boxes must be completed. '✓' indicates that an inspection was carried out and that the result was* ***satisfactory****. 'N/A' indicates that an inspection was* ***not applicable*** *to the particular installation.*

‡ *Where a smoke alarm has been installed, separate certification is required on the appropriate form.*

Page 2 of ☐ DCN7/3

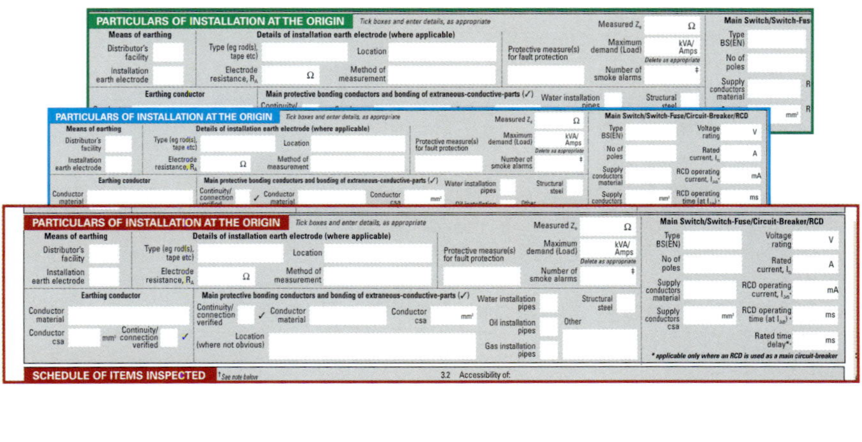

Earthing conductor

The conductor material and cross-sectional area of the earthing conductor must be stated here, followed by a tick to confirm that its continuity has been checked. This confirmation indicates that the inspector has tested the earthing conductor, or inspected it throughout its length, and checked its connections.

Main protective bonding conductors and bonding of extraneous-conductive-parts

The conductor material and cross-sectional area of the main protective bonding conductors must be stated here. Provision is made to record the extraneous-conductive-parts to which protective bonding to the main earthing terminal of the installation has been effected, such as the incoming water, gas and oil installation pipes, followed by a tick to confirm that their continuity has been checked. This confirmation indicates that the inspector has tested such conductors (and their connections) and/or inspected them throughout their length to confirm continuity.

Main Switch/Switch-Fuse/Circuit-Breaker/RCD

Type BS (EN)

This is normally a straightforward process of copying down the details from the installation design, having checked that the device conforms to that design. The types of main switch and circuit-breaker commonly used should have the relevant British Standard or BS EN number clearly marked. If, after checking both the design information and the device, no BS number or any other meaningful identification of the type of the device can be found, the lack of this essential information should be referred to the designer. Do not leave the box blank.

Voltage rating

This is normally a straightforward process of copying down the relevant details from the installation design, having first checked that the device has been selected and installed in accordance with that design.

Number of poles

The number of poles is usually 2 for a single-phase device, and 3 or 4 for a three-phase device. The actual number of poles must be confirmed before writing the number in the box, as a variety of switching arrangements are available.

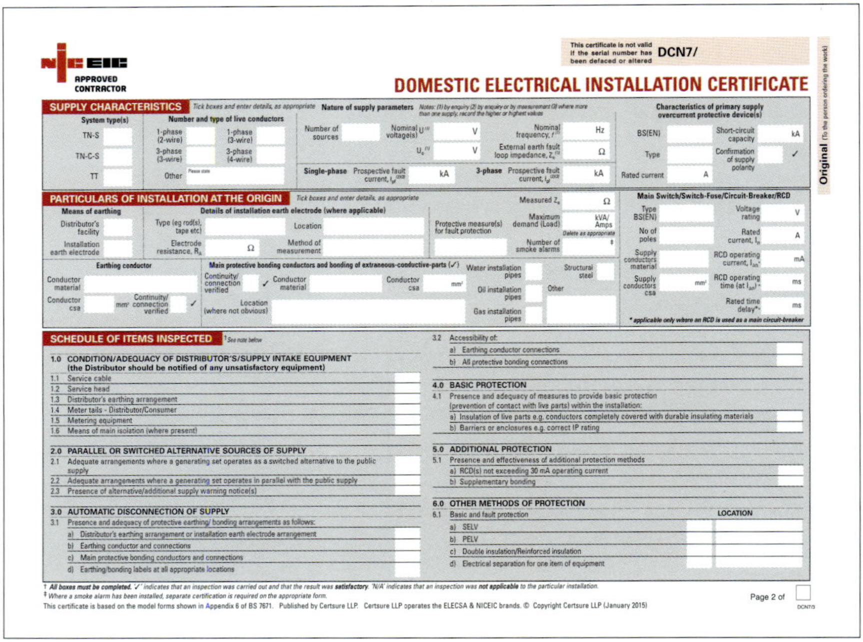

This certificate is not valid if the serial number has been defaced or altered DCN7/

APPROVED CONTRACTOR

Original (To the person ordering the work)

DOMESTIC ELECTRICAL INSTALLATION CERTIFICATE

SUPPLY CHARACTERISTICS *Tick boxes and enter details, as appropriate*

System type(s): TN-S / TN-C-S / TT

Number and type of live conductors: 1-phase (2-wire) / 1-phase (3-wire) / 3-phase (3-wire) / 3-phase (4-wire) / Other (Please state)

Nature of supply parameters *Notes: (1) by enquiry (2) by enquiry or by measurement (3) where more than one supply, record the higher or highest values*

Number of sources | Nominal voltage(s) $U^{(1)}$ V | $U_o^{(1)}$ V | Nominal frequency, $f^{(1)}$ Hz | External earth fault loop impedance, $Z_e^{(2)}$ Ω

Single-phase Prospective fault current, $I_{pf}^{(2)(3)}$ kA | 3-phase Prospective fault current, $I_{pf}^{(2)(3)}$ kA

Characteristics of primary supply overcurrent protective device(s): BS(EN) | Short-circuit capacity kA | Type | Confirmation of supply polarity ✓ | Rated current A

PARTICULARS OF INSTALLATION AT THE ORIGIN *Tick boxes and enter details, as appropriate*

Means of earthing: Distributor's facility / Installation earth electrode

Details of installation earth electrode (where applicable): Type (eg rod(s), tape etc) | Location | Electrode resistance, R_A Ω | Method of measurement

Measured Z_e Ω | Protective measure(s) for fault protection | Maximum demand (Load) kVA/Amps (Delete as appropriate) | Number of smoke alarms ‡

Earthing conductor: Conductor material | Conductor csa mm² | Continuity/connection verified ✓

Main protective bonding conductors and bonding of extraneous-conductive-parts (✓): Continuity/connection verified ✓ | Conductor material | Conductor csa mm² | Location (where not obvious) | Water installation pipes | Oil installation pipes | Gas installation pipes | Structural steel | Other

Main Switch/Switch-Fuse/Circuit-Breaker/RCD: Type BS(EN) | Voltage rating V | No of poles | Rated current, I_n A | Supply conductors material | RCD operating current, $I_{\Delta n}$* mA | Supply conductors csa mm² | RCD operating time (at $I_{\Delta n}$)* ms | Rated time delay* ms

* *applicable only where an RCD is used as a main circuit-breaker*

SCHEDULE OF ITEMS INSPECTED † *See note below*

1.0 CONDITION/ADEQUACY OF DISTRIBUTOR'S/SUPPLY INTAKE EQUIPMENT (the Distributor should be notified of any unsatisfactory equipment)
1.1 Service cable
1.2 Service head
1.3 Distributor's earthing arrangement
1.4 Meter tails - Distributor/Consumer
1.5 Metering equipment
1.6 Means of main isolation (where present)

2.0 PARALLEL OR SWITCHED ALTERNATIVE SOURCES OF SUPPLY
2.1 Adequate arrangements where a generating set operates as a switched alternative to the public supply
2.2 Adequate arrangements where a generating set operates in parallel with the public supply
2.3 Presence of alternative/additional supply warning notice(s)

3.0 AUTOMATIC DISCONNECTION OF SUPPLY
3.1 Presence and adequacy of protective earthing/bonding arrangements as follows:
a) Distributor's earthing arrangement or installation earth electrode arrangement
b) Earthing conductor and connections
c) Main protective bonding conductors and connections
d) Earthing/bonding labels at all appropriate locations
3.2 Accessibility of:
a) Earthing conductor connections
b) All protective bonding connections

4.0 BASIC PROTECTION
4.1 Presence and adequacy of measures to provide basic protection (prevention of contact with live parts) within the installation:
a) Insulation of live parts e.g. conductors completely covered with durable insulating materials
b) Barriers or enclosures e.g. correct IP rating

5.0 ADDITIONAL PROTECTION
5.1 Presence and effectiveness of additional protection methods
a) RCD(s) not exceeding 30 mA operating current
b) Supplementary bonding

6.0 OTHER METHODS OF PROTECTION
6.1 Basic and fault protection — LOCATION
a) SELV
b) PELV
c) Double insulation/Reinforced insulation
d) Electrical separation for one item of equipment

† *All boxes must be completed. '✓' indicates that an inspection was carried out and that the result was **satisfactory**. 'N/A' indicates that an inspection was **not applicable** to the particular installation.*
‡ *Where a smoke alarm has been installed, separate certification is required on the appropriate form.*
This certificate is based on the model forms shown in Appendix 6 of BS 7671. Published by Certsure LLP. Certsure LLP operates the ELECSA & NICEIC brands. © Copyright Certsure LLP (January 2015)

Page 2 of

DCN7/3

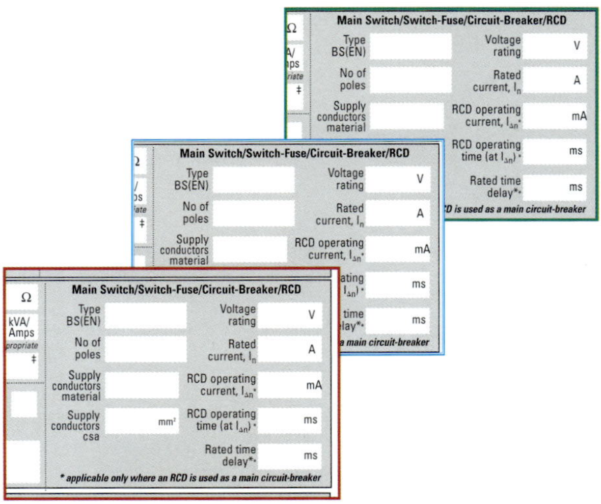

Rated current (I_n)

The information required here is the rated current, which is normally clearly indicated on the device (or on the fuse, if provided). This should be checked against the design information.

Supply conductors: material

The supply conductor material is required to be identified here. This is generally the conductor material of the 'tails' from the electricity distributor's meter to the consumer's installation main switch, and is usually copper.

Supply conductors: csa

This is the cross-sectional area of the supply conductors (for example, 25 mm^2).

Where the main circuit-breaker is a residual current device

The BS (EN) number, voltage rating, number of poles and rated current should be determined by examining both the design information and the device. The rating referred to in this case is the rated current, I_n, and not the rated residual operating (tripping) current, $I_{\Delta n}$, of the device.

RCD residual operating current ($I_{\Delta n}$)

This should be determined from the design information and checked with the marking on the device. The rated residual operating (tripping) current will usually be given in units of mA (for example '30 mA'), but in some instances it may be stated in amperes (for example '0.03 A'). An RCD may operate (trip) at a current just a little more than half its rated residual operating current. Where an RCD is used as a main switch, it should generally not have a low rated residual operating current (i.e. below 100 mA), in order to minimise unwanted tripping.

RCD operating time (at $I_{\Delta n}$)

Guidance on this test, which requires the use of an RCD test instrument, is given in Chapter 9. Record in the box the operating time in milliseconds when subjected to a test current equal to the operating current, $I_{\Delta n}$.

RCD rated time delay

Where the RCD incorporates a set time delay the rated delay in milliseconds should be entered, otherwise N/A should be recorded.

SCHEDULES

The second and third pages of the Domestic Electrical Installation Certificate comprises the Schedule of Items Inspected. Because use of the certificate is subject to particular limitations, it has been possible to omit those inspections covered by the Electrical Installation Certificate which are not generally applicable to dwellings. However, the guidance given in Chapter 6 on the completion of the schedules is largely applicable to the completion of the Domestic Electrical Installation Certificate, as is the guidance on the necessary inspections and tests given in Chapters 7 and 9, respectively.

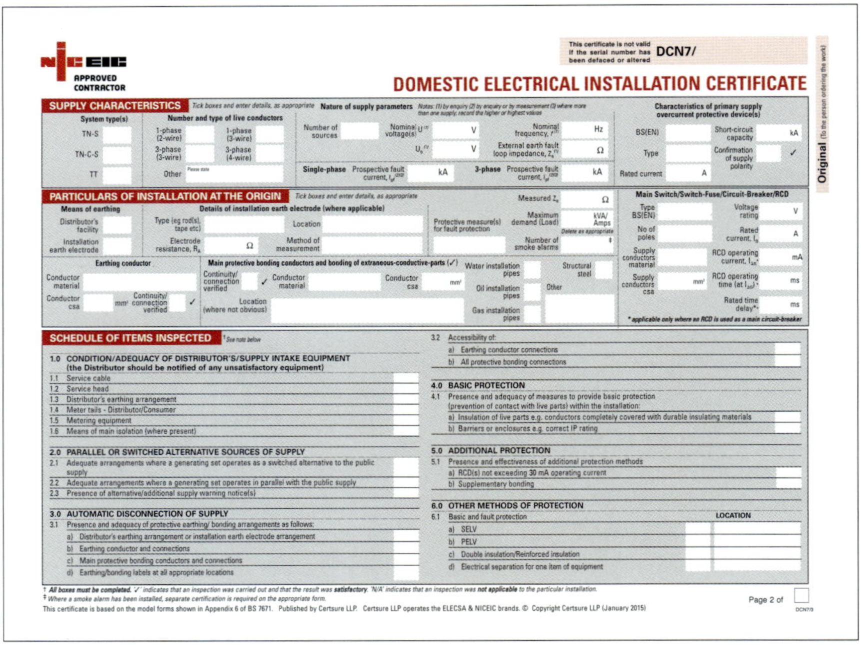
APPROVED CONTRACTOR

This certificate is not valid if the serial number has been defaced or altered DCN7/

Original (To the person ordering the work)

DOMESTIC ELECTRICAL INSTALLATION CERTIFICATE

SUPPLY CHARACTERISTICS *Tick boxes and enter details, as appropriate*

System type(s): TN-S; TN-C-S; TT

Number and type of live conductors: 1-phase (2-wire); 1-phase (3-wire); 3-phase (3-wire); 3-phase (4-wire); Other (Please state)

Nature of supply parameters *Notes: (1) by enquiry (2) by enquiry or by measurement (3) where more than one supply, record the higher or highest values*

Number of sources; Nominal voltage(s) $U^{(1)}$ V; $U_0^{(1)}$ V; Nominal frequency, $f^{(1)}$ Hz; External earth fault loop impedance, $Z_e^{(1)}$ Ω

Single-phase Prospective fault current, $I_{pf}^{(2)(3)}$ kA; 3-phase Prospective fault current, $I_{pf}^{(2)(3)}$ kA

Characteristics of primary supply overcurrent protective device(s): BS(EN); Type; Rated current A; Short-circuit capacity kA; Confirmation of supply polarity ✓

PARTICULARS OF INSTALLATION AT THE ORIGIN *Tick boxes and enter details, as appropriate*

Means of earthing: Distributor's facility; Installation earth electrode

Details of installation earth electrode (where applicable): Type (eg rod(s), tape etc); Location; Electrode resistance, R_A Ω; Method of measurement

Protective measure(s) for fault protection

Measured Z_e Ω; Maximum demand (Load) kVA/Amps *Delete as appropriate*; Number of smoke alarms ‡

Earthing conductor: Conductor material; Conductor csa mm²; Continuity/connection verified ✓

Main protective bonding conductors and bonding of extraneous-conductive-parts (✓): Continuity/connection verified ✓; Conductor material; Conductor csa mm²; Location (where not obvious); Water installation pipes; Oil installation pipes; Gas installation pipes; Structural steel; Other

Main Switch/Switch-Fuse/Circuit-Breaker/RCD: Type BS(EN); No of poles; Supply conductors material; Supply conductors csa mm²; Voltage rating V; Rated current, I_n A; RCD operating current, $I_{\Delta n}$* mA; RCD operating time (at $I_{\Delta n}$)* ms; Rated time delay* ms

* *applicable only where an RCD is used as a main circuit-breaker*

SCHEDULE OF ITEMS INSPECTED † *See note below*

1.0 CONDITION/ADEQUACY OF DISTRIBUTOR'S/SUPPLY INTAKE EQUIPMENT (the Distributor should be notified of any unsatisfactory equipment)
1.1 Service cable
1.2 Service head
1.3 Distributor's earthing arrangement
1.4 Meter tails - Distributor/Consumer
1.5 Metering equipment
1.6 Means of main isolation (where present)

2.0 PARALLEL OR SWITCHED ALTERNATIVE SOURCES OF SUPPLY
2.1 Adequate arrangements where a generating set operates as a switched alternative to the public supply
2.2 Adequate arrangements where a generating set operates in parallel with the public supply
2.3 Presence of alternative/additional supply warning notice(s)

3.0 AUTOMATIC DISCONNECTION OF SUPPLY
3.1 Presence and adequacy of protective earthing/ bonding arrangements as follows:
a) Distributor's earthing arrangement or installation earth electrode arrangement
b) Earthing conductor and connections
c) Main protective bonding conductors and connections
d) Earthing/bonding labels at all appropriate locations
3.2 Accessibility of:
a) Earthing conductor connections
b) All protective bonding connections

4.0 BASIC PROTECTION
4.1 Presence and adequacy of measures to provide basic protection (prevention of contact with live parts) within the installation:
a) Insulation of live parts e.g. conductors completely covered with durable insulating materials
b) Barriers or enclosures e.g. correct IP rating

5.0 ADDITIONAL PROTECTION
5.1 Presence and effectiveness of additional protection methods
a) RCD(s) not exceeding 30 mA operating current
b) Supplementary bonding

6.0 OTHER METHODS OF PROTECTION
6.1 Basic and fault protection — LOCATION
a) SELV
b) PELV
c) Double insulation/Reinforced insulation
d) Electrical separation for one item of equipment

† ***All boxes must be completed.*** *'✓' indicates that an inspection was carried out and that the result was* ***satisfactory****. 'N/A' indicates that an inspection was* ***not applicable*** *to the particular installation.*
‡ *Where a smoke alarm has been installed, separate certification is required on the appropriate form.*

This certificate is based on the model forms shown in Appendix 6 of BS 7671. Published by Certsure LLP. Certsure LLP operates the ELECSA & NICEIC brands. © Copyright Certsure LLP (January 2015)

Page 2 of

DCN7/3

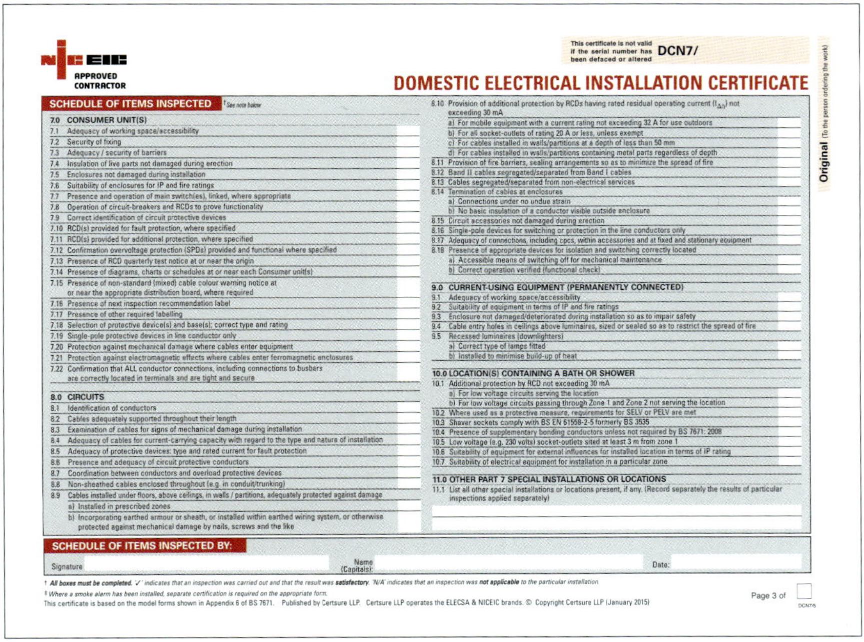

APPROVED CONTRACTOR

This certificate is not valid if the serial number has been defaced or altered DCN7/

Original (To the person ordering the work)

DOMESTIC ELECTRICAL INSTALLATION CERTIFICATE

SCHEDULE OF ITEMS INSPECTED † See note below

7.0 CONSUMER UNIT(S)
7.1 Adequacy of working space/accessibility
7.2 Security of fixing
7.3 Adequacy / security of barriers
7.4 Insulation of live parts not damaged during erection
7.5 Enclosures not damaged during installation
7.6 Suitability of enclosures for IP and fire ratings
7.7 Presence and operation of main switch(es), linked, where appropriate
7.8 Operation of circuit-breakers and RCDs to prove functionality
7.9 Correct identification of circuit protective devices
7.10 RCD(s) provided for fault protection, where specified
7.11 RCD(s) provided for additional protection, where specified
7.12 Confirmation overvoltage protection (SPDs) provided and functional where specified
7.13 Presence of RCD quarterly test notice at or near the origin
7.14 Presence of diagrams, charts or schedules at or near each Consumer unit(s)
7.15 Presence of non-standard (mixed) cable colour warning notice at or near the appropriate distribution board, where required
7.16 Presence of next inspection recommendation label
7.17 Presence of other required labelling
7.18 Selection of protective device(s) and base(s); correct type and rating
7.19 Single-pole protective devices in line conductor only
7.20 Protection against mechanical damage where cables enter equipment
7.21 Protection against electromagnetic effects where cables enter ferromagnetic enclosures
7.22 Confirmation that ALL conductor connections, including connections to busbars are correctly located in terminals and are tight and secure

8.0 CIRCUITS
8.1 Identification of conductors
8.2 Cables adequately supported throughout their length
8.3 Examination of cables for signs of mechanical damage during installation
8.4 Adequacy of cables for current-carrying capacity with regard to the type and nature of installation
8.5 Adequacy of protective devices: type and rated current for fault protection
8.6 Presence and adequacy of circuit protective conductors
8.7 Coordination between conductors and overload protective devices
8.8 Non-sheathed cables enclosed throughout (e.g. in conduit/trunking)
8.9 Cables installed under floors, above ceilings, in walls / partitions, adequately protected against damage
a) Installed in prescribed zones
b) Incorporating earthed armour or sheath, or installed within earthed wiring system, or otherwise protected against mechanical damage by nails, screws and the like
8.10 Provision of additional protection by RCDs having rated residual operating current ($I_{\Delta n}$) not exceeding 30 mA
a) For mobile equipment with a current rating not exceeding 32 A for use outdoors
b) For all socket-outlets of rating 20 A or less, unless exempt
c) For cables installed in walls/partitions at a depth of less than 50 mm
d) For cables installed in walls/partitions containing metal parts regardless of depth
8.11 Provision of fire barriers, sealing arrangements so as to minimize the spread of fire
8.12 Band II cables segregated/separated from Band I cables
8.13 Cables segregated/separated from non-electrical services
8.14 Termination of cables at enclosures
a) Connections under no undue strain
b) No basic insulation of a conductor visible outside enclosure
8.15 Circuit accessories not damaged during erection
8.16 Single-pole devices for switching or protection in the line conductors only
8.17 Adequacy of connections, including cpcs, within accessories and at fixed and stationary equipment
8.18 Presence of appropriate devices for isolation and switching correctly located
a) Accessible means of switching off for mechanical maintenance
b) Correct operation verified (functional check)

9.0 CURRENT-USING EQUIPMENT (PERMANENTLY CONNECTED)
9.1 Adequacy of working space/accessibility
9.2 Suitability of equipment in terms of IP and fire ratings
9.3 Enclosure not damaged/deteriorated during installation so as to impair safety
9.4 Cable entry holes in ceilings above luminaires, sized or sealed so as to restrict the spread of fire
9.5 Recessed luminaires (downlighters)
a) Correct type of lamps fitted
b) Installed to minimise build-up of heat

10.0 LOCATION(S) CONTAINING A BATH OR SHOWER
10.1 Additional protection by RCD not exceeding 30 mA
a) For low voltage circuits serving the location
b) For low voltage circuits passing through Zone 1 and Zone 2 not serving the location
10.2 Where used as a protective measure, requirements for SELV or PELV are met
10.3 Shaver sockets comply with BS EN 61558-2-5 formerly BS 3535
10.4 Presence of supplementary bonding conductors unless not required by BS 7671: 2008
10.5 Low voltage (e.g. 230 volts) socket-outlets sited at least 3 m from zone 1
10.6 Suitability of equipment for external influences for installed location in terms of IP rating
10.7 Suitability of electrical equipment for installation in a particular zone

11.0 OTHER PART 7 SPECIAL INSTALLATIONS OR LOCATIONS
11.1 List all other special installations or locations present, if any. (Record separately the results of particular inspections applied separately)

SCHEDULE OF ITEMS INSPECTED BY:

Signature Name (Capitals): Date:

† *All boxes must be completed. '✓' indicates that an inspection was carried out and that the result was **satisfactory**. 'N/A' indicates that an inspection was **not applicable** to the particular installation.*

‡ *Where a smoke alarm has been installed, separate certification is required on the appropriate form.*

This certificate is based on the model forms shown in Appendix 6 of BS 7671. Published by Certsure LLP. Certsure LLP operates the ELECSA & NICEIC brands. © Copyright Certsure LLP (January 2015)

Page 3 of

DCN7/5

Every circuit, including distribution circuits (sub-mains) must be recorded. The first line of the Schedule of circuit details may be used to record the details of the distribution circuit connecting the meter to the consumer unit at the origin of the installation (the circuit including the meter tails).

An installation may include more than one consumer unit or distribution board. For example, a small consumer unit may be provided in a detached garage. In such a case, the installation will comprise the circuit including the meter tails, the final circuits in the dwelling, the distribution circuit supplying the garage and the final circuits in the garage.

Where an installation consists of more circuits than can be recorded on page 4 of the certificate, one or more continuation schedules should be employed and their page number(s) recorded in the 'Schedule of additional records' box on page 1 of the certificate.

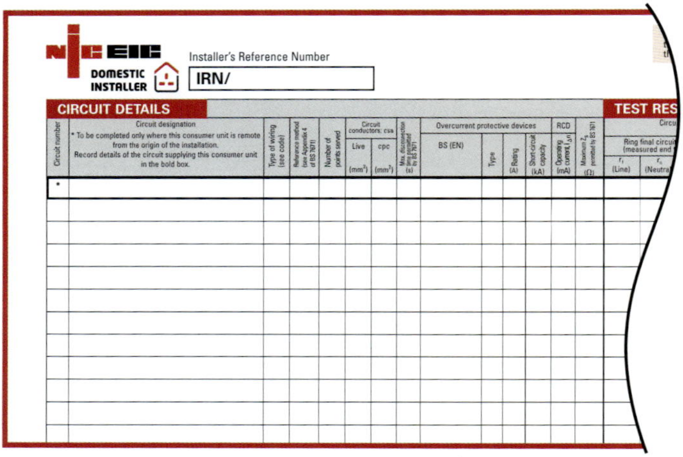

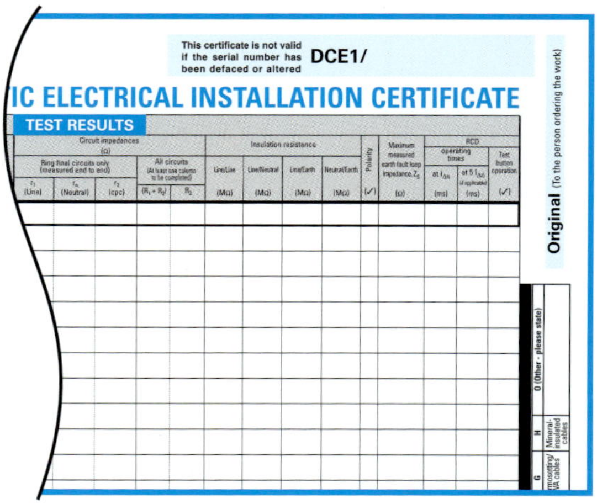

Test instruments (serial numbers) used

At the foot of the page, a panel is provided for recording information about the test instruments used. The serial number of each of the instruments used to obtain the test results should be recorded here. Where a combined instrument such as an insulation/continuity test instrument is used to carry out more than one type of test, the serial number of that instrument should be listed in the space corresponding to each of the relevant types of test.

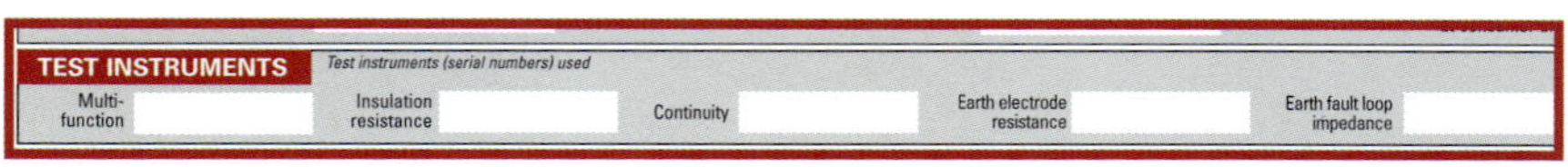

Chapter

4

The Minor Electrical Installation Works Certificate

REQUIREMENTS

USE AND MISUSE OF THE CERTIFICATE

COMPILATION OF THE CERTIFICATE

PART 1: DETAILS OF THE MINOR WORKS

PART 2: DETAILS OF THE MODIFIED CIRCUIT

PART 3: INSPECTION AND TESTING OF THE MODIFIED CIRCUIT AND RELATED PARTS

PART 4: DECLARATION

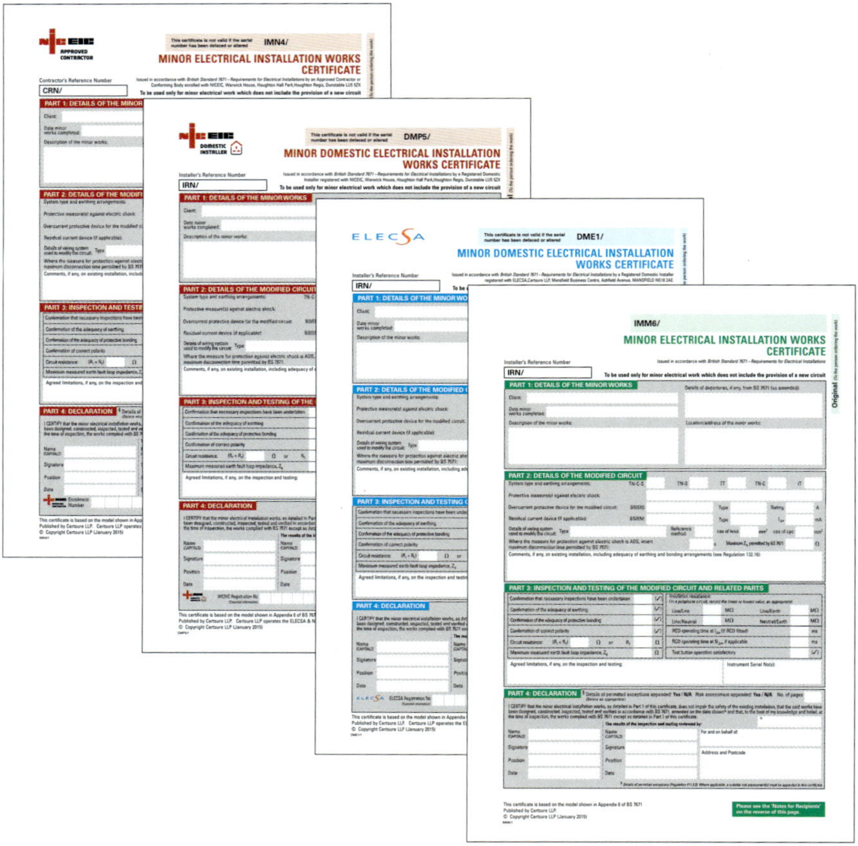

- The NICEIC red MEIWC is available for use by NICEIC registered Approved Contractors.
- The NICEIC red Domestic MEIWC is available for use by NICEIC Registered Domestic Installers
- The ELECSA blue Domestic MEIWC is available for use by ELECSA Registered Domestic Installers
- The green (uncontrolled) Minor Electrical Installation Works Certificate is available for use by:
  - electrical contractors or installers not enrolled or registered with NICEIC or ELECSA, in particular those preparing for enrolment or registration, and
  - for those working outside the scope of their enrolment or registration.

4 THE MINOR ELECTRICAL INSTALLATION WORKS CERTIFICATE

REQUIREMENTS

BS 7671 requires inspection and testing to be carried out, and appropriate certification to be issued, for any alteration or addition to an existing circuit, just as for a new electrical installation. However, provided that the alteration or addition to the installation is **minor** and does **not** include the provision of a new circuit, a Minor Electrical Installation Works Certificate (referred to in this Chapter as a Minor Works Certificate) may be issued instead of an Electrical Installation Certificate or a Domestic Electrical Installation Certificate.

A Minor Works Certificate may be used only for an addition or an alteration to a single circuit that does not extend to the provision of a new circuit (Regulation 631.3).

The Minor Works Certificate therefore has a limited application and must not be used for work outside its scope. Examples of work that would fall within its scope are:

- The addition of a socket-outlet to a ring or radial final circuit.
- Work carried out on a lighting final circuit, including an alteration to the switching arrangements and the addition of a lighting point.
- The replacement of an accessory or luminaire.*

Further examples of proper use of Minor Works Certificates are given in the table on the following page.

Before commencing the minor electrical installation work, it is necessary to check that the rating and condition of any existing equipment, including that of the electricity distributor (which may have to carry additional load), are adequate for the altered circumstances, and the earthing and protective bonding arrangements, if necessary for the protective measures applied for the safety of the work, are also adequate. Where the existence of a dangerous or potentially dangerous situation is discovered in the existing installation (such as the absence of protective bonding where the method of fault protection is ADS), the alteration or addition should not proceed and the client should be advised immediately of the situation, preferably in writing, to satisfy the duties imposed on competent persons by the *Electricity at Work Regulations 1989*.

* *If preferred by a client such as a Local Authority, the client's own documentation (such as a combined works order and certificate) may be used instead of a Minor Works Certificate for the replacement of an accessory or luminaire, provided that the safety declaration, installation details, and the inspection and test results required to be recorded on the alternative documentation are no less comprehensive than those required to be recorded on the Minor Works Certificate, and that a copy of the completed documentation is retained by the contractor.*

ACCEPTABLE AND NON-ACCEPTABLE USE OF MINOR WORKS CERTIFICATES			
Ref	**Examples of electrical work**	**Acceptable use yes/no**	**Comment**
A	Additional lighting point (luminaire and/or switching) on a single existing circuit.	✔	The Minor Works Certificate may be used provided the existing circuit protective device is suitable for protection of the modified circuit, and other safety provisions are adequate.
B	Additional socket-outlet on a single existing radial or ring circuit.	✔	The Minor Works Certificate may be used provided the existing circuit protective device is suitable for protection of the modified circuit, and other safety provisions are adequate.
C	New circuit for lighting.	✘	The Minor Works Certificate must not be used even where the new circuit feeds only one lighting point.
D	New radial or ring circuit for socket-outlets and other accessories such as connection units.	✘	The Minor Works Certificate must not be used even where the circuit feeds only one socket-outlet or other accessory.
E	New radial circuit for fixed equipment.	✘	The Minor Works Certificate must not be used even where the circuit feeds only one item of fixed equipment.
F	New circuit (lighting, power etc.) connected to an existing protective device.	✘	The Minor Works Certificate must not be used.
G	Replacement of an individual item of switchgear, including a control switch, in a like-for-like manner for a single circuit.	✔	
H	Replacement of an individual item of switchgear, including a control switch or a protective device, not in a like-for-like manner (for example, the replacement device has different characteristics).	✔	The Minor Works Certificate must not be used.
I	Replacement of main switchgear, incorporating protective devices, for more than one circuit.	✘	The Minor Works Certificate must not be used.
J	Replacement of an accessory, such as a socket-outlet or a ceiling rose, on a like-for-like basis.	✔	Although such replacement may be regarded as maintenance work, a record of the relevant safety tests undertaken may be recorded on the Minor Works Certificate, though other forms of recording such results are not precluded.
K	Installation of main protective bonding.	✔	
L	Upgrading of main protective bonding.	✔	
M	Installation or upgrading of supplementary bonding.	✔	
N	Replacement of a distribution cable, for a single circuit, damaged, for example, by fire or rodents or impact etc.	✔	On condition that the replacement cable has identical specifications and follows the same route as the damaged cable. Where more than one circuit is connected via a distribution board to the distribution circuit, the Minor Works Certificate is not suitable for test results.
O	Re-fixing, re-lidding existing wiring systems.	✔	On condition that the circuit's protective measures are unaffected.
P	Adding mechanical protection to existing equipment.	✔	On condition that the circuit's protective measures and current-carrying capacity of conductors are unaffected.
Q	A combination of the above items which may individually warrant the use of the certificate.	✘	The use of the certificate for certifying collectively more than one item, which individually may warrant the use of the Minor Works Certificate, is not acceptable.
R	Modifications to more than one circuit.	✘	A single Minor Works Certificate must not be used for modifications to more than circuit. (One Minor Works Certificate must be issued for each circuit altered or extended).
S	Periodic, or other, inspection of an installation.	✘	An Electrical Installation Condition Report must be used.
T	For electrical safety aspects of electrical installation work associated with fire detection and alarm systems.	✔	Where appropriate, a Minor Works Certificate may be used.
U	For electrical safety aspects of electrical installation work associated with emergency lighting systems.	✔	Where appropriate, a Minor Works Certificate may be used.
V	For electrical installation work carried out by others.	✘	
W	Portable appliance inspection and testing.	✘	

NOTE: This table does not represent an exhaustive list, but shows by example the limited scope of the Minor Works Certificate.

With regard to the replacement of accessories and luminaires, it is necessary to satisfy the requirements of *BS 7671*, no matter how minor the works may be. As a minimum, tests to confirm that shock protection has been provided are essential. The essential tests are earth fault loop impedance, polarity and, where an RCD is provided, the correct operation of the RCD. Where it is reasonably practicable, measurements of circuit impedance (R_1 + R_2) and/or R_2, and insulation resistance should also be carried out. The skilled person signing the Minor Works Certificate is responsible for assessing each particular situation, and for deciding whether or not it is reasonable to omit any of the prescribed tests. In any event, a test should be omitted only with the express prior agreement of the client. Where one (or more) of the prescribed tests is not carried out, the contractor should give, on the Minor Works Certificate, brief details of the reasons and technical justifications for omitting the test.

USE AND MISUSE OF THE CERTIFICATE

Except where an Electrical Installation Certificate or a Domestic Electrical Installation Certificate is issued, a separate Minor Works Certificate (based on the model certificate prescribed by *BS 7671*) must be issued to the person who ordered the work, for **each** existing circuit on which minor works are carried out. This requirement applies whether or not the contractor is registered with NICEIC or ELECSA, and whether or not certification has been specifically requested by the client.

As with the Electrical Installation Certificate and the Domestic Electrical Installation Certificate, the Minor Works Certificate is not intended to be issued to confirm the completion of a contract. The certificate is a declaration of electrical safety, and should be compiled before the alteration or addition to the circuit is put into service.

NICEIC and ELECSA strongly prefer contractors registered on their schemes to issue certificates supplied by the Registration Body as this provides a measure of safety assurance and confidence to the recipients. Only those enrolled or registered with NICEIC or ELECSA are authorised to issue their respective certificates. For those not enrolled or registered with NICEIC or ELECSA (green) certificates based on the model given in *BS 7671* are available for use.

An NICEIC or ELECSA Minor Works Certificate may be issued only by the Approved Contractor or Registered Domestic Installer responsible for the installation work. The certificate must not be issued to cover an alteration or addition carried out by another contractor.

The table 'Acceptable and Non-acceptable Use of Minor Works Certificates' shown opposite gives some examples of the circumstances in which the Minor Works Certificate may or may not be used. Most importantly, the certificate may be used only where the work is an alteration or an addition to an existing single circuit and where the work does not entail the provision of a new circuit, as clearly indicated towards the top of the certificate.

NICEIC APPROVED CONTRACTOR

This certificate is not valid if the serial number has been defaced or altered **IMN4/**

MINOR ELECTRICAL INSTALLATION WORKS CERTIFICATE

Contractor's Reference Number

CRN/

Issued in accordance with *British Standard 7671 – Requirements for Electrical Installations* by an Approved Contractor or Conforming Body enrolled with NICEIC, Warwick House, Houghton Hall Park,Houghton Regis, Dunstable LU5 5ZX

To be used only for minor electrical work which does not include the provision of a new circuit

PART 1: DETAILS OF THE MINOR WORKS

Client:

Date minor works completed:

Description of the minor works:

Details of departures, if any, from BS 7671 (as amended):

Location/address of the minor works:

Overcurrent protective device for the modified circuit: BS(EN) Type Rating A

Installer's Reference Number

IRN/

Issued in accordance with *British Standard 7671 – Requirements for Electrical Installations* by a Registered Domestic Installer registered with ELECSA,Certsure LLP, Mansfield Business Centre, Ashfield Avenue, MANSFIELD NG18 2AE.

To be used only for minor electrical work which does not include the provision of a new circuit

PART 1: DETAILS OF THE MINOR WORKS

Client:

Date minor works completed:

Description of the minor works:

Details of departures, if any, from BS 7671 (as amended):

Location/address of the minor works:

PART 4: DECLARATION

§ Details of permitted exceptions appended: **Yes / N/A** Risk assessment appended: **Yes / N/A** No. of pages

(Delete where appropriate)

I CERTIFY that the minor electrical installation works, as detailed in Part 1 of this certificate, does not impair the safety of the existing installation, that the said works have been designed, constructed, inspected, tested and verified in accordance with BS 7671, amended on the date shown* and that, to the best of my knowledge and belief, at the time of inspection, the works complied with BS 7671 except as detailed in Part 1 of this certificate. *

The results of the inspection and testing reviewed by the Qualified Supervisor

Name (CAPITALS) | Name (CAPITALS) | For and on behalf of *(Trading Title of Approved Contractor)*

Signature | Signature

Position | Position | Address and Postcode

Date | Date

NICEIC APPROVED CONTRACTOR Enrolment Number | Branch number (if applicable) | *(The enrolment number is essential information)*

§ *Details of permitted exceptions (Regulation 411.3.3). Where applicable, a suitable risk assessment(s) must be appended to this certificate.*

This certificate is based on the model shown in Appendix 6 of BS 7671

Published by Certsure LLP. Certsure LLP operates the ELECSA & NICEIC brands.

IMN4/1

Please see the 'Notes for Recipients' on the reverse of this page.

COMPILATION OF THE CERTIFICATE

The Minor Works Certificate has four parts. Guidance on the completion of each part is given in the following sections. Generally, irrespective of the method of compilation of the certificate, all unshaded data-entry boxes should be completed by inserting the necessary text, a positive indication such as a '✔' or a numeric value of the measured parameter, or by entering 'N/A' (meaning Not Applicable), where appropriate.

See 'Computer-assisted Preparation of Certificates and Reports' in Chapter 1 for guidance about the compilation of a Minor Works Certificate using a proprietary software package or the NICEIC or ELECSA online certification system(s).

CONTRACTOR'S/INSTALLER'S REFERENCE NUMBER

Contract reference, if any: The client's contract reference, if any, should be stated. In cases where no contract reference has been allocated, the data-entry box should record 'None'.

PART 1: DETAILS OF THE MINOR WORKS

This part of the certificate is where a clear description of the minor works is intended to be given. The minor electrical installation works should be clearly defined such that the work to which the certificate relates can be readily identified. All the data-entry boxes should be completed with the appropriate details that will precisely depict the work, its location and other relevant features, if any.

- **Client:** The name of the client should be stated in the space provided.
- **Date minor works completed:** The date the work was completed should be given.
- **Description of the minor works:** A clear and accurate description of the minor works should be given here, as it is the safety aspects of this particular installation work for which the contractor is taking responsibility. **Failure to clearly and accurately identify the scope of the work could involve the contractor in unforeseen liabilities at a later date.**
- **Details of departures, if any, from *BS 7671*.** Any design departures from *BS 7671* require special consideration by the designer (almost always the contractor in the case of work within the scope of this certificate). Design departures must not result in a degree of safety less than that provided by full compliance with *BS 7671*. Any such departures should be clearly identified and the reason for them clearly explained in this part of the certificate and, in signing the declaration in Part 4, the contractor takes full responsibility for them. In cases where no departures from *BS 7671* are sanctioned by the designer, as will generally be the case, the data-entry box should record 'None'.

APPROVED CONTRACTOR

This certificate is not valid if the serial number has been defaced or altered **IMN4/**

Original (To the person ordering the work)

MINOR ELECTRICAL INSTALLATION WORKS CERTIFICATE

Contractor's Reference Number

CRN/

Issued in accordance with *British Standard 7671 – Requirements for Electrical Installations* by an Approved Contractor or Conforming Body enrolled with NICEIC, Warwick House, Houghton Hall Park,Houghton Regis, Dunstable LU5 5ZX

To be used only for minor electrical work which does not include the provision of a new circuit

PART 1: DETAILS OF THE MINOR WORKS

Client:

Date minor works completed:

Description of the minor works:

Details of departures, if any, from BS 7671 (as amended):

Location/address of the minor works:

PART 2: DETAILS OF THE MODIFIED CIRCUIT

PART 3: INSPECTION AND TESTING OF THE MODIFIED CIRCUIT AND RELATED PARTS

Confirmation that necessary inspections have been undertaken	(✓)	Insulation resistance: (*In a polyphase circuit, record the lower or lowest value, as appropriate*)		
Confirmation of the adequacy of earthing	(✓)	Line/Line MΩ	Line/Earth	MΩ
Confirmation of the adequacy of protective bonding	(✓)	Line/Neutral MΩ	Neutral/Earth	MΩ
Confirmation of correct polarity	(✓)	RCD operating time at $I_{\Delta n}$ (if RCD fitted)		ms
Circuit resistance: $(R_1 + R_2)$ Ω or R_2	Ω	RCD operating time at $5I_{\Delta n}$, if applicable		ms
Maximum measured earth fault loop impedance, Z_S	Ω	Test button operation satisfactory		(✓)

Agreed limitations, if any, on the inspection and testing:

Instrument Serial No(s):

Confirmation of the adequacy of protective bonding	(✓)	Line/Neutral MΩ	Neutral/Earth	MΩ
Confirmation of correct polarity	(✓)	RCD operating time at $I_{\Delta n}$ (if RCD fitted)		ms
Circuit resistance: $(R_1 + R_2)$ Ω or R_2	Ω	RCD operating time at $5I_{\Delta n}$, if applicable		ms
Maximum measured earth fault loop impedance, Z_S	Ω	Test button operation satisfactory		(✓)

Agreed limitations, if any, on the inspection and testing:

Instrument Serial No(s):

PART 4: DECLARATION § Details of permitted exceptions appended: **Yes / N/A** Risk assessment appended: **Yes / N/A** No. of pages

(Delete where appropriate)

I CERTIFY that the minor electrical installation works, as detailed in Part 1 of this certificate, does not impair the safety of the existing installation, that the said works have been designed, constructed, inspected, tested and verified in accordance with BS 7671, amended on the date shown* and that, to the best of my knowledge and belief, at the time of inspection, the works complied with BS 7671 except as detailed in Part 1 of this certificate. *

The results of the inspection and testing reviewed by the Qualified Supervisor

Name (CAPITALS)	Name (CAPITALS)	For and on behalf of *(Trading Title of Approved Contractor)*
Signature	Signature	Address and Postcode
Position	Position	
Date	Date	

Enrolment Number | Branch number (if applicable) | *(The enrolment number is essential information)*

§ *Details of permitted exceptions (Regulation 411.3.3). Where applicable, a suitable risk assessment(s) must be appended to this certificate.*

This certificate is based on the model shown in Appendix 6 of BS 7671

Published by Certsure LLP. Certsure LLP operates the ELECSA & NICEIC brands.

IMN4/1

Please see the 'Notes for Recipients' on the reverse of this page.

- **Location/address of the minor works:** A clear and accurate description of the location and/or details of the address at which the minor works were executed should be recorded here.

PART 2: DETAILS OF THE MODIFIED CIRCUIT

Information concerning the modified circuit should be entered as follows:

- **System type and earthing arrangements:** The system type should be indicated by the insertion of a '✔' in one of the five boxes, as appropriate. Guidance as to the system type and earthing arrangements will be found in Chapter 2. In the United Kingdom, it is likely that the type of system will be TT, TN-S or TN-C-S. One data-entry box only must be completed to indicate the particular system type and earthing arrangement.
- **Protective measure(s) against electric shock:** This refers to the protective measure used for the modified circuit. The applicable protective measure must be selected from the available options as set out in Chapter 41 of *BS 7671*. In many, if not most, cases this will be Automatic Disconnection of Supply (ADS). The protective measure used should be fully described here.
- **Overcurrent protective device for the modified circuit:** The information to be recorded here is the British Standard (or other appropriate Standard) product specification for the existing overcurrent protective device in terms of BS (EN) number, together with the type (if any) and the rated current (I_n). For example, the type of device may be '*BS EN 60898* Type B circuit-breaker' and the rated current in amperes may be '6' or '32' etc.
- **Residual current device (if applicable):** Where a residual current device already exists in the circuit or has been provided as part of the minor works for protection against electric shock, the information to be recorded here is the British Standard (or other appropriate Standard) product specification in terms of *BS (EN)* number, together with the type and the residual operating (tripping) current rating ($I_{\Delta n}$) in units of mA.
- **Details of wiring system used to modify the circuit:** The type of wiring system used should be identified here (e.g. thermoplastic cables in steel conduit) together with the reference method and cross-sectional areas of live and circuit protective conductors. Details of reference methods and associated installation methods are given in Table 4A2 of Appendix 4 of *BS 7671*.

APPROVED CONTRACTOR

This certificate is not valid if the serial number has been defaced or altered **IMN4/**

MINOR ELECTRICAL INSTALLATION WORKS CERTIFICATE

Contractor's Reference Number

CRN/

Issued in accordance with *British Standard 7671 – Requirements for Electrical Installations* by an Approved Contractor or Conforming Body enrolled with NICEIC, Warwick House, Houghton Hall Park,Houghton Regis, Dunstable LU5 5ZX

To be used only for minor electrical work which does not include the provision of a new circuit

Original (To the person ordering the work)

PART 1: DETAILS OF THE MINOR WORKS

Client:

Date minor works completed:

Description of the minor works:

Details of departures, if any, from BS 7671 (as amended):

Location/address of the minor works:

PART 2: DETAILS OF THE MODIFIED CIRCUIT

System type and earthing arrangements: TN-C-S TN-S TT TN-C IT

Protective measure(s) against electric shock:

Overcurrent protective device for the modified circuit: BS(EN) Type Rating A

Residual current device (if applicable): BS(EN) Type $I_{\Delta n}$ mA

Details of wiring system used to modify the circuit: Type Reference method csa of lives mm^2 csa of cpc mm^2

Where the measure for protection against electric shock is ADS, insert maximum disconnection time permitted by BS 7671: s Maximum Z_S permitted by BS 7671 Ω

Comments, if any, on existing installation, including adequacy of earthing and bonding arrangements (see Regulation 132.16):

PART 3: INSPECTION AND TESTING OF THE MODIFIED CIRCUIT AND RELATED PARTS

PART 3: INSPECTION AND TESTING OF THE MODIFIED CIRCUIT AND RELATED PARTS

Confirmation that necessary inspections have been undertaken	(✓)	Insulation resistance: *(In a polyphase circuit, record the lower or lowest value, as appropriate)*	
Confirmation of the adequacy of earthing	(✓)	Line/Line MΩ	Line/Earth MΩ
Confirmation of the adequacy of protective bonding	(✓)	Line/Neutral MΩ	Neutral/Earth MΩ
Confirmation of correct polarity	(✓)	RCD operating time at $I_{\Delta n}$ (if RCD fitted)	ms
Circuit resistance: $(R_1 + R_2)$ Ω or R_2	Ω	RCD operating time at $5I_{\Delta n}$, if applicable	ms
Maximum measured earth fault loop impedance, Z_S	Ω	Test button operation satisfactory	(✓)

Agreed limitations, if any, on the inspection and testing:

Instrument Serial No(s):

Name (CAPITALS)	Name (CAPITALS)	For and on behalf of *(Trading Title of Approved Contractor)*
Signature	Signature	Address and Postcode
Position	Position	
Date	Date	

Enrolment Number Branch number (if applicable) *(The enrolment number is essential information)*

§ *Details of permitted exceptions (Regulation 411.3.3). Where applicable, a suitable risk assessment(s) must be appended to this certificate.*

This certificate is based on the model shown in Appendix 6 of BS 7671

Published by Certsure LLP. Certsure LLP operates the ELECSA & NICEIC brands.

IMN4/1

Please see the 'Notes for Recipients' on the reverse of this page.

- **Maximum disconnection time permitted by *BS 7671*:** Where the protective measure is Automatic Disconnection of Supply (ADS), the maximum time in seconds for automatic disconnection in case of a fault permitted by *BS 7671* should be recorded in the data-box provided.
- **Maximum Z_S permitted by *BS 7671*:** Where a protective device is used for automatic disconnection in case of a fault, the maximum (Z_S) in ohms permitted by *BS 7671* should be recorded in the data-box provided.
- **Comments, if any, on existing installation:** The considerations relating to the completion of this element of the certificate are the same as those applicable to the 'comments on existing installation' section in the Electrical Installation Certificate (see Chapter 2).

PART 3: INSPECTION AND TESTING OF THE MODIFIED CIRCUIT AND RELATED PARTS

The relevant provisions of Part 6 (Inspection and Testing) of *BS 7671* must be applied in full to electrical installation work covered by a Minor Works Certificate.

Generally, all data-entry boxes should be completed to confirm the results of a particular inspection or test by a '✔', indicating the particular inspection or test has been performed and the results are satisfactory, or by the insertion of a measured value where appropriate. Where a particular inspection or test is not applicable, this should be indicated by inserting 'N/A', meaning 'Not Applicable'. Exceptionally, where an inspection or a test is not practicable, the entry should be 'LIM' meaning 'Limitation', indicating that the particular circumstances prevented such an inspection or test procedure from being carried out. In such cases, the limitation(s) should be agreed with the client before the work is undertaken, and identified in the space provided at the bottom of Part 3. The inspections and tests identified on the certificate are considered essential for confirming the safety of all minor electrical installation work involving the alteration or addition of cables and conductors.

The method for carrying out each item of inspection and testing is described in Chapter 7 and Chapter 9, respectively.

The information required for Part 3 of the Minor Works Certificate is as follows:

- **Confirmation that necessary inspections have been undertaken:** A positive entry such as a tick (✔) is necessary here to indicate that all necessary inspections have been carried out with satisfactory outcomes, as appropriate to the particular circuit modification.
- **Confirmation of the adequacy of earthing:** A positive entry such as a tick (✔) here indicates that the adequacy of the earthing has been established by inspection of the earthing conductor and its terminations, and

NICEIC APPROVED CONTRACTOR

This certificate is not valid if the serial number has been defaced or altered IMN4/

MINOR ELECTRICAL INSTALLATION WORKS CERTIFICATE

Original (To the person ordering the work)

Contractor's Reference Number

CRN/

Issued in accordance with *British Standard 7671 – Requirements for Electrical Installations* by an Approved Contractor or Conforming Body enrolled with NICEIC, Warwick House, Houghton Hall Park, Houghton Regis, Dunstable LU5 5ZX

To be used only for minor electrical work which does not include the provision of a new circuit

PART 1: DETAILS OF THE MINOR WORKS

Client:

Date minor works completed:

Description of the minor works:

Details of departures, if any, from BS 7671 (as amended):

Location/address of the minor works:

PART 2: DETAILS OF THE MODIFIED CIRCUIT

System type and earthing arrangements: TN-C-S TN-S TT TN-C IT

Protective measure(s) against electric shock:

Overcurrent protective device for the modified circuit: BS(EN) Type Rating A

Residual current device (if applicable): BS(EN) Type $I_{\Delta n}$ mA

Details of wiring system used to modify the circuit: Type Reference method csa of lives mm² csa of cpc mm²

Where the measure for protection against electric shock is ADS, insert maximum disconnection time permitted by BS 7671: s Maximum Z_s permitted by BS 7671 Ω

Comments, if any, on existing installation, including adequacy of earthing and bonding arrangements (see Regulation 132.16):

PART 3: INSPECTION AND TESTING OF THE MODIFIED CIRCUIT AND RELATED PARTS

Confirmation that necessary inspections have been undertaken		(✓)	Insulation resistance: *(In a polyphase circuit, record the lower or lowest value, as appropriate)*		
Confirmation of the adequacy of earthing		(✓)	Line/Line MΩ	Line/Earth	MΩ
Confirmation of the adequacy of protective bonding		(✓)	Line/Neutral MΩ	Neutral/Earth	MΩ
Confirmation of correct polarity		(✓)	RCD operating time at $I_{\Delta n}$ (if RCD fitted)		ms
Circuit resistance: $(R_1 + R_2)$ Ω or R_2		Ω	RCD operating time at $5I_{\Delta n}$, if applicable		ms
Maximum measured earth fault loop impedance, Z_s		Ω	Test button operation satisfactory		(✓)

Agreed limitations, if any, on the inspection and testing:

Instrument Serial No(s):

(Delete where appropriate)

I CERTIFY that the minor electrical installation works, as detailed in Part 1 of this certificate, does not impair the safety of the existing installation, that the said works have been designed, constructed, inspected, tested and verified in accordance with BS 7671, amended on the date shown* and that, to the best of my knowledge and belief, at the time of inspection, the works complied with BS 7671 except as detailed in Part 1 of this certificate. *

The results of the inspection and testing reviewed by the Qualified Supervisor

Name (CAPITALS)	Name (CAPITALS)	For and on behalf of *(Trading Title of Approved Contractor)*
Signature	Signature	Address and Postcode
Position	Position	
Date	Date	

NICEIC Enrolment Number Branch number (if applicable) *(The enrolment number is essential information)*

§ *Details of permitted exceptions (Regulation 411.3.3). Where applicable, a suitable risk assessment(s) must be appended to this certificate.*

This certificate is based on the model shown in Appendix 6 of BS 7671

Published by Certsure LLP. Certsure LLP operates the ELECSA & NICEIC brands.

IMN4/1

Please see the 'Notes for Recipients' on the reverse of this page.

by measurement of the earth fault loop impedance (Z_e) at the origin of the installation.

- **Confirmation of the adequacy of protective bonding:** A positive entry such as a tick (✔) here confirms that the adequacy of the protective equipotential bonding to all extraneous-conductive-parts has been established by inspection and by continuity checks of the bonding conductors and their terminations.
- **Confirmation of correct polarity:** Correct polarity will have been confirmed during the ($R_1 + R_2$) test procedure or, if the R_2 measurement was taken instead, by other means (described in Chapter 9). A positive indication such as a tick (✔) entered in this part of the certificate signifies that correct polarity has been confirmed.
- **Circuit resistance (R_1 + R_2), or R_2:** Enter the highest measured value of (R_1 + R_2), in ohms, measured at each of the points and/or accessories on the modified circuit. During this test, the line and circuit protective conductors of the circuit should be connected together as described for measurement of (R_1 + R_2) in Chapter 9 (see 'continuity of protective conductors' or, for ring final circuits, 'continuity of ring final circuit conductors'). This test procedure also confirms that polarity is correct and gives an ohmic value of the circuit's contribution to the earth fault loop impedance (Z_S) Alternatively, if preferred, the impedance of the circuit protective conductor R_2 may be recorded instead of (R_1 + R_2), but in this case correct polarity will need to be separately confirmed by other means (see Chapter 9).
- **Maximum measured earth fault loop impedance, Z_S:** Enter the highest value of earth fault loop impedance (Z_S), in ohms, determined at each of the points and/or accessories on the modified circuit. The highest measured value of Z_S must be such as to afford automatic disconnection within the time limit prescribed in *BS 7671.*
- **Insulation resistance:** Enter the measured values of line/line (only applicable for polyphase circuits), line/neutral, line/earth and neutral/earth insulation resistance of the circuit, in megohms. Where the circuit is polyphase circuits (e.g. two-phase or three-phase), the lower or lowest value of measured insulation resistance should be recorded. See Chapter 9 regarding precautions that may be necessary before testing insulation resistance.
- **RCD operating time at $I_{\Delta n}$ (if RCD fitted):** If there is an RCD in the circuit, this should be tested in the manner described in Chapter 9. The operating (tripping) time in milliseconds (ms) when subjected to a test at a current equal to $I_{\Delta n}$ should be recorded in the space provided.

ELECSA

This certificate is not valid if the serial number has been defaced or altered **DME1/**

Original (To the person ordering the work)

MINOR DOMESTIC ELECTRICAL INSTALLATION WORKS CERTIFICATE

Installer's Reference Number

IRN/

Issued in accordance with *British Standard 7671 – Requirements for Electrical Installations* by a Registered Domestic Installer registered with ELECSA,Certsure LLP, Mansfield Business Centre, Ashfield Avenue, MANSFIELD NG18 2AE.

To be used only for minor electrical work which does not include the provision of a new circuit

PART 1: DETAILS OF THE MINOR WORKS

Client:

Date minor works completed:

Description of the minor works:

Details of departures, if any, from BS 7671 (as amended):

Location/address of the minor works:

PART 2: DETAILS OF THE MODIFIED CIRCUIT

System type and earthing arrangements: TN-C-S TN-S TT TN-C IT

Protective measure(s) against electric shock:

Overcurrent protective device for the modified circuit: BS(EN) Type Rating A

Residual current device (if applicable): BS(EN) Type $I_{\Delta n}$ mA

Details of wiring system used to modify the circuit: Type Reference method csa of lives mm^2 csa of cpc mm^2

Where the measure for protection against electric shock is ADS, insert maximum disconnection time permitted by BS 7671: s Maximum Z_s permitted by BS 7671 Ω

Comments, if any, on existing installation, including adequacy of earthing and bonding arrangements (see Regulation 132.16):

PART 3: INSPECTION AND TESTING OF THE MODIFIED CIRCUIT AND RELATED PARTS

Confirmation that necessary inspections have been undertaken	(✓)	Insulation resistance: *(In a polyphase circuit, record the lower or lowest value, as appropriate)*			
Confirmation of the adequacy of earthing	(✓)	Line/Line	MΩ	Line/Earth	MΩ
Confirmation of the adequacy of protective bonding	(✓)	Line/Neutral	MΩ	Neutral/Earth	MΩ
Confirmation of correct polarity	(✓)	RCD operating time at $I_{\Delta n}$ (if RCD fitted)			ms
Circuit resistance: $(R_1 + R_2)$ Ω or R_2	Ω	RCD operating time at $5I_{\Delta n}$, if applicable			ms
Maximum measured earth fault loop impedance, Z_s	Ω	Test button operation satisfactory			(✓)

Agreed limitations, if any, on the inspection and testing:

Instrument Serial No(s):

PART 4: DECLARATION

I CERTIFY that the minor electrical installation works, as detailed in Part 1 of this certificate, does not impair the safety of the existing installation, that the said works have been designed, constructed, inspected, tested and verified in accordance with BS 7671, amended on the date shown* and that, to the best of my knowledge and belief, at the time of inspection, the works complied with BS 7671 except as detailed in Part 1 of this certificate.

*

The results of the inspection and testing reviewed by the Qualified Supervisor

Name (CAPITALS)	Name (CAPITALS)	For and on behalf of *(Trading Title of Registered Domestic Installer)*
Signature	Signature	Address and Postcode
Position	Position	
Date	Date	

ELECSA ELECSA Registration No (Essential information)

This certificate is based on the model shown in Appendix 6 of BS 7671
Published by Certsure LLP. Certsure LLP operates the ELECSA & NICEIC brands.

DME1/1

Please see the 'Notes for Recipients' on the reverse of this page.

- **RCD operating time at $5I_{\Delta n}$, (if applicable):** If there is an RCD in circuit which is intended to provide additional protection, it should be tested in the manner described in Chapter 9. The operating (tripping) time in milliseconds (ms) when subjected to a test at $5I_{\Delta n}$ should be recorded in the space provided. If the RCD is not intended to provide additional protection the test is not essential, and if not undertaken, insert 'N/A' (meaning Not Applicable) in the box.
- **Test button operation satisfactory,** a functional check should be carried out on the RCD to confirm it operates when the the test button is pressed.
- **Agreed limitations, if any, on the inspection and testing:** All limitations imposed on the inspection and testing should be explained to, and agreed with, the client before work commences. Such limitations should be recorded in the space provided together with the technical justifications for taking such decisions. **It should be appreciated that failure to clearly explain and record all of the agreed limitations of the inspection and testing could involve the contractor in unforeseen liabilities at a later date.**
- **Instrument serial No(s),** the serial number of each of the instruments used to obtain the test results should be recorded. If a instrument does not have a serial number, a suitable number should be assigned and permanently marked on the instrument.

With regard to the replacement of accessories and luminaires, it may be impracticable to carry out all the identified tests. However, testing of earth fault loop impedance, polarity and, where an RCD is provided, confirmation of the correct operation of the RCD are considered to be essential. Where practicable (R_1 + R_2) and/or R_2, insulation resistance and earth fault loop impedance tests should also be carried out. The serial number(s) of the test instrument(s) used should be recorded.

For example, where a socket-outlet is added to an existing circuit, it is necessary to:

- Carry out all necessary inspecting and testing of the modified circuit and related parts of the installation and supply on which the circuit depends for protection. This includes inspecting and testing to confirm that the earthing and protective bonding arrangements for the modified circuit are both adequate and reliable.
- Check the continuity and resistance of protective conductor(s) to establish that the earthing contact of the socket-outlet is reliably and effectively connected to the main earthing terminal of the installation via a low impedance circuit protective conductor.
- Measure the insulation resistances, line to line, line to neutral, and line to earth of the circuit that has been modified, and establish that the resistance values comply with Table 61 of *BS 7671*.
- Check that the polarity at the socket-outlet is correct.

NICEIC APPROVED CONTRACTOR

This certificate is not valid if the serial number has been defaced or altered **IMN4/ XXXXXXX**

MINOR ELECTRICAL INSTALLATION WORKS CERTIFICATE

Contractor's Reference Number

CRN/

Issued in accordance with *British Standard 7671 – Requirements for Electrical Installations* by an Approved Contractor or Conforming Body enrolled with NICEIC, Warwick House, Houghton Hall Park,Houghton Regis, Dunstable LU5 5ZX

To be used only for minor electrical work which does not include the provision of a new circuit

Original (To the person ordering the work)

PART 1: DETAILS OF THE MINOR WORKS

Client:

Date minor works completed:

Description of the minor works:

Details of departures, if any, from BS 7671 (as amended):

Location/address of the minor works:

PART 2: DETAILS OF THE MODIFIED CIRCUIT

System type and earthing arrangements: TN-C-S TN-S TT TN-C IT

Protective measure(s) against electric shock:

Overcurrent protective device for the modified circuit: BS(EN) Type Rating A

Residual current device (if applicable): BS(EN) Type $I_{\Delta n}$ mA

Details of wiring system Type Reference csa of lives mm² csa of cpc mm²

PART 4: DECLARATION

I CERTIFY that the minor electrical installation works, as detailed in Part 1 of this certificate, does not impair the safety of the existing installation, that the said works have been designed, constructed, inspected, tested and verified in accordance with BS 7671, amended on the date shown* and that, to the best of my knowledge and belief, at the time of inspection, the works complied with BS 7671 except as detailed in Part 1 of this certificate.

*

The results of the inspection and testing reviewed by the Qualified Supervisor

Name (CAPITALS)		Name (CAPITALS)		For and on behalf of *(Trading Title of Registered Domestic Installer)*
Signature		Signature		Address and Postcode
Position		Position		
Date		Date		

NICEIC DOMESTIC INSTALLER

NICEIC Registration No (Essential information)

PART 4: DECLARATION

§ Details of permitted exceptions appended: **Yes / N/A** Risk assessment appended: **Yes / N/A** No. of pages

(Delete as appropriate)

I CERTIFY that the minor electrical installation works, as detailed in Part 1 of this certificate, does not impair the safety of the existing installation, that the said works have been designed, constructed, inspected, tested and verified in accordance with BS 7671, amended on the date shown* and that, to the best of my knowledge and belief, at the time of inspection, the works complied with BS 7671 except as detailed in Part 1 of this certificate.

*

The results of the inspection and testing reviewed by:

Name (CAPITALS)		Name (CAPITALS)		For and on behalf of:
Signature		Signature		Address and Postcode
Position		Position		
Date		Date		

§ *Details of permitted exceptions (Regulation 411.3.3). Where applicable, a suitable risk assessment(s) must be appended to this certificate.*

This certificate is based on the model shown in Appendix 6 of BS 7671
Published by Certsure LLP.

Please see the 'Notes for Recipients' on the reverse of this page.

- Determine the maximum earth fault loop impedance to establish that the permitted disconnection time is not exceeded - see table provided with NICEIC and ELECSA Minor Works Certificates (and the equivalent green certificates), and
- Check the suitability and effectiveness of the RCD, if the modified circuit is so protected.

PART 4: DECLARATION

In this part of the certificate, the contractor certifies that the work undertaken in connection with the alteration or addition does not impair the safety of the existing installation, and that the new work has been inspected and tested in accordance with *BS 7671*. The contractor also certifies that the alteration or addition complies with the requirements of *BS 7671*, with the exception of any design departures identified in Part 1 of the certificate.

Details of permitted exceptions: For an installation other than a dwelling,(so not applicable to the domestic minor works certificate) a permitted exception may be applied so that an RCD in accordance with Regulation 415.1 is not required for socket-outlets having a rating not exceeding 20 A.

However, where such an exception is applied it must be based on a documented risk assessment, and the skilled person issuing the certificate is required to confirm that the appropriate risk assessment (or a copy of the risk assessment) is appended to the certificate.

***BS 7671* Amendment:** The date of the amendment to *BS 7671* that was current at the date on which the work was carried out should be stated in the relevant space in the text of the declaration.

Name (CAPITALS): The name of the skilled person providing the declaration on behalf of the contractor should be recorded in capital letters in the space provided.

Signature: The signature of the skilled person providing the declaration on behalf of the contractor, and the date of signing, should be inserted in the appropriate spaces. The signatory should be an electrically skilled person who is well informed about the design and construction of the work and competent to confirm whether the requirements of *BS 7671* have been met. The signatory should have personally carried out and verified the work, or have undertaken detailed supervision of the work, so as to be in a position to take with confidence full responsibility for the statements made in the declaration.

Position: The position of the signatory should be identified in the space provided (e.g. NICEIC or ELECSA Qualified Supervisor, director, partner, or supervising electrical engineer).

Date: The date on which the signatory signs the declaration should be recorded in the space provided.

For and on behalf of (Trading Title of Approved Contractor, Registered Domestic Installer or installer): The Contractor's full trading title should be inserted in the space provided.

Address and Postcode: The contractor's full postal address, including the postcode, should be inserted in the space provided.

NICEIC or ELECSA Enrolment or Registration Number: For an NICEIC or ELECSA certificate, it is essential that this information is recorded in the space provided.

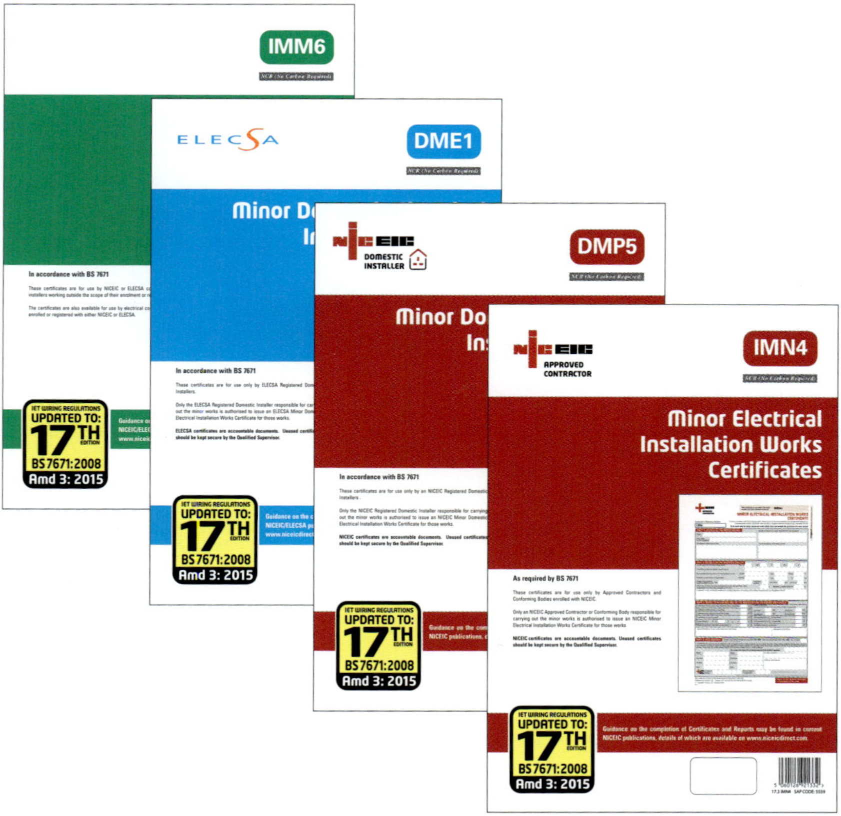

Chapter 5

The Electrical Installation Condition Report

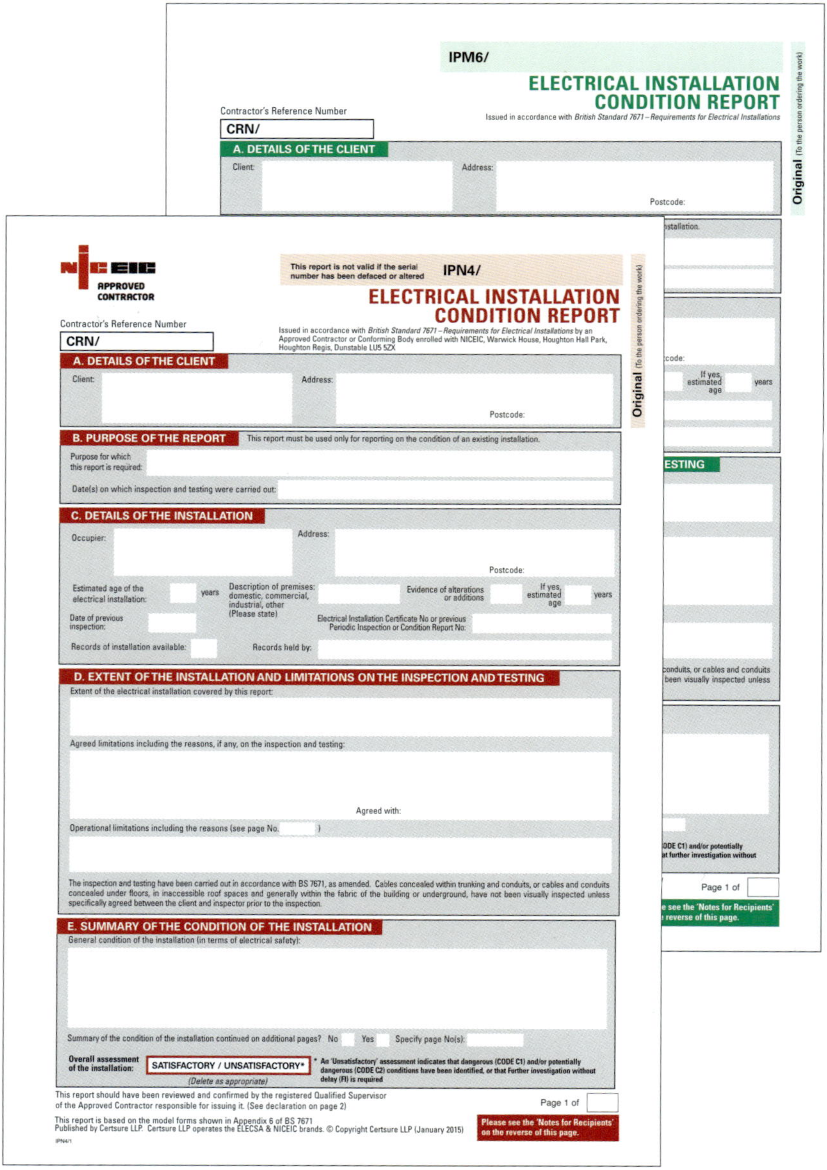

IPM6/

ELECTRICAL INSTALLATION CONDITION REPORT

Issued in accordance with *British Standard 7671 – Requirements for Electrical Installations*

Contractor's Reference Number CRN/

A. DETAILS OF THE CLIENT

Client: Address: Postcode:

Original (To the person ordering the work)

APPROVED CONTRACTOR

This report is not valid if the serial number has been defaced or altered IPN4/

ELECTRICAL INSTALLATION CONDITION REPORT

Issued in accordance with *British Standard 7671 – Requirements for Electrical Installations* by an Approved Contractor or Conforming Body enrolled with NICEIC, Warwick House, Houghton Hall Park, Houghton Regis, Dunstable LU5 5ZX

Original (To the person ordering the work)

Contractor's Reference Number CRN/

A. DETAILS OF THE CLIENT

Client: Address: Postcode:

B. PURPOSE OF THE REPORT This report must be used only for reporting on the condition of an existing installation.

Purpose for which this report is required:

Date(s) on which inspection and testing were carried out:

C. DETAILS OF THE INSTALLATION

Occupier: Address: Postcode:

Estimated age of the electrical installation: years

Description of premises: domestic, commercial, industrial, other (Please state)

Evidence of alterations or additions

If yes, estimated age years

Date of previous inspection:

Electrical Installation Certificate No or previous Periodic Inspection or Condition Report No:

Records of installation available: Records held by:

D. EXTENT OF THE INSTALLATION AND LIMITATIONS ON THE INSPECTION AND TESTING

Extent of the electrical installation covered by this report:

Agreed limitations including the reasons, if any, on the inspection and testing:

Agreed with:

Operational limitations including the reasons (see page No.)

The inspection and testing have been carried out in accordance with BS 7671, as amended. Cables concealed within trunking and conduits, or cables and conduits concealed under floors, in inaccessible roof spaces and generally within the fabric of the building or underground, have not been visually inspected unless specifically agreed between the client and inspector prior to the inspection.

E. SUMMARY OF THE CONDITION OF THE INSTALLATION

General condition of the installation (in terms of electrical safety):

Summary of the condition of the installation continued on additional pages? No Yes Specify page No(s):

Overall assessment of the installation: SATISFACTORY / UNSATISFACTORY* (*Delete as appropriate*)

* An 'Unsatisfactory' assessment indicates that dangerous (CODE C1) and/or potentially dangerous (CODE C2) conditions have been identified, or that Further investigation without delay (FI) is required

This report should have been reviewed and confirmed by the registered Qualified Supervisor of the Approved Contractor responsible for issuing it. (See declaration on page 2)

Page 1 of

This report is based on the model forms shown in Appendix 6 of BS 7671

Published by Certsure LLP. Certsure LLP operates the ELECSA & NICEIC brands. © Copyright Certsure LLP (January 2015)

Please see the 'Notes for Recipients' on the reverse of this page.

IPN4/1

5 THE ELECTRICAL INSTALLATION CONDITION REPORT

THE NEED FOR PERIODIC INSPECTION AND TESTING

Every electrical installation deteriorates with use and age. It is important for the person responsible for the maintenance of the installation to be sure that the safety of the users is not put at risk, and that the installation continues to be in a safe and serviceable condition. It is necessary therefore for the installation to be periodically inspected and tested by a skilled person or persons, competent in such work, and a report on its condition obtained. Deficiencies observed during the inspection and testing may then be remedied such that the installation may continue to be used in safety.

The periodic inspection of an electrical installation may be required for one or more of a variety of reasons, each of which may impose particular requirements or limitations.

PURPOSE OF PERIODIC INSPECTION

The main purpose of periodic inspection and testing is to detect so far as is reasonably practicable, and to report on, any factors impairing the safety of an electrical installation. The aspects to be covered, as stated in Regulation 621.2, include all of the following:

- Safety of persons and livestock against the effects of electric shock and burns
- Protection against damage to property by fire and heat arising from an installation defect
- Confirmation that the installation is not damaged or deteriorated so as to impair safety
- Identification of installation defects and departures from the requirements of *BS 7671*, that may give rise to danger

Unless the circumstances make it unavoidable (for example, if an installer has ceased trading prior to certifying an installation), an Electrical Installation Condition Report should not be issued by one contractor as a substitute for an Electrical Installation Certificate or a Domestic Electrical Installation Certificate for work carried out by another contractor. An Electrical Installation Condition Report does not provide a declaration by the designer or installer that the aspects of the work for which they were responsible comply with *BS 7671*. Also, cables that are concealed cannot be inspected when construction is complete.

If a contractor is called upon to issue an Electrical Installation Condition Report for work designed and installed by others, it would be prudent for that contractor to make the purpose and limitations of the report absolutely clear, in order to avoid unwittingly assuming responsibility for aspects of the work of which the contractor had no knowledge and over which the contractor had no control.

Recommended Initial Frequencies of Inspection of Electrical Installations			
Type of installation	Routine check*	Maximum period between inspections and testing as necessary	Reference (see notes below)
General installations			
Domestic (owner occupied)		Change of occupancy/10 years	
Domestic (rented property)		Change of tenancy/5 years	
Commercial	1 year	Change of occupancy/5 years	1, 2
Educational establishments	4 months	5 years	1, 2
Hospitals	1 year	5 years	1, 2
Offices	1 year	5 years	1, 2
Shops	1 year	5 years	1, 2
Laboratories	1 year	5 years	1, 2
Industrial	1 year	3 years	1, 2
Buildings open to the public			
Cinemas	1 year	1-3 years	2, 6
Leisure complexes excluding swimming pools	1 year	3 years	1, 2, 6
Places of public entertainment	1 year	3 years	1, 2, 6
Places of worship	1 year	5 years	2
Restaurants and hotels	1 year	5 years	1, 2, 6
Theatres	1 year	3 years	2, 6, 7
Public houses	1 year	5 years	1, 2, 6
Village halls/Community centres	1 year	5 years	1, 2
Special installations			
Agricultural & horticultural	1 year	3 years	1, 2
Caravans (infrequently moved)	1 year	3 years	
Caravans (frequently moved)		1 year	
Caravan parks	6 months	1 year	1, 2, 6
Highway power supplies	as convenient	6 years	
Marinas	4 months	1 year	1, 2
Fish farms	4 months	1 year	1, 2
Swimming pools	4 months	1 year	1, 2, 6
Emergency lighting	Daily/monthly	3 years	2, 3, 4
Fire alarms	Daily/weekly/monthly quarterly	1 year	2, 4, 5
Launderettes	1 year	1 year	1, 2, 6
Petrol filling stations	1 year	1 year	1, 2, 6
Construction site installations	3 months	3 months	1, 2

Reference Key

1. Particular attention must be taken to comply with SI 2002 No 2665 The Electrical Safety Quality and Continuity Regulations.
2. SI 1989 No 635. The Electricity at Work Regulations 1989 (Regulation 4 & Memorandum).
3. See BS 5266: Part 1: 2011 Code of practice for the emergency escape lighting of premises and BS EN 50172/BS 5266-8: 2004 Emergency escape lighting systems.
4. Other intervals are recommended for testing operation of batteries and generators.
5. See BS 5839: Part 1: 2013 Code of practice for design, installation, commissioning and maintenance of systems in non-domestic premises (Fire detection and Fire alarm systems for buildings).
6. Local Authority Conditions of Licence.
7. SI 1995 No 1129 (Clause 27) The Cinematograph (Safety) Regulations.

* Refer to sub-clause 3.5 of IET GN 3.

COMPETENCE AND SAFETY

Attention is drawn to the need for all persons undertaking inspection and testing to to be skilled persons competent in such work, and to follow safe working procedures - see Chapter 1

Generally, persons undertaking periodic inspection reporting need to have extensive knowledge and experience of electrical installation matters to enable them to safely and accurately assess the condition of an existing electrical installation, especially when they do not have access to the design information relating to that installation.

If the absence of sufficient installation information prevents the inspection and testing being carried out safely, information (such as diagrams and circuit details) must be obtained from the person responsible for the installation. Alternatively, the information must be prepared for the purpose before work commences, in order to afford compliance with Section 6 of the *Health and Safety at Work etc Act 1974*.

INTERVALS BETWEEN PERIODIC INSPECTION AND TESTING

The interval between periodic inspection and testing will depend on a number of considerations (see Regulation 622.1), including some or all of the factors indicated below, depending on the particular circumstances:

- Age of the installation (It may be reasonable to expect the intervals to become progressively shorter as the installation ages)
- Type of premises
- Environmental conditions (ie external influences)
- Normal life expectancy of the installation
- Level of misuse of the installation (e.g. vandalism)
- Changed usage of the premises (and the installation)
- The extent of any wear and tear, damage or other deterioration.

Determination of the interval to the next inspection will always be a matter of engineering judgement to be exercised by the inspector. However, the table opposite gives recommendations for the maximum initial interval between initial verification and the first periodic inspection. The information given should be used as a guide only and the intervals stated may need to be adjusted to meet the particular circumstances.

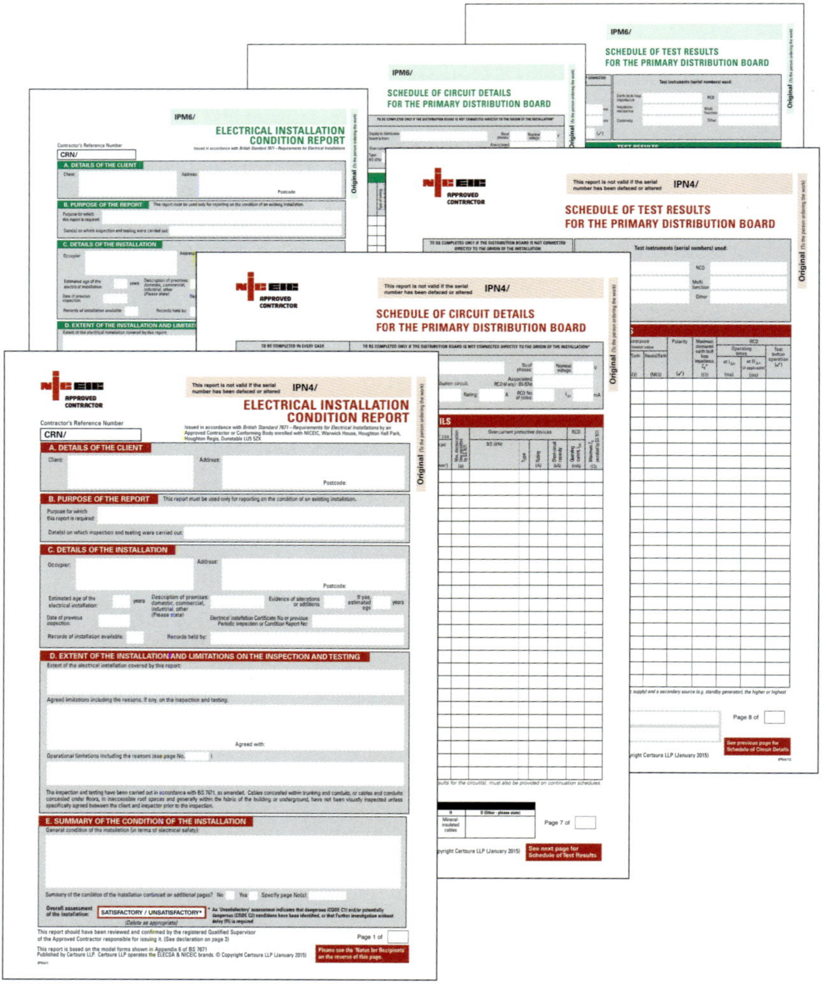

The green (uncontrolled) Electrical Installation Condition Report form is available for use by:

- electrical contractors not enrolled/registered with NICEIC or ELECSA, in particular those preparing for enrolment or registration, and
- NICEIC and ELECSA contractors or installers working outside the scope of their enrolment/registeration

REQUIREMENTS

BS 7671 requires that an Electrical Installation Condition Report is issued following the in-service periodic inspection and testing of an electrical installation. The report is required to include details of the extent of the installation inspected and of any limitations (including the reasons for these limitations) of the inspection and testing, together with a record of the inspection and the results of testing. A separate report is required for each distinct installation examined. The report provides a formal declaration that, within the stated and agreed limitations, the details recorded, including the observations and recommendations and the completed schedules of inspection and test results, give an accurate assessment of the condition of the electrical installation at the time it was inspected and tested.

Wherever possible, before undertaking periodic inspection and testing, it is important for the skilled person undertaking the work of inspection to have sight of the records associated with the installation. Such records would include the Electrical Installation Certificate or a Domestic Electrical Installation Certificate issued when the installation was originally completed, and any subsequent Minor Electrical Installation Works Certificates, Periodic Inspection Reports and Electrical Installation Condition Reports. Depending on the complexity of the installation, the records might also include 'as-fitted' drawings and single-line distribution drawings.

A report (based on the model form prescribed by *BS 7671*) should be issued to the person ordering the inspection and testing , whether or not the contractor is enrolled or registered with NICEIC or ELECSA, and whether or not a written report has been specifically requested by the client. NICEIC and ELECSA strongly prefer their contractors/installers to issue the report forms supplied by their respective bodies, as this provides a measure of safety assurance and confidence to the recipients. For contractors not authorised to issue NICEIC or ELECSA Electrical Installation Condition Report forms, similar (green) report forms based on the model form given in *BS 7671* are available from NICEIC.

The Electrical Installation Condition Report is, as its title indicates, a report and not a certificate. It relates to an assessment of the in-service condition of an electrical installation against the requirements of the issue of *BS 7671* current at the time of the inspection, irrespective of the age of the installation. The criteria for assessing the compliance of each part of an older installation with *BS 7671* are, therefore, the same as for new installation work. The report is for the benefit of the person ordering the work, and of persons subsequently involved in additional or remedial work, or further inspections.

The Electrical Installation Condition Report form is to be used only for reporting on the condition of an existing installation. It must not be used instead of an Electrical Installation Certificate or a Domestic Electrical Installation Certificate for certifying new electrical installation work, or as a substitute for a Minor Electrical Installation Works Certificate for certifying an addition or an alteration to an existing installation.

APPROVED CONTRACTOR

Contractor's Reference Number

CRN/

This continuation sheet is not valid if the serial number is not the same as the corresponding certificate or report ICN/IPN Delete as appropriate

SCHEDULE OF CIRCUIT DETAILS FOR THE INSTALLATION - CONTINUATION

Original (To the person ordering the work)

TO BE COMPLETED IN EVERY CASE	TO BE COMPLETED ONLY IF THE DISTRIBUTION BOARD IS NOT CONNECTED DIRECTLY TO THE ORIGIN OF THE INSTALLATION*
Location of distribution board:	Supply to distribution board is from: No of phases: Nominal voltage: V
	Overcurrent protective device for the distribution circuit: Associated RCD (if any): BS(EN)
Distribution board designation:	Type: BS(EN) Rating: A RCD No of poles: $I_{\Delta n}$ mA

CIRCUIT DETAILS

Circuit number and line	Circuit designation	Type of wiring (see code below)	Reference method †	Number of points served	Circuit conductors: csa Live (mm²)	Circuit conductors: csa cpc (mm²)	Max. disconnection time permitted by BS 7671 (s)	Overcurrent protective devices BS (EN)	Type	Rating (A)	Short-circuit capacity (kA)	RCD Operating current, $I_{\Delta n}$ (mA)	Maximum Z_s permitted by BS 7671 (Ω)

† *See Table 4A2 of Appendix 4 of BS 7671*

CODES FOR TYPE OF WIRING

A	B	C	D	E	F	G	H	O (Other - please state)
Thermoplastic insulated/ sheathed cables	Thermoplastic cables in metallic conduit	Thermoplastic cables in non-metallic conduit	Thermoplastic cables in metallic trunking	Thermoplastic cables in non-metallic trunking	Thermoplastic /SWA cables	Thermosetting/ SWA cables	Mineral-insulated cables	

se state)

Page of

* *In such cases, details of the distribution (sub-main) circuit(s), together with the test results for the circuit(s), must also be provid*

be provided on continuation schedules.

This certificate is based on the model forms shown in Appendix 6 of BS 7671

Published by Certsure LLP. Certsure LLP operates the ELECSA & NICEIC brands. © Copyright Certsure LLP (January 2015)

See next page for Schedule of Test Results

ISN4/1

Continuation schedules are available.

For installations having more than one distribution board, or more circuits than can be recorded on Pages 7 and 8, one or more additional pages of the Schedule of Circuit Details for the Installation and the Schedule of Test Results for the Installation will be required. Continuation schedules are available from NICEIC and ELECSA. The additional pages are to be given the same unique serial number as the other pages of the report. For an NICEIC condition report this is achieved by first striking out 'ICN' and then adding the remainder of the unique serial number in the space allocated (see the following page). Only the version of the continuation schedules intended for use in conjunction with the current version of the Electrical Installation Condition Report should be used. Superseded versions of continuation schedules must not be used. The page number for each additional schedule is to be inserted, together with the total number of pages comprising the report (e.g. Page 9 of 10).

Generally, irrespective of the method of compilation (by hand, computer software or using NICEIC's online certification system) all unshaded data-entry boxes must be completed by inserting the necessary text, or a '✔' to indicate that the task has been completed and that the result was satisfactory, or a numeric value of the measured parameter, or by entering 'N/A' meaning 'Not Applicable', where appropriate. Exceptionally, where a limitation on a particular inspection or test has been agreed, and has been recorded in Section D, the appropriate data-entry box(es) should be completed by inserting 'LIM', indicating that an agreed limitation has prevented the inspection or test being carried out.

The total number of pages which make up the report must be inserted in the box provided at the foot of each of the pages on the right-hand side.

PERIODIC INSPECTION AND TESTING PROCEDURES

The procedures for periodic inspection and testing differ in some respects from those for the initial verification of new installation work. This is because the subject of a periodic inspection is usually an installation which has been energised and in use for some time, and particular attention therefore needs to be given during the inspection process to assessing the condition of the installation in respect of:

- Safety
- Wear and tear
- Corrosion
- Damage and deterioration
- Excessive loading
- Age
- External influences
- Suitability (taking account of any changes in use or building layout etc).

Also, for reasons beyond the inspector's control, the inspector may be unable to gain access to parts of the existing installation. For example, it is usually impossible to inspect cables that have been installed within the fabric of the building. It may also not be permitted to switch off certain parts of an existing installation due to

Initial Sequence of Tests
For initial testing (From *BS 7671*)
(i) Before the supply is connected, or with the supply disconnected as appropriate • Continuity of protective conductors including main and supplementary equipotential bonding. • Continuity of ring final circuit conductors. • Insulation resistance. • Protection by separation of circuits, includes SELV, PELV and electrical separation. • Basic protection by a barrier or an enclosure provided during erection. • Insulation of non-conducting floors and walls. • Polarity. • Earth electrode resistance. (ii) With the electrical supply connected (re-check polarity before further testing) • Earth fault loop impedance. • Prospective fault current. • Verification of phase sequence. • Functional testing of RCDs (the test to be independent of any test facility incorporated in the device) • Functional testing of switchgear and controlgear, assemblies, drives, controls and interlocks.

Figure 1

Periodic Tests
For periodic testing
With the supply disconnected as appropriate • Continuity of circuit protective conductors. • Continuity of main and supplementary equipotential bonding conductors. • Continuity of ring final circuit conductors. • Insulation resistance. • Polarity. • Earth electrode resistance. • Earth fault loop impedance. • Verification of phase sequence. • Functional test of RCDs. • Functional test of circuit-breakers, isolators and switching devices. • Verification of voltage drop (if necessary). Note 1: The person carrying out the testing is required to decide which of the above tests are appropriate by using their experience and knowledge of the installation being inspected and tested and by consulting any available records. Note 2: The tests need not be carried out in the order shown.

Figure 2

operational restrictions imposed by the client. Such restrictions are likely to result in the inspection and testing of those parts of the installation being very limited, or the parts may have to be omitted entirely from the process.

Some degree of sampling may be involved in the inspection and testing process. Such sampling requires careful consideration being given to the selection of the parts of the installation to be inspected and tested. In the event of deficiencies being discovered in the initial sample, the size of the sample should be increased as described in *IET Guidance Note 3*. The sampling technique used, and the parts of the installation sampled, should be carefully recorded so that a different sample can be selected for the next and subsequent periodic inspections.

A further distinction between periodic inspection and initial verification relates to the range of tests required and the order in which the testing is carried out. For periodic testing the range and order may differ to that which is given in *BS 7671* for new installation work (including work involving an addition or an alteration). For comparison purposes both the Initial Sequence of Tests for initial testing (Fig1) and the Periodic Tests for periodic testing (Fig 2), are shown on the opposite page.

Where, during the course of inspection or testing, a real and immediate danger is found to be present in an installation (from an exposed live part, for example), immediate action will be necessary before continuing. It is not sufficient simply to draw attention to the danger when submitting a condition report. At the very least, the inspector must ensure that a person with responsibility for the safety of the installation is made aware of the danger that exists. An agreement should be made with this person as to the appropriate action to be taken to remove the source of danger (for example, by switching off and isolating the affected part of the installation until remedied), before continuing with the inspection or testing.

Contractors should note that the *Electricity at Work Regulations 1989* effectively require them to endeavour to make safe, before leaving site and with the agreement of the user or owner, any dangerous conditions found in an installation. For example, where blanks are missing from a distribution board, suitable temporary barriers should be installed to protect persons from contact with live parts.

COMPILING THE FORM

Parts of the Electrical Installation Condition Report form are identical or similar to parts of the Electrical Installation Certificate and the Domestic Electrical Installation Certificate, the preparation of which is described in Chapter 2 and Chapter 3, respectively. Where each of these parts is reached in this chapter, the reader is referred to Chapter 2 in order to avoid repetition.

APPROVED CONTRACTOR

This report is not valid if the serial number has been defaced or altered **IPN4/**

Original (To the person ordering the work)

ELECTRICAL INSTALLATION CONDITION REPORT

Contractor's Reference Number

CRN/

Issued in accordance with *British Standard 7671 – Requirements for Electrical Installations* by an Approved Contractor or Conforming Body enrolled with NICEIC, Warwick House, Houghton Hall Park, Houghton Regis, Dunstable LU5 5ZX

A. DETAILS OF THE CLIENT

Client:

Address:

Postcode:

B. PURPOSE OF THE REPORT

This report must be used only for reporting on the condition of an existing installation.

Purpose for which this report is required:

Date(s) on which inspection and testing were carried out:

C. DETAILS OF THE INSTALLATION

Occupier:

Address:

Postcode:

Estimated age of the electrical installation: years

Description of premises: domestic, commercial, industrial, other (Please state)

Evidence of alterations or additions

If yes, estimated age years

Date of previous inspection:

Electrical Installation Certificate No or previous Periodic Inspection or Condition Report No:

Records of installation available:

Records held by:

Agreed limitations including the reasons, if any, on the inspection and testing:

Agreed with:

Operational limitations including the reasons (see page No.)

The inspection and testing have been carried out in accordance with BS 7671, as amended. Cables concealed within trunking and conduits, or cables and conduits concealed under floors, in inaccessible roof spaces and generally within the fabric of the building or underground, have not been visually inspected unless specifically agreed between the client and inspector prior to the inspection.

E. SUMMARY OF THE CONDITION OF THE INSTALLATION

General condition of the installation (in terms of electrical safety):

Summary of the condition of the installation continued on additional pages? No Yes Specify page No(s):

Overall assessment of the installation: SATISFACTORY / UNSATISFACTORY*

(Delete as appropriate)

* **An 'Unsatisfactory' assessment indicates that dangerous (CODE C1) and/or potentially dangerous (CODE C2) conditions have been identified, or that Further investigation without delay (FI) is required**

This report should have been reviewed and confirmed by the registered Qualified Supervisor of the Approved Contractor responsible for issuing it. (See declaration on page 2)

Page 1 of

This report is based on the model forms shown in Appendix 6 of BS 7671

Please see the 'Notes for Recipients' on the reverse of this page.

IPN4/1

The client's contract reference number, if any, should be recorded in the box provided.

SECTION A: DETAILS OF THE CLIENT

Client and/Address

Insert details as described in Chapter 2 under 'Details of Client'.

SECTION B: PURPOSE OF THE REPORT

Purpose for which this report is required

It is important, for all concerned, that a clear statement of the purpose of the report is made in this part of the form. A report may be required, for example, in connection with a proposed house purchase or for an application for an entertainments licence. Alternatively, a report may be required on the condition of an installation following a fire or flood. A report may be required at the end of the period recommended in the original Electrical Installation Certificate or Domestic Electrical Installation Certificate, or a previous Periodic Inspection Report or Electrical Installation Condition Report, or for an assessment of the condition of an installation in relation to current standards.

SECTION C: DETAILS OF THE INSTALLATION

Occupier

The occupier may or may not be the client as described in Section A. An appropriate name or title should be obtained and recorded in this box.

Address and postcode

The complete postal address is necessary, sufficient to clearly identify the premises containing the installation concerned.

Estimated age of the installation

This may be determined from information relating to the original installation. Otherwise a reasonable estimate should be made by other means, such as the appearance of the installed equipment.

Description of premises

'Domestic', 'Commercial' or 'Industrial' should be ticked as appropriate or, if the type of premises does not fall within any of these categories (such as a construction site), a brief description should be entered in the box.

Evidence of alterations or additions

If there is clear evidence as to whether or not alterations or additions have been made to the installation since the previous inspection (or from new, if no subsequent information is available), this should be indicated by stating 'Yes' or 'No' in the box as appropriate.

NICEIC APPROVED CONTRACTOR

This report is not valid if the serial number has been defaced or altered **IPN4/**

Original (To the person ordering the work)

ELECTRICAL INSTALLATION CONDITION REPORT

Issued in accordance with *British Standard 7671 – Requirements for Electrical Installations* by an Approved Contractor or Conforming Body enrolled with NICEIC, Warwick House, Houghton Hall Park, Houghton Regis, Dunstable LU5 5ZX

Contractor's Reference Number

CRN/

A. DETAILS OF THE CLIENT

Client: Address: Postcode:

B. PURPOSE OF THE REPORT

This report must be used only for reporting on the condition of an existing installation.

Purpose for which this report is required:

C. DETAILS OF THE INSTALLATION

Occupier: Address: Postcode:

Estimated age of the electrical installation: years

Description of premises: domestic, commercial, industrial, other (Please state)

Evidence of alterations or additions

If yes, estimated age years

Date of previous inspection:

Electrical Installation Certificate No or previous Periodic Inspection or Condition Report No:

Records of installation available:

Records held by:

D. EXTENT OF THE INSTALLATION AND LIMITATIONS ON THE INSPECTION AND TESTING

D. EXTENT OF THE INSTALLATION AND LIMITATIONS ON THE INSPECTION AND TESTING

Extent of the electrical installation covered by this report:

Agreed limitations including the reasons, if any, on the inspection and testing:

Agreed with:

Operational limitations including the reasons (see page No.)

The inspection and testing have been carried out in accordance with BS 7671, as amended. Cables concealed within trunking and conduits, or cables and conduits concealed under floors, in inaccessible roof spaces and generally within the fabric of the building or underground, have not been visually inspected unless specifically agreed between the client and inspector prior to the inspection.

Overall assessment of the installation: SATISFACTORY / UNSATISFACTORY*

(Delete as appropriate)

* An 'Unsatisfactory' assessment indicates that dangerous (CODE C1) and/or potentially dangerous (CODE C2) conditions have been identified, or that Further investigation without delay (FI) is required

This report should have been reviewed and confirmed by the registered Qualified Supervisor of the Approved Contractor responsible for issuing it. (See declaration on page 2)

Page 1 of

This report is based on the model forms shown in Appendix 6 of BS 7671
Published by Certsure LLP. Certsure LLP operates the ELECSA & NICEIC brands. © Copyright Certsure LLP (January 2015)

IPN4/1

Please see the 'Notes for Recipients' on the reverse of this page.

If there is clear evidence of alterations or additions either visually or by reference to subsequent certificates, their actual or estimated age should be given in the space available. Otherwise write 'N/A' (meaning 'Not Applicable').

Date of previous inspection

It may be possible to ascertain the date of the previous inspection from a Periodic Inspection Report or the original Electrical Installation Certificate or equivalent. Alternatively, the 'Periodic Inspection Notice' fixed at the origin of the installation (to comply with Regulation 514.12.1) should provide an indication of the previous inspection. If the information cannot be ascertained, then 'not known' should be entered.

Electrical Installation Certificate No. or previous Periodic Inspection or Condition Report No.

Where the inspector has details of the original Electrical Installation Certificate or Domestic Electrical Installation Certificate, or a subsequent Periodic Inspection or Condition Report for the particular installation, the serial number of the latest document should be recorded in the space provided. If the information cannot be ascertained, then 'not known' should be entered.

Records of installation available

This refers to the availability of records of original certification, previous periodic inspection(s), operating and maintenance manuals, as-installed drawings etc. Indicate 'yes' or 'no', as appropriate.

Records held by

If the previous indication was 'yes', give the name of the person, company or organisation that is holding the records of the previous inspection(s). If the previous indication was 'no', write 'N/A'.

SECTION D: EXTENT OF THE INSTALLATION AND LIMITATIONS OF THE INSPECTION AND TESTING

Extent of electrical installation covered by this report

Before commencing an inspection, it is essential to agree with the client the exact extent of the installation to be inspected, taking into account the requirements of any third party involved (such as a licensing authority). It might be necessary to make a cursory inspection of the installation and available inspection records before discussing with the client the scope of the detailed inspection required, and the available options.

NICEIC APPROVED CONTRACTOR

This report is not valid if the serial number has been defaced or altered **IPN4/**

Original (To the person ordering the work)

ELECTRICAL INSTALLATION CONDITION REPORT

Contractor's Reference Number

CRN/

Issued in accordance with *British Standard 7671 – Requirements for Electrical Installations* by an Approved Contractor or Conforming Body enrolled with NICEIC, Warwick House, Houghton Hall Park, Houghton Regis, Dunstable LU5 5ZX

A. DETAILS OF THE CLIENT

Client:

Address:

Postcode:

B. PURPOSE OF THE REPORT

This report must be used only for reporting on the condition of an existing installation.

Purpose for which this report is required:

Date(s) on which inspection and testing were carried out:

C. DETAILS OF THE INSTALLATION

Occupier:

Address:

Postcode:

Estimated age of the electrical installation: years

Description of premises: domestic, commercial, industrial, other (Please state)

Evidence of alterations or additions

If yes, estimated age years

Date of previous inspection:

Electrical Installation Certificate No or previous Periodic Inspection or Condition Report No:

D. EXTENT OF THE INSTALLATION AND LIMITATIONS ON THE INSPECTION AND TESTING

Extent of the electrical installation covered by this report:

Agreed limitations including the reasons, if any, on the inspection and testing:

Agreed with:

Operational limitations including the reasons (see page No.)

The inspection and testing have been carried out in accordance with BS 7671, as amended. Cables concealed within trunking and conduits, or cables and conduits concealed under floors, in inaccessible roof spaces and generally within the fabric of the building or underground, have not been visually inspected unless specifically agreed between the client and inspector prior to the inspection.

Summary of the condition of the installation continued on additional pages? No Yes Specify page No(s):

Overall assessment of the installation: SATISFACTORY / UNSATISFACTORY*

(Delete as appropriate)

* An 'Unsatisfactory' assessment indicates that dangerous (CODE C1) and/or potentially dangerous (CODE C2) conditions have been identified, or that Further investigation without delay (FI) is required

This report should have been reviewed and confirmed by the registered Qualified Supervisor of the Approved Contractor responsible for issuing it. (See declaration on page 2)

Page 1 of

This report is based on the model forms shown in Appendix 6 of BS 7671

IPN4/1

Please see the 'Notes for Recipients' on the reverse of this page.

The agreed extent of the installation covered by the inspection should be fully recorded in this part of Section D. The extent of the installation covered by the report might be the whole of the installation in the premises described in Section C, or it might be only a part of that installation. The part could, for example, be a particular area (such as the second floor only) or particular circuits (such as all lighting circuits). The extent could also be indicated by exclusions from the whole electrical installation, such as all high bay lighting or the fire alarm system. The wording will need to be tailored exactly to detail the extent of each inspection requirement and, in some instances, a continuation sheet (appropriately numbered, and identified here and in Section H) may be necessary.

Agreed limitations including the reasons, if any, on the inspection and testing

The limitations imposed on the inspection and testing should also be explained to, and agreed with, the client before work commences. Section D of the Electrical Installation Condition Report form includes standard text which states that concealed cables in certain parts of the building's structure will not be visually inspected. However, inspection should be made within accessible roof spaces housing electrical equipment which needs to be maintained, such as pumps, motors or inverters. Consequently, all limitations should be agreed with the client before commencing the inspection and be clearly recorded (including the reasons for these limitations) on the report.

A periodic inspection must include a thorough visual inspection of all the electrical equipment that comprises the extent of the installation described in the previous section, and which is not concealed or inaccessible. However, in most cases, it will be appropriate to apply a sampling process to the detailed inspection of the internal condition of equipment, the condition of joints and terminations etc. It may also be appropriate to apply a sampling process to the inspection and testing of the installation.

If sampling is intended, this should be made clear to the client, and the initial degree of sampling for both the inspection and the testing elements should be agreed before the work commences. IET *Guidance Note 3* provides recommendations for the minimum degree of sampling for both inspection and testing. Should the actual degree of sampling carried out be different from that agreed initially (because, for example, increased sampling was necessary due to deficiencies being found during the initial sampling), the actual degree should be recorded on the report. Details of the sampling technique and identification of the equipment selected for inspection and testing on a sampling basis should also be fully identified, on an additional page if necessary.

Neither the contractor nor the customer should set unnecessary limitations on the inspection. The aim should be to produce a description that is both fair to the client and reasonable for the contractor. **It should be remembered that the greater the limitations applying to a report, the less its value from the safety aspect.**

NICEIC APPROVED CONTRACTOR

This report is not valid if the serial number has been defaced or altered **IPN4/**

ELECTRICAL INSTALLATION CONDITION REPORT

Original (To the person ordering the work)

Contractor's Reference Number

CRN/

Issued in accordance with *British Standard 7671 – Requirements for Electrical Installations* by an Approved Contractor or Conforming Body enrolled with NICEIC, Warwick House, Houghton Hall Park, Houghton Regis, Dunstable LU5 5ZX

A. DETAILS OF THE CLIENT

Client:

Address:

Postcode:

B. PURPOSE OF THE REPORT

This report must be used only for reporting on the condition of an existing installation.

Purpose for which this report is required:

Date(s) on which inspection and testing were carried out:

C. DETAILS OF THE INSTALLATION

Occupier:

Address:

Postcode:

Estimated age of the electrical installation: years

Description of premises: domestic, commercial, industrial, other (Please state)

Evidence of alterations or additions

If yes, estimated age years

Date of previous inspection:

Electrical Installation Certificate No or previous Periodic Inspection or Condition Report No:

Records of installation available:

Records held by:

D. EXTENT OF THE INSTALLATION AND LIMITATIONS ON THE INSPECTION AND TESTING

Extent of the electrical installation covered by this report:

Agreed limitations including the reasons, if any, on the inspection and testing:

Agreed with:

Operational limitations including the reasons (see page No.)

E. SUMMARY OF THE CONDITION OF THE INSTALLATION

General condition of the installation (in terms of electrical safety):

Summary of the condition of the installation continued on additional pages? No Yes Specify page No(s):

Overall assessment of the installation: SATISFACTORY / UNSATISFACTORY*

(Delete as appropriate)

* **An 'Unsatisfactory' assessment indicates that dangerous (CODE C1) and/or potentially dangerous (CODE C2) conditions have been identified, or that Further investigation without delay (FI) is required**

This report should have been reviewed and confirmed by the registered Qualified Supervisor of the Approved Contractor responsible for issuing it. (See declaration on page 2)

Page 1 of

This report is based on the model forms shown in Appendix 6 of BS 7671

Please see the 'Notes for Recipients' on the reverse of this page.

IPN4/1

Operational limitations including the reasons

Details of any circumstances that have prevented the inspection and testing from being performed as previously agreed with the person ordering the work, such as inability to gain access to a part of an installation for reasons beyond the control of the inspector, should be provided. Where necessary, details of the particular circumstances causing the operational limitation should be provided on a separate page attached to the report.

Liabilities arising from inadequate description:

It should be appreciated that failure to clearly describe and record the extent of the installation inspected and the agreed limitations (including giving reasons for these limitations) of the inspection and testing could involve the contractor in unforeseen liabilities at a later date. For example, if a contractor failed to clearly record that all high bay lighting had been excluded from a periodic inspection, the contractor might be held responsible if an electrical fault in that part of the installation later resulted in danger or damage.

If there is insufficient space in Section D to provide full details of the extent of the work to which the condition report refers, the details should be provided on an additional page attached to the report, and reference to the additional page should be included in the relevant data entry fields in Section D.

SECTION E: SUMMARY OF THE CONDITION OF THE INSTALLATION

The summary should adequately describe the overall condition of the installation, taking into account the specific observations made. It is essential to provide a clear summary of the condition of the installation having considered, for example:

- The adequacy of the earthing and bonding
- The suitability of the switchgear and control gear
- The type(s) of wiring system, and its condition
- The serviceability of equipment, including accessories
- The presence of adequate identification and notices
- The extent of any wear and tear, damage or other deterioration
- Changes in use of the building which have led to, or might lead to, deficiencies in the installation.

Minimal descriptions such as 'poor', and superficial statements such as 'Recommend a rewire' are considered unacceptable as they do not indicate the true condition of the installation. It will, however, often be necessary or appropriate to explain the implications of an Electrical Installation Condition Report in a covering letter, for the benefit of recipients who require additional advice and guidance about their installation. For example, where an installation has deteriorated or been damaged to such an extent that its safe serviceable life can reasonably be considered to be at an end, a

F. OBSERVATIONS AND RECOMMENDATIONS FOR ACTIONS TO BE TAKEN

Referring to the attached schedules of inspection and test results, and subject to the limitations at D:

There are **no** items adversely affecting electrical safety ☐ **or** The following observations and recommendations for action are made ☐

Item No	Observations	Code†
1		

Additional pages? No ☐ Yes ☐ Specify page No(s):

† *One of the following codes, as appropriate, has been allocated to each of the observations made above to indicate to the person(s) responsible for the installation the degree of urgency for remedial action:*

Code C1 ***'Danger present'.*** *Risk of injury. Immediate remedial action required.*
Code C2 ***'Potentially dangerous'.*** *Urgent remedial action required.*
Code C3 ***'Improvement recommended'.***
Code FI ***'Further investigation required without delay'.***

Please see the reverse of this page for guidance regarding the Classification codes.

Immediate remedial action required for items:

Urgent remedial action required for items:

Further investigation required without delay for items:

Improvement recommended for items:

G. DECLARATION

I/We, being the person(s) responsible for the inspection and testing of the electrical installation (as indicated by my/our signatures below), particulars of which are described on page 1 (see C), having exercised reasonable skill and care when carrying out the inspection and testing, hereby declare that the information in this report, including the observations (see F) and the attached schedules (see H), provides an accurate assessment of the condition of the electrical installation taking into account the stated extent of the installation and the limitations of the inspection and testing (see D).

I/We further declare that in my/our judgement, the overall assessment of the installation in terms of its suitability for continued use is

SATISFACTORY / UNSATISFACTORY* **(see F) at the time the inspection was carried out, and that it should be further inspected as recommended (see I).**

Delete as appropriate

* **An 'Unsatisfactory' assessment indicates that dangerous (CODE C1) and/or potentially dangerous (CODE C2) conditions have been identified, or that Further investigation without delay (FI) is required.**

INSPECTION, TESTING AND ASSESSMENT BY:

Signature:

Name: (CAPITALS)

Position:

Date:

REPORT REVIEWED AND CONFIRMED BY:

Signature:

Name: (CAPITALS)

(Registered Qualified Supervisor for the Approved Contractor at J)

Date:

This report is based on the model forms shown in Appendix 6 of BS 7671
Published by Certsure LLP. Certsure LLP operates the ELECSA & NICEIC brands.

IPN4/3

Page 2 of ☐

Please see the 'Guidance for Recipients on the Classification codes' on the reverse of this page.

recommendation for renewal should be made in a covering letter, giving adequate supporting reasons. Reference to the covering letter should be made in the report.

At the bottom of Section E of the report, a box is provided for the overall assessment of the condition of the installation to be given. After due consideration, the overall condition should be given as either 'satisfactory' or 'unsatisfactory'. **It would not be reasonable to indicate a 'satisfactory' assessment if any observation in the report had been given a 'Code C1' or 'Code C2' recommendation, or if an observation requires further investigation without delay (FI), to determine whether danger or potential danger exists.**

Where the space provided for the description of the general condition of the installation is inadequate for the purpose and it is necessary to continue the description on an additional page(s), the page number(s) of the additional page(s) should be recorded in this space, as indicated on the form.

SECTION F: OBSERVATIONS AND RECOMMENDATIONS FOR ACTIONS TO BE TAKEN

Any items in the Inspection Schedule or Schedule of Test Results that have been identified as being dangerous (code C1) or potentially dangerous (code C2), that would result in a significant enhancement of safety if improved (code C3), or that require further investigation without delay to determine whether danger or potential danger exists (code FI), should be brought forward to this section of the condition report in the form of observations on the safety of the installation.

The observations and classifications should take due account of the results of the inspection and testing, and be based on the requirements of the issue of *BS 7671* current at the time of the inspection (**not** the requirements of an earlier standard current at the time the installation was originally constructed).

This section includes two small unshaded data-entry boxes at the top, one of which must be completed with a '✔' to indicate that 'there are no items adversely affecting electrical safety' or, alternatively, 'the following observations and recommendations for action are made'. The data-entry box which does not attract a positive entry should be completed by recording 'N/A', meaning 'Not Applicable'.

In cases where observations and classifications are appropriate, these are to be itemised and given a numerical reference under the left-hand column headed 'Item No'. The observation(s) must be provided in the wide column second from the left in an accurate, concise and easily-understandable manner. Each observation must be attributed with a Classification code C1,C2, C3 or FI, which is to be recorded in the appropriate column.

GUIDANCE FOR RECIPIENTS ON THE CLASSIFICATION CODES

Only one Classification code should have been given for each recorded observation.

Classification code C1 ***(Danger present)***

Where an observation has been given a Classification code C1, the safety of those using the installation is at risk and immediate remedial action is required.

The person responsible for the maintenance of the installation is advised to take action without delay to remedy the observed deficiency in the installation, or to take other appropriate action (such as switching off and isolating the affected part(s) of the installation) to remove the danger. The NICEIC Approved Contractor issuing this report will be able to provide further advice.

NICEIC makes available 'Electrical Danger Notification' forms to enable inspectors to record, and then to communicate to the person ordering the report, any dangerous condition discovered.

Classification code C2 ***(Potentially dangerous)***

Classification code C2 indicates that, whilst those using the installation may not be at immediate risk, **urgent remedial action is required to remove potential danger**. The NICEIC Approved Contractor issuing this report will be able to provide further advice.

Classification code C3 ***(Improvement recommended)***

Where an observation has been given a Classification code C3, the inspection and/or testing has revealed a non-compliance with the current safety standard which, whilst not presenting immediate or potential danger, would result in a significant safety improvement if remedied. Careful consideration should be given to the safety benefits of improving these aspects of the installation. The NICEIC Approved Contractor issuing this report will be able to provide further advice.

It is important to note that the recommendation given at Section I of this report (Next Inspection) for the maximum interval until the next inspection is conditional upon all items which have been given a Classification code C1 and code C2 being remedied immediately and as a matter of urgency, respectively.

It would not be reasonable for the inspector to indicate that the installation is in a satisfactory condition if any observation in this report has been given a code C1 or code C2 classification.

Code FI (*Further investigation required without delay*)

It should usually be possible for the inspector to attribute a Classification code to each observation without indicating a need for further investigation.

However, where **'FI'** has been entered against an observation the inspector considers that further investigation of that observation is likely to reveal danger or potential danger that, due to the agreed extent or limitations of the inspection and/or testing, could not be fully identified at the time.

It would not be appropriate for the inspector to indicate that the installation is in a satisfactory condition if there is reasonable doubt as to whether danger or potential danger exists. Consequently, where the inspector has indicated 'Further investigation required without delay' (FI) the overall assessment of the installation (Section E) should be marked as 'Unsatisfactory'.

If the inspector has indicated that an observation requires further investigation without delay, the person ordering this report is advised to arrange for the NICEIC Approved Contractor issuing the report (or another skilled person or persons competent in such work) to undertake further examination of that aspect of the installation as a matter of urgency, to determine whether or not danger or potential danger exists.

Further information

Further information on the application of Classification codes, primarily aimed at inspectors but of possible interest to persons ordering condition reports, can be found in Electrical Safety First's Best Practice Guide entitled *Electrical installation condition reporting: Classification Codes for domestic and similar electrical installations.* The guide can be viewed or downloaded free of charge from **www.electricalsafetyfirst.org.uk**

IPN4/3&4B

Guidance for recipients provided on the reverse of Periodic Inspection Reports.

It should usually be possible for the inspector to attribute an outcome to each observation without requiring further investigation. Further investigation required without delay (FI) should not be called for unless the inspector has reason to believe that further investigation of an observation is likely to reveal danger or potential danger that, due to the agreed extent or limitations of the inspection and/or testing, could not be fully identified at the time. **If there is reasonable doubt as to whether danger or potential danger exists, the condition of the installation must be reported to be 'unsatisfactory'.** The person ordering the report should be advised that any observations for which further investigation is considered necessary should be investigated without delay after the inspection, by a skilled person or persons, competent in such work.

Where during inspection and testing a real and immediate danger is observed that puts the safety of those using the installation at risk, Classification code C1 (danger present) must be given.

Where no items adversely affecting safety have been observed and recorded, each of the four data-entry boxes at the bottom right-hand side of the section should be completed by entering the word 'None'.

Where one or more items that do adversely affect safety have been observed and recorded, the four boxes should be completed as follows:

- Observations that have been attributed a Classification code C1 (danger present) should be highlighted by inserting the relevant item numbers in the first box adjacent to the words 'Immediate remedial work required for items:' Where no observation has been attributed with a Classification code C1, the entry should read 'None'
- Observations that have been attributed a Classification code C2 (potentially dangerous) should be highlighted by inserting the relevant item numbers in the second box adjacent to the words 'Urgent remedial action required for items:' Where no observation has been attributed with a Classification code C2, the entry should read 'None'
- Observations for which further investigation code FI is required should be highlighted by inserting the relevant item numbers in the third box adjacent to the words 'Further investigation required without delay for items:' Where no observation requires further investigation, the entry should read 'None'
- Observations that have been attributed a Classification code C3 (improvement recommended) should be highlighted by inserting the relevant item numbers in the fourth box adjacent to the words 'Improvement recommended for items:' Where no observation has been attributed with a Classification code C3, the entry should read 'None'.

Where a Classification code C1 is considered appropriate for an observation, the person ordering the report is to be advised immediately (that is, before the report is issued), and also in writing, that immediate remedial action is required (or has been taken) by skilled person(s) competent in electrical installation work to remove the danger. This action is necessary to satisfy the duties imposed on the inspector and other duty holders by the Health and Safety at Work etc Act 1974 and the Electricity at Work Regulations 1989.

If the space in Section F is insufficient to record all the observations adversely affecting safety, additional numbered pages should be provided as necessary. For NICEIC Electrical Installation Condition Reports, additional pages should be identified by the unique Electrical Installation Condition Report serial number. Continuation sheets for this purpose are available from NICEIC.

Observations:

Each recorded observation should describe a specific defect or omission in the electrical installation. The observation should detail what the situation is, and not what is considered necessary to put it right. For example, 'excessive external damage to the enclosure of Distribution Board F2/7' would be appropriate, whereas 'Distribution Board F2/7 to be replaced' would not. **Remember that this is a factual report on the condition of an installation, not a proposal for remedial work.**

Only observations that can be supported by one or more regulations in the current issue of *BS 7671* should be recorded. The particular regulation number(s) need not be entered on the report (unless specifically required by the client), but should serve to remind the inspector that it is only compliance with *BS 7671* that is to be considered. Observations based solely on personal preference or 'custom and practice' should not be included.

Each observation should be written in a manner that is likely to be understood by the client. Comments should be clear and unambiguous, but the use of technical terms should be avoided unless it is known that the recipient is an electrical engineer or electrician, for example.

The lists of Classification codes below are not exhaustive, and there are other observations that could be considered by the inspector to require immediate attention, urgent attention or improvement.

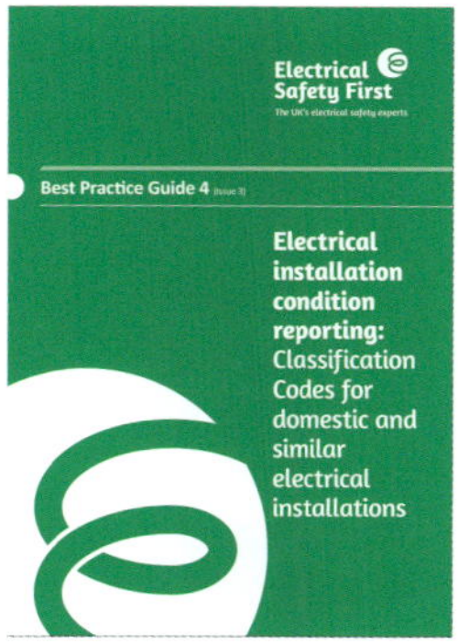

Further guidance on the application of the Classification codes can be found in the Electrical Safety First's Best Practice Guide – *Electrical Installation condition reporting: Classification codes for domestic and similar electrical installations* - produced in collaboration with other leading industry bodies including NICEIC and ELECSA. The guide can be downloaded from **www.electricalsafetyfirst.org.uk**

Although the guidance in the Best Practice Guide is for 'domestic and similar electrical installations', the same principles can be applied to other types of electrical installation, such as in some commercial and industrial premises.

Code C1 (Danger present)
Observations that would almost certainly warrant a Code C1 classification include:

- Exposed live parts that are accessible to touch, such as where:
  - a fuse carrier or circuit-breaker is missing from a distribution board and a blanking piece is not fitted in its place
  - terminations or connections have no (or damaged) barriers or enclosures
  - live conductors have no (or damaged) insulation
  - an accessory is badly damaged.
- Conductive parts that have become live as the result of a fault
- Incorrect polarity

Code C2 (Potentially dangerous)
Observations that would usually warrant a Code C2 classification include:

- Absence of an effective means of earthing for the installation
- A public utility water pipe being used as the means of earthing for the installation
- A gas or oil pipe being used as the means of earthing for the installation
- Cross-sectional area of the earthing conductor does not satisfy adiabatic requirements (that is, does not comply with Regulation 543.1.1)
- Absence of a circuit protective conductor for a lighting circuit supplying one or more items of Class I equipment, or connected to switches having metallic face plates
- Absence of a notice warning that lighting circuits have no circuit protective conductor
- Absence of a circuit protective conductor for a circuit, other than a lighting circuit, supplying one or more items of Class I equipment
- Absence of earthing at a socket-outlet
- Absence of main protective bonding
- Inadequate cross-sectional area of a main protective bonding conductor where the conductor is less than 6 mm^2 or where there is evidence of thermal damage
- Absence of supplementary bonding where required, such as in a location containing a bath or shower, where **any** of the following three conditions are not satisfied:
  - All final circuits of the location comply with the requirements of Regulation 411.3.2 for automatic disconnection, **and**
  - All final circuits of the location have additional protection by means of a 30 mA RCD, **and**
  - All extraneous-conductive-parts of the location are effectively connected to the protective equipotential bonding (main earthing terminal)

Code C3 (Improvement recommended)
Observations that would usually warrant a Code C3 classification include:

- Absence of RCD protection for a socket-outlet that is unlikely to supply portable or mobile equipment for use outdoors, does not serve a location containing a bath or shower, and the use of which is otherwise not considered by the inspector to result in potential danger. (Note: Code C2 would apply if the circuit supplied a socket-outlet in a location containing a bath or shower in accordance with Regulation 701.512.3)
- Absence of RCD protection for cables installed at a depth of less than 50 mm from a surface of a wall or partition where the cables do not incorporate an earthed metallic covering, are not enclosed in earthed metalwork, or are not mechanically protected against penetration by nails and the like
- Reliance on a voltage-operated earth-leakage circuit-breaker for fault protection (protection against indirect contact), subject to the device being proved to operate correctly. (If the circuit-breaker relies on a water pipe not permitted by Regulation 542.2.6 as the means of earthing, this would attract a Code C2 classification.)
- Absence of RCD or voltage-operated earth-leakage circuit-breaker quarterly test notice
- Absence of circuit protective conductors in circuits having only Class II (or all-insulated) luminaires and switches
- Absence of 'Safety Electrical Connection — Do Not Remove' notice
- Sheath of an insulated and sheathed non-armoured cable not taken inside the enclosure of an accessory, such as at a socket-outlet or lighting switch. (Note: Code C2 would apply if unsheathed cores are accessible to touch and/or likely to come into contact with metalwork)
- Bare protective conductor of an insulated and sheathed cable not sleeved with insulation, colour coded to indicate its function
- Electrical equipment having an inadequate degree of ingress protection (IP rating) for the external influences likely to occur in the location, if this does not result in potential danger
- Socket-outlet mounted in such a position as to result in potential damage to socket, plug and/or flex
- Absence of a notice indicating that the installation has wiring colours to two versions of *BS 7671* (if appropriate).

Classification codes:

Each observation must be given an appropriate Classification code, selected from the standard codes C1, C2, C3 and FI, as defined in the note near the foot of Section F. Each code has a particular meaning, as follows:

Classification codes:	
Code C1	**Danger present**
Code C2	**Potentially dangerous**
Code C3	**Improvement recommended**
Code FI	**Further investigation required without delay**

One, and only one, of the standard Classification codes should be attributed to each observation. If more than one classification could be applied to an observation, only the most serious classification should be used (Code C1 being the most serious). In general terms, the Classification codes should be used as follows:

- **Code C1 (Danger present)** – to be used to indicate that real and immediate danger exists, requiring immediate remedial action. The persons using the installation are at immediate risk. The person ordering the report should be advised to take action without delay to remedy the observed deficiency in the installation, or to take other appropriate action (such as switching off and isolating the affected parts of the installation) to remove the danger. The inspector should not wait for the full report to be issued before giving this advice. NICEIC 'Electrical Danger Notification' forms are available to NICEIC registrants for this purpose. Examples of items that would usually warrant a Code C1 classification are given in the Table on page 121.
- **Code C2 (Potentially dangerous)** – to be used to indicate that, whilst an observed deficiency is not considered to be dangerous at the time of the periodic inspection, it would become a real and immediate danger if a fault or other foreseeable event was to occur in the installation or connected equipment, and that urgent remedial action is required. The person ordering the report should be advised that, whilst the safety of those using the installation may not be at immediate risk, remedial action should be taken as a matter of urgency, by skilled person(s) competent in electrical installation work, to remove the source of potential danger. Examples of items that NICEIC considers would usually warrant a Code C2 classification are given in the Table on page 122.
- **Code C3 (Improvement recommended)** – to be used to indicate that, whilst an observed deficiency is not considered to be a source of immediate or potential danger, improvement would contribute to a significant enhancement of the safety of the electrical installation. Examples of items that would usually warrant a Code C3 classification are given in the Table on page 123.

GUIDANCE FOR RECIPIENTS ON THE CLASSIFICATION CODES

Only one Classification code should have been given for each recorded observation.

Classification code C1 ***(Danger present)***

Where an observation has been given a Classification code C1, the safety of those using the installation is at risk and immediate remedial action is required.

The person responsible for the maintenance of the installation is advised to take action without delay to remedy the observed deficiency in the installation, or to take other appropriate action (such as switching off and isolating the affected part(s) of the installation) to remove the danger. The NICEIC Approved Contractor issuing this report will be able to provide further advice.

NICEIC makes available 'Electrical Danger Notification' forms to enable inspectors to record, and then to communicate to the person ordering the report, any dangerous condition discovered.

Classification code C2 ***(Potentially dangerous)***

Classification code C2 indicates that, whilst those using the installation may not be at immediate risk, **urgent remedial action is required to remove potential danger**. The NICEIC Approved Contractor issuing this report will be able to provide further advice.

Classification code C3 ***(Improvement recommended)***

Where an observation has been given a Classification code C3, the inspection and/or testing has revealed a non-compliance with the current safety standard which, whilst not presenting immediate or potential danger, would result in a significant safety improvement if remedied. Careful consideration should be given to the safety benefits of improving these aspects of the installation. The NICEIC Approved Contractor issuing this report will be able to provide further advice.

It is important to note that the recommendation given at Section I of this report (Next Inspection) for the maximum interval until the next inspection is conditional upon all items which have been given a Classification code C1 and code C2 being remedied immediately and as a matter of urgency, respectively.

It would not be reasonable for the inspector to indicate that the installation is in a satisfactory condition if any observation in this report has been given a code C1 or code C2 classification.

Code FI (*Further investigation required without delay*)

It should usually be possible for the inspector to attribute a Classification code to each observation without indicating a need for further investigation.

However, where '**FI**' has been entered against an observation the inspector considers that further investigation of that observation is likely to reveal danger or potential danger that, due to the agreed extent or limitations of the inspection and/or testing, could not be fully identified at the time.

It would not be appropriate for the inspector to indicate that the installation is in a satisfactory condition if there is reasonable doubt as to whether danger or potential danger exists. Consequently, where the inspector has indicated 'Further investigation required without delay' (FI) the overall assessment of the installation (Section E) should be marked as 'Unsatisfactory'.

If the inspector has indicated that an observation requires further investigation without delay, the person ordering this report is advised to arrange for the NICEIC Approved Contractor issuing the report (or another skilled person or persons competent in such work) to undertake further examination of that aspect of the installation as a matter of urgency, to determine whether or not danger or potential danger exists.

Further information

Further information on the application of Classification codes, primarily aimed at inspectors but of possible interest to persons ordering condition reports, can be found in Electrical Safety First's Best Practice Guide entitled *Electrical installation condition reporting: Classification Codes for domestic and similar electrical installations.* The guide can be viewed or downloaded free of charge from **www.electricalsafetyfirst.org.uk**

IPN4/3&4B

Guidance for recipients provided on the reverse of Periodic Inspection Reports.

NICEIC APPROVED CONTRACTOR

This report is not valid if the serial number has been defaced or altered **IPN4/**

Original (To the person ordering the work)

ELECTRICAL INSTALLATION CONDITION REPORT

F. OBSERVATIONS AND RECOMMENDATIONS FOR ACTIONS TO BE TAKEN

Referring to the attached schedules of inspection and test results, and subject to the limitations at D:

There are **no** items adversely affecting electrical safety ☐ **or** The following observations and recommendations for action are made ☐

Item No	Observations	Code†
1		

G. DECLARATION

I/We, being the person(s) responsible for the inspection and testing of the electrical installation (as indicated by my/our signatures below), particulars of which are described on page 1 (see C), having exercised reasonable skill and care when carrying out the inspection and testing, hereby declare that the information in this report, including the observations (see F) and the attached schedules (see H), provides an accurate assessment of the condition of the electrical installation taking into account the stated extent of the installation and the limitations of the inspection and testing (see D).

I/We further declare that in my/our judgement, the overall assessment of the installation in terms of its suitability for continued use is

SATISFACTORY / UNSATISFACTORY* **(see F) at the time the inspection was carried out, and that it should be further inspected as recommended (see I).**

Delete as appropriate

* **An 'Unsatisfactory' assessment indicates that dangerous (CODE C1) and/or potentially dangerous (CODE C2) conditions have been identified, or that Further investigation without delay (FI) is required.**

INSPECTION, TESTING AND ASSESSMENT BY:		REPORT REVIEWED AND CONFIRMED BY:	
Signature:		Signature:	
Name: (CAPITALS)		Name: (CAPITALS)	
Position:			*(Registered Qualified Supervisor for the Approved Contractor at J)*
Date:		Date:	

Page 2 of ☐

This report is based on the model forms shown in Appendix 6 of BS 7671
Published by Certsure LLP. Certsure LLP operates the ELECSA & NICEIC brands.

IPN4/3

Please see the 'Guidance for Recipients on the Classification codes' on the reverse of this page.

installation taking into account the stated extent of the installation and the limitations of the inspection and testing (see D).

I/We further declare that in my/our judgement, the overall assessment of the installation in terms of its suitability for continued use is

SATISFACTORY / UNSATISFACTORY* (see F) at the time the inspection was carried out, and that it should be further inspected as recommended (see I).

Delete as appropriate

* An 'Unsatisfactory' assessment indicates that dangerous (CODE C1) and/or potentially dangerous (CODE C2) conditions have been identified, or that Further investigation without delay (FI) is required.

INSPECTION, TESTING AND ASSESSMENT BY: Signature: Name: (CAPITALS) Position: Date:

REPORT REVIEWED AND CONFIRMED BY: Signature: Name: (CAPITALS) (Registered Qualified Supervisor for the Approved Contractor at J) Date:

Page 2 of

This report is based on the model forms shown in Appendix 6 of BS 7671
Published by Certsure LLP. Certsure LLP operates the ELECSA & NICEIC brands.
© Copyright Certsure LLP (January 2015)
IPN4/3

Please see the 'Guidance for Recipients on the Classification codes' on the reverse of this page.

- **Code FI (Further investigation required without delay)** – to be used to indicate that an observation requires further investigation to determine whether danger or potential danger exists. Further investigation should not be called for unless the inspector has reason to believe that further investigation of an observation is likely to reveal danger or potential danger that, due to the agreed extent or limitations of the inspection and/or testing, could not be fully identified at the time. The person ordering the report should be advised that any observations for which further investigation is considered necessary should be investigated without delay after the inspection.

It is entirely a matter for the skilled person conducting the inspection to decide on the Classification code to be attributed to a given observation. The skilled person's judgement should not be unduly influenced by the person ordering the work. The persons signing the report are fully responsible for its content and accuracy.

Further explanation of each Classification code is given on the reverse of NICEIC Electrical Installation Condition Report forms, and NICEIC and ELECSA Domestic Electrical Installation Condition Report forms (and the equivalent green forms) for the benefit of recipients, as previously indicated.

SECTION G: DECLARATION

Section G is a declaration that the report gives an accurate assessment of the condition of the installation within the extent and limitations specified at Section D. The declaration should be signed by the skilled person competent to undertake the inspection, and then by a skilled person, competent to review the report and verify if it has been correctly compiled. In the case of an NICEIC Electrical Installation Condition Report, the reviewer should be the Approved Contractor's registered Qualified Supervisor.

Where the Qualified Supervisor has personally conducted the inspection and testing, and has compiled the report, that person should sign in both places.

For the uncontrolled (green) version of the Electrical Installation Condition Report, the completed report should preferably be reviewed by another skilled person or persons, competent to confirm that the declared overall condition of the electrical installation is consistent with the inspection and testing results, and with the observations and recommendations for action (if any) made in the report.

The data-entry box for the overall condition of the installation must be completed by deleting either 'SATISFACTORY' or 'UNSATISFACTORY' as appropriate. This declaration of the condition of the installation should reiterate the detailed entry given in Section E: *Summary of the Inspection*, which itself should summarise the observations and recommendations made in Section F.

NICEIC APPROVED CONTRACTOR

This report is not valid if the serial number has been defaced or altered **IPN4/**

ELECTRICAL INSTALLATION CONDITION REPORT

H. SCHEDULES AND ADDITIONAL PAGES

Inspection Schedule: Page(s) No 4, 5, 6 Additional pages, including additional source(s) data sheets: Page No(s)

H. SCHEDULES AND ADDITIONAL PAGES

Inspection Schedule: Page(s) No 4, 5, 6

Additional pages, including additional source(s) data sheets: Page No(s)

Schedule of Circuit Details for the Installation: Page No(s) 7

Schedule of Test Results for the Installation: Page No(s) 8

The pages identified are an essential part of this report. The report is valid only if accompanied by all the schedules and additional pages identified above.

I. NEXT INSPECTION

I/We recommend that this installation is further inspected and tested after an interval of not more than *(Enter interval in terms of years, months or weeks, as appropriate)*

provided that any items at F which have been attributed a Classification code C1 (danger present) are remedied immediately and that any items which have been attributed a code C2 (potentially dangerous) or FI (further investigation required without delay) are remedied or investigated respectively as a matter of urgency. Items which have been attributed a Classification code C3 should be improved as soon as practicable (see F).

Postcode:

NICEIC APPROVED CONTRACTOR Enrolment number: (Essential information)

Branch number: (if applicable)

K. SUPPLY CHARACTERISTICS AND EARTHING ARRANGEMENTS

System type(s)	Number and type of live conductors			Nature of supply parameters		Characteristics of primary supply overcurrent protective device(s)	
TN-S	a.c.		d.c.	Nominal voltage(s): $U^{(1)}$ V	$U_0^{(1)}$ V	BS(EN)	
TN-C-S	1-phase (2-wire)	1-phase (3-wire)	2-pole	Nominal frequency, $f^{(1)}$ Hz	Notes: (1) by enquiry	Type	
TN-C	2-phase (3-wire)		3-pole	Prospective fault current, $I_{pf}^{(2)(3)}$ kA	(2) by enquiry or by measurement	Rated current	A
TT	3-phase (3-wire)	3-phase (4-wire)	other	External earth fault loop impedance, $Z_e^{(3)(4)}$ Ω	(3) where more than one supply, record the higher or highest values	Short-circuit capacity	kA
IT	Other	Please state		Number of sources	(4) by measurement	Confirmation of supply polarity	(✓)

L. PARTICULARS OF INSTALLATION AT THE ORIGIN

Means of earthing		Details of installation earth electrode (where applicable)			
Distributor's facility:		Type: (eg rod(s), tape(s) etc)		Location:	
Installation earth electrode:		Electrode resistance, R_A:	(Ω)	Method of measurement:	

Main Switch/Switch-Fuse/Circuit-Breaker/ RCD

Type: BS(EN)		Voltage rating	V
No of poles		Rated current, I_n	A
Primary supply conductors: material		RCD operating current, $I_{\Delta n}$*	mA
Primary supply conductors: csa	mm²	Rated time delay*	ms
		RCD operating time (at $I_{\Delta n}$)*	ms

(applicable only where an RCD is suitable and is used as a main circuit-breaker)

Earthing and protective bonding conductors

Earthing conductor		Main protective bonding conductors		Bonding of extraneous-conductive-parts (✓)	
Conductor material		Conductor material		Water installation pipes	Lightning protection
Conductor csa	mm²	Conductor csa	mm²	Oil installation pipes	Structural steel
Connection/ continuity verified	(✓)	Connection/ continuity verified	(✓)	Gas installation pipes	
				Other	

Page 3 of

This report is based on the model forms shown in Appendix 6 of BS 7671

Please see the 'Notes for Recipients' on the reverse of this page.

IPN4/5

the person ordering the work)

The date (or dates if the inspection and testing were undertaken over a number of days) should be entered in the left-hand box at the bottom of this section. This is intended to be the date(s) when the inspection and testing was actually carried out, rather than when the report was issued.

SECTION H: SCHEDULES AND ADDITIONAL PAGES

This section is provided for the purpose of recording additional data sheets, including all the schedules relating to the report. Additional pages may be required where there is a need to record supplementary information about, for example, particular aspects of the installation or its source(s), which may include data sheets relating to the characteristics of additional sources where appropriate. The page number(s) of such additional sheets should be recorded in the top right-hand data-entry box ('Pages No(s)') provided for this purpose.

Where additional schedules are used for the circuit details and associated test results, the page numbers should be recorded in the two data-entry boxes (after the printed page numbers which represent the minimum number of pages for the two schedules) provided to record the existence of these additional schedules which form part of the report. For this purpose NICEIC and ELECSA supply continuation sheets.

SECTION I: NEXT INSPECTION

The inspector should, in accordance with Regulation 622.1 and as described in Chapter 2 of this book, make an appropriate recommendation for the time interval to the next periodic inspection. The Table given earlier in this Chapter gives some guidance in terms of maximum intervals. The guidance may be used directly if it is appropriate to the age, condition and usage of the installation. However, the inspector may decide to recommend a shorter interval than the maximum recommended in the table, due to the particular circumstances relating to the installation. This is acceptable if the inspector can properly justify such a recommendation. For example, a shorter period may be considered appropriate if an installation is old or perhaps subject to more rapid deterioration than usual.

The recommendation for the interval to the next inspection is conditional upon all observations that have been attributed a Classification code C1 (danger present) being remedied immediately and all observations that have been attributed a code C2 (potentially dangerous) or FI (further investigation required without delay) being remedied or investigated respectively as a matter of urgency. It is also stated that observations that have been attributed a Classification code C3 should be improved as soon as practicable.

APPROVED CONTRACTOR

This report is not valid if the serial number has been defaced or altered **IPN4/**

(To the person ordering the work)

ELECTRICAL INSTALLATION CONDITION REPORT

H. SCHEDULES AND ADDITIONAL PAGES

Inspection Schedule: Page(s) No 4, 5, 6		Additional pages, including additional source(s) data sheets:	Page No(s)
Schedule of Circuit Details for the Installation: Page No(s)	7	Schedule of Test Results for the Installation: Page No(s)	8

J. DETAILS OF NICEIC APPROVED CONTRACTOR

Trading title:

Address:

Postcode:

Telephone number:

Email address:

APPROVED CONTRACTOR Enrolment number: (Essential information)

Branch number: (if applicable)

K. SUPPLY CHARACTERISTICS AND EARTHING ARRANGEMENTS

System type(s)	Number and type of live conductors						Nature of supply parameters					Characteristics of primary supply overcurrent protective device(s)		
TN-S		a.c.		d.c.			Nominal voltage(s): $U^{(1)}$		V	$U_o^{(1)}$	V	BS(EN)		
TN-C-S	1-phase (2-wire)		1-phase (3-wire)		2-pole		Nominal frequency, $f^{(1)}$		Hz	*Notes:* *(1) by enquiry*		Type		
TN-C	2-phase (3-wire)				3-pole		Prospective fault current, $I_{pf}^{(2)(3)}$		kA	*(2) by enquiry or by measurement*		Rated current		A
TT	3-phase (3-wire)		3-phase (4-wire)		other		External earth fault loop impedance, $Z_e^{(3)(4)}$		Ω	*(3) where more than one supply, record the higher or highest values*		Short-circuit capacity		kA
IT	Other	Please state					Number of sources			*(4) by measurement*		Confirmation of supply polarity		(✓)

L. PARTICULARS OF INSTALLATION AT THE ORIGIN

Means of earthing		Details of installation earth electrode (where applicable)			
Distributor's facility:		Type: (eg rod(s), tape(s) etc)		Location:	
Installation earth electrode:		Electrode resistance, R_A:	(Ω)	Method of measurement:	

Main Switch/Switch-Fuse/Circuit-Breaker/ RCD

Type: BS(EN)		Voltage rating		V
No of poles		Rated current, I_n		A
Primary supply conductors: material		RCD operating current, $I_{\Delta n}$*		mA
Primary supply conductors: csa	mm²	Rated time delay*		ms
		RCD operating time (at $I_{\Delta n}$)*		ms

* *(applicable only where an RCD is suitable and is used as a main circuit-breaker)*

Earthing and protective bonding conductors

Earthing conductor		Main protective bonding conductors		Bonding of extraneous-conductive-parts (✓)	
Conductor material		Conductor material		Water installation pipes	Lightning protection
Conductor csa	mm²	Conductor csa	mm²	Oil installation pipes	Structural steel
Connection/ continuity verified	(✓)	Connection/ continuity verified	(✓)	Gas installation pipes	
				Other	

* *(applicable only where an RCD is suitable and is used as a main circuit-breaker)*

Page 3 of

This report is based on the model forms shown in Appendix 6 of BS 7671

Published by Certsure LLP. Certsure LLP operates the ELECSA & NICEIC brands. © Copyright Certsure LLP (January 2015)

Please see the 'Notes for Recipients' on the reverse of this page.

IPN4/5

SECTION J: DETAILS OF NICEIC APPROVED CONTRACTOR/ CONTRACTOR

On an NICEIC Electrical Installation Condition Report, the Approved Contractor's trading title as registered with NICEIC (not necessarily the Contractor's name), postal address and NICEIC Enrolment Number and Branch Number, where applicable, should be given here. The recording of the Approved Contractor's telephone number and email address is optional.

For the uncontrolled (green) version of the Electrical Installation Condition Report, the Electrical Contractor's trading title, address and postcode should be given here.

SECTION K: SUPPLY CHARACTERISTICS AND EARTHING ARRANGEMENTS

The supply characteristics and earthing arrangements should be obtained and inserted generally as described in Chapter 2. Note, however, that the Electrical Installation Condition Report form requires the value for the external earth fault loop impedance (Z_e) to be obtained by measurement only. However, the determination of this parameter by calculation or enquiry is not appropriate for an existing installation, and these options are therefore not catered for on the form.

Where, due to operational considerations, it is truly impracticable to measure the external earth fault loop impedance (Z_e), it would be acceptable to obtain a value from up-to-date records of the installation, provided there can be no doubt that the intended means of earthing is present and suitable for the installation. Such records should be available from the person responsible for the safety of the installation. Such considerations could, for example, apply to a hospital installation, where it might be unacceptable for the supply to be disconnected to enable a measurement of Z_e to be made for the purpose of periodic inspection. In such an exceptional case, the words 'by enquiry' should be included adjacent to the value of Z_e so obtained, and reference to the operational restriction should be included in the agreed limitations (of the inspection) part of Section D.

SECTION L: PARTICULARS OF INSTALLATION AT THE ORIGIN

The particulars of the installation at the origin should be ascertained and inserted in the data-entry boxes as described in Chapter 2.

Schedules for the Periodic Inspection Report

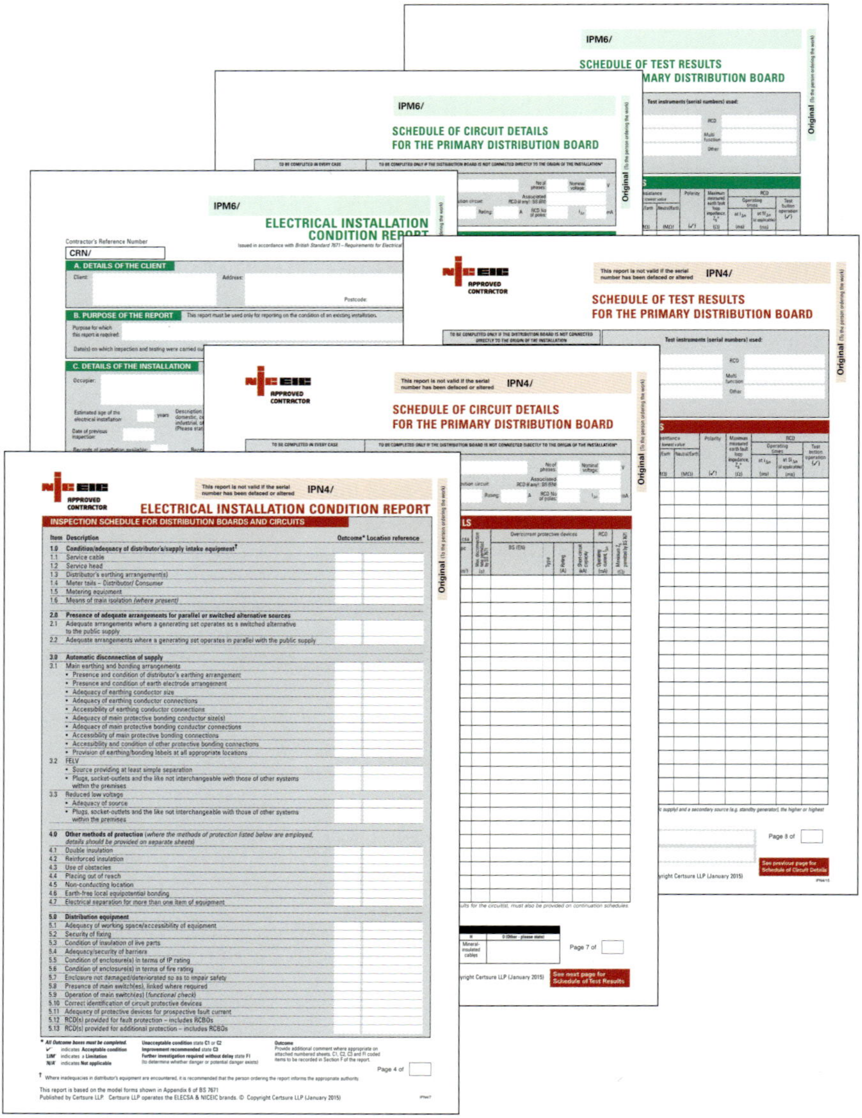

SCHEDULES (Pages 4, 5, 6, 7 and 8)

The remainder of the Electrical Installation Condition Report consists of the following schedules:

- Inspection schedule for distribution boards and circuits (see Chapter 8)
- Schedule of circuit details for the primary distribution board (see Chapter 6)
- Schedule of test results for the primary distribution board (see Chapter 6)

Guidance on the completion of the Schedule of Circuit Details and the Schedule of Test Results is given in Chapter 6. Guidance on the process of inspection and testing necessary to complete the schedules is given in Chapters 8 and 9 respectively.

Where a distribution board has more circuits than can be accommodated on the Schedule of Circuit Details and the Schedule of Test Results, continuation schedules will be required.

Where, in addition to the primary distribution board, an installation includes one or more distribution boards that are not connected directly to the origin of the installation, details of the distribution (sub-main) circuits, together with the test results for the circuits connected to those sub-distribution boards, must be provided on separate schedules,

Continuation schedules for Electrical Installation Condition Reports are available from NICEIC. All additional pages should be identified by the unique NICEIC serial number or in the case of the uncontrolled (green) version of the Electrical Installation Condition Report, the Contractor's Reference Number.

Due to its functional design, continuation sheets should not be necessary for the Inspection Schedule that forms part of NICEIC Electrical Installation Condition Reports.

It should be noted that an Electrical Installation Condition Report must be issued with all its associated schedules, even where, due to operational or other restrictions, the work comprised a visual inspection only. The schedules should be completed to the fullest extent possible with regard to the limitations of the inspection. Where, due to the particular limitations placed on a periodic inspection, a schedule or parts of a schedule are not applicable, this should be indicated by 'N/A' or 'Not Applicable'. NICEIC Electrical Installation Condition Reports issued without appropriately compiled schedules are incomplete, and therefore invalid.

Test instruments (serial numbers) used

At the top of the Schedules of Test Results, a panel is provided for recording information about the test instruments used. The serial number of each of the instruments used to obtain the test results should be recorded here. If any instrument does not have a serial number, a suitable number should be assigned and permanently marked on the instrument for traceability purposes. Where a combined instrument such as an insulation/continuity test instrument is used to carry out more than one type of test, the serial number of that instrument should be listed in the space corresponding to each of the relevant types of test.

REPORTING ON THE CONDITION OF DOMESTIC PREMISES

For the purpose of reporting on the condition of an existing electrical installation in a domestic property, NICEIC and ELECSA provide respective Electrical Installation Condition Reports, for use only by those authorised by the scope of their enrolment or registration.

The red NICEIC and blue ELECSA Domestic Electrical Installation Condition Reports may be used only where all the following conditions apply:

- The inspection and testing work relates to a single dwelling (house or individual flat)
- The installation forms part of a TT, TN-S or TN-C-S (PME) system
- The distributor's cut-out incorporates an HBC fuse rated at 100 A or less
- The protective measure against electric shock is by Automatic Disconnection of Supply (ADS)

Compilation of the NICEIC and the ELECSA Domestic Electrical Installation Condition Reports closely follow the red and green condition reports covered in this chapter. However, more detailed information on periodic inspection and testing of domestic premises is provided in the NICEIC and ELECSA publication: *Domestic Periodic Inspection, Testing and Reporting.*

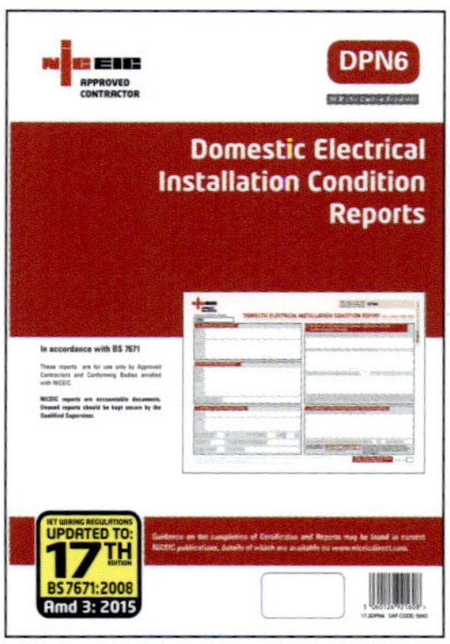

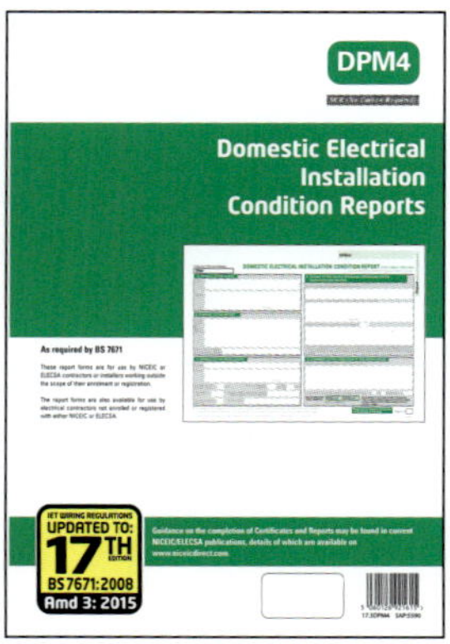

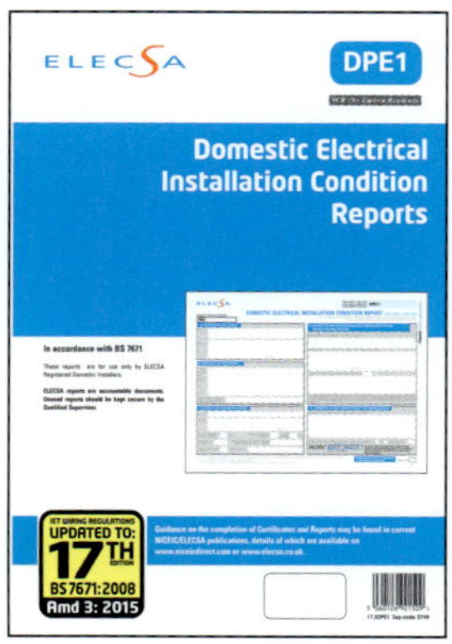

Chapter 6

The Schedule of Circuit Details and the Schedule of Test Results for new installation work and condition reporting

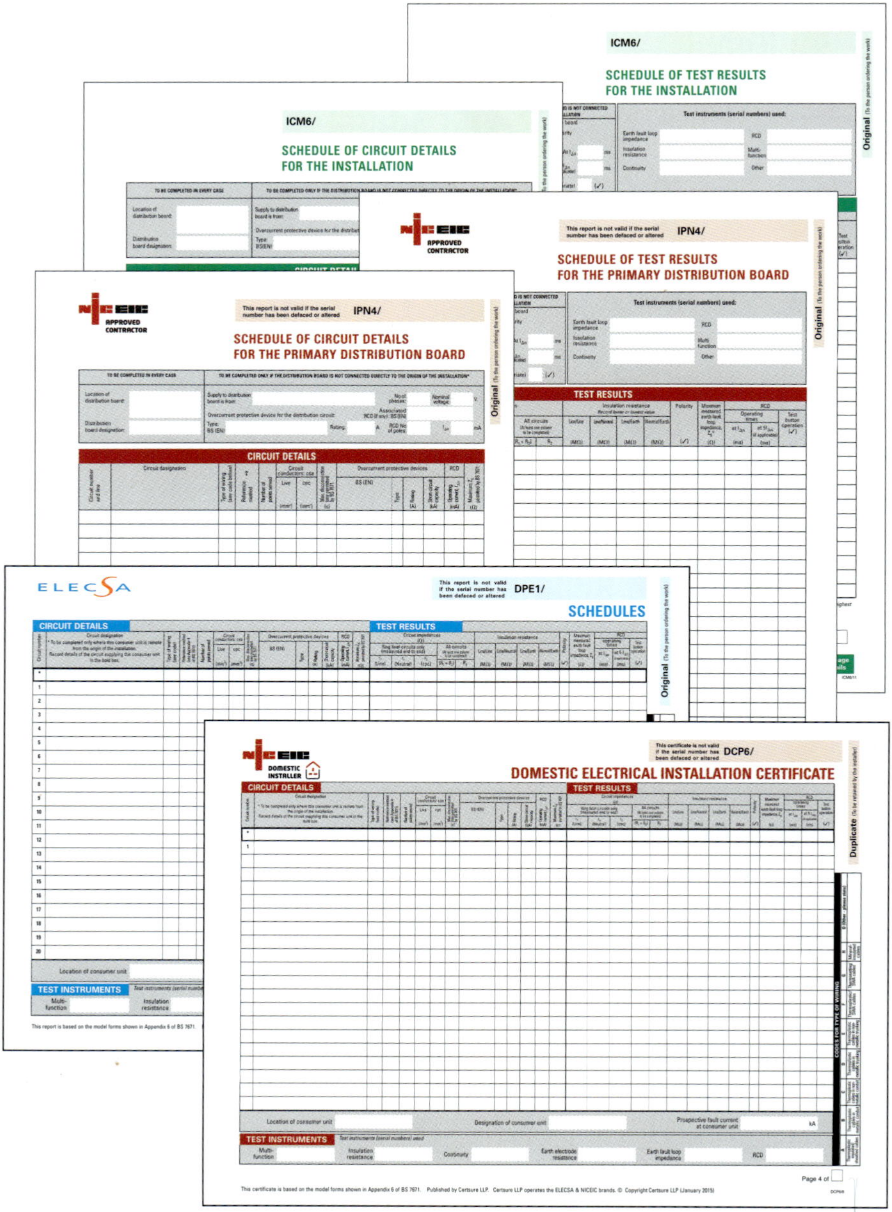
ICM6/

SCHEDULE OF TEST RESULTS FOR THE INSTALLATION

Test instruments (serial numbers) used:

Earth fault loop impedance
Insulation resistance
Continuity
RCD
Multi-function
Other

Original (To the person ordering the work)

ICM6/

SCHEDULE OF CIRCUIT DETAILS FOR THE INSTALLATION

TO BE COMPLETED IN EVERY CASE

Location of distribution board:
Distribution board designation:

Supply to distribution board is from:
Overcurrent protective device for the distribution circuit:
Type: BS(EN)

NICEIC APPROVED CONTRACTOR

This report is not valid if the serial number has been defaced or altered

IPN4/

SCHEDULE OF TEST RESULTS FOR THE PRIMARY DISTRIBUTION BOARD

Test instruments (serial numbers) used:

TEST RESULTS

Insulation resistance
Polarity
Maximum measured earth fault loop impedance, Z_s
RCD
Operating times
Test button operation

Original (To the person ordering the work)

NICEIC APPROVED CONTRACTOR

This report is not valid if the serial number has been defaced or altered

IPN4/

SCHEDULE OF CIRCUIT DETAILS FOR THE PRIMARY DISTRIBUTION BOARD

TO BE COMPLETED IN EVERY CASE

TO BE COMPLETED ONLY IF THE DISTRIBUTION BOARD IS NOT CONNECTED DIRECTLY TO THE ORIGIN OF THE INSTALLATION*

Location of distribution board:
Distribution board designation:
Supply to distribution board is from:
No of phases:
Nominal voltage:
Overcurrent protective device for the distribution circuit:
Associated RCD (if any): BS (EN)
Type: BS (EN)
Rating: A
RCD No of poles:
mA

CIRCUIT DETAILS

Circuit number and line
Circuit designation
Circuit conductors: csa
Live
cpc
Overcurrent protective devices
BS (EN)
Type
Rating (A)
Short-circuit capacity (kA)
RCD
Operating current (mA)

Original (To the person ordering the work)

ELECSA

This report is not valid if the serial number has been defaced or altered

DPE1/

SCHEDULES

CIRCUIT DETAILS

TEST RESULTS

1 2 3 4 5 6 7 8 9 10 11 12 13 14 15 16 17 18 19 20

Location of consumer unit

TEST INSTRUMENTS

Multi-function
Insulation resistance

This report is based on the model forms shown in Appendix 6 of BS 7671.

Original (To the person ordering the work)

NICEIC DOMESTIC INSTALLER

This certificate is not valid if the serial number has been defaced or altered

DCP6/

DOMESTIC ELECTRICAL INSTALLATION CERTIFICATE

CIRCUIT DETAILS

TEST RESULTS

Location of consumer unit
Designation of consumer unit
Prospective fault current at consumer unit
kA

TEST INSTRUMENTS

Test instruments (serial numbers) used

Multi-function
Insulation resistance
Continuity
Earth electrode resistance
Earth fault loop impedance
RCD

CODES FOR TYPE OF WIRING

Page 4 of

This certificate is based on the model forms shown in Appendix 6 of BS 7671. Published by Certsure LLP. Certsure LLP operates the ELECSA & NICEIC brands. © Copyright Certsure LLP (January 2015)

Duplicate (To be retained by the installer)

CHAPTER 6. THE SCHEDULE OF CIRCUIT DETAILS AND THE SCHEDULE OF TEST RESULTS

This chapter gives guidance on how to complete the Schedule of Circuit Details and the Schedule of Test Results. The guidance is equally applicable if the schedules form part of an Electrical Installation Certificate or an Electrical Installation Condition Report.

The guidance is also generally applicable to the completion of the similar schedules that form a part of the Domestic Electrical Installation Certificate and Domestic Electrical Installation Condition Report.

Both Electrical Installation Certificates and Electrical Installation Condition Reports should be accompanied by schedules of test results to provide details of the circuits under test as required by Sections 632 and 634 of *BS 7671*.

In the case of the Electrical Installation Certificate and Domestic Electrical Installation Certificate, the Schedule of Items Inspected are used to identify the particular protective measures and other safety features that are applicable to the installation, and to confirm that these have been inspected as required by *BS 7671*. The Schedule of Circuit Details and Schedule of Test Results must be issued as a pair, giving details of each circuit of the installation. The former records information about the design, such as the composition of each circuit and the type and rating of each protective device, and the latter records the test results for each of those circuits.

Each of the two schedules have a number of unshaded boxes which must be completed. No box should be left blank.

SCHEDULE OF CIRCUIT DETAILS

A Schedule of Circuit Details must be compiled for each switchboard, distribution board, consumer unit, control panel and the like within the installation covered by the Electrical Installation Certificate or Electrical Installation Condition Report. Reference to the 'distribution board' in this chapter should be taken as meaning any of the aforementioned items of switchgear, or composite assemblies of such items.

The schedule relates mainly to the design information for the installation, and should be completed in all possible respects prior to any testing being carried out on site. Each schedule includes essential details about the item of distribution equipment to which it relates, and about the outgoing final or distribution circuits. It is important to record the presence of spare ways, identified in the sequence of the other circuits. In the case of new installation work, the schedule can be used to confirm that the installation complies with the intended design.

One Schedule of Circuit Details and one Schedule of Test Results is provided as part of each certificate or report. Where the installation has more than one distribution board, additional schedules are required in the form of continuation sheets. Each continuation sheet must be numbered in sequence with all the other sheets making up the certificate or report. See the 'Continuation Schedules, section at the end of this chapter.

NICEIC APPROVED CONTRACTOR

This report is not valid if the serial number has been defaced or altered **IPN4/**

Original (To the person ordering the work)

SCHEDULE OF CIRCUIT DETAILS FOR THE PRIMARY DISTRIBUTION BOARD

TO BE COMPLETED IN EVERY CASE	TO BE COMPLETED ONLY IF THE DISTRIBUTION BOARD IS NOT CONNECTED DIRECTLY TO THE ORIGIN OF THE INSTALLATION*
Location of distribution board:	Supply to distribution board is from: No of phases: Nominal voltage: V
	Overcurrent protective device for the distribution circuit: Associated RCD (if any): BS (EN)
Distribution board designation:	Type: BS (EN) Rating: A RCD No of poles: $I_{\Delta n}$ mA

NICEIC APPROVED CONTRACTOR

This report is not valid if the serial number has been defaced or altered **IPN4/**

Original (To the person ordering the work)

SCHEDULE OF CIRCUIT DETAILS FOR THE PRIMARY DISTRIBUTION BOARD

TO BE COMPLETED IN EVERY CASE | TO BE COMPLETED ONLY IF THE DISTRIBUTION BOARD IS NOT CONNECTED DIRECTLY TO THE ORIGIN OF THE INSTALLATION*

Location of distribution board: | Supply to distribution board is from: No of phases: Nominal voltage: V

Overcurrent protective device for the distribution circuit: Associated RCD (if any): BS (EN)

Distribution board designation: | Type: BS (EN) Rating: A RCD No of poles: $I_{\Delta n}$ mA

* *In such cases, details of the distribution (sub-main) circuit(s), together with the test results for the circuit(s), must also be provided on continuation schedules.*

† *See Table 4A2 of Appendix 4 of BS 7671*

CODES FOR TYPE OF WIRING								
A	B	C	D	E	F	G	H	O (Other - please state)
Thermoplastic insulated/ sheathed cables	Thermoplastic cables in metallic conduit	Thermoplastic cables in non-metallic conduit	Thermoplastic cables in metallic trunking	Thermoplastic cables in non-metallic trunking	Thermoplastic /SWA cables	Thermosetting/ SWA cables	Mineral-insulated cables	

Page 7 of

This report is based on the model forms shown in Appendix 6 of BS 7671

See next page for Schedule of Test Results

IPN4/13

At the top of the schedule are a number of boxes. Two of these must be completed irrespective of whether or not the distribution board is connected directly to the origin:

- **Location of the distribution board:** Clearly identify the location.
- **Distribution board designation:** Give the reference number or other identifying mark. This designation should be different from that of any other distribution board forming part of the installation.

The other boxes at the top of the schedule should be completed only if the distribution board is not connected directly to the origin of the installation.

- **Supply to the distribution board is from:** Identify the equipment from which the distribution circuit feeding the distribution board is directly supplied. For example, 'Switchboard No 1'.
- **Overcurrent protective device for the distribution circuit:** State the type and rating of the overcurrent device protecting the distribution circuit that feeds the distribution board. For example, Type BS (EN): '*BS 88-2*', Rating: '63 A'.
- **No of phases:** Typically this will be either '1' or '3'.
- **Nominal voltage:** Record the nominal voltage to earth, U_0, typically '230 V'.
- **Associated RCD (if any):** BS (EN): State the product specification number. For example '*BS EN 61008*'
- **RCD No of poles:** Record the number of poles. For example, '2', '3', or '4'.
- $\mathbf{I_{\Delta n}}$**:** Record the nominal operating (tripping) current of the RCD , in units of mA.

CIRCUIT DETAILS

The details of each outgoing circuit must be entered in the body of the schedule, one row being used for each circuit. The details to be entered under each column heading are as follows:

- **Circuit number and line:** The circuit number and line should be identified using a scheme which is compatible with that used at the actual distribution board on site. For example: '1L1, 1L2, 1L3'.
- **Circuit designation:** The entry should be as descriptive as possible so that it cannot be confused with any other circuit of the distribution board. Designations such as 'lighting' or 'power' would not be acceptable.
- **Type of wiring:** Details of the type of wiring, such as 'thermoplastic insulated / sheathed' or 'thermosetting' should be entered. A table at the bottom of the schedule lists a set of codes for use in this respect. Where code O (other) is used, a note must be added in the space provided in the table to identify the specific type of wiring.

NICEIC APPROVED CONTRACTOR

This report is not valid if the serial number has been defaced or altered **IPN4/**

Original (To the person ordering the work)

SCHEDULE OF CIRCUIT DETAILS FOR THE PRIMARY DISTRIBUTION BOARD

TO BE COMPLETED IN EVERY CASE	TO BE COMPLETED ONLY IF THE DISTRIBUTION BOARD IS NOT CONNECTED DIRECTLY TO THE ORIGIN OF THE INSTALLATION*
Location of distribution board:	Supply to distribution board is from: No of phases: Nominal voltage: V
	Overcurrent protective device for the distribution circuit: Associated RCD (if any): BS (EN)
Distribution board designation:	Type: BS (EN) Rating: A RCD No of poles: $I_{\Delta n}$ mA

CIRCUIT DETAILS

Circuit number and line	Circuit designation	Type of wiring (see code below)	Reference method †	Number of points served	Circuit conductors: csa Live (mm²)	Circuit conductors: csa cpc (mm²)	Max. disconnection time permitted by BS 7671 (s)	Overcurrent protective devices BS (EN)	Type	Rating (A)	Short-circuit capacity (kA)	RCD Operating current, $I_{\Delta n}$ (mA)	Maximum Z_s permitted by BS 7671 (Ω)

TO BE COMPLETED IN EVERY CASE	TO BE COMPLETED ONLY IF THE DISTRIBUTION BOARD IS NOT CONNECTED DIRECTLY TO THE ORIGIN OF THE INSTALLATION*
Location of distribution board:	Supply to distribution board is from: No of phases: Nominal voltage: V
	Overcurrent protective device for the distribution circuit: Associated RCD (if any): BS (EN)
Distribution board designation:	Type: BS (EN) Rating: A RCD No of poles: $I_{\Delta n}$ mA

Original

* *In such cases, details of the distribution (sub-main) circuit(s), together with the test results for the circuit(s), must also be provided on continuation schedules.*

† *See Table 4A2 of Appendix 4 of BS 7671*

CODES FOR TYPE OF WIRING								
A	B	C	D	E	F	G	H	O (Other - please state)
Thermoplastic insulated/ sheathed cables	Thermoplastic cables in metallic conduit	Thermoplastic cables in non-metallic conduit	Thermoplastic cables in metallic trunking	Thermoplastic cables in non-metallic trunking	Thermoplastic /SWA cables	Thermosetting/ SWA cables	Mineral-insulated cables	

Page 7 of

This report is based on the model forms shown in Appendix 6 of BS 7671

See next page for Schedule of Test Results

IPN4/13

- **Reference method:** The reference method(s) used for the installation of the circuit, as detailed in Appendix 4 of *BS 7671*, must be recorded here.
- **Number of points served:** Record the number of items of current-using equipment, socket-outlets or similar on the circuit.
- **Circuit conductors (csa)**: Completion of this column is straightforward for the live conductors (line and neutral), and for the circuit protective conductor (cpc) if this is a single-core cable or a core of a multi-core cable. It is not so straightforward if the cpc is provided by the steel wire armouring of an armoured cable, the copper sheath of a mineral insulated cable, or by steel conduit or trunking. In such cases, the cpc should be indicated by its type, such as 'Arm', 'Con', 'Trun' and so on, rather than by its cross-sectional area. In specifying the use of armouring etc. as a protective conductor, the designer of the circuit will have taken responsibility for ensuring its suitability for that purpose.
- **Maximum disconnection time permitted by *BS 7671* (s):** The maximum permitted disconnection time is determined by the requirements of *BS 7671*, having regard to factors such as the type and location of equipment supplied by the circuit. For example, in the case of circuits forming part of a TN system a single-phase final circuit not exceeding 32 A would have a maximum permitted disconnection time of 0.4 seconds in the case of a fault, whilst a final circuit exceeding 32 A or a distribution circuit would be subject to a maximum disconnection time of 5 seconds.
- **Overcurrent protective devices:** There are four columns under this heading:
  - **BS (EN):** For example, circuit-breaker to *BS EN 60898*
  - **Type:** In the case of a circuit-breaker to *BS EN 60898*, this may be 'B', 'C' or 'D'. Where the device does not have a 'type' as is the case for *BS 3036* (rewireable fuses), an entry of N/A would be appropriate.
  - **Rating:** To be recorded in Amperes.
  - **Short-circuit capacity:** The maximum fault current that the device can interrupt safely should be recorded in kA.
- **RCD: Operating current, $I_{\Delta n}$ (mA):** The figure to be inserted in this column is the rated residual operating (tripping) current, in mA, of any RCD that may be in circuit. If there is no RCD present, then **'N/A'** should be entered.
- **Maximum Z_s permitted by *BS 7671* (Ω):** This column should record the maximum permitted values given for Z_s, by reference to the limiting earth fault loop impedance values given in Chapter 41 of *BS 7671*, not to other tabulated 'corrected' values used for comparison with measured values.

Many distribution boards and consumer units do not have sufficient space to record all the information required by Regulations 514.8.1 and 514.9.1. For an installation for

NICEIC APPROVED CONTRACTOR

This report is not valid if the serial number has been defaced or altered **IPN4/**

Original (To the person ordering the work)

SCHEDULE OF TEST RESULTS FOR THE PRIMARY DISTRIBUTION BOARD

TO BE COMPLETED ONLY IF THE DISTRIBUTION BOARD IS NOT CONNECTED DIRECTLY TO THE ORIGIN OF THE INSTALLATION

Characteristics at this distribution board

Confirmation of supply polarity

* See note below

Z_s * Ω — Operating times of associated RCD (if any): At $I_{\Delta n}$ ms

I_{pf} * kA — At $5I_{\Delta n}$ (if applicable) ms

Phase sequence confirmed (where appropriate) (✓)

Test instruments (serial numbers) used:

Earth fault loop impedance		RCD	
Insulation resistance		Multi function	
Continuity		Other	

TEST RESULTS

...ber	Circuit impedances (Ω)	Insulation resistance Record lower or lowest value	Polarity	Maximum measured	RCD Operating...	Test...

TO BE COMPLETED ONLY IF THE DISTRIBUTION BOARD IS NOT CONNECTED DIRECTLY TO THE ORIGIN OF THE INSTALLATION

Characteristics at this distribution board

Confirmation of supply polarity

* See note below

Z_s * Ω — Operating times of associated RCD (if any): At $I_{\Delta n}$ ms

I_{pf} * kA — At $5I_{\Delta n}$ (if applicable) ms

Phase sequence confirmed (where appropriate) (✓)

Test instruments (serial numbers) used:

Earth fault loop impedance — RCD

Insulation resistance — Multi function

Continuity — Other

Original (To th

* *Note: Where the installation can be supplied by more than one source, such as a primary source (e.g. public supply) and a secondary source (e.g. standby generator), the higher or highest values must be recorded.*

TESTED BY

Signature:		Position:	
Name: (CAPITALS)		Date of testing:	

Page 8 of

See previous page for Schedule of Circuit Details

This report is based on the model forms shown in Appendix 6 of BS 7671

IPN4/15

which the issue of a Domestic Electrical Installation Certificate is appropriate, an additional copy of the completed schedules comprising the fourth page of the certificate is likely to provide most of the required information. For other simple installations, an additional copy of the 'Schedule of Circuit Details', which forms part of the Electrical Installation Certificate, is likely to serve the same purpose. More complex installations will require more comprehensive information.

When an additional copy of the schedule is used to provide a record of the installation details, it should be protected from damage (for example by enclosing it in a clear plastic folder or encapsulation), and be fixed within or adjacent to the distribution board or consumer unit. The 'original' and 'duplicate' of the schedule should not be used for this purpose, but should be retained as part of the certificate by the client and contractor respectively.

SCHEDULE OF TEST RESULTS FOR THE INSTALLATION

In addition to the Schedule of Circuit Details previously discussed, a Schedule of Test Results should be compiled for each distribution board included in the installation covered by the Electrical Installation Certificate or Electrical Installation Condition Report.

One such schedule is provided as part of each NICEIC or ELECSA certificate or report. Where the installation has more than one distribution board, additional schedules are required in the form of continuation sheets. There should be a corresponding Schedule of Test Results for each Schedule of Circuit Details. Each sheet should be numbered in sequence with all the other sheets making up the certificate or report. See the 'Continuation Schedules' section at the end of this chapter.

The boxes relating to characteristics at the distribution board at the top left-hand side of the schedule should be completed only if the distribution board is not connected directly to the origin of the installation.

- **Characteristics at this distribution board:** The supply polarity should be confirmed and together with the values of earth fault loop impedance (Z_s) and maximum prospective fault current (I_{pf}), measured at the incoming terminals of the distribution board or control panel etc, should be recorded here, together with the respective operating times (ms) of an associated RCD (if fitted) when subject to a test current of $I_{\Delta n}$ and, where the RCD is providing additional protection, a test current of $5I_{\Delta n}$. For polyphase supplies, the phase sequence should also be confirmed, otherwise N/A should be recorded.

On the right-hand side at the top of the schedule is a panel where information concerning the test instruments used should be recorded:

NICEIC APPROVED CONTRACTOR

This report is not valid if the serial number has been defaced or altered **IPN4/**

Original (To the person ordering the work)

SCHEDULE OF TEST RESULTS FOR THE PRIMARY DISTRIBUTION BOARD

TO BE COMPLETED ONLY IF THE DISTRIBUTION BOARD IS NOT CONNECTED DIRECTLY TO THE ORIGIN OF THE INSTALLATION

Characteristics at this distribution board

Confirmation of supply polarity

* See note below

Z_s* Ω Operating times of associated RCD (if any) At $I_{\Delta n}$ ms

I_{pf}* kA At $5I_{\Delta n}$ (if applicable) ms

Phase sequence confirmed (where appropriate) (✓)

Test instruments (serial numbers) used:

Earth fault loop impedance | RCD

Insulation resistance | Multi function

Continuity | Other

TEST RESULTS

Circuit number and line	Circuit impedances (Ω)					Insulation resistance *Record lower or lowest value*				Polarity	Maximum measured earth fault loop impedance, Z_s*	RCD		
	Ring final circuits only (measured end to end)			All circuits (At least one column to be completed)		Line/Line	Line/Neutral	Line/Earth	Neutral/Earth			Operating times		Test button operation (✓)
	r_1 (Line)	r_n (Neutral)	r_2 (cpc)	$(R_1 + R_2)$	R_2	(MΩ)	(MΩ)	(MΩ)	(MΩ)	(✓)	(Ω)	at $I_{\Delta n}$ (ms)	at $5I_{\Delta n}$ (if applicable) (ms)	

* Note: *Where the installation can be supplied by more than one source, such as a primary source (e.g. public supply) and a secondary source (e.g. standby generator), the higher or highest values must be recorded.*

TESTED BY

Signature: | Position:

Name: (CAPITALS) | Date of testing:

Page 8 of

See previous page for Schedule of Circuit Details

This report is based on the model forms shown in Appendix 6 of BS 7671

IPN4/15

- **Test instruments (serial numbers) used:** The serial number of each of the instruments used to obtain the test results recorded in this schedule should be given here. If any instrument does not have a serial number, a suitable number should be assigned and permanently marked on the instrument. Where a combined instrument such as an insulation resistance/continuity test instrument is used to carry out more than one type of test, the serial number of that instrument should be given in the space corresponding to each of the relevant types of test. Where instruments have been used which are 'other' than those listed, delete the word 'other' and insert a brief description of each such instrument, followed by its serial number in the space provided.

TEST RESULTS

The test results for each outgoing circuit must be entered in the body of the schedule, in the same rows and in the same order as the corresponding circuits appear on the Schedule of Circuit Details. This alignment is essential in order to enable the Schedule of Circuit Details and the Schedule of Test Results for each distribution board to be read in conjunction with each other. The method for carrying out each test is described in Chapter 9. The information to be entered under each column heading is indicated below:

- **Circuit number and line:** The circuit number and line here should be identical to those used in the corresponding Schedule of Circuit Details.
- **Circuit impedances: ring final circuits only, r_1, r_n, r_2:** Where the circuit is a ring final circuit, the resistance of each of the circuit's conductors, measured from end to end, should be recorded in the three columns provided, one each for the line conductor ring (r_1), the neutral conductor ring (r_n) and the circuit protective conductor ring (r_2), in units of ohms. For circuits other than ring final circuits, '**N/A**' should be entered in these columns to indicate that they were not applicable to the circuit.
- **Circuit impedances: (R_1 + R_2):** Enter the measured resistance, in ohms, of the line conductor and circuit protective conductor connected together as described for the measurement of (R_1 + R_2) in Chapter 9 (see 'continuity of protective conductors' or, for ring final circuits, 'continuity of ring final circuit conductors'). For a ring final circuit, these test procedures also confirm that polarity is correct.
- **Circuit impedances: (R_2):** Where R_2 has been determined using the 'wander lead' method, or where for other reasons it is not practicable to record (R_1 + R_2), it is permissible to record R_2 values in this column.

An entry in at least one of the two columns (R_1 + R_2) or R_2, is necessary for all circuits, including ring final circuits. If, for technically justifiable reasons, data is not recorded in either of the two columns of a Schedule of Test Results forming a part of an Electrical

NICEIC APPROVED CONTRACTOR

This report is not valid if the serial number has been defaced or altered **IPN4/**

Original (To the person ordering the work)

SCHEDULE OF TEST RESULTS FOR THE PRIMARY DISTRIBUTION BOARD

TO BE COMPLETED ONLY IF THE DISTRIBUTION BOARD IS NOT CONNECTED DIRECTLY TO THE ORIGIN OF THE INSTALLATION				
Characteristics at this distribution board				
	Confirmation of supply polarity			
* See note below				
Z_s*	Ω	Operating times of associated RCD (if any)	At $I_{\Delta n}$	ms
I_{pf}*	kA		At $5I_{\Delta n}$ (if applicable)	ms
Phase sequence confirmed (where appropriate)				(✓)

Test instruments (serial numbers) used:			
Earth fault loop impedance		RCD	
Insulation resistance		Multi function	
Continuity		Other	

TEST RESULTS

Circuit number and line	Circuit impedances (Ω)					Insulation resistance *Record lower or lowest value*				Polarity	Maximum measured earth fault loop impedance, Z_s*	RCD		
	Ring final circuits only (measured end to end)			All circuits (At least one column to be completed)		Line/Line	Line/Neutral	Line/Earth	Neutral/Earth			Operating times		Test button operation
	r_1 (Line)	r_n (Neutral)	r_2 (cpc)	$(R_1 + R_2)$	R_2	(MΩ)	(MΩ)	(MΩ)	(MΩ)	(✓)	(Ω)	at $I_{\Delta n}$ (ms)	at $5I_{\Delta n}$ (if applicable) (ms)	(✓)

* Note: *Where the installation can be supplied by more than one source, such as a primary source (e.g. public supply) and a secondary source (e.g. standby generator), the higher or highest values must be recorded.*

TESTED BY

Signature:		Position:	
Name: (CAPITALS)		Date of testing:	

Page 8 of

See previous page for Schedule of Circuit Details

IPN4/15

Installation Condition Report, **'Lim'** (meaning limitation) should be entered. In such cases, an explanation of why the testing could not be performed should be given in Section D of the Electrical Installation Condition Report. Such a situation should not arise in the case of new work covered by an Electrical Installation Certificate or Domestic Electrical Installation Certificate.

- **Insulation resistance:** There are four columns under this heading. For a single-phase circuit, all but the first column are used (**'N/A'** being entered in the first column). For a 2-phase or 3-phase circuit, all columns are used, and the lower or lowest insulation resistance measured is recorded for line/line, line/neutral and line/earth. Enter measured values of insulation resistance in megohms. If the measured insulation resistance exceeds the maximum range of the instrument being used to perform the test, record the measurement as being greater than the maximum range by, for example '> 200' or '200+' or similar. Do not record the value as '∞' or 'infinity'.
- **Polarity:** If polarity is found to be correct throughout the circuit by testing, a positive indication such as a tick (✔) should be entered. If polarity is found to be incorrect in any part of the circuit, a negative indication such as a cross (✗) should be entered. it is important to appreciate that an indication of incorrect polarity must never be included on a schedule of test results for new installation work; such a dangerous deficiency must always be corrected before the installation is put into service. Only in the case of an Electrical Installation Condition Report can it ever be acceptable to issue a schedule of test results showing incorrect polarity. However, even in the event of incorrect polarity being discovered during a periodic inspection it should, as a Code C1 departure, be the subject of immediate remedial action.
- **Maximum measured earth fault loop impedance, Z_s:** Enter the measured value of earth fault loop impedance at the point or accessory which is electrically most remote from the origin of the circuit.
- **RCD operating times:** There are two columns under this heading. The left-hand column is used to record the operating (tripping) time of any RCD which is in circuit when tested at its rated residual operating current ($I_{\Delta n}$). The right-hand column is applicable where the RCD has a rated residual operating current of 30 mA or less, and has been installed to provide additional protection. This second test is carried out at a current of $5I_{\Delta n}$.

Any items in the Schedule of Test Results that have been identified as being dangerous (code C1) or potentially dangerous (code C2), that would result in a significant enhancement of safety if improved (code C3), or that require further investigation to determine whether danger or potential danger exists (code FI), should be carried forward to Section F of the condition report in the form of observations on

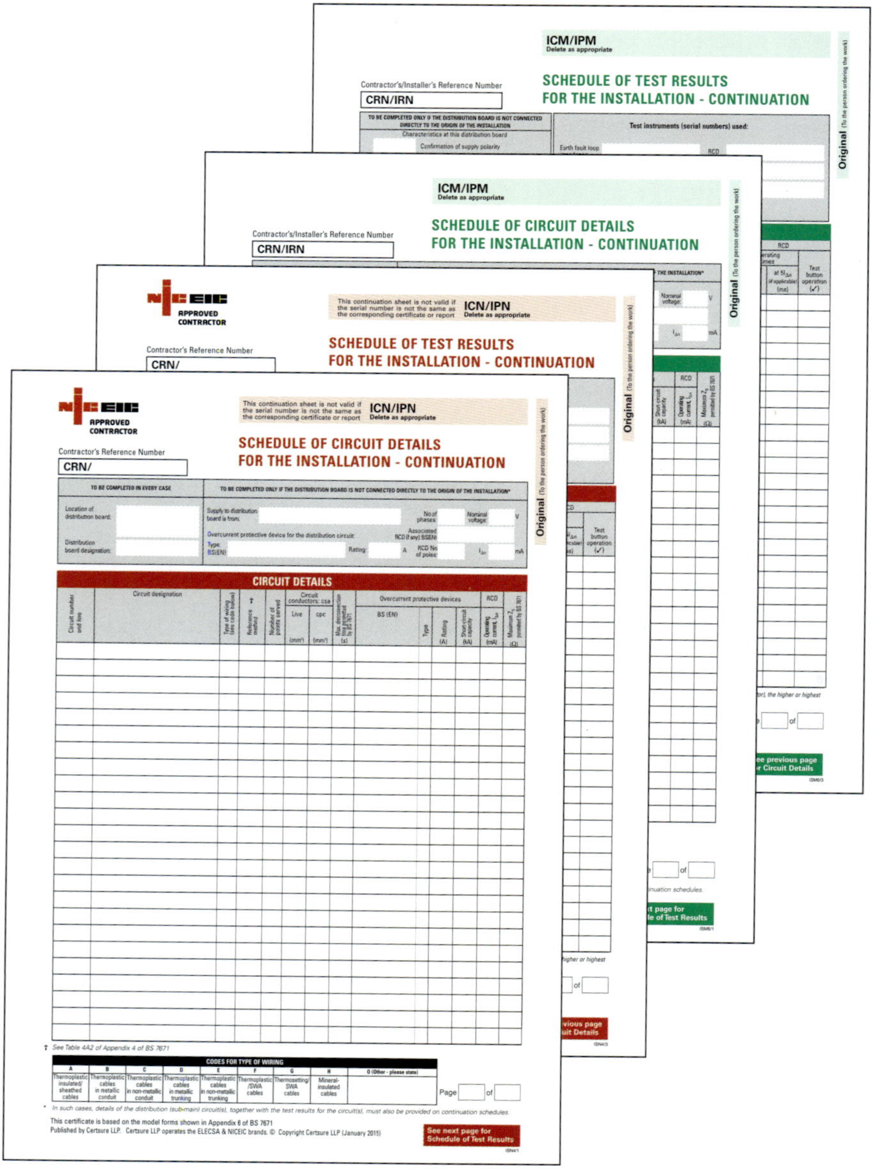

APPROVED CONTRACTOR

Contractor's Reference Number

CRN/

This continuation sheet is not valid if the serial number is not the same as the corresponding certificate or report

ICN/IPN
Delete as appropriate

SCHEDULE OF CIRCUIT DETAILS
FOR THE INSTALLATION - CONTINUATION

Original (To the person ordering the work)

TO BE COMPLETED IN EVERY CASE

Location of distribution board:

Distribution board designation:

TO BE COMPLETED ONLY IF THE DISTRIBUTION BOARD IS NOT CONNECTED DIRECTLY TO THE ORIGIN OF THE INSTALLATION*

Supply to distribution board is from:

No of phases:

Nominal voltage: V

Overcurrent protective device for the distribution circuit:

Associated RCD (if any): BS(EN)

Type: BS(EN)

Rating: A

RCD No of poles:

$I_{\Delta n}$ mA

CIRCUIT DETAILS

Circuit number and line	Circuit designation	Type of wiring (see code below)	Reference method †	Number of points served	Circuit conductors: csa Live (mm²)	Circuit conductors: csa cpc (mm²)	Max. disconnection time permitted by BS 7671 (s)	Overcurrent protective devices BS (EN)	Type	Rating (A)	Short-circuit capacity (kA)	RCD Operating current, $I_{\Delta n}$ (mA)	Maximum Z_s permitted by BS 7671 (Ω)

† See Table 4A2 of Appendix 4 of BS 7671

CODES FOR TYPE OF WIRING

A	B	C	D	E	F	G	H	O (Other - please state)
Thermoplastic insulated/ sheathed cables	Thermoplastic cables in metallic conduit	Thermoplastic cables in non-metallic conduit	Thermoplastic cables in metallic trunking	Thermoplastic cables in non-metallic trunking	Thermoplastic /SWA cables	Thermosetting/ SWA cables	Mineral-insulated cables	

Page of

* In such cases, details of the distribution (sub-main) circuit(s), together with the test results for the circuit(s), must also be provided on continuation schedules.

This certificate is based on the model forms shown in Appendix 6 of BS 7671
Published by Certsure LLP. Certsure LLP operates the ELECSA & NICEIC brands. © Copyright Certsure LLP (January 2015)

See next page for Schedule of Test Results

the safety of the installation.

Where an RCD protects a number of circuits, the RCD (on no load) can be tested by connecting the test instrument immediately downstream of the device, and the test currents and corresponding disconnection times may be recorded for the group of circuits so protected. Alternatively, the tests may be carried out on each circuit with the corresponding disconnection times recorded separately for each circuit. In both cases, test results are recorded in milliseconds (ms).

- **RCD test button operation**: This column relates to the operation of the integral test button. In the case of an Electrical Installation Certificate covering a new installation, or an addition or alteration, only correct operation of the RCD, indicated by a tick (✔) is acceptable. However, in the case of a periodic inspection of an existing installation, either a tick (✔) or a cross (✗) could be entered, as appropriate.

CONTINUATION SCHEDULES

As previously indicated, only one Schedule of Circuit Details and one Schedule of Test Results is supplied as part of each NICEIC or ELECSA Electrical Installation Certificate and Electrical Installation Condition Report (and the equivalent green forms).

Where the certificate or report relates to an installation having more than one distribution board or consumer unit, more than 24 circuits (21 in the case of the Domestic Electrical Installation Certificate or Domestic Electrical Installation Condition Report, or where the installation includes one or more distribution ('sub-main') circuits, additional 'continuation' schedules are required.

Sets of continuation schedules are available from NICEIC. Only ELECSA and NICEIC continuation schedules intended to be used with the current versions of their certificates or report forms should be used. Superseded versions should not be used.

For NICEIC Electrical Installation Certificates or Electrical Installation Condition Reports the continuation schedules should be given the same unique serial number, by first striking out 'ICN or IPN' prefix (as appropriate) at the top of the additional schedules and then adding the remainder of the serial number in the spaces allocated. In the case of an NICEIC or ELECSA Domestic Electrical Installation Certificate or Domestic Electrical Installation Condition Report, the certificate or report serial number should be written on each page of any continuation schedules.

The page number for each additional schedule should be inserted at the foot of the schedule, together with the total number of pages comprising the certificate or report (e.g. page 7 of 8).

C	D	E	F	G	H	O (Other - please state)	
ermoplastic cables non-metallic conduit	Thermoplastic cables in metallic trunking	Thermoplastic cables in non-metallic trunking	Thermoplastic /SWA cables	Thermosetting/ SWA cables	Mineral-insulated cables		Page ☐ of ☐

e distribution (sub-main) circuit(s), together with the test results for the circuit(s), must also be provided on continuation schedules.

the model forms shown in Appendix 6 of BS 7671

See next page for Schedule of Test Results

ISN4/1

There is a tendency to overlook the need to record circuit details and test results for distribution circuits (commonly referred to as 'sub-mains'), where such circuits form part of an installation. For example, where the switchboard at the origin of an installation incorporates a number of fused-switches feeding distribution circuits to remote distribution boards, the information relating to those distribution circuits will need to be recorded on a Schedule of Circuit Details and a Schedule of Test Results. Such additional schedules are also required for the distribution circuit where a main switch at the origin of an installation feeds a single, remote distribution board.

The Electrical Installation Certificate or Electrical Installation Condition Report must also include an additional Schedule of Circuit Details and Schedule of Test Results for each of the distribution boards, including their final circuits.

Chapter 7

The Schedule of Items Inspected for new installation work

PURPOSE OF INITIAL INSPECTION

SAFETY

INSPECTION OF NEW INSTALLATION WORK

THE SEQUENCE OF INSPECTIONS

CONDITION OF ELECTRICAL INTAKE EQUIPMENT

PARALLEL OR SWITCHED ALTERNATIVE SOURCES OF SUPPLY

AUTOMATIC DISCONNECTION OF SUPPLY

BASIC PROTECTION

ADDITIONAL PROTECTION

OTHER METHODS OF PROTECTION

DISTRIBUTION EQUIPMENT

CIRCUITS

ISOLATION AND SWITCHING

CURRENT-USING EQUIPMENT (PERMANENTLY CONNECTED)

SPECIAL INSTALLATIONS OR LOCATIONS

OTHER

NICEIC APPROVED CONTRACTOR

This certificate is not valid if the serial number has been defaced or altered **ICN4/**

Original (To the person ordering the work)

SCHEDULE OF ITEMS INSPECTED

† *See note below*

1.0 CONDITION OF ELECTRICAL INTAKE EQUIPMENT (the Distributor should be notified of any unsatisfactory equipment)

1.1 Service cable
1.2 Service head
1.3 Distributor's earthing arrangement
1.4 Meter tails - Distributor/Consumer
1.5 Metering equipment
1.6 Isolator

2.0 PARALLEL OR SWITCHED ALTERNATIVE SOURCES OF SUPPLY

2.1 Presence of adequate arrangements where generator to operate as a switched alternative
- a) Dedicated earthing arrangement independent of that of the public supply

2.2 Presence of adequate arrangements where generator to operate in parallel with public supply system
- a) Correct connection of generator in parallel
- b) Compatibility of characteristics of means of generation
- c) Means to provide automatic disconnection of generator in the event of loss of public supply system or voltage or frequency deviation beyond declared values
- d) Means to prevent connection of generator in the event of loss of public supply system or voltage or frequency deviation beyond declared values
- e) Means to isolate generator from the public supply system

2.3 Presence of alternative/additional supply warning notices at:
- a) The origin
- b) The meter position, if remote from origin
- c) The consumer unit/distribution board to which the alternative/additional sources are connected
- d) All points of isolation of ALL sources of supply

3.0 AUTOMATIC DISCONNECTION OF SUPPLY

3.1 Presence and adequacy of protective earthing/ bonding arrangements as follows:
- a) Distributor's earthing arrangement or installation earth electrode arrangement
- b) Earthing conductor and connections
- c) Main protective bonding conductors and connections
- d) Earthing/bonding labels at all appropriate locations

3.2 Accessibility of:
- a) Earthing conductor connections
- b) All protective bonding connections

3.3 FELV – requirements satisfied
3.4 Reduced low voltage – requirements satisfied

4.0 BASIC PROTECTION

4.1 Presence and adequacy of protective measures to provide basic protection
- a) Insulation of live parts
- b) Barriers or enclosures
- c) Obstacles**
- d) Placing out of reach**

5.0 ADDITIONAL PROTECTION

5.1 The presence and effectiveness of additional protection methods used, as follows:
- a) RCDs not exceeding 30 mA operating current
- b) Supplementary bonding

6.0 OTHER METHODS OF PROTECTION (insert location in box provided)

The presence and effectiveness of other methods of protection against electric shock where used, as follows:

		LOCATION
6.1	Basic and fault protection	
	a) SELV	
	b) PELV	
	c) Double insulation/ Reinforced insulation	
	d) Electrical separation for one item of equipment	
6.2	Fault protection	
	a) Non-conducting location/Earth-free local equipotential bonding**	
	b) Electrical separation for more than one item of equipment**	

7.0 DISTRIBUTION EQUIPMENT

7.1 Adequacy of working space/accessibility
7.2 Security of fixing
7.3 Insulation of live parts not damaged during erection
7.4 Adequacy / security of barriers
7.5 Suitability of enclosures for IP and fire ratings
7.6 Enclosures not damaged during installation
7.7 Presence and effectiveness of obstacles
7.8 Presence of main switch(es), linked where required
7.9 Operation of main switch(es) (functional check)
7.10 Operation of circuit-breakers and RCDs to prove functionality
7.11 RCD(s) provided for fault protection, where specified
7.12 RCD(s) provided for protection against fire
7.13 RCD(s) provided for additional protection, where specified
7.14 Confirmation overvoltage protection (SPDs) provided where specified
7.15 Confirmation of indication that SPD is functional
7.16 Presence of RCD quarterly test notice at or near the origin
7.17 Presence of diagrams, charts or schedules at or near each distribution board, where required
7.18 Presence of non-standard (mixed) cable colour warning notice at or near the appropriate distribution board, where required
7.19 Presence of next inspection recommendation label
7.20 Presence of other required labelling
7.21 Selection of protective device(s) and base(s); correct type and rating
7.22 Single-pole protective devices in line conductor only
7.23 Protection against mechanical damage where cables enter equipment
7.24 Protection against electromagnetic effects where cables enter ferromagnetic enclosures
7.25 Confirmation that ALL conductor connections, including connections to busbars are correctly located in terminals and are tight and secure

8.0 CIRCUITS

8.1 Identification of conductors
8.2 Cables correctly supported throughout their length
8.3 Examination of cables for signs of mechanical damage during installation
8.4 Examination of insulation of live parts, not damaged during erection

** *For use in controlled supervised/conditions only*

† ***All boxes must be completed.*** *'✓' indicates that an inspection was carried out and that the result was* ***satisfactory****. 'N/A' indicates that an inspection was* ***not applicable*** *to the particular installation.*

* *Where the electrical work to which this certificate relates includes the installation of a fire alarm system and/or an emergency lighting system (or a part of such systems), this electrical safety certificate should be accompanied by the particular certificate(s) for the system(s).*

Page 3 of

This certificate is based on the model forms shown in Appendix 6 of BS 7671

ICN4/5

Inspections may follow the sequence embodied in the NICEIC schedule

7 INSPECTION

PURPOSE OF INITIAL INSPECTION

Before an installation is tested, it is necessary to carry out a careful and thorough inspection using the senses of sight, hearing, smell and touch. Such inspection may reveal deficiencies that are unlikely to be detected by testing, such as incomplete enclosures, damaged accessories or cable sheaths, unsuitable erection and installation methods, overheating, absence of fire barriers, adverse external influences etc.

The main purpose of initial inspection is to verify that the installed equipment and other associated materials:

- comply with appropriate British, European or equivalent product standards, and
- have been correctly selected and erected, and
- are not visibly damaged or defective so as to impair safety, and
- are suitable for the environment in which they are installed.

SAFETY

Wherever possible, inspection should be carried out when the installation is not energised, in accordance with the *Electricity at Work Regulations 1989*. Where diagrams, schedules and other relevant information relating to the installation are not available, a degree of exploratory work may be necessary so that the inspection (and subsequent testing) can be carried out safely.

INSPECTION OF NEW INSTALLATION WORK

BS 7671 requires that every installation, and every alteration or addition to an installation, is inspected during erection and on completion before being put into service to verify, so far as is reasonably practicable, that the requirements of the regulations have been met.

It is almost always necessary for some inspection work to be carried out during the process of constructing an installation, because some of the items requiring inspection are likely to be inaccessible on completion. For example, the condition of cables concealed in the fabric of a building cannot be inspected after completion of the building work. Inspection during the construction stage will also enable unsatisfactory work to be identified at an early stage, so that it can be remedied before becoming a serious and costly problem to the contractor.

It is a requirement of *BS 7671* that the relevant design information is made available to those carrying out the inspection and testing of new installation work, irrespective of whether the design was carried out by the contractor or by another party, such as a consulting engineer (see Regulation 610.2). Unless such information is made available at the appropriate time, it is unlikely that inspection and testing can be completed satisfactorily.

ICM6/

Original (To the person ordering the work)

SCHEDULE OF ITEMS INSPECTED

† See note below

1.0 CONDITION OF ELECTRICAL INTAKE EQUIPMENT (the Distributor should be notified of any unsatisfactory equipment)

1.1	Service cable	
1.2	Service head	
1.3	Distributor's earthing arrangement	
1.4	Meter tails - Distributor/Consumer	
1.5	Metering equipment	
1.6	Isolator	

2.0 PARALLEL OR SWITCHED ALTERNATIVE SOURCES OF SUPPLY

2.1	Presence of adequate arrangements where generator to operate as a switched alternative	
	a) Dedicated earthing arrangement independent of that of the public supply	
2.2	Presence of adequate arrangements where generator to operate in parallel with public supply system	
	a) Correct connection of generator in parallel	
	b) Compatibility of characteristics of means of generation	
	c) Means to provide automatic disconnection of generator in the event of loss of public supply system or voltage or frequency deviation beyond declared values	
	d) Means to prevent connection of generator in the event of loss of public supply system or voltage or frequency deviation beyond declared values	
	e) Means to isolate generator from the public supply system	
2.3	Presence of alternative/additional supply warning notices at:	
	a) The origin	
	b) The meter position, if remote from origin	
	c) The consumer unit/distribution board to which the alternative/additional sources are connected	
	d) All points of isolation of ALL sources of supply	

3.0 AUTOMATIC DISCONNECTION OF SUPPLY

3.1	Presence and adequacy of protective earthing/ bonding arrangements as follows:	
	a) Distributor's earthing arrangement or installation earth electrode arrangement	
	b) Earthing conductor and connections	
	c) Main protective bonding conductors and connections	
	d) Earthing/bonding labels at all appropriate locations	
3.2	Accessibility of:	
	a) Earthing conductor connections	
	b) All protective bonding connections	
3.3	FELV – requirements satisfied	
3.4	Reduced low voltage – requirements satisfied	

4.0 BASIC PROTECTION

4.1	Presence and adequacy of protective measures to provide basic protection	
	a) Insulation of live parts	
	b) Barriers or enclosures	
	c) Obstacles**	
	d) Placing out of reach**	

5.0 ADDITIONAL PROTECTION

5.1	The presence and effectiveness of additional protection methods used, as follows:	
	a) RCDs not exceeding 30 mA operating current	
	b) Supplementary bonding	

6.0 OTHER METHODS OF PROTECTION (insert location in box provided)

The presence and effectiveness of other methods of protection against electric shock where used, as follows:

			LOCATION
6.1	Basic and fault protection		
	a) SELV		
	b) PELV		
	c) Double insulation/ Reinforced insulation		
	d) Electrical separation for one item of equipment		
6.2	Fault protection		
	a) Non-conducting location/Earth-free local equipotential bonding**		
	b) Electrical separation for more than one item of equipment**		

7.0 DISTRIBUTION EQUIPMENT

7.1	Adequacy of working space/accessibility	
7.2	Security of fixing	
7.3	Insulation of live parts not damaged during erection	
7.4	Adequacy / security of barriers	
7.5	Suitability of enclosures for IP and fire ratings	
7.6	Enclosures not damaged during installation	
7.7	Presence and effectiveness of obstacles	
7.8	Presence of main switch(es), linked where required	
7.9	Operation of main switch(es) (functional check)	
7.10	Operation of circuit-breakers and RCDs to prove functionality	
7.11	RCD(s) provided for fault protection, where specified	
7.12	RCD(s) provided for protection against fire	
7.13	RCD(s) provided for additional protection, where specified	
7.14	Confirmation overvoltage protection (SPDs) provided where specified	
7.15	Confirmation of indication that SPD is functional	
7.16	Presence of RCD quarterly test notice at or near the origin	
7.17	Presence of diagrams, charts or schedules at or near each distribution board, where required	
7.18	Presence of non-standard (mixed) cable colour warning notice at or near the appropriate distribution board, where required	
7.19	Presence of next inspection recommendation label	
7.20	Presence of other required labelling	
7.21	Selection of protective device(s) and base(s); correct type and rating	
7.22	Single-pole protective devices in line conductor only	
7.23	Protection against mechanical damage where cables enter equipment	
7.24	Protection against electromagnetic effects where cables enter ferromagnetic enclosures	
7.25	Confirmation that ALL conductor connections, including connections to busbars are correctly located in terminals and are tight and secure	

8.0 CIRCUITS

8.1	Identification of conductors	
8.2	Cables correctly supported throughout their length	
8.3	Examination of cables for signs of mechanical damage during installation	
8.4	Examination of insulation of live parts, not damaged during erection	

** *For use in controlled supervised/conditions only*

† ***All boxes must be completed.*** *'✓' indicates that an inspection was carried out and that the result was* ***satisfactory****. 'N/A' indicates that an inspection was* ***not applicable*** *to the particular installation.*

* *Where the electrical work to which this certificate relates includes the installation of a fire alarm system and/or an emergency lighting system (or a part of such systems), this electrical safety certificate should be accompanied by the particular certificate(s) for the system(s).*

Page 3 of

This certificate is based on the model forms shown in Appendix 6 of BS 7671

ICM6/5

THE SEQUENCE OF INSPECTIONS FOR A NEW INSTALLATION, ADDITIONS OR ALTERATIONS

Guidance on the sequence for the various inspections in the remainder of this chapter closely follows that of the items of inspection embodied in the Schedule of Items Inspected, which forms part of the NICEIC *Electrical Installation Certificate*. NICEIC and ELECSA *Domestic Electrical Installation Certificates* also incorporate a modified form of this schedule. However, it is recognised that it may not always be appropriate to follow such a sequence in undertaking the inspections.

1.0 CONDITION OF ELECTRICAL INTAKE EQUIPMENT

Aspects of the supply intake equipment listed on the Inspection Schedule, which are readily accessible, should be inspected for signs of mechanical damage, evidence of overheating and other forms of deterioration. The **metering equipment** and any connection boxes provided by the distributor as a part of their installation should be securely fixed with all outer casings/enclosures undamaged. Meter tails should be correctly sized, and clearly and unambiguously identified.

Where a switch is provided by the distributor as a means of main isolation, it should be confirmed that the switch is functional and its condition satisfactory.

Note: Where inadequacies in the electricity distributor's or supplier's equipment are observed, the person ordering the inspection should be advised to inform the relevant authority.

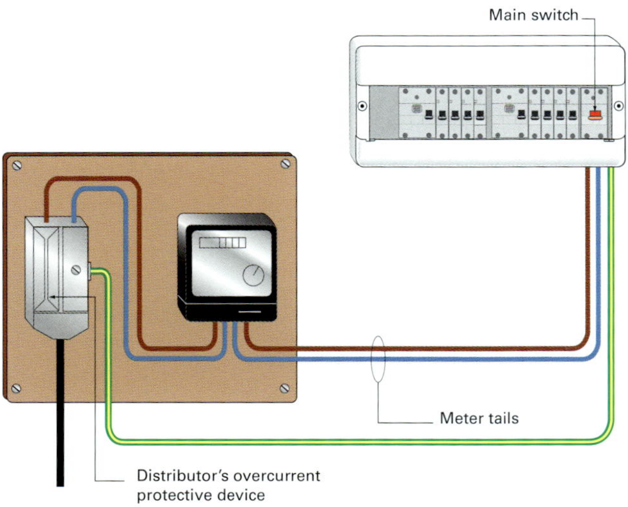

2.0 PARALLEL OR SWITCHED ALTERNATIVE SOURCES OF SUPPLY

Where a supply to the installation is available from more than one source, the inspector should check that adequate arrangements in terms of protection for safety are present, including appropriate provision for isolation, manual and automatic switching, and any necessary interlocking.

Adequate arrangements for parallel operation

The particular requirements for generators, including those used as parallel and standby sources, are given in Section 551 of *BS 7671*. Where a generator operates in parallel with the public supply system the additional requirements of Regulation 551.7.1 must be satisfied.

Inspection should confirm that thermal and overcurrent protection are provided in accordance with Chapter 42 and Chapter 43 of *BS 7671* and remain effective in all situations (Regulation 551.7.1). Where an RCD provides additional protection in accordance with Regulation 415.1.1 for the circuit connecting the generator set to the installation, the device should disconnect all live conductors (line and neutral).

For a generator installed on the load side of all the circuit protective devices, the inspector should verify that the requirements of Regulation 551.7.2 are satisfied.

Presence of alternative/additional supply warning notices

As required by Regulation 514.15.1, where an installation includes an additional/alternative source of supply such as where a solar photovoltaic system or a generating boiler is used as an additional source of supply in parallel with the distributor's supply, warning notices should be affixed at the following locations in the installation:

- At the installation's origin
- At the meter position, where this is remote from the origin
- At the consumer unit or distribution board to which the generating set is connected
- At all points of isolation of all sources.

The warning notice is required to have the wording given in this example.

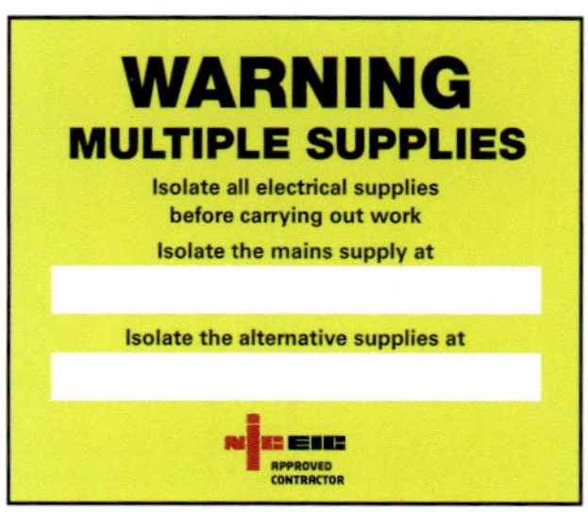

A warning label is required where installation has alternative supplies

3.0 AUTOMATIC DISCONNECTION OF SUPPLY

Presence and adequacy of protective earthing and bonding arrangements

Distributor's earthing arrangement or installation earth electrode arrangement

Electricity distributors will make available, in many instances, a means of earthing for an electrical installation. However, ensuring an installation is adequately connected to Earth is always the responsibility of the installation owner, who usually delegates the task to an electrical contractor. For first-time supplies, the electricity distributor is obliged under the Electricity Safety, Quality and Continuity Regulations 2002 (as amended) to make available an earthing facility for the consumer's installation, unless there are reasons of safety which preclude such a provision.

The designer of an electrical installation, or of any alteration or addition to an installation, is responsible for assessing the intended means of earthing, by inspection, testing and, where appropriate, enquiry to the distributor, to ensure that it is suitable for the needs of the installation in terms of safety (Regulations 132.16 and 313.1 refer).

Earthing conductor and connections

The earthing conductor is the protective conductor which connects the Main Earthing Terminal (MET) of the installation to the means of earthing (e.g. the installation earth electrode for a TT system). The earthing conductor is a vitally important part of the earth fault loop path, and it must be confirmed by inspection that the earthing conductor is present and properly connected. The inspection must also confirm that the earthing conductor has a cross-sectional area of at least that required by *BS 7671*. Testing alone is not sufficient to determine that the earthing conductor has been correctly selected and installed.

The minimum cross-sectional area of the earthing conductor should have been determined by the designer in the same way as for any other protective conductor. This may have been by calculation, or by selection in accordance with Table 54.7 of *BS 7671*. Additionally, where the earthing conductor is buried in the ground, its cross-sectional area must not be less than that given in Table 54.1 of *BS 7671*.

If the cross-sectional area of the earthing conductor is less than that indicated in Table 54.7 (or Table 54.1, if applicable), the inspector should consult the designer to confirm the adequacy of the earthing conductor arrangement.

Presence of earthing conductor

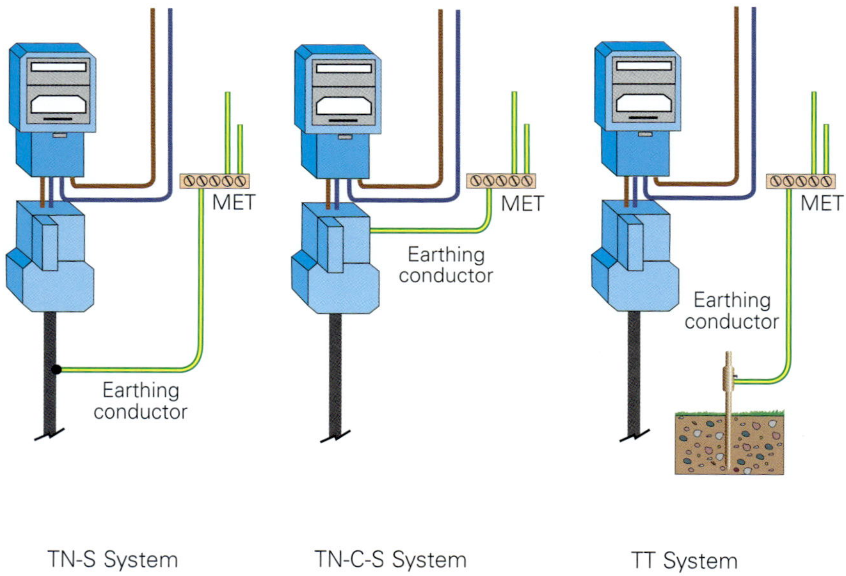

The earthing conductor connects the Main Earthing Terminal (MET) of an installation to the means of earthing.

Main protective bonding conductors and connections

Main protective bonding conductors are bonding conductors connecting the main earthing terminal of the installation to extraneous-conductive-parts entering the installation which may include:

- water installation pipes
- gas installation pipes
- other service pipework and ducting
- central heating and air conditioning systems
- exposed metallic structural parts of buildings
- a lightning protection system.

Where plumbing and/or wet central heating systems employ non-metallic pipework, it is difficult for the inspector to decide whether or not such pipework (or the liquid within it) constitutes an extraneous-conductive-part. For a new installation, cases of doubt should be referred to the installation designer for consideration and confirmation as to the requirement for main, and where applicable, supplementary bonding.

For an inspection of an existing installation, the inspector will need to make an assessment based on all the relevant circumstances. Guidance issued in the NICEIC/ELECSA publication *Connections* and *IET Guidance Note 8: Earthing and Bonding* give advice to help determine whether or not a conductive part is an extraneous-conductive-part.

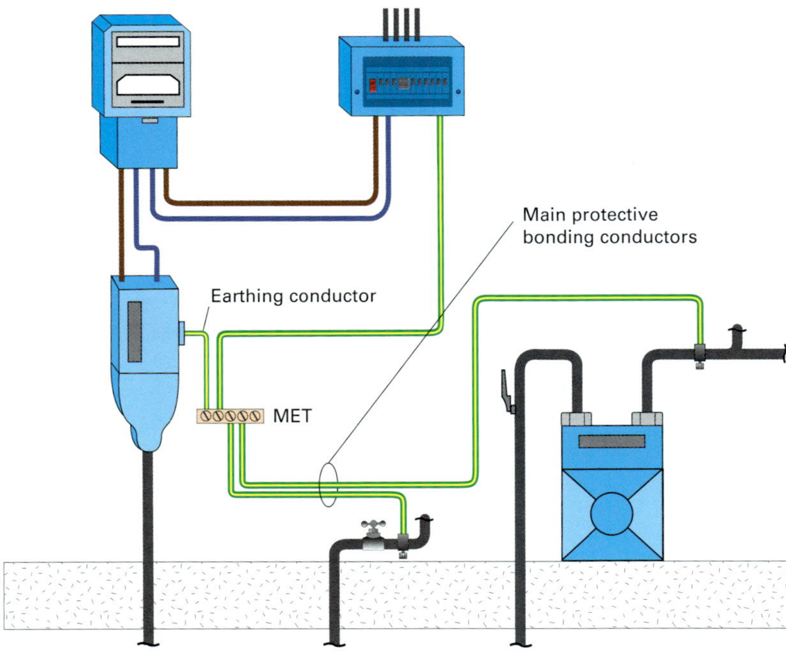

Except where Protective Multiple Earthing (PME) conditions apply, the cross-sectional area of main protective bonding conductors must be not less than half the cross-sectional area required by *BS 7671* for the earthing conductor, with a minimum of 6 mm^2. The cross-sectional area need not exceed 25 mm^2 if the bonding conductor is of copper. If the bonding conductor is not of copper, its cross-sectional area must be such that its conductance is not less than that of the required size of copper conductor.

For an installation connected to a PME supply (a TN-C-S system), the cross-sectional area of the main protective bonding conductors must be not less than that given in Table 54.8 of *BS 7671*. The data shown in this table are minimum cross-sectional areas of main protective bonding conductors. The electricity distributor may require a larger cross-sectional area in some instances.

In the case of a service pipe, the main protective bonding conductor should have been connected as near as practicable to the point at which the particular service enters the premises. The connection must be made on hard installation pipework, before any branch, on the consumer's side of any meter or insulating section. Where practicable, the connection should be made within 600 mm of the meter outlet. Where the meter is external, the bonding connection should be made at the point(s) of entry of the service into the building.

Minimum cross-sectional area (csa) of main protective bonding conductors for installations served by PME supplies

Copper equivalent csa of the supply neutral conductor	Minimum copper equivalent* csa of the main protective bonding conductors
35 mm^2 or less	10 mm^2
over 35 mm^2 up to 50 mm^2	16 mm^2
over 50 mm^2 up to 95 mm^2	25 mm^2
over 95 mm^2 up to 150 mm^2	35 mm^2
over 150 mm^2	50 mm^2

Notes:
The above data has been reproduced from Table 54.8 of *BS 7671* by kind permission of the IET. This Table should be used as a guide only. The specific advice of the electricity distributor should always be sought if any doubt exists as to their requirements.

* The minimum copper equivalent cross-sectional area is given by a copper bonding conductor of the tabulated cross-sectional area or a bonding conductor of another metal affording equivalent conductance.

Where the inspector finds, in an existing installation, that the main protective bonding conductors have a cross-sectional area of say 6 mm^2, rather than (say) 10 mm^2 as required by *BS 7671*, the inspector may, having carefully considered all the circumstances, conclude that the deficiency does not pose a serious risk to the users. For example, where the installation has been modified by an addition or alteration, and where the existing protective bonding satisfies the requirements of *BS 7671* except in terms of cross-sectional area and colour-coding, it may have been reasonable for the designer to have relied on that bonding as part of the protective measures for that addition or alteration. However, the deficiency must be recorded, together with the reasons why the inspector has concluded that the deficiency does not pose a serious risk to the users and an appropriate recommendation, on the Electrical Installation Certificate, Domestic Electrical Installation Certificate or *Minor Electrical Installation Works Certificate*, as appropriate.

This dispensation is not applicable to a new installation, including a rewire. Neither is the dispensation applicable to an existing installation served by a PME supply which was commenced, or in certain cases has been worked upon, by the electricity distributor on or after 1 October 1988. Even where a PME supply was commenced before this date, careful consideration should be given to any decision to rely on existing main protective bonding conductors with cross-sectional areas less than that required by Table 54.8 of *BS 7671.* There is always the possibility that main protective bonding conductors may have to carry network circulating currents continuously or for long periods.

Earthing/bonding labels at all appropriate locations

In accordance with Regulation 514.13.1, a permanent label to *BS 951* with the words 'Safety Electrical Connection - Do Not Remove' must be permanently fixed in a position at or near:

- The connection of an earthing conductor to an installation earth electrode.
- The connection of a protective bonding conductor to an extraneous-conductive-part.
- The main earthing terminal, where it is separate from the main switchgear.

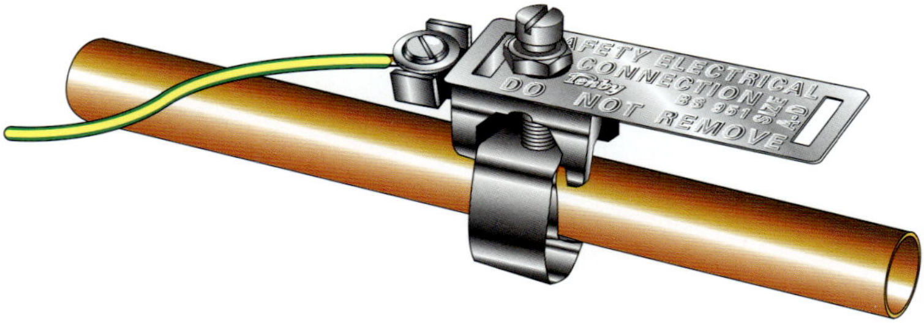

Accessibility of earthing/bonding connections

Inspection should confirm that all earthing and protective bonding connections are accessible for the purposes of inspection and testing, and to facilitate maintenance and repair.

Functional Extra-Low Voltage (FELV) – requirements satisfied

A functional extra-low voltage system is a system where not all of the protective measures required for SELV and PELV have been applied. A FELV system may be used for both basic and fault protection provided the following have been applied:

- Basic protection is provided by basic insulation of live parts and/or barriers or enclosures.
- Fault protection - the exposed-conductive-parts of the equipment of the FELV circuit are connected to the protective conductor of the primary circuit of the source. The primary circuit is to have automatic disconnection of supply.

The inspector should check that the protective provisions for basic and fault protection and the other requirements detailed in Section 411.7 have been provided.

Reduced low voltage requirements (RLV) – requirements satisfied

Where an RLV system is installed the inspector should confirm the requirements for fault and basic protection are satisfied in accordance with Section 411.8. In particular, it should be confirmed that any connecting method, such as a plug, socket or other connecting device forming part of a reduced low voltage system is not dimensionally compatible with those of any other system present in the installation.

4.0 Basic Protection

Presence and adequacy of protective measures to provide basic protection

Insulation of live parts

Inspection of this protective provision includes checking that live parts are completely covered with insulation. When inspecting equipment, the insulation must comply with the relevant standard for such electrical equipment. Basic insulation is intended to prevent contact with live parts.

Paint, varnish, lacquer or similar products are generally not considered to provide adequate insulation for basic protection in normal service.

Barriers or enclosures

An understanding of *BS EN 60529: Specification for degrees of protection provided by enclosures (IP code)*, and of the particular requirements of *BS 7671*, is required for the inspection of barriers and enclosures. For the purpose of this book, however, the basic requirements are that:

- Barriers or enclosures containing live parts must provide a degree of protection of at least IP2X or IPXXB (with certain exceptions).
  - IP2X means no contact with live parts by a British Standard test finger having a diameter of 12 mm and 80 mm long, and that the enclosure will not permit the insertion of any object 12.5 mm or more in diameter.
  - IPXXB means no contact with hazardous parts is possible with a British Standard test finger having a diameter of 12 mm and 80 mm long.

A barrier provides protection from contact with live parts from any usual direction of access; an enclosure provides protection from contact with live parts from any direction.

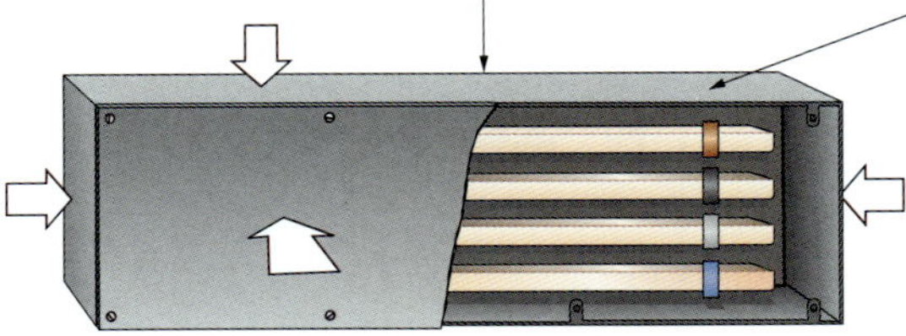

Protection by enclosures

International Protection (IP) Code

FIRST NUMERAL		SECOND NUMERAL	
a PROTECTION OF PERSONS AGAINST CONTACT WITH HAZARDOUS PARTS INSIDE ENCLOSURE b PROTECTION OF EQUIPMENT AGAINST INGRESS OF SOLID BODIES AND DUST		PROTECTION OF EQUIPMENT AGAINST INGRESS OF WATER	
No./ SYMBOL	**DEGREE OF PROTECTION**	**No./ SYMBOL**	**DEGREE OF PROTECTION**
0	a No special protection. b No special protection.	**0**	No special protection.
1	a Protection against accidental or inadvertent contact by a large surface of the body, e.g. hand, but not against deliberate access. b Protection against ingress of large solid objects >50mm diameter.	**1**	Protection against drops of water. Drops of water falling on enclosure shall have no harmful effect.
2	a Protection against contact by standard finger. b Protection against ingress of medium size bodies >12mm diameter or not longer than 80mm.	**2**	**Drip Proof**:- Protection against water. Vertically dripping water shall have no harmful effect when the enclosure is tilted at any angle up to 15° from the vertical.
3	a Protection against contact by tools, wires or suchlike more than 2.5mm thick. b Protection against ingress of solid objects >2.5mm.	**3**	**Rain Proof**:- Water falling as rain at any angle up to 60° from vertical shall have no harmful effect.
4	a As 3 above but against contact by wires of 1 mm diameter. b Protection against ingress of small foreign bodies.	**4**	**Splash Proof**:- Water splashed from any direction shall have no harmful effect.
5	a As 4 above. b DUSTPROOF:- Protection against harmful deposits of dust. Dust may enter but not in amount sufficient to interfere with satisfactory operation.	**5**	**Jet Proof**:- Water projected by a nozzle from any direction (under stated conditions) shall have no harmful effect.
6	a As 4 above. b DUST-TIGHT No ingress of dust.	**6**	**Watertight Equipment**:- Protection against conditions on ships decks, etc. Water from heavy seas or power jets shall not enter the enclosures under prescribed conditions.
IP CODE NOTES - Degree of protection is stated in form IPXX. - Protection against contact or ingress of water respectively is specified by replacing first or second X by digit number tabled e.g. -IP2X defines an enclosure giving protection against finger contact but without any specific protection against ingress of water or liquid.		**7**	**Protection Against Immersion in Water**:- It shall not be possible for water to enter the enclosure under stated conditions of pressure and time.
		8	**Protection Against Indefinite Immersion in Water Under Specified Pressure**:- It shall not be possible for water to enter the enclosure, to harmful effect.

Note - Use this table for General Guidance only - refer to BS EN 60529:1992 for full information on degrees of protection provided by enclosures.

Distribution board having bare live parts placed behind barriers

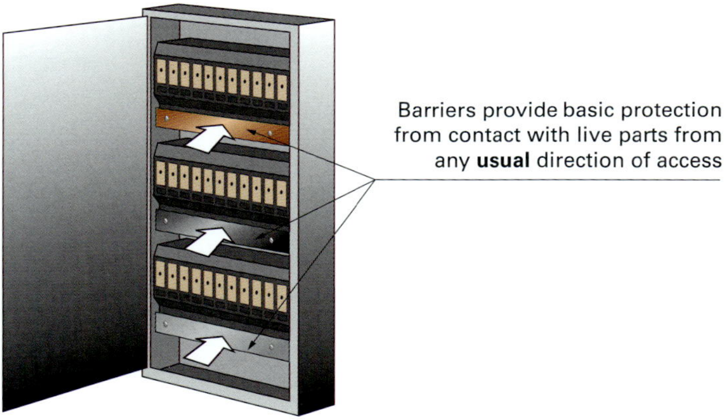

Protection by barriers

- The horizontal top surface of a barrier or enclosure which is readily accessible must provide a degree of protection of at least IP4X or IPXXD.
  - IP4X means at no point on the surface must the insertion of a wire or object having a diameter 1 mm or greater be possible, and that the enclosure will not permit the ingress of small foreign bodies.
  - IPXXD means that no contact with hazardous parts is possible with a wire or object having a diameter of 1 mm and length of 150 mm.

The letter 'X' in these IP Codes indicates that no particular degree of protection against ingress of liquids has been specified. It does not necessarily mean that no such protection is provided.

Generally, it should be possible to confirm by thorough visual inspection alone that barriers and enclosures provide the necessary minimum degree of protection against the ingress of solid objects. For example, it should be verified that all unused entries in enclosures have been closed, and that no blanks are missing from spare ways in consumer units and distribution boards.

Obstacles and placing out of reach

Obstacles

An obstacle can be as simple as a set of railings, the *BS 7671* definition being 'a part preventing unintentional contact with live parts but not preventing deliberate contact'. An obstacle may be removed without the use of a tool or key, but it should be secured so as to prevent unintentional removal. This protective measure may be used only in locations to which access is restricted to persons under the supervision of a skilled person. The presence of warning notices associated with such restriction must be verified.

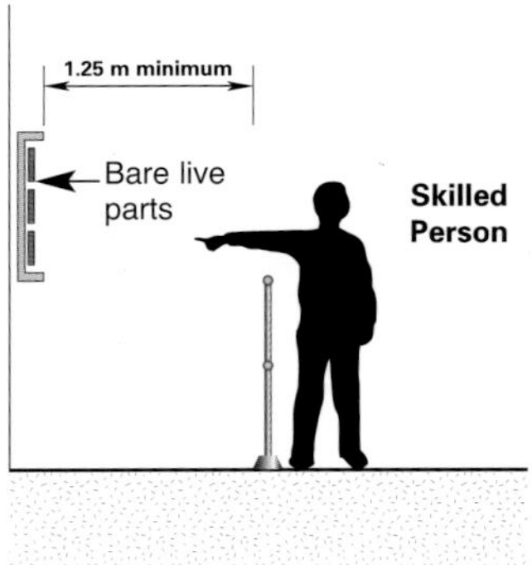

Placing out of reach

This protective measure is intended to prevent unintentional contact with a bare live part by placing it out of reach. The measure may be used only in locations which are under the control of skilled persons. The presence of such restriction must be verified.

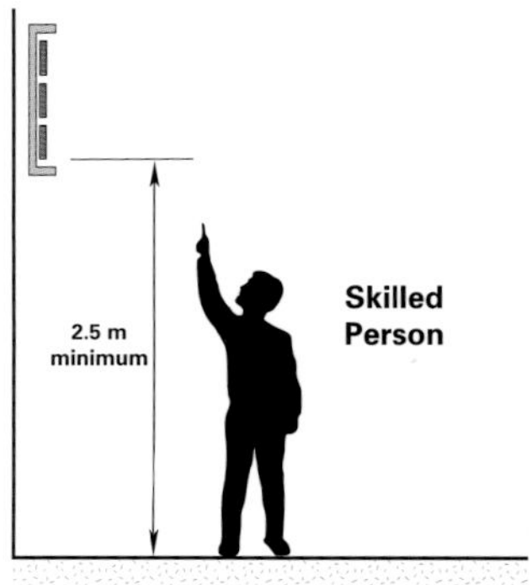

Inspection of this protective measure will include verifying that the minimum clearance distances satisfy the definition of 'arms reach' given in Regulation group 417.3 and Fig 417 of *BS 7671*. Where long or bulky objects, such as aluminium ladders or scaffold poles, are likely to be handled in the location and there is a risk of contact with live parts, the designer should have allowed for suitably increased clearance distances, and the continued maintenance of such increased distances must be verified by inspection.

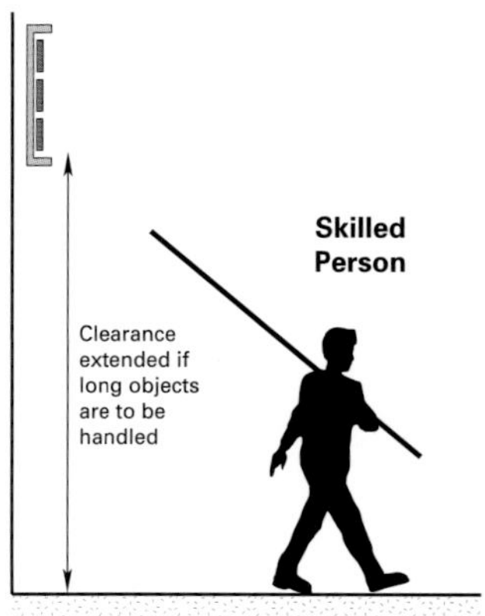

5.0 Additional Protection

Presence and effectiveness of additional protection methods used

Presence of 30 m A RCD protection

The inspector should check that additional protection has been provided by an RCD having the operating characteristics given in Regulation 415.1.1 for the following, as required by *BS 7671*, (Regulation 411.3.3 refers):

i) Socket-outlets with a rated current not exceeding 20 A.

ii) Mobile equipment with a current rating not exceeding 32 A for use outdoors.

Exceptions to (i) are permitted under the following conditions:

- For an installation other than a dwelling where a documented risk assessment has determined that the provision of additional protection is unnecessary, or
- for a specific labelled or otherwise suitably identified socket-outlet provided for connection of a particular item of equipment, such as a freezer.

RCDs are also required to provide additional protection for concealed cables as specified in Regulation Group 522.6, and at designated points or circuits in the special installations or locations covered by Part 7 of *BS 7671*.

Each RCD provided for additional protection should be inspected to confirm that it has a rated residual operating current ($I_{\Delta n}$) not exceeding 30 mA and must be tested to confirm that its operating time does not exceed 40 ms at a residual current of 5 $I_{\Delta n}$. An RCD must not be used as the sole means of protection against electric shock (see Regulation 415.1.2), one or more of the protective measures covered in this Chapter must also be provided.

Inspection should verify that the number of points or circuits controlled by a single RCD are such that the operation of that RCD would not result in unreasonable hazards or inconvenience (Regulation 314.1 refers).

Presence of supplementary bonding

The requirement for supplementary equipotential bonding (see Regulation 415.2) is generally applicable only to installations and locations where there is an increased risk of electric shock. Supplementary equipotential bonding is required as additional protection for several of the locations and installations covered by Part 7 of *BS 7671*, the most common of these being locations containing a bath or shower. In some circumstances the designer may decide that an increased risk of electric shock exists, which warrants the provision of supplementary equipotential bonding.

6.0 Other methods of protection

The presence and effectiveness of other methods of protection against electric shock

Basic and fault protection

Separated Extra Low Voltage (SELV)

Inspection of this protective measure includes checking that the system source is suitable. Several types of source for SELV systems are recognised by *BS 7671*, but the most common is a safety isolating transformer complying with *BS EN 61558-2-6*, having no connection to Earth on the secondary extra-low voltage winding. Such transformers are designed to provide an output of no more than 50 V a.c.

Other types of source for SELV systems recognised in *BS 7671* are:

- A motor-driven generator in which the windings provide separation equivalent to double or reinforced insulation.
- An electrochemical source, such as a battery, or another source independent of a higher voltage circuit, such as an engine-driven generator.
- Certain electronic devices which meet the constraints laid down in *BS 7671* and which are deemed to be suitable for the purpose.

A socket-outlet on a SELV circuit must be dimensionally incompatible with those used for other systems. Additionally, live parts of a SELV circuit, including the transformer secondary winding and socket-outlets, must have no connection to Earth, or to a live part, or to any protective conductor forming part of another electrical system.

Protective Extra-Low Voltage (PELV)

A PELV system is similar to a SELV system, except that the extra-low voltage circuit is generally connected to Earth at one point. This means that a PELV system will not be suitable in situations where a SELV system has been specified, such as for certain zones of a swimming pool. The visual inspection should therefore confirm that a PELV (Protective Extra-Low Voltage) system (i.e. an Extra-low Voltage (ELV) system which is not electrically separated from Earth but does otherwise comply with the requirements for a SELV system) is not installed in a location where the design specifically requires a SELV system (as may be the case for a special installation or location in Part 7 of *BS 7671*).

SELV

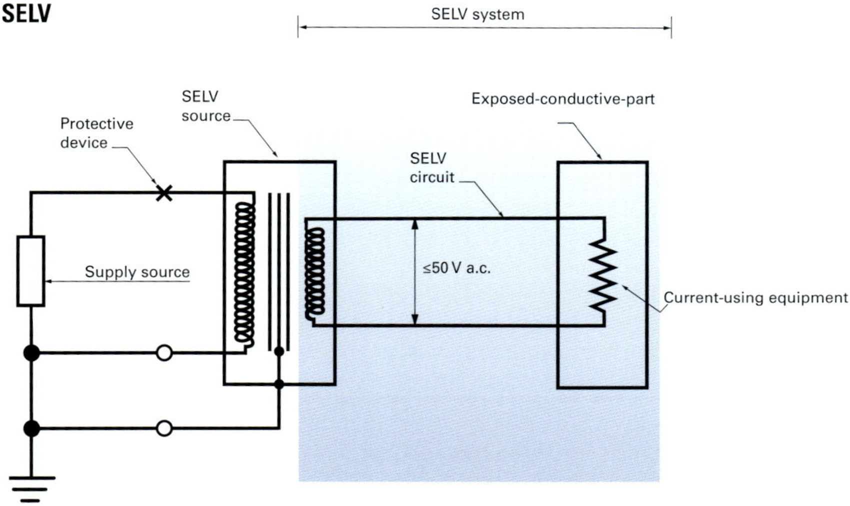
SELV system
SELV
source
Protective
device
Exposed-conductive-part
SELV
circuit
Supply source
≤50 V a.c.
Current-using equipment

PELV

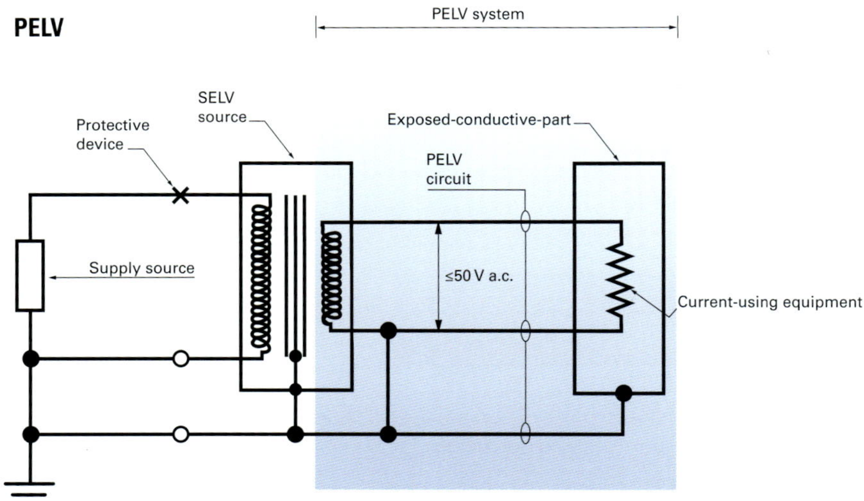
PELV system
SELV
source
Protective
device
Exposed-conductive-part
PELV
circuit
Supply source
≤50 V a.c.
Current-using equipment

Double or reinforced insulation

1. Basic protection is provided by basic insulation of live parts, and fault protection is provided by supplementary insulation, or
2. Both basic and fault protection are provided by reinforced insulation between live parts and accessible parts.

The protective measures of double or reinforced insulation are generally applicable in all situations, unless limitations are given in Part 7 of *BS 7671*. Where double or reinforced insulation is to be used as the sole protective measure (for example where the whole installation or circuit is intended to consist entirely of equipment with double insulation or reinforced insulation), to meet the requirements of Regulation 412.1.3, it must be verified that the installation or circuit concerned will be under effective supervision in normal use. This is to prevent changes being made to the installation or circuit that could impair the effectiveness of the protective measure.

The protective measures of double insulation and reinforced insulation must not be applied to any circuit that includes a socket-outlet, luminaire supporting coupler (LSC), a device for connecting a luminaire (DCL) or cable coupler, where the user might change items of equipment without authorisation.

Double Insulation

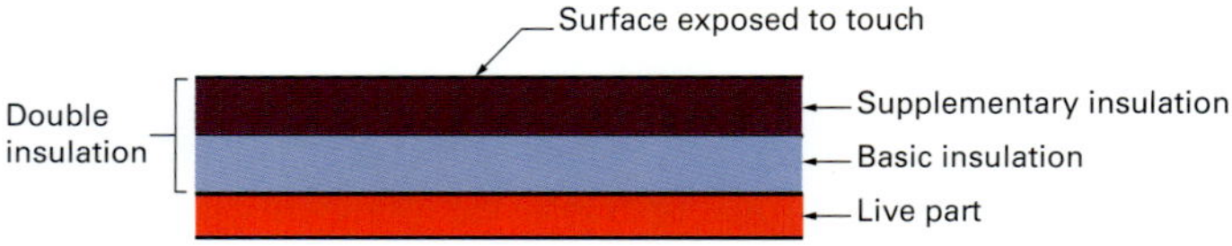

Reinforced Insulation

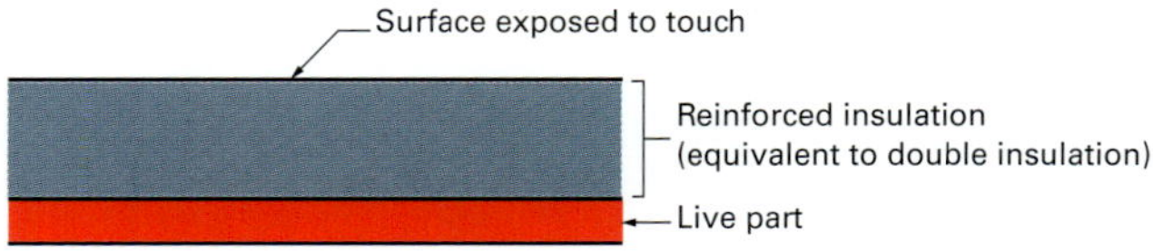

Note: Reinforced insulation may in practice, comprise two or more layers which are incapable of being tested separately.

The terms basic insulation, double insulation, reinforced insulation and supplementary insulation are all defined in Part 2 of *BS 7671*.

Electrical separation for one item of equipment

Electrical separation is a protective measure that may be applied to circuits operating at a voltage of up to 500 V. It should not be confused with extra-low voltage systems, SELV or PELV.

Electrical separation is a protective measure in which:

- Basic protection is provided by basic insulation of live parts or by barriers or enclosures in accordance with Section 416 of *BS 7671*. Inspection of these provisions should be carried out as discussed earlier in this chapter.
- Fault protection is provided by simple separation of the separated circuit from other circuits and from Earth. The inspector should check that the requirements of Regulations 413.3.2 to 413.3.6 are met in order to establish that this is the case.

Particular attention should be given to checking the following:

- The separated circuit is supplied from a source of supply with at least simple separation. This could for example be a double-wound transformer the secondary winding of which is not earthed.
- That no live part is connected at any point to another circuit or to Earth, or to a protective conductor either deliberately or unintentionally, as could occur due to a damaged cable.
- Flexible cables liable to mechanical damage are visible throughout their length.
- The wiring comprises either a separate wiring system (preferably) or one of the alternatives given in Regulation 413.3.5 (such as suitable cables in insulating conduit); the rated voltage is not less than the highest nominal voltage; overcurrent protection is provided; and electrical separation from other circuits is provided – see Chapter 9 (Testing).

Where electrical separation is used to supply an individual item of equipment, the inspector should verify that no exposed-conductive-part of the separated circuit, such as any metal casing of an item of equipment fed by the circuit, is connected to the protective conductor or exposed-conductive-parts of another circuit, or to Earth.

Fault protection

Non-conducting location/Earth-free local equipotential bonding

These two protective measures, although included in *BS 7671*, are not recognised as being suitable for common use. They are intended to be applied only in special situations where effective supervision is provided, and their use is prohibited in certain installations and locations of increased shock risk as covered in Part 7 of *BS 7671*.

NICEIC APPROVED CONTRACTOR

This certificate is not valid if the serial number has been defaced or altered **ICN4/**

Original (To the person ordering the work)

SCHEDULE OF ITEMS INSPECTED

† See note below

1.0 CONDITION OF ELECTRICAL INTAKE EQUIPMENT (the Distributor should be notified of any unsatisfactory equipment)

1.1	Service cable	
1.2	Service head	
1.3	Distributor's earthing arrangement	
1.4	Meter tails - Distributor/Consumer	
1.5	Metering equipment	
1.6	Isolator	

2.0 PARALLEL OR SWITCHED ALTERNATIVE SOURCES OF SUPPLY

2.1	Presence of adequate arrangements where generator to operate as a switched alternative	
	a) Dedicated earthing arrangement independent of that of the public supply	
2.2	Presence of adequate arrangements where generator to operate in parallel with public supply system	
	a) Correct connection of generator in parallel	
	b) Compatibility of characteristics of means of generation	
	c) Means to provide automatic disconnection of generator in the event of loss of public supply system or voltage or frequency deviation beyond declared values	
	d) Means to prevent connection of generator in the event of loss of public supply system or voltage or frequency deviation beyond declared values	
	e) Means to isolate generator from the public supply system	
2.3	Presence of alternative/additional supply warning notices at:	
	a) The origin	
	b) The meter position, if remote from origin	
	c) The consumer unit/distribution board to which the alternative/additional sources are connected	
	d) All points of isolation of ALL sources of supply	

3.0 AUTOMATIC DISCONNECTION OF SUPPLY

3.1	Presence and adequacy of protective earthing/ bonding arrangements as follows:	
	a) Distributor's earthing arrangement or installation earth electrode arrangement	
	b) Earthing conductor and connections	
	c) Main protective bonding conductors and connections	
	d) Earthing/bonding labels at all appropriate locations	
3.2	Accessibility of:	
	a) Earthing conductor connections	
	b) All protective bonding connections	
3.3	FELV – requirements satisfied	
3.4	Reduced low voltage – requirements satisfied	

4.0 BASIC PROTECTION

4.1	Presence and adequacy of protective measures to provide basic protection	
	a) Insulation of live parts	
	b) Barriers or enclosures	
	c) Obstacles**	
	d) Placing out of reach**	

5.0 ADDITIONAL PROTECTION

5.1	The presence and effectiveness of additional protection methods used, as follows:	
	a) RCDs not exceeding 30 mA operating current	
	b) Supplementary bonding	

6.0 OTHER METHODS OF PROTECTION (insert location in box provided)

The presence and effectiveness of other methods of protection against electric shock where used, as follows:

			LOCATION
6.1	Basic and fault protection		
	a) SELV		
	b) PELV		
	c) Double insulation/ Reinforced insulation		
	d) Electrical separation for one item of equipment		
6.2	Fault protection		
	a) Non-conducting location/Earth-free local equipotential bonding**		
	b) Electrical separation for more than one item of equipment**		

7.0 DISTRIBUTION EQUIPMENT

7.1	Adequacy of working space/accessibility	
7.2	Security of fixing	
7.3	Insulation of live parts not damaged during erection	
7.4	Adequacy / security of barriers	
7.5	Suitability of enclosures for IP and fire ratings	
7.6	Enclosures not damaged during installation	
7.7	Presence and effectiveness of obstacles	
7.8	Presence of main switch(es), linked where required	
7.9	Operation of main switch(es) (functional check)	
7.10	Operation of circuit-breakers and RCDs to prove functionality	
7.11	RCD(s) provided for fault protection, where specified	
7.12	RCD(s) provided for protection against fire	
7.13	RCD(s) provided for additional protection, where specified	
7.14	Confirmation overvoltage protection (SPDs) provided where specified	
7.15	Confirmation of indication that SPD is functional	
7.16	Presence of RCD quarterly test notice at or near the origin	
7.17	Presence of diagrams, charts or schedules at or near each distribution board, where required	
7.18	Presence of non-standard (mixed) cable colour warning notice at or near the appropriate distribution board, where required	
7.19	Presence of next inspection recommendation label	
7.20	Presence of other required labelling	
7.21	Selection of protective device(s) and base(s); correct type and rating	
7.22	Single-pole protective devices in line conductor only	
7.23	Protection against mechanical damage where cables enter equipment	
7.24	Protection against electromagnetic effects where cables enter ferromagnetic enclosures	
7.25	Confirmation that ALL conductor connections, including connections to busbars are correctly located in terminals and are tight and secure	

8.0 CIRCUITS

8.1	Identification of conductors	
8.2	Cables correctly supported throughout their length	
8.3	Examination of cables for signs of mechanical damage during installation	
8.4	Examination of insulation of live parts, not damaged during erection	

** *For use in controlled supervised/conditions only*

† ***All boxes must be completed.*** *'✓' indicates that an inspection was carried out and that the result was* ***satisfactory****. 'N/A' indicates that an inspection was* ***not applicable*** *to the particular installation.*

* *Where the electrical work to which this certificate relates includes the installation of a fire alarm system and/or an emergency lighting system (or a part of such systems), this electrical safety certificate should be accompanied by the particular certificate(s) for the system(s).*

Page 3 of

This certificate is based on the model forms shown in Appendix 6 of BS 7671

ICN4/5

Owing to their specialised nature and comparative rarity of application, these protective measures are not included within the scope of this book.

Reference should be made to Section 418 of *BS 7671* for the main requirements relating to protection by non-conducting location and Earth-free equipotential bonding. Some guidance on the particular requirements for inspection and testing for these protective measures is given in IET *Guidance Note 3*.

Use of electrical separation to supply more than one item of equipment

The use of electrical separation to supply several items of equipment from a single source is recognised in *BS 7671* for applications where the installation is controlled or under the supervision of skilled or instructed persons. To meet the requirements of *BS 7671* for protection by electrical separation for the supply to more than one item of equipment, compliance with Regulation Group 418.3 is required.

7.0 Distribution equipment

Adequacy of working space/accessibility

It must be confirmed that adequate and safe means of access and working space have been afforded to every piece of electrical equipment and switchgear to facilitate operation, inspection, testing, fault detection, maintenance and repair.

Section 729 in Part 7 of *BS 7671* contains requirements for operating and maintenance gangways, locations to which access is restricted to skilled or instructed persons only. It states the

- minimum acceptable clearances that are applicable where basic protection is provided by barriers or enclosures or by obstacles
- acceptable arrangements for access to gangways
- minimum passing widths between electrical equipment and walls

Each of the above, where relevant, may be confirmed by inspection.

Security of fixing

Inspection should confirm that all installed equipment is securely fixed using appropriate methods and taking into account the equipment manufacturers instructions.

Insulation of live parts not damaged during erection

It is important to recognise that the risk of mechanical damage and other damaging influences such as dust and water may be greater during the construction process than when the installation is in service. Consequently, the inspector should confirm that insulation intended to protect against contact with live parts has not been impaired during construction of the installation.

Adequacy/security of barriers

It should be verified that barriers intended to prevent contact with live parts are present and undamaged. For example, consumer units and distribution boards should be checked to confirm that blanks have been inserted in all spare ways and all unused entries have been suitably closed.

Suitability of enclosures for IP and fire ratings

Inspection should confirm that enclosures provide the necessary minimum degree of protection against the ingress of solid objects and liquids (see 4.0 Basic Protection).

The inspector should seek to confirm that the enclosures of installed distribution equipment and switchgear comply with the appropriate British Standard or equivalent, and are suitable for the particular location.

Where a consumer unit is installed in a domestic premises it should be confirmed that the unit and assembly complies with *BS EN 61439-3* and is made of non-combustible material (metal is an example of non-combustible material) or located in an enclosure constructed of non-combustible material (Regulation 421.1.201 refers).

The requirements of Regulation 421.1.201 are to be implemented on 1st January 2016, whilst this does not preclude compliance with this regulation prior to this date.

For purposes of protection against fire and thermal effects, every joint or connection in a live conductor or PEN conductor must be made in an enclosure complying with the requirements of Section 526 of *BS 7671*. It should be noted that this requirement applies not only to connections in low voltage circuits, but also those in extra-low voltage circuits. The enclosure must also provide adequate protection against mechanical damage and any other external influence or stress to which it may be subjected.

Enclosures not damaged during Installation

The risk of mechanical damage to enclosures is greater during the construction process than when the installation is in service. Consequently, inspection should confirm that enclosures have not been cracked, broken or otherwise impaired.

Presence and effectiveness of obstacles

Where used, the inspector should verify that the obstacle has been properly secured to prevent unintentional contact with live parts, and is located in an area that is controlled or supervised by skilled persons (Section 417 of *BS 7671*).

Presence of main switch(es), linked where required

The inspector should confirm that the installation has a main linked switch or linked circuit-breaker positioned as near as practicable to the origin (Regulation 537.1.4). This is intended as a means of switching the supply on load, and as a means of isolation. Where the installation is supplied from more than one source (such as where a microgenerator is installed), a main switch or main circuit-breaker is required for each source together with a durable notice to warn persons that may need to isolate the installation (Regulation 537.1.6).

The inspector should verify the presence of the correct number of poles in the main switch or circuit-breaker, and where the main switch is intended for operation by ordinary persons, as will be the case in domestic or similar installations, it should be confirmed that the main switch interrupts both the line and neutral conductors of a single-phase supply (Regulation 537.1.4 refers).

Functional check of circuit-breakers and RCDs

The satisfactory operation of all circuit-breakers and RCDs should be confirmed.

Provision of RCD(s)

Provision of RCD(s), including RCBO(s), to provide fault, fire or additional protection should be verified.

Where an RCD is used to provide earth fault protection in an installation having a TT earthing arrangement the inspector should confirm that overcurrent protection is provided in accordance with Chapter 43 of *BS 7671*, and the conditions specified in Regulation 411.5.3 are satisfied.

Where the earth fault loop impedance (Z_s) of the final circuit protected by the RCD meets the requirements of Table 41.5 of *BS 7671* the requirements of Regulation 411.5.3 are met.

Where an RCD is used to provide protection against fire such as, for example, for a wiring system installed in a location with an increased risk of fire due to the nature of processed or stored materials (Section 422.3 of *BS 7671*) the inspector should confirm that the type and rating of the installed RCD, or RCBO, is suitable (Regulation 422.3.9 refers).

Where the design requires additional protection to be provided, each RCD, or RCBO, should be inspected to confirm that it has a rated residual operating current ($I_{\Delta n}$) not exceeding 30 mA and that it meets a product standard which requires the device to operate under type-test conditions within 40 ms at a residual current of 5 $I_{\Delta n}$ (Regulation 415.1.1 refers).

Overvoltage protection

Where protection against overvoltage is provided by surge protective devices (SPDs), the inspector should confirm such devices are installed in accordance with Regulation 534.2.1 and remain functional (Regulation 534.2.8 refers). Details on protection against overvoltage are contained in Section 534 and Appendix 16 of *BS 7671*.

Presence of RCD quarterly test notice at or near the origin

The presence of a notice at (or near) the origin of an installation which incorporates one or more residual current devices should be confirmed (Regulation 514.12.2 refers).

> This installation, or part of it, is protected by a device which automatically switches off the supply if an earth fault develops. Test quarterly by pressing the button marked 'T' or 'Test'. The device should switch off the supply and should then be switched on to restore the supply. If the device does not switch off the supply when the button is pressed, seek expert advice.

Presence of circuit charts or schedules,

The presence of the necessary diagrams, charts or tables, as required by Regulation 514.9.1 of *BS 7671*, or an equivalent form of information for the work being inspected, should be verified. The form of information should be legible and durable, and should indicate all of the following.

- The type and composition of each circuit (that is, the points of utilisation served, number and size of conductors, type of wiring)
- The method used for compliance with Regulation 410.3.2 (that is, the protective measures used for basic and fault protection)
- The information necessary for the identification of each device performing the functions of protection, isolation and switching, and its location
- Any circuit or equipment vulnerable to a typical test.

For an installation for which the issue of a Domestic Electrical Installation Certificate has been appropriate, an additional copy of the completed schedules comprising the fourth page of the certificate, fixed within or adjacent to the consumer unit, is likely to provide most of the above information necessary for compliance with *BS 7671*. For other simple installations, an additional copy of the 'Schedule of Circuit Details', which forms part of the Electrical Installation Certificate, is likely to serve the same purpose. More complex installations will require more comprehensive information. In all cases, each switchboard, distribution board and consumer unit should have a copy of the relevant installation details provided in or adjacent to it.

Presence of non-standard (mixed) cable colour warning notice

In accordance with Regulation 514.14.1, if wiring alterations, additions, extensions or repairs are made to an installation such that some of the wiring uses the new or harmonised colours and there is also wiring to previous versions of *BS 7671*, a warning notice must be fixed at or near the appropriate distribution board or consumer unit (see 8.0 - Identification of conductors)

Presence of next inspection recommendation label

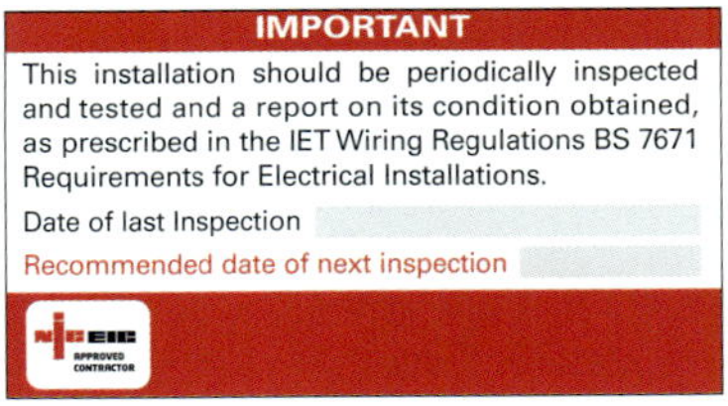

A label should be fitted on completion of installation work (including alterations and additions) and on each completion of periodic inspection, in a prominent position at or near the origin, giving the recommended date by which the installation should be re-inspected (Regulation 514.12.1 refers).

Presence of other required labelling

The inspector should verify that all relevant warning notices and labels have been fitted in the appropriate locations, in accordance with Section 514 of *BS 7671*.

The most commonly required notices are as follows:

- Alternative supplies (covered in 2.0 - Parallel or switched alternative sources of supply)
- Earthing and bonding labels (covered in 3.0 - Automatic disconnection of supply)
- Voltage warning (Regulation 514.10.1)

This warning is to be visible before gaining access to live parts in an enclosure where a nominal voltage exceeding 230 V to earth exists but would not normally be expected.

- High protective conductor currents (Regulation 543.7.1.205)

Where a circuit has, or is likely to have, a high protective conductor current, information should be provided at the distribution board or consumer unit indicating the circuit having or likely to have a high protective conductor current and such information must be so positioned as to be visible to a person modifying or extending the circuit.

Labelling of protective devices, switches and terminals

Each fuse, circuit-breaker and RCD should be checked to ensure that:

- it is arranged and identified so that the circuit protected may be easily recognised, and
- its rated current is indicated on or adjacent to it.

For protective devices incorporated in a distribution board, the above details may be given on the chart within or adjacent to the board, provided the devices themselves are identified and arranged to correspond with the chart.

- Switches etc:

The inspector should verify that, except where there is no possibility of confusion, each item of switching apparatus for operation, regulation or other control has a label or other suitable means of identification to indicate its purpose and the installation, or circuit, it controls.

This isolator disconnects the supply to **No 1 BUCKET ELEVATOR**	**No 1 BUCKET ELEVATOR** The isolator for this machine is situated in Plant Room B

Selection of protective device(s) and base(s): correct type and rating

This item is concerned with fuses, circuit-breakers, RCDs and any current monitoring relays which control separate circuit-breakers. Their rated current, settings (where applicable) and characteristics must be checked to verify conformity with the design information for the installation.

For each fuse and circuit-breaker, a check should be made of not only the rated current and the time/current characteristics but also the type (such as gG for a fuse to *BS EN 88-2* and *BS 88-3*, or Type B for a circuit-breaker to *BS EN 60898*).

It should be noted that on some circuit-breakers, both the time/current characteristics and the rated current are adjustable. These must be checked against the design information.

For each RCD, a check should be made of the rated residual operating current. The time/residual current characteristics should also be checked where the device is to be used for additional protection, or where an intended time delay is incorporated.

Single-pole protective devices in line conductor only

Inspection should confirm that all single-pole switching and control devices are connected in the line conductor only. No single-pole switching device, circuit-breaker, fuse or solid link which can be removed without the use of a tool or key or the like should interrupt or control the neutral. This check is made in addition to the polarity testing carried out later.

Protection against mechanical damage where cables enter equipment

Cables entering metal enclosures should not be exposed to strain or abrasion. In particular inspection should confirm, where necessary, that bushes and glands have been selected and installed correctly.

Protection against electromagnetic effects where cables enter ferromagnetic enclosures

Single cables of a.c. circuits run in steel conduit or any other form of steel enclosure should be installed so that all associated line, neutral and, where provided, separate protective conductors are together within the same enclosure. This requirement also applies to cables passing through holes in ferromagnetic enclosures (such as steel trunking). Single-core cables armoured with steel wire or tape are not permitted in a.c. circuits due to the adverse thermal and electromagnetic effects associated with such use.

Example of incorrect use of ferrous enclosures

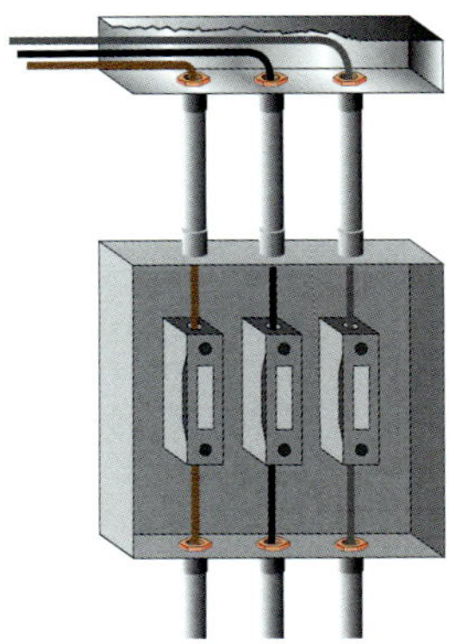

Warning!

This arrangement is
NOT
permitted

To avoid adverse electromagnetic effects, conductors of an a.c. circuit should not be installed in separate steel conduits (see Regulation 521.5.1).

Confirmation that ALL conductor connections, including connections to busbars are correctly located in terminals and are tight and secure

The consequences of loose or poorly terminated conductors can cause high resistance connections leading to arcing and in some cases fire. Therefore, the electrical and mechanical integrity of connections in consumer units/distribution boards and similar equipment should be checked and confirmed.

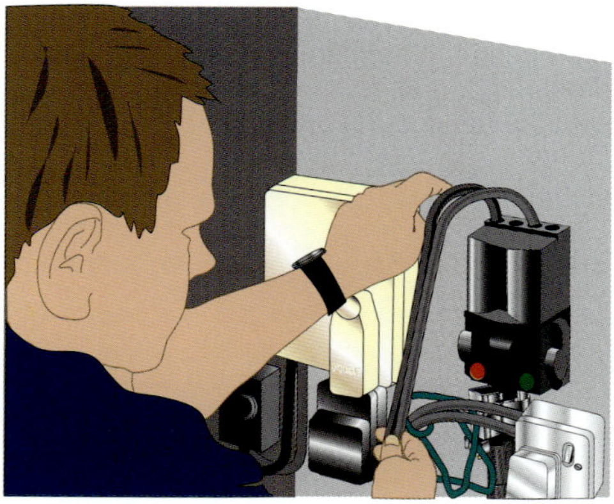

8.0 Circuits

Identification of conductors

The inspector should verify that, so far as is reasonably practicable, the wiring is arranged and/or marked so that it may be readily identified for the purposes of operation, inspection, testing, fault detection, maintenance and repair of the installation.

Taking a distribution board or consumer unit as an example, the wiring within the equipment should be identified by arrangement. This usually means connection of the neutral and cpc of each circuit to the terminals which relate specifically to the associated outgoing fuse or circuit-breaker, by sequence or terminal marking. Where the arrangement does not identify the wiring sufficiently, the terminations of the conductors should be marked with codings such as '1, 2, 3' or '1L1, 1L2, 1L3' etc, as appropriate. Similarly, conductors connected to a main earthing terminal which is separate from the main switchgear should be identified by arrangement or marking.

TABLE 51 - Identification of conductors

Function	Colour	Alpha numeric
Protective conductors	Green-and-yellow	
Functional earthing conductor	Cream	
a.c. power circuit[(1)]		
Line of single-phase circuit	Brown	L
Neutral of single- or three-phase circuit	Blue	N
Line 1 of three-phase circuit	Brown	L1
Line 2 of three-phase circuit	Black	L2
Line 3 of three-phase circuit	Grey	L3
Two-wire unearthed d.c. power circuit		
Positive of two-wire circuit	Brown	L+
Negative of two-wire circuit	Grey	L-
Two-wire earthed d.c. power circuit		
Positive (of negative earthed) circuit	Brown	L+
Negative (of negative earthed) circuit[(2)]	Blue	M
Positive (of positive earthed) circuit[(2)]	Blue	M
Negative (of positive earthed) circuit	Grey	L-
Three-wire d.c. power circuit		
Outer positive of two-wire circuit derived from three-wire system	Brown	L+
Outer negative of two-wire circuit derived from three-wire system	Grey	L-
Positive of three-wire circuit	Brown	L+
Mid-wire of three-wire circuit[(2)(3)]	Blue	M
Negative of three-wire circuit	Grey	L-
Control circuits, ELV and other applications		
Line conductor	Grey	L
Brown, Orange	White	
Black, Yellow	Pink, or	
Red, Violet	Turquoise	
Neutral or mid-wire[(4)]	Blue	N or M

NOTES: [(1)] Power circuits include lighting circuits.
[(2)] M identifies either the mid-wire of a three-wire d.c. circuit, or the earthed conductor of a two-wire earthed dc circuit.
[(3)] Only the middle wire of three-wire circuits may be earthed.
[(4)] An earthed PELV conductor is blue.

Identification of conductors

(Regulation Group 514.3 refers)

The correct identification of the conductors of cables, and of any bare conductors, in terms of their polarity or protective function, should be verified. This is in addition to the requirements for identification of terminals and connections referred to in the preceding paragraphs.

With certain permitted exceptions*, cores of cables must be identified by colour and/or lettering and/or numbering. Every core of a cable must be identifiable at its terminations and preferably throughout its length. Binding or sleeves used for identification must comply with *BS 3858* where appropriate (Regulations 514.3.1, 514.3.2 and 514.6.1 refer).

Identification by colour

Line conductors

For a single-phase installation where identification is to be by colour, the line conductors should be identified by the colour brown. For a three-phase installation where identification is by colour, the line conductors should be identified by the colours of brown, black and grey.

Neutral conductors

Where a circuit includes a neutral conductor which is identified by colour, the colour must be blue (Regulation 514.4.1).

Protective conductors

The colours of green-and-yellow must be used for protective conductors and must not be used for any other purpose (Regulation 514.4.2). The single colour green must not be used (Regulation 514.4.5). The combination of the colours must be such that one of the colours covers at least 30 % and at most 70 % of the surface, while the other colour must cover the remainder of the surface.

A bare conductor or busbar used as a protective conductor must be identified, where necessary, by equal green-and-yellow stripes, each not less than 15 mm and not more than 100 mm wide, close together, either throughout the length of the conductor or in each compartment and unit and at each accessible position.

* The permitted exceptions are concentric conductors of cables, metal sheath or armour of cables where used as a protective conductor, certain bare conductors where identification is not practicable, extraneous-conductive-parts used as a protective conductor and exposed-conductive-parts used as a protective conductor (Regulation 514.6.1).

Single-core cables that are coloured green-and-yellow throughout their length must only be used as a protective conductor and, unless they are PEN conductors, they must not be overmarked at their terminations (Regulations 514.4.2 and 514.4.3 refer).

Identification by lettering and/or numbering

Lettering and/or numbering must be in letters or Arabic numerals, must be clearly legible and durable and, in order to avoid confusion, unattached numerals 6 and 9 must be underlined (see Regulation 514.5.1). Where identification is by numbers, the number 0 (zero) is reserved for the neutral conductor (Regulation 514.5.4).

The identification of conductors is summarised in Table 51.

Bare conductors

A bare conductor must be identified, where necessary, by the application of tape, sleeve or disc or by painting with such a colour (Regulation 514.4.6 refers).

Older installations

Single-phase older installations are identified, in general, by the colours of red, black and green-and-yellow for the line, neutral and protective conductors respectively. Three-phase installations are identified by the colours of red, yellow, blue for the three line conductors and black and green-and-yellow for the neutral and protective conductors, respectively.

Except where there is no possibility of confusion, unambiguous marking must be provided at the interface between conductors identified in accordance with *BS 7671* (the 'new' colours) and wiring to previous versions of the Regulations (the 'old' colours).

In a single-phase installation at the wiring interface between new and old colours, providing the existing cables are correctly identified by the colours of red for the line conductor and black for the neutral conductor and the new cables are correctly identified by the colours of brown for the line conductor and blue for the neutral conductor then the extension, alteration, addition or repair can be considered to be unambiguously marked and further marking at the interface would not be necessary. Note that a 'Caution' notice in accordance with Regulation 514.14.1 must be provided at the appropriate consumer unit or distribution board.

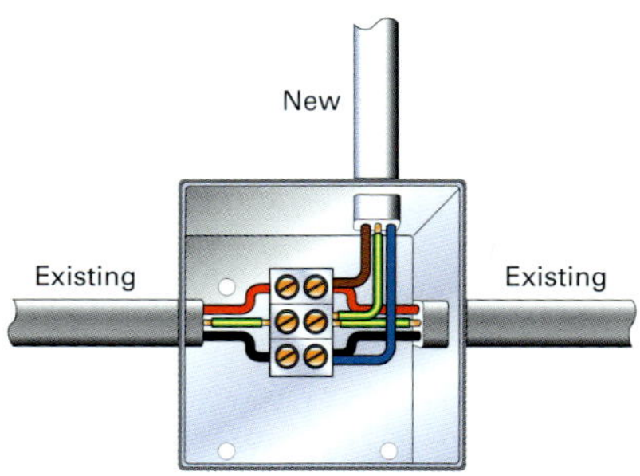

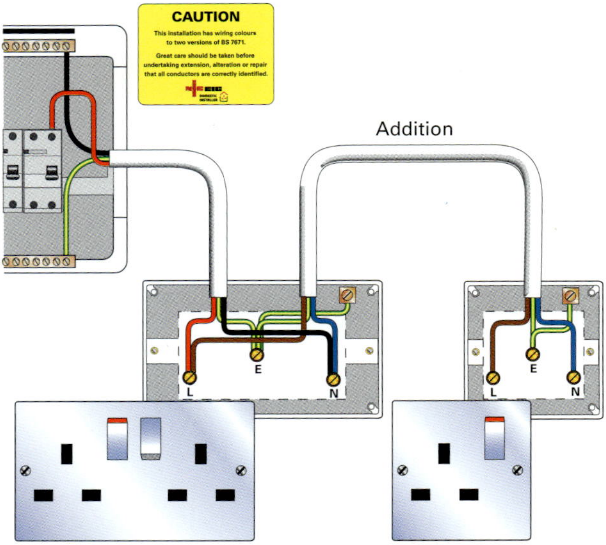

In a three-phase installation, at the wiring interface between new and old colours, where an extension, alteration, addition or repair is made with the new colours, to an installation wired in the old colours, unambiguous identification is required at the interface. Neutral conductors, where identified by colour, must be identified by the colour blue. Both the old line conductors (red, yellow and blue) and new line conductors (brown, black and grey) should be fitted with sleeves marked L1, L2 and L3 and neutral conductors should be fitted with sleeves marked N to avoid any possibility of confusion. Once again a 'Caution' notice must be provided at the appropriate consumer unit or distribution board.

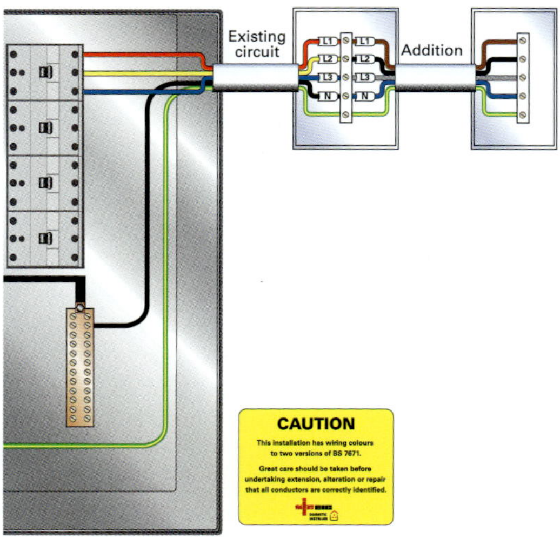

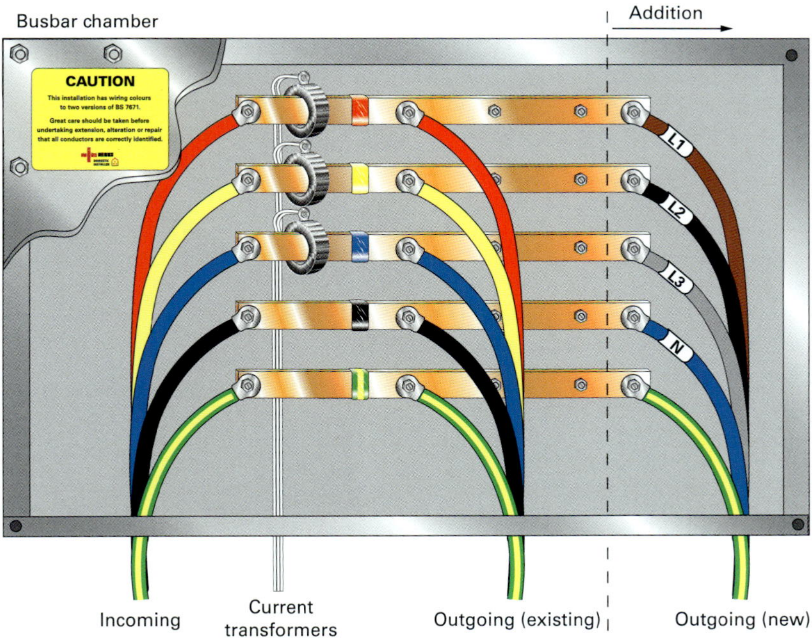

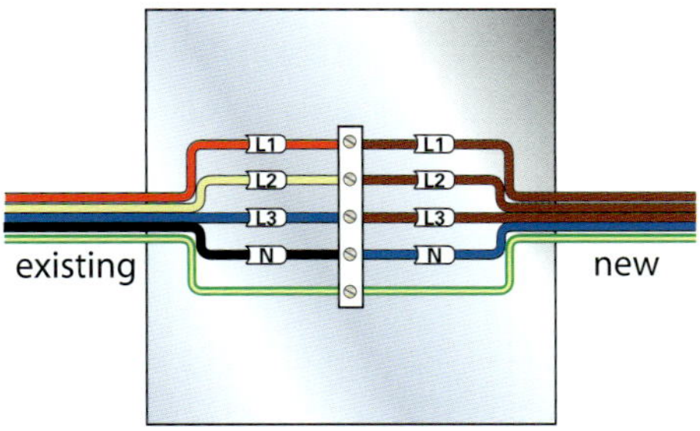

A permitted alternative arrangement is to use three single cores with insulation of the same colour, but unambiguous identification must be provided at the terminations. This could be achieved by using numbering or lettering.

Cables correctly supported throughout their length

It should be confirmed that cable supports are sufficient in number to prevent the cables from being damaged by their own weight or by electromechanical forces associated with fault conditions, and that no appreciable strain is placed on the terminals (Regulation 522.8.5 refers).

Where the cable support system is installed along/above a route that is used as a means of escape in the event of an emergency, the means of support should be sufficient to prevent premature collapse of the cabling and subsequent obstruction of the escape route (521.11.201 refers). This effectively precludes the use of plastic cable ties as the sole means of support for cabling, and requires a suitable fire-resistant means of support/retention to be provided for non-metallic trunking/conduit. Such requirements already exist for the cable supports of both fire alarm systems[1] and emergency escape lighting systems[2].

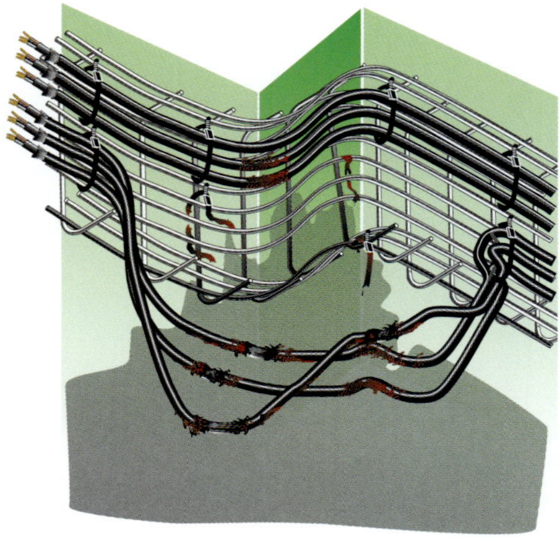

Examination of cables for signs of mechanical damage during installation

Generally, the risk of mechanical damage to cables is greater during construction than when the installation is in service. Consequently, during its construction the installation, especially those parts not accessible on completion, should be inspected at appropriate intervals. In particular, cables should be inspected before being enclosed within the fabric of the building.

Inspection should verify that the radii of bends in cables are not less than the minimum recommended for the particular type and overall diameter of cable, and confirm that cable sheaths, which are intended to provide mechanical protection, extend into enclosures.

1 See clause 26.2f of BS 5839-1: 2013

2 See clause 8.2.3 of BS 5266-1: 2011

Examination of insulation of live parts, not damaged during erection

To minimise the risk of conductor insulation being damaged during the drawing in process, prior to the installation of cables, the inspector should check that conduits are free from burrs and conductors are protected from any sharp edges in containment systems. To minimise the risk of insulation damage being caused by abrasion or excessive pulling forces, a sufficient number of access boxes should be provided to facilitate the drawing in of conductors.

Non-sheathed cables protected by enclosure in conduit, ducting or trunking

It should be confirmed that non-sheathed cables are enclosed in conduit, ducting or trunking in accordance with Regulation 521.10.1. This requirement does not apply to a protective conductor complying with Section 543.

Before cables are installed in a conduit or ducting system buried in the building structure the conduit or duct should be fully erected.

Suitability of containment systems (including flexible conduit)

Conduit, trunking and all other types of containment should be checked against the installation design to confirm their suitability for the conditions likely to be encountered (as required by Section 522 of *BS 7671*).

Inspection should confirm, for example, that a conduit or trunking installed in an environment prone to damp/wetness is adequately protected against corrosion, such as a galvanised type, and fitted with the appropriate seals or gaskets, in accordance with the manufacturer's instructions, to prevent ingress of water. The inspector should not only verify that all installed containment complies with the appropriate British or Harmonised standard applicable to the environment, but should also confirm that any protective coatings/coverings that may have been removed during the installation process (say, as a result of a running coupling being made in a conduit) have been reinstated, such as by applying a galvanised paint.

Where containment is installed in an environment of high ambient temperature allowance is required for expansion. In particular, where plastic conduit is installed in an area exposed to high ambient temperatures, expansion couplers should be installed at appropriate intervals according to the conduit manufacturer's instructions.

Where a conduit is connected to an item of equipment that is subject to vibration in normal use, such as a motor, a flexible type conduit should be used. Where the flexible conduit is of metallic construction, inspection should confirm that metallic parts of the conduit are not used to perform the function of a protective conductor (Regulation 543.2.3). Additionally, it should be confirmed that flexible conduit, metallic construction or otherwise, is not used to achieve compliance with the requirements

Choice and setting of protective and monitoring devices
Examples of devices which should be checked.

The BS (EN) number, type (e.g. general-purpose or selective) and rated residual current of each RCD.

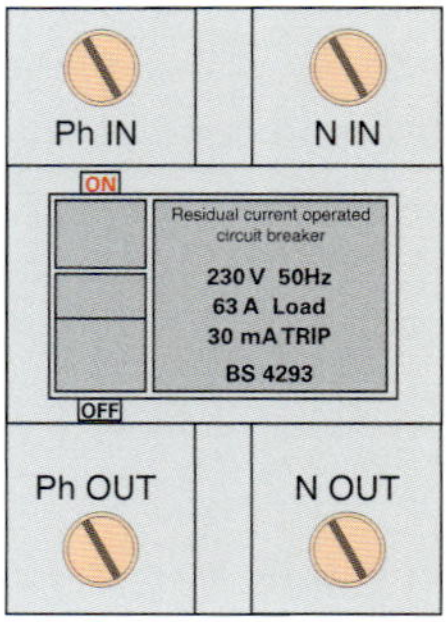

The BS (EN) number, type and rated current of each fuse.

The BS (EN) number, type and rated current of each circuit-breaker.

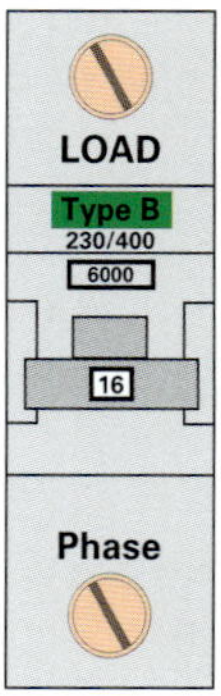

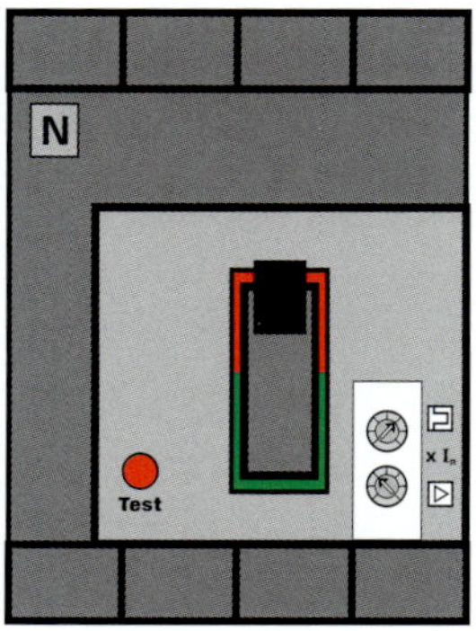

The BS (EN) number, type (characteristics) and, where appropriate, settings of each circuit-breaker.

Note: Drawings not to scale.

of Regulation 522.6.204 for mechanical protection of concealed cables (see - *cables installed under floors above ceilings, in walls/partitions, adequately protected against damage*).

Correct temperature rating of cable insulation

The current to be carried by any conductor for sustained periods during normal operation (including any harmonic current) should be such that the temperature limit, specified in Table 52.1 of *BS 7671*, is not exceeded (Regulation 523.1 refers).

It should be noted that both non-sheathed and sheathed cables, selected in accordance with the current carrying capacities given in Appendix 4 of *BS 7671* are considered to satisfy the requirements of Regulation 523.1.

Adequacy of cables for current-carrying capacity with regard to the type and nature of installation

The sizes and types of all the installed cables should be checked against the installation design information, to confirm that they have been correctly selected and installed to meet the requirements of Sections 523, 524 and 525 of *BS 7671* with regard to selection of conductors for current-carrying capacity and voltage drop respectively.

It is a requirement of *BS 7671* that this design information is made available to those carrying out the inspection and testing of new installation work, irrespective of whether the design was carried out by the contractor or by another party such as a consulting engineer. Particular attention should be given to cables in contact with thermally insulating material.

Adequacy of protective devices: type and rated current for fault protection

This item is concerned with fuses, circuit-breakers, RCDs and any current monitoring relays which control separate circuit-breakers. Their rated current, settings (where applicable) and characteristics must be checked to verify conformity with the design information for the installation.

For each fuse and circuit-breaker, a check should be made of not only the rated current but also the type (such as gG for a fuse to *BS EN 88-2* and *BS 88-3*, or Type B for a circuit-breaker to *BS EN 60898*).

For each circuit-breaker, a check should be made of the rated current or current setting, where appropriate, and the time/current characteristics. It should be noted that on some circuit-breakers, both the time/current characteristics and the rated current are adjustable. These must be checked against the design information.

For each RCD, a check should be made of the rated residual operating current. The time/residual current characteristics should also be checked where the device is to be used for additional protection, or where an intended time delay is incorporated.

NICEIC APPROVED CONTRACTOR

This certificate is not valid if the serial number has been defaced or altered **ICN4/**

Original (To the person ordering the work)

SCHEDULE OF ITEMS INSPECTED

† See note below

8.5	Non-sheathed cables protected by enclosure in conduit, ducting or trunking	
8.6	Suitability of containment systems (including flexible conduit)	
8.7	Correct temperature rating of cable insulation	
8.8	Adequacy of cables for current-carrying capacity with regard to the type and nature of installation	
8.9	Adequacy of protective devices: type and rated current for fault protection	
8.10	Presence and adequacy of circuit protective conductors	
8.11	Coordination between conductors and overload protective devices	
8.12	Wiring systems and cable installation methods / practices appropriate to the type and nature of installation and external influences	
8.13	Cables installed under floors, above ceilings, in walls / partitions, adequately protected against damage	
	• installed in prescribed zones	
	• incorporating earthed armour or sheath, or installed within earthed wiring system, or otherwise protected against mechanical damage by nails, screws and the like	
8.14	Provision of additional protection by RCDs having rated residual operating current ($I_{\Delta n}$) not exceeding 30 mA	
	a) for mobile equipment with a current rating not exceeding 32 A for use outdoors	
	b) For all socket-outlets of rating 20 A or less, unless exempt	
	c) For cables installed in walls/partitions at a depth of less than 50 mm	
	d) For cables installed in walls/partitions containing metal parts regardless of depth	
8.15	Provision of fire barriers, sealing arrangements so as to minimize the spread of fire	
8.16	Band II cables segregated/separated from Band I cables	
8.17	Cables segregated/separated from non-electrical services	
8.18	Termination of cables at enclosures	
	a) Connections under no undue strain	
	b) No basic insulation of a conductor visible outside enclosure	
	c) Connections of live conductors adequately enclosed	
	d) Adequately connected at point of entry to enclosure (glands, bushes etc.)	
8.19	Suitability of circuit accessories for external influences	
8.20	Circuit accessories not damaged during erection	
8.21	Single-pole devices for switching in line conductor only	
8.22	Adequacy of connections, including cpcs, within accessories and at fixed and stationary equipment	
9.0	**ISOLATION AND SWITCHING**	
9.1	Isolators	
	a) Presence and location of appropriate devices	
	b) Capable of being secured in the OFF position	
	c) Correct operation verified (functional check)	
	d) The installation, circuit or part thereof that will be isolated is clearly identified by location and/or durable marking	
	e) Warning label posted in situations where live parts cannot be isolated by the operation of a single device	
9.2	Switching off for mechanical maintenance	
	a) Presence of appropriate devices	
	b) Acceptable location (state if local or remote)	
	c) Capable of being secured in the OFF position	
	d) Correct operation verified (functional check)	
	e) The circuit or part thereof to be disconnected clearly identified by location and/or durable marking	
9.3	Emergency switching/stopping	
	a) Presence of appropriate devices	
	b) Readily accessible for operation where danger might occur	
	c) Correct operation verified (functional check)	
	d) The installation, circuit or part thereof to be disconnected, clearly identified by location and/or durable marking	
9.4	Functional switching	
	a) Presence of appropriate devices	
	b) Correct operation verified (functional check)	
10.0	**CURRENT-USING EQUIPMENT (PERMANENTLY CONNECTED)**	
10.1	Suitability of equipment in terms of IP and fire ratings	
10.2	Enclosure not damaged/deteriorated during installation so as to impair safety	
10.3	Suitability for the environment and external influences	
10.4	Security of fixing	
10.5	Cable entry holes in ceilings above luminaires, sized or sealed so as to restrict the spread of fire	
10.6	Recessed luminaires (downlighters)	
	a) Correct type of lamps fitted	
	b) Installed to minimise build-up of heat	
10.7	Provision of undervoltage protection, where specified	
10.8	Provision of overload protection, where specified	
10.9	Adequacy of working space/accessibility to equipment	

11.0 SPECIAL INSTALLATIONS OR LOCATIONS

List below any Special Installations or Locations which are part of the installation to be verified, and confirm that the additional requirements given in the respective section of Part 7 are fulfilled.

12.0 OTHER

SCHEDULE OF ADDITIONAL RECORDS* (See attached schedule)

Page No(s)

Note: Additional page(s) must be identified by the Electrical Installation Certificate serial number and page number(s).

† ***All boxes must be completed.*** *'✓' indicates that an inspection was carried out and that the result was* ***satisfactory****. 'N/A' indicates that an inspection was* ***not applicable*** *to the particular installation.*

* *Where the electrical work to which this certificate relates includes the installation of a fire alarm system and/or an emergency lighting system (or a part of such systems), this electrical safety certificate should be accompanied by the particular certificate(s) for the system(s).*

Page 4 of

This certificate is based on the model forms shown in Appendix 6 of BS 7671

ICN4/7

Presence and adequacy of circuit protective conductors

A visual inspection must be made to check that circuit protective conductors, where required, have been correctly selected and installed. The designer may have determined the cross-sectional area of the circuit protective conductors either by calculation or by application of Table 54.7 of *BS 7671*. The chosen method of determination, together with other design information including the intended cross-sectional areas of each protective conductor, should be made available to the inspector.

Connections in protective conductors should not be overlooked in the inspection process. Particular attention should be paid to situations where some, or all, of the protective conductor is formed from metallic wiring systems, enclosures and the like, as would be the case for a glanded connection between a steel wire armoured cable and the metallic casing of a distribution board. In such cases, an inspection of the connection will not be sufficient to confirm continuity, which could be detrimentally affected not only by the degree of tightness of the connection but also by factors such as the presence of paint, corrosion or other elements within the joint. As such, where any doubt exists, the continuity of such connections should be verified by testing.

Coordination between conductors and overload protective devices

It should be confirmed that each protective device providing overload protection satisfies the conditions specified in Regulation 433.1.1. Where the device is a semi-enclosed fuse to *BS 3036*, Regulation 433.1.202 should be taken into account.

Wiring systems and cable installation methods/practices appropriate to the type and nature of installation and external influences

Owing to production (or cleaning) processes, for example, the electrical Installation may be exposed to water or chemical sprays, solvents, steam, or a variety of other external influences. Therefore, as required by Section 522, inspection should confirm that installed cables and wiring systems and their method of installation are suitable for the environment and the external influences likely to be present.

Where cables are installed in areas that are, or are liable to be, inhabited by rodents, such as might be found in the roof voids and cellars of some premises, the wiring system must be capable of resisting damage caused by gnawing.

The enclosures of electrical switchgear, accessories and wiring systems (such as trunking) should be inspected to confirm they are free of any openings through which rodents could gain entry to build nests and cause damage to cables or other equipment. Cable entries to equipment, such as luminaires, must be effected through correctly selected cable entries using, if necessary, cable glands.

A list of external influences is given in Appendix 5 of *BS 7671 - Classification of external influences*.

Cables installed under floors, above ceilings, in walls/partitions, adequately protected against damage

Regulation 522.6.201 requires that a cable installed under a floor or above a ceiling is run in such a position that it is not liable to be damaged by contact with the floor, the ceiling or any of their fixings. The regulation also requires that where a cable has to pass through a timber joist within a floor or ceiling construction, or through a ceiling batten, the cable must either:

1. be at least 50 mm measured vertically from the top, or bottom, as appropriate, of the joist or batten,

or

2. comply with Regulation 522.6.204.

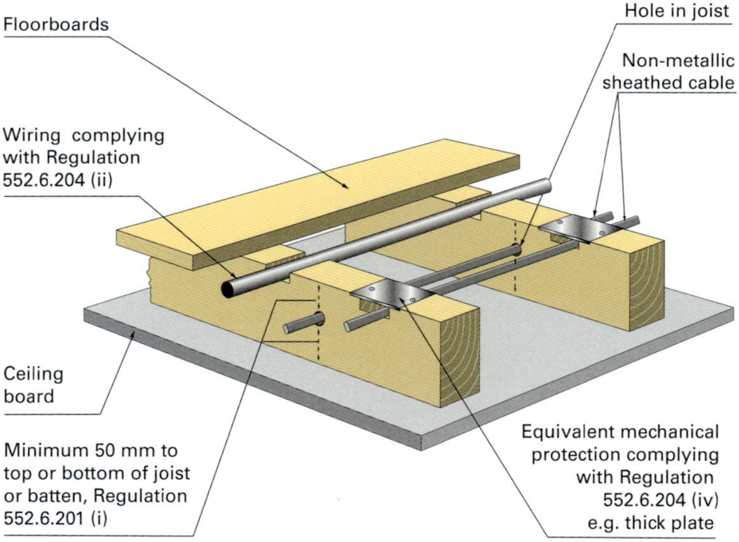

Cables in floor joists

Installed in prescribed zones

A cable installed in a wall or partition can be vulnerable to penetration by nails, screws and the like, which can lead to the danger of electric shock or fire. Therefore, inspection should be carried out at appropriate intervals during installation to confirm that cables installed in walls/partitions, less than 50 mm from the surface, are routed within the prescribed zones of Regulation 522.6.202, unless they are cables of a permitted type (see Regulation 522.6.204).

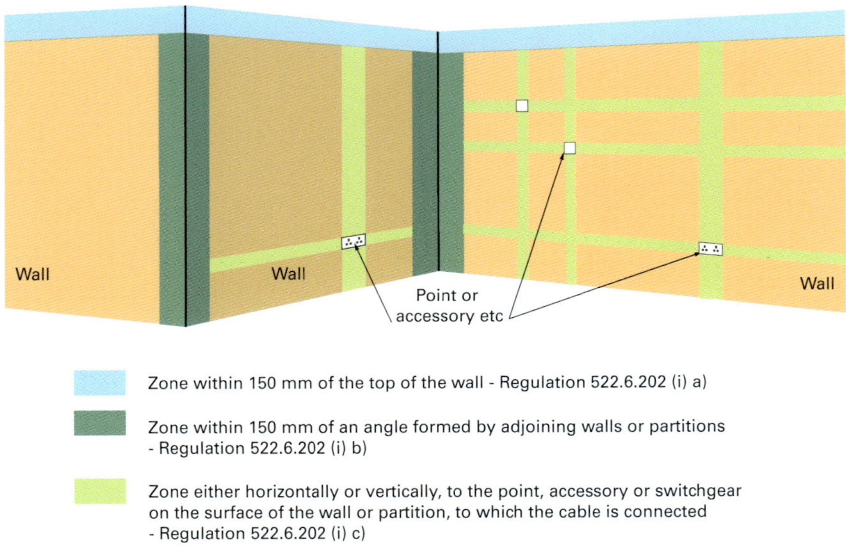

The zones detailed in Regulation 522.6.202 (i)

Generally, a zone created on one side of a wall or partition does not extend to the reverse side. However, where the location of the accessory, point or switchgear can be determined from the reverse side, a zone formed on one side of a wall or partition of 100 mm thickness or less extends to the reverse side.

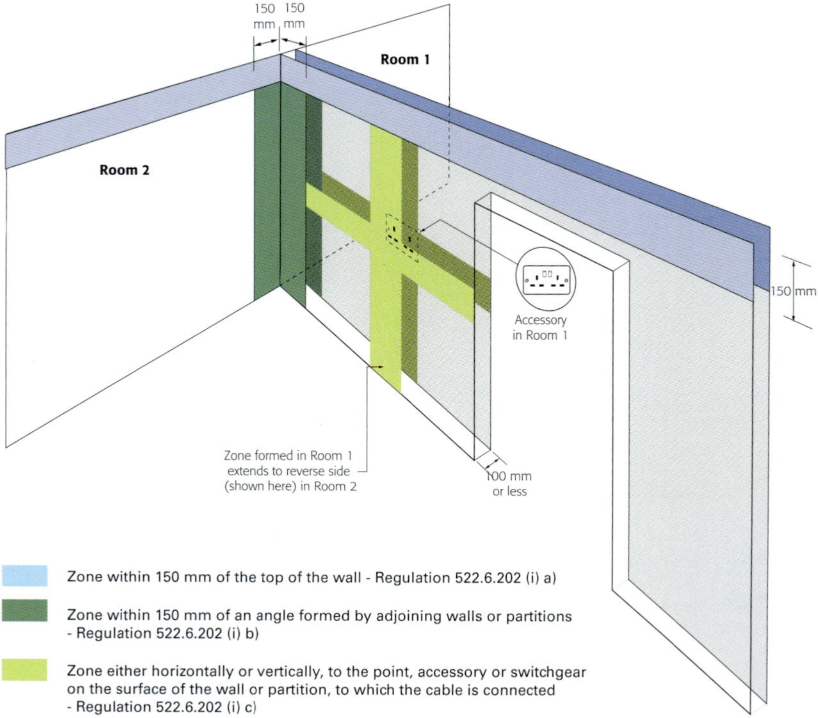

An example of where the location of an accessory can be determined from the reverse side of a wall

The presence of a doorway means that a person intending to drive a nail, screw or the like into the wall can reasonably determine the location of the accessory from the reverse side of the wall. A mirror image of the permitted cross-shaped zone created in the room with the accessory (room 1) is therefore considered to exist in the other room. Thus, the concealed wiring connected to the accessory is permitted to be within 50 mm of surface of the reverse side of the wall (just as it is permitted to be within 50 mm of the surface with the accessory), provided it is within the mirror image zone.

Apart from where the location of accessories, switchgear and the like can be determined from the reverse side, a cable that is installed at a depth of less than 50 mm from either side of a wall or partition has to be in at least one of the permitted zones with respect to that side.

The installation of a cable in such a zone, but passing through the box of an accessory rather than connecting to the accessory, is generally considered acceptable.

Protection of cables by earthed armour/sheath or wiring system

Inspection should confirm that concealed cables installed in walls/partitions less than 50 mm from the surface, which do not satisfy the requirements of Regulation 522.6.204, are both routed in zones and also provided with additional protection by means of an RCD having the characteristics specified in Regulation 415.1.1. Where this is not the case, the inspector should confirm that a cable type or wiring system complying with the requirements of Regulation 522.6.204 is installed.

Where additional mechanical protection is used to satisfy the requirements of 522.6.204 to prevent penetration of a cable by nails, screws and the like, it must be sufficient to prevent such penetration. A protective plate provided to prevent penetration of a cable should be at least 3 mm thick.

Provision of additional protection by RCDs having rated residual operating current ($I_{\Delta n}$) not exceeding 30 mA

The inspector should check that additional protection has been provided by an RCD for the following, as required by Regulation 411.3.3, and Regulations 522.6.202 and 522.6.203:

1. mobile equipment with a current rating not exceeding 32 A for use outdoors, and
2. all socket-outlets with a rated current not exceeding 20 A, unless exempt, and
3. cables installed in walls or partitions at a depth of less than 50 mm, unless complying with 522.6.204, and
4. cables installed in walls or partitions containing significant metal parts regardless of depth, unless complying with 522.6.204.

Each RCD should be inspected to confirm that it has a rated residual operating current ($I_{\Delta n}$) not exceeding 30 mA and that it meets a product standard which requires the device to operate under type-test conditions within 40 ms at a residual current of 5 $I_{\Delta n}$ (Regulation 415.1.1).

Where a cable is concealed in a wall or partition that is constructed of, or contains, significant metal parts, there is a risk that damage to the cable could result in causing the metalwork of the wall or partition to become live. Owing to this risk, *BS 7671* requires additional protection to be provided for cables in walls or partitions containing significant metal parts irrespective of depth, unless complying with 522.6.204.

It should be confirmed that the number of socket-outlets or items of equipment controlled by a single RCD are such that the operation of that RCD does not result in unreasonable inconvenience in the event of a fault or, exceptionally, due to excessive protective conductor currents (Regulation 314.1).

Provision of fire barriers, sealing arrangements so as to minimise the spread of fire

Where the wiring system passes through an element of building construction (such as a wall or floor) having a specified fire resistance, the space around the wiring system must be sealed to a degree of fire resistance which is no less than that (if any) prescribed for the building element concerned. Similarly, where a wiring system having an internal space, such as trunking, passes through an element of a building having a specified fire resistance, the wiring system must be sealed internally to the appropriate degree of fire resistance. The exceptions to this requirement are:

- A non-flame-propagating wiring system, with an internal cross-sectional area of not more than 710 mm^2. This is equivalent to the internal cross-sectional area of a 32 mm diameter conduit.
- A wiring system that has passed a relevant type test meeting the requirements of Regulation 527.2.3.

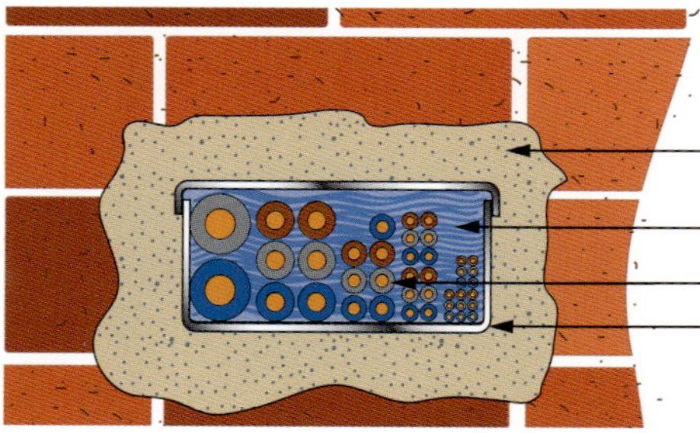

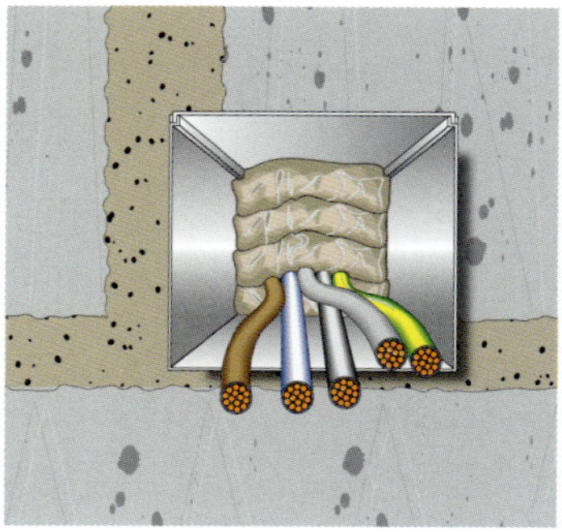

Internal barriers may be made from intumescent material which expands to fill the space when heated to the temperatures likely to occur under fire conditions. Suitable solidifying foam may also be used.

For new installations, the presence of the required fire barriers must be verified during the construction stage, when access to all the wiring system penetrations should be readily available.

Protection against thermal effects, such as the proximity of hot surfaces to electrical equipment, must be checked. Sufficient clearance or an appropriate form of permanent heat shield or barrier may need to be provided during construction to prevent adverse effects on wiring systems.

Band II cables segregated/separated from Band I cables

It is necessary to verify by inspection that Band I and Band II circuits are separated or segregated from each other either by containment in separate wiring systems or by adopting a method of insulating (either individually or collectively) the Band I conductors for the highest voltage present according to Regulation 528.1.

Voltage Band I covers installations where protection against electric shock is provided under certain conditions by the value of voltage. It extends also to installations where the voltage is limited for operational reasons such as in telecommunication, signalling, bell, control and alarm installations. Circuits operating at voltages not exceeding extra-low voltage (50 V a.c. or 120 V ripple-free d.c.) will normally fall within Band I.

Voltage Band II includes low-voltage supplies to household, commercial and industrial installations. Low voltage is defined as exceeding extra-low voltage but not exceeding 1000 V a.c. or 1500 V d.c. between conductors, or 600 V a.c. or 900 V d.c. between conductors and Earth.

Segregation or separation may be achieved in the following ways.

- Where every cable or conductor is insulated for the highest voltage present.
- By containment of a Band I circuit, insulated for its system voltage, in a separate conduit, trunking or ducting system.
- By containment of Band I and Band II circuits insulated for their respective system voltage in separate compartments of a common trunking or ducting system.
- By installation of Band I and Band II circuits on tray or ladder where physical separation is provided by a partition.
- Where Band I and Band II circuits are contained in a common wiring system, by using circuit conductors all having an insulation rating suitable for the highest voltage present.
- Where Band I and Band II circuits are contained in a multicore cable, by having the cores for Band I circuits suitably insulated for the highest voltage present, either individually or collectively. Alternatively, the cores of the Band I circuits must be separated from the Band II circuits by an earthed metal screen having a current-carrying capacity not less than that of the largest core of the Band II circuits.

Where outlets or controls for Band I and Band II circuits are mounted in or on a common box, block or switchplate of wiring systems formed by conduit, trunking or ducting, verification by inspection is required to check that the necessary segregation is maintained by an effective partition and that, where the partition is metal, it is earthed.

Segregation of safety services

Fire alarm and emergency lighting circuits are required to be segregated from other circuits and from each other in accordance with the relevant parts of the *BS 5266* and *BS 5839* series.

This segregation is to avoid for example:

- a breakdown of the cable insulation of the fire alarm circuits and/or other circuits, or
- a fire caused by a fault on another circuit, or
- electromagnetic interference to a fire alarm circuit as a result of the proximity of another circuit, or
- damage resulting from the need for other circuits to be installed in, or removed from conduit, ducts or trunking containing a fire alarm circuit.

The segregation requirements may also apply to the mains supply to fire alarm and emergency lighting systems.

Though not directly related to segregation, it must be appreciated that the *BS 5266* and *BS 5839* series also contain specific requirements concerning the selection and erection of emergency lighting and fire alarm wiring systems.

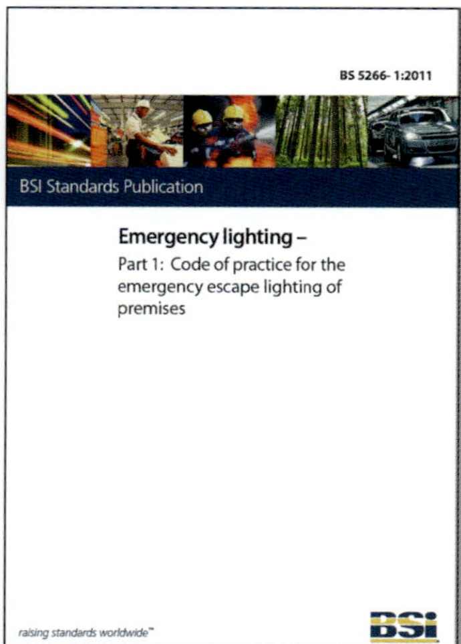

BS 5839: Part 1 and BS 5266: Part 1 contain requirements for segregation of the wiring of fire alarm and centralised emergency lighting systems.

Cables segregated/separated from non-electrical services

It should be verified that no destructive, damaging or harmful effects are likely to occur because of the proximity of any part of the electrical installation to non-electrical services or other influences. For example, it should be checked that any heat, steam, smoke, fumes or condensation is not likely to damage the electrical installation, or that electrolytic corrosion is not likely to occur between dissimilar metal parts of the electrical installation and the building structure or mechanical plant which are in contact with each other in damp situations, such as outdoors.

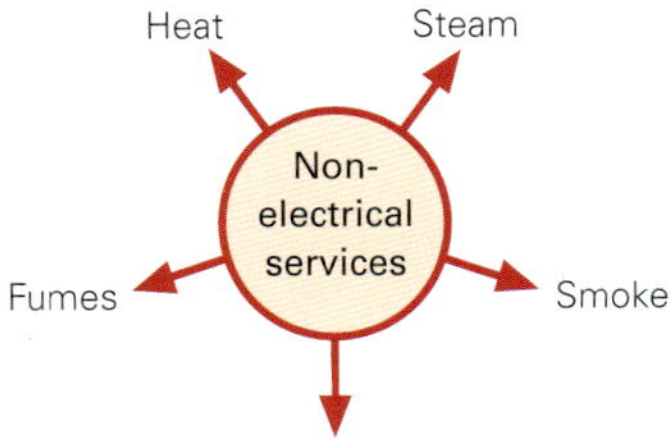

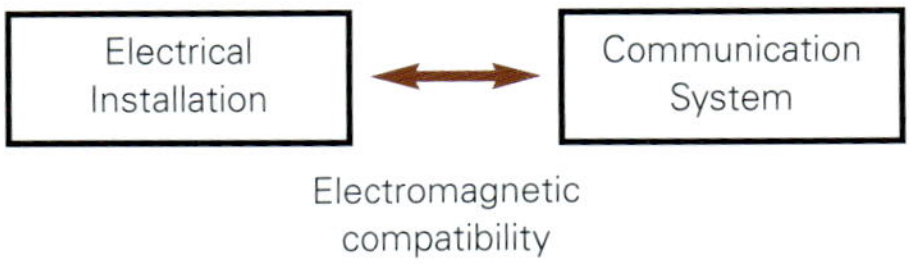

Examples of possible influences

Where the equipment or wiring of an electrical installation is in the vicinity of a communication or control system (say), it should be checked that the relevant electromagnetic compatibility (EMC) requirements have been complied with, so that one system will not cause interference to the other.

Where there is a lift, a check should be made to verify that the lift well/shaft has not been used as a route for cables which do not form part of the lift installation, as defined in *BS EN 81*. This restriction on the use of the lift well/shaft is mainly due to considerations of fire risk and to the problems of gaining safe access for inspection, testing and maintenance of parts not related to the lift installation, rather than to the existence of mutual detrimental influences. This is, however, a convenient heading under which to include this check.

Termination of cables at enclosures

Every connection between conductors and between a conductor and equipment must be sound, both mechanically and electrically. The conductor(s) and insulation must be undamaged and the standard of workmanship must be such that the connection is likely to remain secure for the lifetime of the installation. The method of connection should take account of external influences such as moisture, vibration and thermal cycling, and there should be no appreciable mechanical strain on the terminations.

Connections must remain accessible throughout the lifetime of an installation. The only types of connection or joint which may be excused from this requirement at a periodic inspection (but not during the initial inspection) are those which are:

- designed to be installed buried in the ground, or
- compound filled or encapsulated, or
- between a cold-tail (as defined in Part 2 of *BS 7671*) and a heating element, or
- formed by brazing, compression tool, soldering or welding, or
- made in equipment by a product manufacturer which are not intended to be inspected or maintained, or
- made in an accessory meeting the requirements to be maintenance free given in *BS 5733*.

For purposes of protection against fire and thermal effects, every joint or connection in a live conductor or PEN conductor must be made in an enclosure complying with the requirements of Section 526 of *BS 7671*. It should be noted that this requirement applies not only to connections in low voltage circuits, but also those in extra-low voltage circuits.

The enclosure must also provide adequate protection against mechanical damage and any other external influence or stress to which it may be subjected. The cores of sheathed cables from which the sheath has been removed must not extend outside the enclosure.

Where a cable is connected to an enclosure using a gland or bush, inspection should confirm that the correct type of gland or bush has been installed to prevent strain. In particular, armoured cable glands must not be used as a means of support for cables.

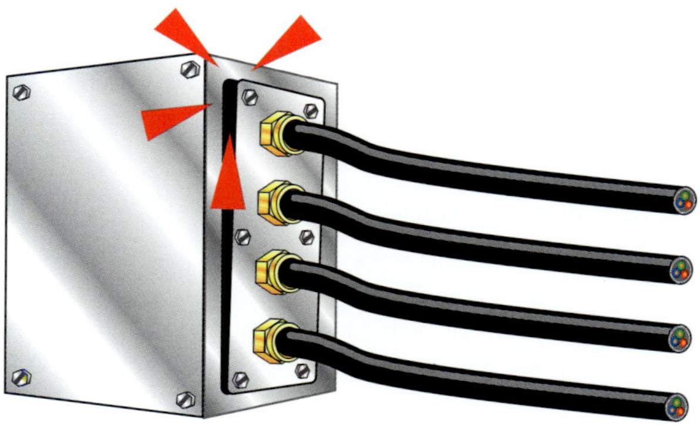

Suitability of circuit accessories for external influences

It should be confirmed that accessories are suitable (comply with the appropriate British Standard and required IP rating) for the external influences likely to be encountered. Where accessories are located in an enclosure or cabinet to protect against external influences, the inspector should check that the enclosure or cabinet does not cause overheating of the protected accessory, impair its operation, nor impede its inspection, testing and maintenance.

Circuit accessories not damaged during erection

The inspector should verify that installed accessories have not been damaged during construction.

Single-pole devices for switching in line conductor only

This is a visual check to verify that all single-pole switching and control devices are connected in the line conductor only. No single-pole switching device, circuit-breaker, fuse, solid link which can be removed without the use of a tool or key, or the like should interrupt or control the neutral conductor. This check should be made in addition, and not as an alternative, to the polarity test which will be conducted later in the verification process.

Adequacy of connections, including cpcs, within accessories and at fixed and stationary equipment

The inspector should examine the installation to verify that the conductors, including circuit protective conductors, at accessories and other items of equipment are connected to the correct terminals, and that the connections are well made in both electrical and mechanical terms.

Table 53.4 - Guidance on the selection of protective, isolation and switching devices

Device	Standard	Isolation[4]	Emergency switching[2]	Functional switching
Switching devices	BS EN 50428 BS EN 60669-1 BS EN 60669-2-1 BS EN 60669-2-2 BS EN 60669-2-3 BS EN 60669-2-4 BS EN 60947-3 BS EN 60947-5-1	No No No No No Yes[3] Yes[1,3] No	No Yes No Yes Yes Yes Yes Yes	Yes Yes Yes Yes Yes Yes Yes Yes
Contactors	BS EN 60947-4-1 BS EN 61095	Yes[1,3] No	Yes No	Yes Yes
Circuit-breakers	BS EN 60898 BS EN 60947-2 BS EN 61009-1	Yes[3] Yes[1,3] Yes[3]	Yes Yes Yes	Yes Yes Yes
RCDs	BS EN 60947-2 BS EN 61008-1 BS EN 61009-1	Yes[1,3] Yes[3] Yes[3]	Yes Yes Yes	Yes Yes Yes
Isolating switches	BS EN 60669-2-4 BS EN 60947-3	Yes[3] Yes[1,3]	Yes Yes	Yes Yes
Plugs and socket-outlets (≤ 32 A)	BS EN 60309	Yes[3] Yes[3] Yes[3]	No No No	Yes Yes Yes
Plugs and socket-outlets (>32 A)	BS EN 60309	Yes[3]	No	No
Devices for the connection of luminaires	IEC 61995-1	Yes[3]	No	No
Control and protective switching devices for equipment (CPS)	BS EN 60947-6-1 BS EN 60947-6-2	Yes[1,3] Yes[1,3]	Yes Yes	Yes Yes
Fuses	BS 88 series	Yes	No	No
Devices with semi-conductors	BS EN 50428 BS EN 60669-2-1	No No	No No	Yes Yes
Luminaire Support coupler	BS 6972	Yes[3]	No	No
Plugs and unswitched socket-outlets	BS 1363-1 BS 1363-2	Yes[3] Yes[3]	No No	Yes Yes
Plugs and switched socket-outlets	BS 1363-1 BS 1363-2	Yes[3] Yes[3]	No No	Yes Yes
Plugs and socket-outlets	BS 5733	Yes[3]	No	Yes
Switched fused connection unit	BS 1363-4	Yes[3]	Yes	Yes
Unswitched fused connection unit	BS 1363-4	Yes[3] (Removal of fuse link)	No	No
Fuse	BS 1362	Yes	No	No
Cooker Control Unit switch	BS 4177	Yes[3]	Yes	Yes

Yes Function provided No Function not provided

(1) Function provided if the device is suitable and marked with the symbol for isolation (see BS EN 60617 identity number S00288.)

(2) See 537.4.2.5

(3) Device is suitable for on-load isolation, i.e. disconnection whilst carrying load current.

(4) In an installation forming part of a TT or IT system, isolation requires disconnection of all live conductors. (See Regulation 537.2.2.1.)

Note 1: An entry of (1,3) means that the device is suitable for on-load isolation only if it is marked with the symbol for **on-load** isolation

Note 2: In the above table, the functions provided by the devices for isolation and switching are summarized, together with the indication of the relevant product standards.

9.0 ISOLATION AND SWITCHING

This is the general term used to cover four basic functions; isolation, switching off for mechanical maintenance, emergency switching and functional switching. It should be appreciated that two or more of these functions may be performed by a single device, provided that the arrangement and characteristics of the device satisfy all the requirements of *BS 7671* for the particular functions concerned (see table 53.4).

Whilst checking the items listed on the schedule, the inspector should also confirm that all devices for isolation and switching are suitable for the currents they will have to carry and, where appropriate, make or break, under normal and fault conditions.

Isolators

The purpose of isolation is to enable persons to carry out work on, or in the vicinity of, parts that are normally live in service without risk of injury from electric shock from those parts. *BS 7671* requires that every circuit must be capable of being isolated.

It should be confirmed that the installation has a means of isolation capable of switching the supply on load positioned as near as practicable to the origin. This means of isolation should preferably be provided by a multi-pole switching device that disconnects all poles of the supply when operated. Where the installation is supplied from more than one source, a main switch or main circuit-breaker is required for each source.

It should be verified that it is possible to interrupt all live conductors of the supply except as follows:

- In a TN-S or TN-C-S system, the neutral conductor generally need not be switched where this can reliably be regarded as being connected to earth through a suitable low impedance. However, a main switch intended for operation by ordinary persons (such as in a consumer unit) must interrupt all live conductors.
- In a TN-C system, the PEN conductor must not be isolated or switched.

Where the main switch or circuit-breaker does not interrupt the neutral conductor, *BS 7671* requires provision to be made for the disconnection of the conductor for testing purposes.

Although the main switch/switch-fuse/circuit-breaker or RCD provides a means of isolation for the whole installation, it is probable that other isolating devices need to be present so that individual items of equipment, circuits or groups of circuits can be isolated independently. The presence of these other devices, where appropriate, should be verified. It is likely that, for operational reasons, additional isolating devices will form part of the design of any large installation, so that a section can be safely worked on without necessarily having to isolate the whole installation.

The additional isolating devices must interrupt all live conductors except, generally, the neutral conductor in TN-S and TN-C-S systems where this can reliably be regarded as being at earth potential. In a TN-C system, the PEN conductor must not be isolated or switched.

It should be checked that each device used for isolation is of a type which *BS 7671* permits for this purpose. Such devices include an isolator (disconnector), isolating switch (switch-disconnector), suitable circuit-breaker, plug and socket-outlet, (withdrawable) fuse, or disconnectable link.

The isolating distance between contacts or other means of isolation when in the open position is to be not less than that determined for an isolator (disconnector) in accordance with the requirements of *BS 1363-4, BS EN 60669-2-4, BS EN 60898, BS EN 60947-2, BS EN 60947-3, BS EN 61008-1* or *BS EN 61009-1*. The position of the contacts must be either externally visible or clearly and reliably indicated when the specified isolation has been obtained in each pole. As a rule of thumb, a contact separation of 3 mm is generally considered to be sufficient, but if there is any doubt as to whether a device is designed to provide isolation, its suitability must be confirmed by enquiry.

All isolating devices should be selected and/or installed in such a way as to prevent unintentional re-closure (such as by mechanical shock or vibration). Means should be provided to secure, in the open position, any isolating devices which are placed remotely from the equipment to be isolated, and to secure any off-load isolating devices, to prevent inadvertent or unauthorised operation.

Where live parts cannot be isolated by a single device, isolation is required at each position (Regulation 514.11.1). The location of each isolating device must be indicated unless there is no possibility of confusion.

Switching off for mechanical maintenance

The purpose of switching off for mechanical maintenance is to enable persons to safely replace, refurbish or clean lamps, and to maintain non-electrical parts of electrical equipment, plant and machinery.

It should be verified that a means of switching off for mechanical maintenance is provided where any of the above operations may involve a risk of burns, or a risk of injury from mechanical movement. For example, a means of switching off for mechanical maintenance would be required to enable maintenance personnel to clean luminaires having lamps that may cause burns, or to enable a mechanical fitter to work on the normally moving parts of an electrically-driven machine. It should be noted, however, that a suitable means of isolation would also be required if any of these operations were likely to involve a need to work on or near live parts, such as could be the case if the maintenance operations involved dismantling the equipment.

The devices used for switching off for mechanical maintenance should be checked to ensure that they are of the types permitted for this function by *BS 7671*, namely switches or suitable socket-outlets. Switches must be capable of cutting off the full load current of the relevant part of the installation, and either have an externally visible contact gap, or give a clear and reliable indication of the OFF or OPEN position when each pole of the contacts is properly opened. Plugs and socket-outlets are permitted for such purposes only if their rating does not exceed 16 A. (Regulation 537.3.2.6 refers).

Devices for switching off for mechanical maintenance must be suitably positioned for ready operation. This often means that the device has to be positioned adjacent to the equipment requiring maintenance. Unless the device is to be continuously under the control of the person performing the maintenance, suitable provisions (for example, locking off facilities on the device) must be available to prevent the equipment from being reactivated during mechanical maintenance. In any event, each device must have been selected and/or installed such that unintentional re-closure by mechanical shock and so on is unlikely to occur.

It should be confirmed that each device for switching off for mechanical maintenance is connected in the main supply circuit. Such a device may only be connected in the control circuit where supplementary precautions have been taken to provide a degree of safety equivalent to that of interruption of the main supply.

Emergency switching/stopping

The purpose of emergency switching is to remove, as quickly as possible, danger which may have occurred unexpectedly. It should be verified that a means of emergency switching is provided for every part of the installation for which it may be necessary to cut off the supply rapidly to prevent or remove danger. For example, an emergency switching device would be required for a drilling machine in a factory machine shop. Where an electrically-driven machine may give rise to danger, *BS 7671* requires that a means of emergency stopping be provided; that is, emergency switching intended to stop the operation whilst, if necessary for safety, leaving certain parts of the equipment energised.

Emergency switching devices must be suitably positioned for ready operation and must not be sited where access to them is likely to be impeded in any foreseen emergency. The operating means (for example a handle or push-button) must be clearly identifiable, capable of being restrained in the OFF or STOP position and preferably be coloured red. *BS 7671* does not permit the selection of a plug and socket-outlet as an emergency switching device. However, this does not preclude their use for this purpose where a plug and socket-outlet provides a readily accessible means of so doing.

APPROVED CONTRACTOR

This certificate is not valid if the serial number has been defaced or altered **ICN4/**

Original (To the person ordering the work)

SCHEDULE OF ITEMS INSPECTED

† See note below

8.5	Non-sheathed cables protected by enclosure in conduit, ducting or trunking	
8.6	Suitability of containment systems (including flexible conduit)	
8.7	Correct temperature rating of cable insulation	
8.8	Adequacy of cables for current-carrying capacity with regard to the type and nature of installation	
8.9	Adequacy of protective devices: type and rated current for fault protection	
8.10	Presence and adequacy of circuit protective conductors	
8.11	Coordination between conductors and overload protective devices	
8.12	Wiring systems and cable installation methods / practices appropriate to the type and nature of installation and external influences	
8.13	Cables installed under floors, above ceilings, in walls / partitions, adequately protected against damage	
	• installed in prescribed zones	
	• incorporating earthed armour or sheath, or installed within earthed wiring system, or otherwise protected against mechanical damage by nails, screws and the like	
8.14	Provision of additional protection by RCDs having rated residual operating current ($I_{\Delta n}$) not exceeding 30 mA	
	a) for mobile equipment with a current rating not exceeding 32 A for use outdoors	
	b) For all socket-outlets of rating 20 A or less, unless exempt	
	c) For cables installed in walls/partitions at a depth of less than 50 mm	
	d) For cables installed in walls/partitions containing metal parts regardless of depth	
8.15	Provision of fire barriers, sealing arrangements so as to minimize the spread of fire	
8.16	Band II cables segregated/separated from Band I cables	
8.17	Cables segregated/separated from non-electrical services	
8.18	Termination of cables at enclosures	
	a) Connections under no undue strain	
	b) No basic insulation of a conductor visible outside enclosure	
	c) Connections of live conductors adequately enclosed	
	d) Adequately connected at point of entry to enclosure (glands, bushes etc.)	
8.19	Suitability of circuit accessories for external influences	
8.20	Circuit accessories not damaged during erection	
8.21	Single-pole devices for switching in line conductor only	
8.22	Adequacy of connections, including cpcs, within accessories and at fixed and stationary equipment	

9.0 ISOLATION AND SWITCHING

9.1	Isolators	
	a) Presence and location of appropriate devices	
	b) Capable of being secured in the OFF position	
	c) Correct operation verified (functional check)	
	d) The installation, circuit or part thereof that will be isolated is clearly identified by location and/or durable marking	
	e) Warning label posted in situations where live parts cannot be isolated by the operation of a single device	
9.2	Switching off for mechanical maintenance	
	a) Presence of appropriate devices	
	b) Acceptable location (state if local or remote)	
	c) Capable of being secured in the OFF position	
	d) Correct operation verified (functional check)	
	e) The circuit or part thereof to be disconnected clearly identified by location and/or durable marking	
9.3	Emergency switching/stopping	
	a) Presence of appropriate devices	
	b) Readily accessible for operation where danger might occur	
	c) Correct operation verified (functional check)	
	d) The installation, circuit or part thereof to be disconnected, clearly identified by location and/or durable marking	
9.4	Functional switching	
	a) Presence of appropriate devices	
	b) Correct operation verified (functional check)	

10.0 CURRENT-USING EQUIPMENT (PERMANENTLY CONNECTED)

10.1	Suitability of equipment in terms of IP and fire ratings	
10.2	Enclosure not damaged/deteriorated during installation so as to impair safety	
10.3	Suitability for the environment and external influences	
10.4	Security of fixing	
10.5	Cable entry holes in ceilings above luminaires, sized or sealed so as to restrict the spread of fire	
10.6	Recessed luminaires (downlighters)	
	a) Correct type of lamps fitted	
	b) Installed to minimise build-up of heat	
10.7	Provision of undervoltage protection, where specified	
10.8	Provision of overload protection, where specified	
10.9	Adequacy of working space/accessibility to equipment	

11.0 SPECIAL INSTALLATIONS OR LOCATIONS

List below any Special Installations or Locations which are part of the installation to be verified, and confirm that the additional requirements given in the respective section of Part 7 are fulfilled.

12.0 OTHER

SCHEDULE OF ADDITIONAL RECORDS* (See attached schedule)

Page No(s)

Note: Additional page(s) must be identified by the Electrical Installation Certificate serial number and page number(s).

† ***All boxes must be completed.*** *'✓' indicates that an inspection was carried out and that the result was* ***satisfactory****. 'N/A' indicates that an inspection was* ***not applicable*** *to the particular installation.*

* *Where the electrical work to which this certificate relates includes the installation of a fire alarm system and/or an emergency lighting system (or a part of such systems), this electrical safety certificate should be accompanied by the particular certificate(s) for the system(s).*

Page 4 of

This certificate is based on the model forms shown in Appendix 6 of BS 7671

ICN4/7

It should be confirmed that the means of interrupting the supply is capable of cutting off the full load current of the relevant part of the installation. This may, for example, be a contactor used in conjunction with the emergency switching device. Due account must be taken of any stalled motor conditions.

Functional switching

The inspector should verify that devices for switching 'on' and 'off' or installed to vary the supply of electrical energy for normal operating purposes are appropriate in quantity, type, function and location.

Functional switching is required for any circuit or part of a circuit that may require to be controlled independently of other parts of the installation. Devices for functional switching may be single-pole or multi-pole; they need not control all live conductors but must not solely control the neutral. Suitable devices include switches, plugs and socket-outlets rated at up to 16 A (except for control of d.c.) and semiconductor devices. Off-load isolators, fuses or links etc. must not be used for functional switching.

10.0 Current-using equipment (permanently connected)

Permanently connected current-using equipment must be inspected to verify that it does not present a hazard in terms of electric shock or fire.

Suitability of equipment in terms of IP and fire ratings

The inspector should confirm that the installed equipment provides adequate protection against contact with live parts (Regulation 416.2 refers), and will not constitute a fire hazard - Section 421.

Enclosure not damaged/deteriorated during installation so as to impair safety

It should be confirmed that the installed equipment has not suffered damage during the installation process, which may increase the risk of contact with live parts.

Suitability for the environment and external influences

The installation should be inspected during construction and on completion to confirm that the installed equipment is suitably selected and erected to operate safely, given whatever external influences are reasonably likely to occur during the lifetime of the installation.

An external influence is defined in Part 2 of *BS 7671* as '*any influence external to an electrical installation which affects the design and safe operation of that installation*'. Examples of external influences include ambient temperature, external heat sources, solar radiation, impact, vibration, presence of water, high humidity, solid foreign bodies, corrosive or polluting substances, or other factors such as structural movement.

BS 7671 requires that all wiring and other equipment must be of a design appropriate to the situation in which it is to be used, and/or that its mode of installation must take account of the conditions likely to be encountered. Moreover, any equipment which does not meet these requirements by its own construction must be provided with appropriate additional protection. For example, in an installation in industrial premises where there are dusty or wet conditions, the selected luminaires and wiring system may, by their own construction, be suitable for the arduous conditions, whereas the distribution boards may be of a standard pattern, but housed within suitable cabinets.

Where there is doubt about the types or severity of the external influence(s) which are likely to act on an installation, reference should be made to the designer of the installation, who should have made an assessment of these influences as part of the design process in accordance with Part 3 of *BS 7671*.

Security of fixing

Equipment should be securely fixed using appropriate methods and taking into account the equipment manufacturers instructions.

Cable entry holes in ceilings above luminaires, sized or sealed so as to restrict the spread of fire

Cable entry holes made in the fabric of the building should, where necessary, be sealed to restrict the spread of fire (refer to - 8.0 Provision of fire barriers, sealing arrangements so as to minimise the spread of fire).

Recessed luminaires (downlighters)

Where an installation contains recessed luminaires, it should be confirmed that the lamps are of the correct type and rating for the luminaire, and the arrangement to prevent a build-up of heat above the luminaire is appropriate for the particular design.

Whilst no additional measures may be necessary in the case of so called 'fire rated' luminaires, where open-backed type luminaires have been installed, an insulation displacement box or similar may be necessary.

Provision of undervoltage protection

The inspector should examine the installation for undervoltage protective devices which are provided to disconnect equipment in the event of a significant reduction in the supply voltage. These devices are not uncommon. They are found, for instance, in starter units controlling and protecting electric motors. They may also be found in emergency stop systems and in automatic control systems to bring standby supplies into operation.

The inspector should check that any undervoltage devices installed conform to the design requirements for the installation and Section 445 of *BS 7671*. The presence of any necessary arrangements to prevent automatic re-closure of undervoltage devices should also be verified. Such arrangements are required where the re-closure of an undervoltage device is likely to cause danger, for example, where the unexpected restarting of a machine could cause danger.

Provision of overload protection, where specified

The type and rating of overload protection provided for current-using equipment should be checked against the design. For example, the inspector should confirm that the current-settings of motor overloads have been adjusted and installed in accordance with the requirements of *BS 7671* and the electrical designers intentions (Regulation 612.13.2 refers).

Adequacy of working space/accessibility to equipment

It must be confirmed that adequate and safe means of access and working space have been afforded to every piece of electrical equipment and switchgear to facilitate operation, inspection, testing, fault detection, maintenance and repair.

11.0 SPECIAL INSTALLATIONS OR LOCATIONS

The special installations or locations contained in Part 7 of *BS 7671* are those where the risks associated with electric shock are increased due to wetness; absence of, or minimal clothing; presence of earthed metal; arduous conditions; and where other risks, such as that of fire, may also be increased.

The requirements included in the particular sections of special installations or locations supplement those contained in the other parts of the regulations. Therefore in addition to those requirements the inspector should confirm that the particular requirements of Part 7 of *BS 7671* for the special location or Installation have been met.

11.0 SPECIAL INSTALLATIONS OR LOCATIONS

List below any Special Installations or Locations which are part of the installation to be verified, and confirm that the additional requirements given in the respective section of Part 7 are fulfilled.

'Special installations or locations' are fairly common, and the inspector will need to think carefully before putting an N/A in the relevant box on the Electrical Installation Certificate or Domestic Electrical Installation Certificate. It should be remembered that a location containing a bath or shower is a special location and normally applicable for every domestic installation. For these reasons, the inspection schedule relating to the Domestic Electrical Installation Certificate includes items applicable for a location containing a bath or shower.

12.0 Other

The installations and locations included in Part 7 of *BS 7671*, such as locations containing a bath or shower, and agricultural and horticultural premises are not the only ones where there may be increased risk of electric shock. The designer of an installation may have identified other locations of increased shock risk and decided to use additional measures such as 30 mA RCD protection for certain equipment or supplementary bonding.

and at fixed and stationary equipment

9.0 ISOLATION AND SWITCHING

9.1 Isolators

a) Presence and location of appropriate devices

b) Capable of being secured in the OFF position

c) Correct operation verified (functional check)

d) The installation, circuit or part thereof that will be isolated is clearly identified by location and/or durable marking

e) Warning label posted in situations where live parts cannot be isolated by the operation of a single device

12.0 OTHER

SCHEDULE OF ADDITIONAL RECORDS* (See attached schedule)

Page No(s)

Note: Additional page(s) must be identified by the Electrical Installation Certificate serial number and page number(s).

† ***All boxes must be completed.*** *'✓' indicates that an inspection was carried out and that the result was* ***satisfactory****. 'N/A' indicates that an inspection was* ***not applicable*** *to the particular installation.*

* *Where the electrical work to which this certificate relates includes the installation of a fire alarm system and/or an emergency lighting system (or a part of such systems), this electrical safety certificate should be accompanied by the particular certificate(s) for the system(s).*

Page 4 of

This certificate is based on the model forms shown in Appendix 6 of BS 7671

Published by Certsure LLP. Certsure LLP operates the ELECSA & NICEIC brands. © Copyright Certsure LLP (January 2015)

ICN4/7

Chapter

8

The Inspection Schedule for condition reporting

IPM6/

ELECTRICAL INSTALLATION CONDITION REPORT

INSPECTION SCHEDULE FOR DISTRIBUTION BOARDS AND CIRCUITS

Item	Description	Outcome*	Location reference
1.0	**Condition/adequacy of distributor's/supply intake equipment†**		
1.1	Service cable		
1.2	Service head		
1.3	Distributor's earthing arrangement(s)		
1.4	Meter tails – Distributor/ Consumer		
1.5	Metering equipment		

Original (To the person ordering the work)

appropriate on
C3 and FI coded
the report.

Page 4 of

ority.

IPM6/7

APPROVED CONTRACTOR

This report is not valid if the serial number has been defaced or altered **IPN4/**

ELECTRICAL INSTALLATION CONDITION REPORT

INSPECTION SCHEDULE FOR DISTRIBUTION BOARDS AND CIRCUITS

Original (To the person ordering the work)

Item	Description	Outcome*	Location reference
1.0	**Condition/adequacy of distributor's/supply intake equipment†**		
1.1	Service cable		
1.2	Service head		
1.3	Distributor's earthing arrangement(s)		
1.4	Meter tails – Distributor/ Consumer		
1.5	Metering equipment		
1.6	Means of main isolation *(where present)*		
2.0	**Presence of adequate arrangements for parallel or switched alternative sources**		
2.1	Adequate arrangements where a generating set operates as a switched alternative to the public supply		
2.2	Adequate arrangements where a generating set operates in parallel with the public supply		
3.0	**Automatic disconnection of supply**		
3.1	Main earthing and bonding arrangements		
	• Presence and condition of distributor's earthing arrangement		
	• Presence and condition of earth electrode arrangement		
	• Adequacy of earthing conductor size		
	• Adequacy of earthing conductor connections		
	• Accessibility of earthing conductor connections		
	• Adequacy of main protective bonding conductor size(s)		
	• Adequacy of main protective bonding conductor connections		
	• Accessibility of main protective bonding connections		
	• Accessibility and condition of other protective bonding connections		
	• Provision of earthing/bonding labels at all appropriate locations		
3.2	FELV		
	• Source providing at least simple separation		
	• Plugs, socket-outlets and the like not interchangeable with those of other systems within the premises		
3.3	Reduced low voltage		
	• Adequacy of source		
	• Plugs, socket-outlets and the like not interchangeable with those of other systems within the premises		
4.0	**Other methods of protection** *(where the methods of protection listed below are employed, details should be provided on separate sheets)*		
4.1	Double insulation		
4.2	Reinforced insulation		
4.3	Use of obstacles		
4.4	Placing out of reach		
4.5	Non-conducting location		
4.6	Earth-free local equipotential bonding		
4.7	Electrical separation for more than one item of equipment		
5.0	**Distribution equipment**		
5.1	Adequacy of working space/accessibility of equipment		
5.2	Security of fixing		
5.3	Condition of insulation of live parts		
5.4	Adequacy/security of barriers		
5.5	Condition of enclosure(s) in terms of IP rating		
5.6	Condition of enclosure(s) in terms of fire rating		
5.7	Enclosure not damaged/deteriorated so as to impair safety		
5.8	Presence of main switch(es), linked where required		
5.9	Operation of main switch(es) *(functional check)*		
5.10	Correct identification of circuit protective devices		
5.11	Adequacy of protective devices for prospective fault current		
5.12	RCD(s) provided for fault protection – includes RCBOs		
5.13	RCD(s) provided for additional protection – includes RCBOs		

* ***All Outcome boxes must be completed.***
'✔' indicates **Acceptable condition**
'LIM' indicates a **Limitation**
'N/A' indicates **Not applicable**

Unacceptable condition state **C1** or **C2**
Improvement recommended state **C3**
Further investigation required without delay state **FI**
(to determine whether danger or potential danger exists)

Outcome
Provide additional comment where appropriate on attached numbered sheets. C1, C2, C3 and FI coded items to be recorded in Section F of the report.

Page 4 of

† Where inadequacies in distributor's equipment are encountered, it is recommended that the person ordering the report informs the appropriate authority.

This report is based on the model forms shown in Appendix 6 of BS 7671

IPN4/7

8 CHAPTER 8. THE INSPECTION SCHEDULE FOR CONDITION REPORTING

Electrical installations deteriorate with age, as well as with wear and tear. Every installation therefore needs to be inspected at appropriate intervals during its service life to check that its condition is such that it is safe to remain in service, and is likely to remain safe at least until the next inspection is due. Periodic inspection also enables the need for any remedial work to be identified and drawn to the attention of those responsible for the safety of the installation.

Generally, persons undertaking periodic inspection and subsequent installation condition reporting need to have extensive knowledge and experience of electrical installation matters to enable them to safely and accurately assess the condition of an existing electrical installation, especially when they do not have access to the design information relating to that installation.

SEQUENCE OF INSPECTIONS FOR A PERIODIC INSPECTION

Guidance on the range of inspections in this chapter closely follows the sequence of the items listed in the Inspection Schedule for Distribution Boards and Circuits that forms part of the NICEIC Electrical Installation Condition Report.

An entry should be made in every unshaded box in the 'Outcome' column of the Inspection Schedule for Distribution Boards and Circuits to indicate the condition of that element of the installation or other appropriate factor (such as 'not applicable'), using one of the following options:

✔	the result was **satisfactory**
C1	an **unsatisfactory** condition was observed, such that **danger was present**
C2	an **unsatisfactory** condition was observed which was **potentially dangerous**
C3	means **improvement recommended** and should be used to indicate that, whilst an observed deficiency was not considered to be a source of immediate or potential danger, improvement would contribute to a significant enhancement of the safety of the electrical installation.
FI	indicates that **further investigation without delay** is required to determine whether danger or potential danger exists.
Lim	indicates that, exceptionally, a **limitation** agreed with the person ordering the work prevented the inspection being carried out.
N/A	means that an item on the inspection schedule was not applicable to the particular installation.

Note: If further investigation is required, the condition of the installation must be reported to be unsatisfactory.

NICEIC APPROVED CONTRACTOR

This report is not valid if the serial number has been defaced or altered **IPN4/**

riginal (To the person ordering the work)

ELECTRICAL INSTALLATION CONDITION REPORT

INSPECTION SCHEDULE FOR DISTRIBUTION BOARDS AND CIRCUITS

Item	Description	Outcome*	Location reference
1.0	**Condition/adequacy of distributor's/supply intake equipment†**		
1.1	Service cable		
1.2	Service head		
1.3	Distributor's earthing arrangement(s)		
1.4	Meter tails – Distributor/ Consumer		

INSPECTION SCHEDULE FOR DISTRIBUTION BOARDS AND CIRCUITS

Item	Description	Outcome*	Location reference
1.0	**Condition/adequacy of distributor's/supply intake equipment†**		
1.1	Service cable		
1.2	Service head		
1.3	Distributor's earthing arrangement(s)		
1.4	Meter tails – Distributor/ Consumer		
1.5	Metering equipment		
1.6	Means of main isolation *(where present)*		
2.0	**Presence of adequate arrangements for parallel or switched alternative sources**		
2.1	Adequate arrangements where a generating set operates as a switched alternative to the public supply		
2.2	Adequate arrangements where a generating set operates in parallel with the public supply		
3.0	**Automatic disconnection of supply**		
3.1	Main earthing and bonding arrangements		
	• Presence and condition of distributor's earthing arrangement		
	• Presence and condition of earth electrode arrangement		
	• Adequacy of earthing conductor size		
	• Adequacy of source		
	• Plugs, socket-outlets and the like not interchangeable with those of other systems within the premises		
4.0	**Other methods of protection** (*where the methods of protection listed below are employed, details should be provided on separate sheets*)		
4.1	Double insulation		
4.2	Reinforced insulation		
4.3	Use of obstacles		
4.4	Placing out of reach		
4.5	Non-conducting location		
4.6	Earth-free local equipotential bonding		
4.7	Electrical separation for more than one item of equipment		
5.0	**Distribution equipment**		
5.1	Adequacy of working space/accessibility of equipment		
5.2	Security of fixing		
5.3	Condition of insulation of live parts		
5.4	Adequacy/security of barriers		
5.5	Condition of enclosure(s) in terms of IP rating		
5.6	Condition of enclosure(s) in terms of fire rating		
5.7	Enclosure not damaged/deteriorated so as to impair safety		
5.8	Presence of main switch(es), linked where required		
5.9	Operation of main switch(es) (*functional check*)		
5.10	Correct identification of circuit protective devices		
5.11	Adequacy of protective devices for prospective fault current		
5.12	RCD(s) provided for fault protection – includes RCBOs		
5.13	RCD(s) provided for additional protection – includes RCBOs		

* ***All Outcome boxes must be completed.***
'✓' indicates **Acceptable condition**
'LIM' indicates a **Limitation**
'N/A' indicates **Not applicable**

Unacceptable condition state **C1** or **C2**
Improvement recommended state **C3**
Further investigation required without delay state **FI**
(to determine whether danger or potential danger exists)

Outcome
Provide additional comment where appropriate on attached numbered sheets. C1, C2, C3 and FI coded items to be recorded in Section F of the report.

Page 4 of

† Where inadequacies in distributor's equipment are encountered, it is recommended that the person ordering the report informs the appropriate authority.

This report is based on the model forms shown in Appendix 6 of BS 7671

IPN4/7

1.0 Condition/adequacy of distributor's/supply intake equipment

This section requires the inspector to look into the following aspects of the supply intake equipment which are readily accessible:

The service cable should be inspected for signs of mechanical damage, evidence of overheating and other forms of deterioration.

An inspection should be performed to assess the general condition of the **service cut-out** assembly. In general, it will be possible to ascertain the type of fuse employed but not its rating, which will probably need to be ascertained by reference to the original design or specification, or the Electrical Installation Certificate issued on completion of the original electrical installation.

The type and rating of the service fuse(s) should be entered in the appropriate boxes of the 'characteristics of primary supply overcurrent protective device(s)' section of Part K of the Electrical Installation Condition Report.

Under no circumstances should the inspector attempt to access or withdraw the cut-out fuse(s) as a part of this inspection, unless authorised to do so.

Distributor's earthing arrangement(s) The suppliers earthing arrangement should be inspected to confirm it is suitable for the particular supply system Type, TN-S, TN-C-S or TT being the most common systems used. For a TN-S supply system the arrangement should include a separate earth return path to the supply transformer, usually via the metallic sheath of the distributor's supply cable. Whereas for a TN-C-S system the earth return path is achieved by connection of the installation earthing conductor to the supplier's neutral, or more accurately Combined Neutral and Earth (CNE) conductor (also known as a PEN conductor).

The **meter tails** belonging to the **distributor** and the **consumer** should be inspected for signs of mechanical damage, evidence of overheating and other forms of deterioration in a manner similar to the service cable. The results of this inspection will play an important part in the decision-making process regarding the suitability of the meter tails for continued use, especially where the tails are of cross-sectional area smaller than that required by the current edition of the *BS 7671*. The inspector should also confirm whether or not the tails are correctly, clearly and unambiguously identified.

The **metering equipment** and any connection boxes provided by the distributor as a part of their installation should be inspected. In particular such equipment should be inspected for security of fixings and signs of damage to outer casings/enclosures. Where signs of significant damage are observed these should be noted in Section F of the report 'Observations and recommendations for actions to be taken'.

Some installations will incorporate an isolating switch provided by the distributor. Where this is the case, it should be confirmed that the switch functions correctly in addition to confirming its overall condition.

NICEIC APPROVED CONTRACTOR

This report is not valid if the serial number has been defaced or altered **IPN4/**

(To the person ordering the work) ...riginal

ELECTRICAL INSTALLATION CONDITION REPORT

INSPECTION SCHEDULE FOR DISTRIBUTION BOARDS AND CIRCUITS

Item	Description	Outcome*	Location reference
1.0	**Condition/adequacy of distributor's/supply intake equipment**†		
1.1	Service cable		
1.2	Service head		
1.3	Distributor's earthing arrangement(s)		
1.4	Meter tails – Distributor/ Consumer		

Item	Description	Outcome*	Location reference
2.0	**Presence of adequate arrangements for parallel or switched alternative sources**		
2.1	Adequate arrangements where a generating set operates as a switched alternative to the public supply		
2.2	Adequate arrangements where a generating set operates in parallel with the public supply		
3.0	**Automatic disconnection of supply**		
3.1	Main earthing and bonding arrangements		
	• Presence and condition of distributor's earthing arrangement		
	• Presence and condition of earth electrode arrangement		
	• Adequacy of earthing conductor size		
	• Adequacy of earthing conductor connections		
	• Accessibility of earthing conductor connections		
	• Adequacy of main protective bonding conductor size(s)		
	• Adequacy of main protective bonding conductor connections		
	• Accessibility of main protective bonding connections		
	• Accessibility and condition of other protective bonding connections		
	• Provision of earthing/bonding labels at all appropriate locations		
3.2	FELV		
	• Source providing at least simple separation		
	• Plugs, socket-outlets and the like not interchangeable with those of other systems within the premises		

Item	Description	Outcome*	Location reference
	• Adequacy of source		
	• Plugs, socket-outlets and the like not interchangeable with those of other systems within the premises		
4.0	**Other methods of protection** (*where the methods of protection listed below are employed, details should be provided on separate sheets*)		
4.1	Double insulation		
4.2	Reinforced insulation		
4.3	Use of obstacles		
4.4	Placing out of reach		
4.5	Non-conducting location		
4.6	Earth-free local equipotential bonding		
4.7	Electrical separation for more than one item of equipment		
5.0	**Distribution equipment**		
5.1	Adequacy of working space/accessibility of equipment		
5.2	Security of fixing		
5.3	Condition of insulation of live parts		
5.4	Adequacy/security of barriers		
5.5	Condition of enclosure(s) in terms of IP rating		
5.6	Condition of enclosure(s) in terms of fire rating		
5.7	Enclosure not damaged/deteriorated so as to impair safety		
5.8	Presence of main switch(es), linked where required		
5.9	Operation of main switch(es) (*functional check*)		
5.10	Correct identification of circuit protective devices		
5.11	Adequacy of protective devices for prospective fault current		
5.12	RCD(s) provided for fault protection – includes RCBOs		
5.13	RCD(s) provided for additional protection – includes RCBOs		

* ***All Outcome boxes must be completed.***
'✔' indicates **Acceptable condition**
'*LIM*' indicates a **Limitation**
'*N/A*' indicates **Not applicable**

Unacceptable condition state **C1** or **C2**
Improvement recommended state **C3**
Further investigation required without delay state **FI**
(to determine whether danger or potential danger exists)

Outcome
Provide additional comment where appropriate on attached numbered sheets. C1, C2, C3 and FI coded items to be recorded in Section F of the report.

Page 4 of

† Where inadequacies in distributor's equipment are encountered, it is recommended that the person ordering the report informs the appropriate authority.

This report is based on the model forms shown in Appendix 6 of BS 7671

IPN4/7

The person who ordered the inspection should be advised to inform the distributor and/or meter operator, as appropriate, of any inadequacies in the equipment forming a part of their installation that have been observed during the inspection. Where any departures deserving of a code C1 (danger present) or code C2 (potentially dangerous) classification have been found, the person who ordered the inspection should be informed immediately, or as a matter of urgency, respectively.

2.0 Presence of adequate arrangements for parallel or switched alternative sources

Where, as is increasingly the case even in domestic installations, there are parallel or switched sources of supply to, or within, the installation, the inspector should confirm that the connection and operation of the generating set complies with the requirements detailed in Regulation 551.6 and 551.7 as appropriate.

3.0 Automatic disconnection of supply

The majority of electrical installations within the UK rely primarily on automatic disconnection of supply (ADS) for protection against electric shock.

Section 3.1 requires confirmation of the presence, condition and adequacy of the main earthing and protective bonding arrangements for the installation. It also asks for confirmation that the labelling required by Regulation 514.13.1 has been provided at the relevant points within the installation. Earthing and bonding was discussed at greater length in Chapter 7.

Section 3.2 is only applicable where functional extra-low voltage (FELV) has been employed within an installation as part of the protective measure of automatic disconnection of supply (ADS). FELV is considered further in Chapter 7.

Section 3.3 is applicable to the use of reduced low voltage (RLV) in accordance with the requirements of Regulation group 411.8.

- **Adequacy of source:** Confirm the use of a source permitted by Regulation 411.8.4. Typically this will be a double-wound isolating transformer meeting the requirements of *BS EN 61558-1* and *BS EN 61558-2-23*, although supplies derived from a motor-generator providing isolation equivalent to that of the aforementioned transformer or from engine-driven generator sets may also be used.
- **Plugs, socket-outlets and the like not interchangeable with those of other systems within the premises:** Inspect the plugs, socket-outlets and other accessories forming part of the RLV system to confirm the presence of a protective conductor contact. Appropriately rated (in terms of voltage and current) plugs, socket-outlets and couplers meeting the constructional requirements of *BS EN 60309-2* will be dimensionally non-interchangeable with such accessories used for other systems in use within the premises.

NICEIC APPROVED CONTRACTOR

This report is not valid if the serial number has been defaced or altered **IPN4/**

riginal (To the person ordering the work)

ELECTRICAL INSTALLATION CONDITION REPORT

INSPECTION SCHEDULE FOR DISTRIBUTION BOARDS AND CIRCUITS

Item	Description	Outcome*	Location reference
1.0	**Condition/adequacy of distributor's/supply intake equipment†**		
1.1	Service cable		
1.2	Service head		
1.3	Distributor's earthing arrangement(s)		
1.4	Meter tails – Distributor/ Consumer		

Item	Description	Outcome*	Location reference
4.0	**Other methods of protection** (*where the methods of protection listed below are employed, details should be provided on separate sheets*)		
4.1	Double insulation		
4.2	Reinforced insulation		
4.3	Use of obstacles		
4.4	Placing out of reach		
4.5	Non-conducting location		
4.6	Earth-free local equipotential bonding		
4.7	Electrical separation for more than one item of equipment		
5.0	**Distribution equipment**		
5.1	Adequacy of working space/accessibility of equipment		
5.2	Security of fixing		
5.3	Condition of insulation of live parts		
5.4	Adequacy/security of barriers		
5.5	Condition of enclosure(s) in terms of IP rating		
5.6	Condition of enclosure(s) in terms of fire rating		
5.7	Enclosure not damaged/deteriorated so as to impair safety		
5.8	Presence of main switch(es), linked where required		
5.9	Operation of main switch(es) (*functional check*)		
5.10	Correct identification of circuit protective devices		

Item	Description	Outcome*	Location reference
	• Adequacy of source		
	• Plugs, socket-outlets and the like not interchangeable with those of other systems within the premises		
4.0	**Other methods of protection** (*where the methods of protection listed below are employed, details should be provided on separate sheets*)		
4.1	Double insulation		
4.2	Reinforced insulation		
4.3	Use of obstacles		
4.4	Placing out of reach		
4.5	Non-conducting location		
4.6	Earth-free local equipotential bonding		
4.7	Electrical separation for more than one item of equipment		
5.0	**Distribution equipment**		
5.1	Adequacy of working space/accessibility of equipment		
5.2	Security of fixing		
5.3	Condition of insulation of live parts		
5.4	Adequacy/security of barriers		
5.5	Condition of enclosure(s) in terms of IP rating		
5.6	Condition of enclosure(s) in terms of fire rating		
5.7	Enclosure not damaged/deteriorated so as to impair safety		
5.8	Presence of main switch(es), linked where required		
5.9	Operation of main switch(es) (*functional check*)		
5.10	Correct identification of circuit protective devices		
5.11	Adequacy of protective devices for prospective fault current		
5.12	RCD(s) provided for fault protection – includes RCBOs		
5.13	RCD(s) provided for additional protection – includes RCBOs		

* ***All Outcome boxes must be completed.***
'✓' indicates **Acceptable condition**
'*LIM*' indicates a **Limitation**
'*N/A*' indicates **Not applicable**

Unacceptable condition state **C1** or **C2**
Improvement recommended state **C3**
Further investigation required without delay state **FI**
(to determine whether danger or potential danger exists)

Outcome
Provide additional comment where appropriate on attached numbered sheets. C1, C2, C3 and FI coded items to be recorded in Section F of the report.

Page 4 of

† Where inadequacies in distributor's equipment are encountered, it is recommended that the person ordering the report informs the appropriate authority.

This report is based on the model forms shown in Appendix 6 of BS 7671
Published by Certsure LLP. Certsure LLP operates the ELECSA & NICEIC brands. IPN4/7

4.0 Other methods of protection

Where a method of protection other than ADS is employed, one of the outcome options listed at the beginning of this chapter should be entered in the appropriate data entry box and details of those aspects of the protective measure(s) which have been subjected to an inspection should be provided on separate sheets to be attached to the report. Where this is not the case, N/A should be entered.

5.0 Distribution equipment

25 suggested inspection items are listed under this heading including:

- **adequacy of working space/accessibility of equipment**
- **security of fixing**
- a number of aspects relating to
  - **the condition of enclosures**
  - **presence and operation of main switches**
  - **suitability of protective devices in terms of fault current rating**
- provision of RCD protection
- confirmation that **circuit-breakers/RCDs provide disconnection** when switched to the OFF position
- **provision of identification and/or labelling**, such as:
  - circuit protective devices
  - RCD retest notice
  - charts, diagrams etc at/near equipment (where required)
  - cables utilising different colour-coding arrangements
  - presence of alternative supply arrangements
  - next inspection recommendation
- **examination of protective devices and, where applicable, their bases** for signs of notable deterioration
- suitability of cable entries in terms of protection against:
  - **mechanical damage:** such as the use of paxolene or similar inserts, grommet strip, bushes etc.
  - **electromagnetic effects:** all associated conductors passing through the same entry of a metallic enclosure.

NICEIC APPROVED CONTRACTOR

This report is not valid if the serial number has been defaced or altered IPN4/

ELECTRICAL INSTALLATION CONDITION REPORT

Original (To the person ordering the work)

INSPECTION SCHEDULE FOR DISTRIBUTION BOARDS AND CIRCUITS

Item	Description	Outcome*	Location reference
5.14	RCD(s) provided for protection against fire – includes RCBOs		
5.15	Manual operation of circuit-breakers and RCDs to prove disconnection		
5.16	Presence of RCD retest notice at or near equipment where required		
5.17	Presence of diagrams, charts or schedules at or near equipment, where required		
5.18	Presence of non-standard (mixed) cable colour warning notice at or near equipment where required		
5.19	Presence of alternative/additional s… where required		
5.20	Presence of replacement next ins…		
5.21	Presence of other required labelli…		
5.22	Examination of protective device(… (*no signs of unacceptable therma…*)		
5.23	Single-pole switching or protectiv…		
5.24	Protection against mechanical da…		
5.25	Protection against electromagnet…		
6.0	**Distribution/final circuits**		
6.1	Identification of conductors		
6.2	Cables correctly supported throu…		
6.3	Condition of insulation of live part…		
6.4	Non-sheathed cables protected b…		
6.5	Suitability of containment system…		
6.6	Cables correctly terminated in en…		
6.7	Confirmation of indication that SP…		
6.8	Confirmation that ALL conductor … located in terminals and are tight		
6.9	Examination of cables for signs of…		
6.10	Adequacy of cables for current-ca…		
6.11	Adequacy of protective devices; t…		
6.12	Presence and adequacy of circuit…		
6.13	Co-ordination between conductor…		
6.14	Cable installation methods/practic… and external influences		
6.15	Cables where exposed to direct s…		
6.16	Cables installed under floors, abo… adequately protected against dam…		
	• installed in prescribed zones (s…		
	• incorporating earthed armour o… or otherwise protected against… (see Section D. Extent and limit…		
6.17	Provision of additional protection…		
	• †for mobile equipment not excee…		
	• †for all socket-outlets of rating 2…		
	• †for cables installed in walls / pa…		
	• †for cables installed in walls / pa…		
6.18	Provision of fire barriers, sealing…		
6.19	Band II cables segregated/separa…		
6.20	Cables segregated/separated fro…		
6.21	Termination of cables at enclosure…		
	• Connections under no undue st…		
	• No basic insulation of a conduc…		
	• Connections of live conductors…		
	• Adequacy of connection at poi…		
6.22	General condition of wiring syste…		
6.23	Temperature rating of cable insula…		
6.24	Condition of accessories includin…		
6.25	Suitability of accessories for exte…		
6.26	Single-pole switching or protectiv…		
6.27	Adequacy of connections, includi… equipment – identify /record num…		

†*Note: Older installations designed prior to …for additional protection*

* *All Outcome boxes must be completed.* '✓' indicates **Acceptable condition**; 'LIM' indicates a **Limitation**; 'N/A' indicates **Not applicable**. Unacce… Improve… Further… (to dete…

This report is based on the model forms shown …
Published by Certsure LLP. Certsure LLP operat…
IPN4/9

NICEIC APPROVED CONTRACTOR

This report is not valid if the serial number has been defaced or altered IPN4/

ELECTRICAL INSTALLATION CONDITION REPORT

Original (To the person ordering the work)

INSPECTION SCHEDULE FOR DISTRIBUTION BOARDS AND CIRCUITS

Item	Description	Outcome*	Location reference
7.0	**Isolation and switching**		
7.1	Isolators		
	• presence and condition of appropriate devices		
	• acceptable location (state if local or remote)		
	• capable of being secured in the OFF position		
	• correct operation verified		
	• clearly identified by position and/or durable marking(s)		
	• Warning label posted in situations where live parts cannot be isolated by the operation of a single device		
7.2	Switching off for mechanical maintenance		
	• presence and condition of appropriate devices		
	• acceptable location		
	• capable of being secured in the OFF position		
	• correct operation verified		
	• clearly identified by position and/or durable marking(s)		
7.3	Emergency switching/stopping		
	• presence and condition of appropriate devices		
	• readily accessible for operation where danger might occur		
	• correct operation verified		
	• clearly identified by position and/or durable marking(s)		
7.4	Functional switching		
	• presence and condition of appropriate devices		
	• correct operation verified		
8.0	**Current-using equipment (*permanently connected*)**		
8.1	Condition of equipment in terms of IP rating		
8.2	Equipment does not constitute a fire hazard		
8.3	Enclosure not damaged/deteriorated so as to impair safety		
8.4	Suitability for the environment and external influences		
8.5	Security of fixing		
8.6	Cable entry holes in ceiling above luminaires, sized or sealed so as to restrict the spread of fire (*indicate extent of sampling in Section D of report*)		
8.7	Recessed luminaires (e.g. downlighters)		
	• correct type of lamps fitted		
	• installed to minimise build-up of heat by use of "fire rated" fittings, insulation displacement box or similar		
	• no signs of overheating to surrounding building fabric		
	• no signs of overheating to conductors/terminations		
9.0	**Location(s) containing a bath or shower**		
9.1	Additional protection by RCD not exceeding 30 mA		
	• for low voltage circuits serving the location		
	• for low voltage circuits passing through Zone 1 and Zone 2 not serving the location		
9.2	Where used as a protective measure, requirements for SELV or PELV are met		
9.3	Shaver sockets comply with BS EN 61558-2-5 or BS 3535		
9.4	Presence of supplementary bonding conductors unless not required by BS 7671: 2008		
9.5	Low voltage (e.g. 230 volts) socket-outlets sited at least 3 m from zone 1		
9.6	Suitability of equipment for external influences for installed location in terms of IP rating		
9.7	Suitability of equipment for installation in a particular zone		
9.8	Suitability of current-using equipment for a particular position within the location		
10.0	**Other special installations or locations**		
	List special locations present, if any. List the results of particular inspections applied (a separate page is required for each location).		

* *All Outcome boxes must be completed.* '✓' indicates **Acceptable condition**; 'LIM' indicates a **Limitation**; 'N/A' indicates **Not applicable**

Unacceptable condition state **C1** or **C2**
Improvement recommended state **C3**
Further investigation required without delay state **FI** (to determine whether danger or potential danger exists)

Outcome
Provide additional comment where appropriate on attached numbered sheets. C1, C2, C3 and FI coded items to be recorded in Section F of the report.

Page 6 of

This report is based on the model forms shown in Appendix 6 of BS 7671
Published by Certsure LLP. Certsure LLP operates the ELECSA & NICEIC brands. © Copyright Certsure LLP (January 2015)
IPN4/11

6.0 Distribution/final circuits

This section of the schedule lists 27 items relating to circuits which might require inspection in a typical installation, most of which are self-explanatory.

7.0 Isolation and switching

This section has four parts listing a number of inspection items relating to devices providing:

- isolation
- switching off for mechanical maintenance
- emergency switching/stopping
- functional switching

It should be noted that a single device or collection of devices may provide more than one of the functions listed above. Where this is the case it will be necessary that the device meets all the relevant requirements of *BS 7671* for each of the functions it is intended to provide. In such situations, prior knowledge of the installation and/or availability of relevant information relating to the design of the installation will be highly beneficial.

8.0 Current-using equipment (permanently connected)

This section of the inspection schedule calls for the inspection of permanently connected current-using equipment (including electrical equipment present in accessible roof spaces) to verify that it does not present a hazard in terms of shock or fire.

Equipment enclosures should be inspected to confirm their continued adequacy in terms of IP rating and to identify any damage/deterioration that has occurred whilst in service. A sample inspection should be made of cable entry holes through ceilings and details of the location of the sample should be provided in the 'location reference' column on the inspection schedule.

Where an installation contains recessed luminaires, it should be confirmed that the lamps currently fitted are of the correct type and rating for the luminaire. This may require reference to manufacturer's data where the relevant information is not given on the luminaire. A sample of luminaires so installed should be inspected to confirm the arrangements for preventing a build-up of heat above the luminaire as appropriate to their particular design.

Whilst no additional measures may be necessary in the case of so-called 'fire rated' luminaires, where open backed type luminaires have been installed, an insulation displacement box or similar may be necessary.

NICEIC APPROVED CONTRACTOR

This report is not valid if the serial number has been defaced or altered **IPN4/**

riginal (To the person ordering the work)

ELECTRICAL INSTALLATION CONDITION REPORT

INSPECTION SCHEDULE FOR DISTRIBUTION BOARDS AND CIRCUITS

Item	Description	Outcome*	Location reference
7.0	**Isolation and switching**		
7.1	Isolators		
	• presence and condition of appropriate devices		
	• acceptable location (state if local or remote)		

9.0	**Location(s) containing a bath or shower**		
9.1	Additional protection by RCD not exceeding 30 mA		
	• for low voltage circuits serving the location		
	• for low voltage circuits passing through Zone 1 and Zone 2 not serving the location		
9.2	Where used as a protective measure, requirements for SELV or PELV are met		
9.3	Shaver sockets comply with BS EN 61558-2-5 or BS 3535		
9.4	Presence of supplementary bonding conductors unless not required by BS 7671: 2008		
9.5	Low voltage (e.g. 230 volts) socket-outlets sited at least 3 m from zone 1		
9.6	Suitability of equipment for external influences for installed location in terms of IP rating		
9.7	Suitability of equipment for installation in a particular zone		
9.8	Suitability of current-using equipment for a particular position within the location		
10.0	**Other special installations or locations**		
	List special locations present, if any. List the results of particular inspections applied (a separate page is required for each location).		

* ***All Outcome boxes must be completed.*** **Unacceptable condition** state **C1** or **C2** **Outcome** Provide additional comment where appropriate on

8.5	Security of fixing		
8.6	Cable entry holes in ceiling above luminaires, sized or sealed so as to restrict the spread of fire (*indicate extent of sampling in Section D of report*)		
8.7	Recessed luminaires (e.g. downlighters)		
	• correct type of lamps fitted		
	• installed to minimise build-up of heat by use of "fire rated" fittings, insulation displacement box or similar		
	• no signs of overheating to surrounding building fabric		
	• no signs of overheating to conductors/terminations		
9.0	**Location(s) containing a bath or shower**		
9.1	Additional protection by RCD not exceeding 30 mA		
	• for low voltage circuits serving the location		
	• for low voltage circuits passing through Zone 1 and Zone 2 not serving the location		
9.2	Where used as a protective measure, requirements for SELV or PELV are met		
9.3	Shaver sockets comply with BS EN 61558-2-5 or BS 3535		
9.4	Presence of supplementary bonding conductors unless not required by BS 7671: 2008		
9.5	Low voltage (e.g. 230 volts) socket-outlets sited at least 3 m from zone 1		
9.6	Suitability of equipment for external influences for installed location in terms of IP rating		
9.7	Suitability of equipment for installation in a particular zone		
9.8	Suitability of current-using equipment for a particular position within the location		
10.0	**Other special installations or locations**		
	List special locations present, if any. List the results of particular inspections applied (a separate page is required for each location).		

* ***All Outcome boxes must be completed.***
'✓' indicates **Acceptable condition**
'*LIM*' indicates a **Limitation**
'*N/A*' indicates **Not applicable**

Unacceptable condition state **C1** or **C2**
Improvement recommended state **C3**
Further investigation required without delay state **FI**
(to determine whether danger or potential danger exists)

Outcome
Provide additional comment where appropriate on attached numbered sheets. C1, C2, C3 and FI coded items to be recorded in Section F of the report.

Page 6 of

This report is based on the model forms shown in Appendix 6 of BS 7671
Published by Certsure LLP. Certsure LLP operates the ELECSA & NICEIC brands. © Copyright Certsure LLP (January 2015)
IPN4/11

Whilst it might be possible to inspect a number of recessed luminaires from above via an accessible loft space, it is recommended that a number of luminaires installed in inaccessible floor/ceiling voids are also withdrawn for inspection. Again, details of those luminaires that have been so inspected should be provided in the 'location reference' column of the inspection schedule.

9.0 Locations containing a bath or shower

This section lists eight items that should be verified by inspection, as appropriate.

Regulation 701.411.3.3 requires additional protection to be provided by an RCD having a rated residual current ($I_{\Delta n}$) not exceeding 30 m A for all low voltage circuits:

- serving the location
- passing through zones 1 and/or 2 of the location but not serving the location.

Typically this requirement will be met if the protective measures of SELV or PELV have been employed, the inspector should confirm that the relevant general requirements for these protective measures applicable for example to the source of supply, have been met as well as those specific to such locations contained within Section 701.

Where shaver socket-outlets have been installed within the location, it should be verified that they comply with *BS EN 61558-2-5* or *BS 3535* and that they have NOT been installed in zone 0 or zone 1.

Where inspection and/or testing indicates that no supplementary bonding has been installed within the location, the inspector should confirm that:

- all final circuits of the location meet the requirements of *BS 7671* for automatic disconnection, **and**
- all final circuits of the location have additional protection, in accordance with 701.411.3.3, provided by an RCD having a residual operating current not exceeding ($I_{\Delta n}$) 30 mA, **and**
- there is an effective connection of the extraneous-conductive-parts of the installation to the protective equipotential bonding.

If low voltage (230 V) socket-outlets have been installed within the location it should be confirmed that they are located at least 3 m horizontally from the boundary of zone 1.

All installed equipment within the location should be inspected for suitability for installation within the particular zone in which it is situated in terms of both the requirements relating to zoning and resistance to external influences. In some cases, this may require reference to manufacturers' information.

10.0 Other special installations or locations

No space has been allocated in the schedule for types of special installation or location other than a location containing a bath or shower. Where any of these locations are encountered, it is for the inspector to produce a suitable report or schedule in order to describe any pertinent details to the person who ordered the inspection.

Any items in the Inspection Schedule that have been identified as being dangerous (code C1) or potentially dangerous (code C2), or that would result in a significant enhancement of safety if improved (code C3), or any items that require further investigation without delay to determine whether danger or potential danger exists (code FI), should be carried forward to Section F of the condition report in the form of observations on the safety of the installation.

9.8	Suitability of current-using equipment for a particular position within the location		
10.0	**Other special installations or locations** List special locations present, if any. List the results of particular inspections applied (a separate page is required for each location).		

*** *All Outcome boxes must be completed.***
'✓' indicates **Acceptable condition**
'*LIM*' indicates a **Limitation**
'*N/A*' indicates **Not applicable**

Unacceptable condition state **C1** or **C2**
Improvement recommended state **C3**
Further investigation required without delay state **FI**
(to determine whether danger or potential danger exists)

Outcome
Provide additional comment where appropriate on attached numbered sheets. C1, C2, C3 and FI coded items to be recorded in Section F of the report.

Page 6 of

This report is based on the model forms shown in Appendix 6 of BS 7671
Published by Certsure LLP. Certsure LLP operates the ELECSA & NICEIC brands. © Copyright Certsure LLP (January 2015)
IPN4/11

Chapter 9

TESTING

1.2 Monthly instrument accuracy log for test equipment

Checkbox		Multifunction		Continuity / I
Serial No.	98968	Serial No.	A302417	Serial No. N/A
Make	ANY	Make	ANY	Make N/A
Model	X1000	Model	TF42A	Model N/A

TESTS	Month 1	Month 2	Month 3	Month 4	Month 5
Continuity resistance (Ω)					
1 Test value (e.g. 0.5 Ω) (0.5)*	Ω	Ω	Ω	Ω	Ω
Measured value	0.51	N/A	0.50	N/A	0.51
2 Test value (e.g. 100 Ω) (100)*	Ω	Ω	Ω	Ω	Ω
Measured value	100.1	N/A	100.1	N/A	100.1
Insulation resistance (MΩ)					
1 Test value (e.g. 0.5 Ω) (0.5)*	MΩ	MΩ	MΩ	MΩ	MΩ
Measured value	0.51	N/A	0.50	N/A	0.51

1.2 Monthly instrument accuracy log for test equipment

Checkbox		Multifunction		Continuity / Insulation		Earth Fault Loop impedence		RCD	
Serial No.	98968	Serial No.	A302417	Serial No.	N/A	Serial No.	N/A	Serial No.	N/A
Make	ANY	Make	ANY	Make	N/A	Make	N/A	Make	N/A
Model	X1000	Model	TF42A	Model	N/A	Model	N/A	Model	N/A

TESTS	Month 1	Month 2	Month 3	Month 4	Month 5	Month 6	Month 7	Month 8	Month 9	Month 10	Month 11	Month 12
Continuity resistance (Ω)												
1 Test value (e.g. 0.5 Ω) (0.5)*	Ω	Ω	Ω	Ω	Ω	Ω	Ω	Ω	Ω	Ω	Ω	Ω
Measured value	0.51	N/A	0.50	N/A	0.51							
2 Test value (e.g. 100 Ω) (100)*	Ω	Ω	Ω	Ω	Ω	Ω	Ω	Ω	Ω	Ω	Ω	Ω
Measured value	100.1	N/A	100.1	N/A	100.1							
Insulation resistance (MΩ)												
1 Test value (e.g. 0.5 Ω) (0.5)*	MΩ	MΩ	MΩ	MΩ	MΩ	MΩ	MΩ	MΩ	MΩ	MΩ	MΩ	MΩ
Measured value	0.51	N/A	0.50	N/A	0.51							
2 Test value (e.g. 100 MΩ) (100)*	MΩ	MΩ	MΩ	MΩ	MΩ	MΩ	MΩ	MΩ	MΩ	MΩ	MΩ	MΩ
Measured value	99.9	N/A	99.9	N/A	99.9							
Earth fault loop impedance (Ω)	**Test conducted at designated socket-outlet:** Room 3A socket under window											
Measured value at socket-outlet	1.12	N/A	1.12	N/A	1.10							
RCD (ms)	**Rated residual operating current of designated RCD:** 30 mA											
1/2 x the rated residual operating current of the designated RCD – to confirm RCD does not trip												
RCD did not trip (Y or ✔)	✔	N/A	✔	N/A	✔							
1 x the rated residual operating current of the designated RCD												
Operating time (ms)	37	N/A	36	N/A	37							
5 x the rated residual operating current of the designated RCD												
Operating time (ms)	10	N/A	11	N/A	10							

Notes: Instruments tested every other month, due to type and quantity of work

(____)* Insert value of Ω/MΩ

Full details of the results of the accuracy tests, including any calibration certificates, are to be retained for record purposes in support of this summary.

9 TESTING

SAFETY

Electrical testing inherently involves a degree of risk. Persons carrying out electrical testing have a duty to ensure the safety of themselves and others from any possible danger resulting from the tests or from access to live parts. This requires strict adherence to safe working practice, including checking that the test equipment and leads are safe and suitable for the intended purpose, that the equipment to be tested is safe for the tests, and that the working environment does not impair safety. It is important to appreciate there is a potential danger of electric shock not only from electricity supplies, but also from voltages generated within test instruments, from stored energy devices such as uninterruptible power supplies, and from capacitive loads. Particular care is needed where there are alternative sources, such as from standby generators and uninterruptible power supplies.

General advice on such safety matters is given in HSE Guidance Note GS 38: *Electrical Test Equipment for use by Electricians.* Regulation 14 *(work on or near live conductors)* of the *Electricity at Work Regulations 1989* will often apply to electrical testing.

INSTRUMENT ACCURACY

It is essential to ensure the accuracy and consistency of test instruments used to carry out the range of tests and measurements required by *BS 7671* for certification and reporting purposes.

There should be a system in place which enables confirmation of the continuing accuracy and consistency of all test instruments used for certification and reporting purposes.

There are several alternatives for such a system, including:

- Maintaining records over time of comparative cross-checks with other test instruments.
- Maintaining records over time of measurements of the characteristics of designated reference circuits or devices. For example, the consistency of continuity, insulation resistance and earth electrode test instruments can be checked against a proprietary resistance box or a set of suitable resistors. Earth fault loop impedance test instruments can be checked by carrying out tests on a designated socket-outlet (on a non-RCD protected circuit) in a particular office. RCD test instruments can be checked by carrying out tests on an RCD unit plugged into the designated socket-outlet.

Either of these systems will provide a measure of confidence in the consistency of test measurements over time. However, before any reliance is placed in such systems, the accuracy of each test instrument first needs to be confirmed, such as by

Initial Sequence of Tests

For initial testing
(From *BS 7671*)

(i) Before the supply is connected, or with the supply disconnected as appropriate

- Continuity of protective conductors including main and supplementary equipotential bonding.
- Continuity of ring final circuit conductors.
- Insulation resistance.
- Protection by separation of circuits, includes SELV, PELV and electrical separation.
- Basic protection by a barrier or an enclosure provided during erection.
- Insulation of non-conducting floors and walls.
- Polarity.
- Earth electrode resistance.

(ii) With the electrical supply connected (re-check polarity before further testing)

- Earth fault loop impedance.
- Prospective fault current.
- Verification of phase sequence.
- Functional testing of RCDs (the test to be independent of any test facility incorporated in the device)
- Functional testing of switchgear and controlgear, assemblies, drives, controls and interlocks.

Figure 1

Periodic Tests

For periodic testing

With the supply disconnected as appropriate

- Continuity of circuit protective conductors.
- Continuity of main and supplementary bonding conductors.
- Continuity of ring final circuit conductors.
- Insulation resistance.
- Polarity.
- Earth electrode resistance.
- Earth fault loop impedance.
- Verification of phase sequence.
- Functional testing of RCDs.
- Functional testing of circuit-breakers, isolators and switching devices.
- Verification of voltage drop (if required).

Note 1:
The person carrying out the testing is required to decide which of the above tests are appropriate by using their experience and knowledge of the installation being inspected and tested and by consulting any available records.

Note 2:
The tests need not be carried out in the order shown.

Figure 2

formal calibration/re-calibration supported by calibration certificates issued by recognised organisations, with measurements traceable to national standards. Certificates issued by UKAS accredited laboratories are preferable. It should be noted that new or repaired test instruments may not be supplied with calibration certificates unless specifically requested.

Another alternative is simply to maintain records of the formal calibration/re-calibration of test instruments at the intervals recommended by the instrument manufacturers, supported by calibration certificates. However, given the arduous conditions in which test instruments often have to be used, such a system will not provide any assurance of continuing accuracy and consistency over the period between the formal calibration checks.

REQUIRED TESTS

As mentioned in Chapter 5, the range of tests required and the order the testing is carried out for periodic testing may differ to that which is given in *BS 7671* for new installation work (including work involving an addition or an alteration). The comparison tables given in Chapter 5, listing both the Initial Sequence of Tests for initial testing (Fig 1) and the Periodic Tests for periodic testing (Fig 2), are repeated opposite for ease of reference.

NOTE: The Initial Sequence of Tests, as applicable to the particular installation, should be conducted in the appropriate sequence shown opposite (Fig 1) for reasons of safety.

If any test carried out during the initial verification of installation work indicates a failure to comply, that test, and any preceding test which may have been affected by the defect, must be repeated after the defect has been rectified.

If any test carried out during periodic inspection and testing of an installation indicates a failure to comply, then (unless there is evidence of real and immediate danger which requires immediate remedial action as discussed in Chapter 5) the result of that test must be duly recorded on the Electrical Installation Condition Report together with appropriate observations, recommendations and, where appropriate, comments in the summary section of the report.

Measurement of prospective fault current using a two-lead test instrument

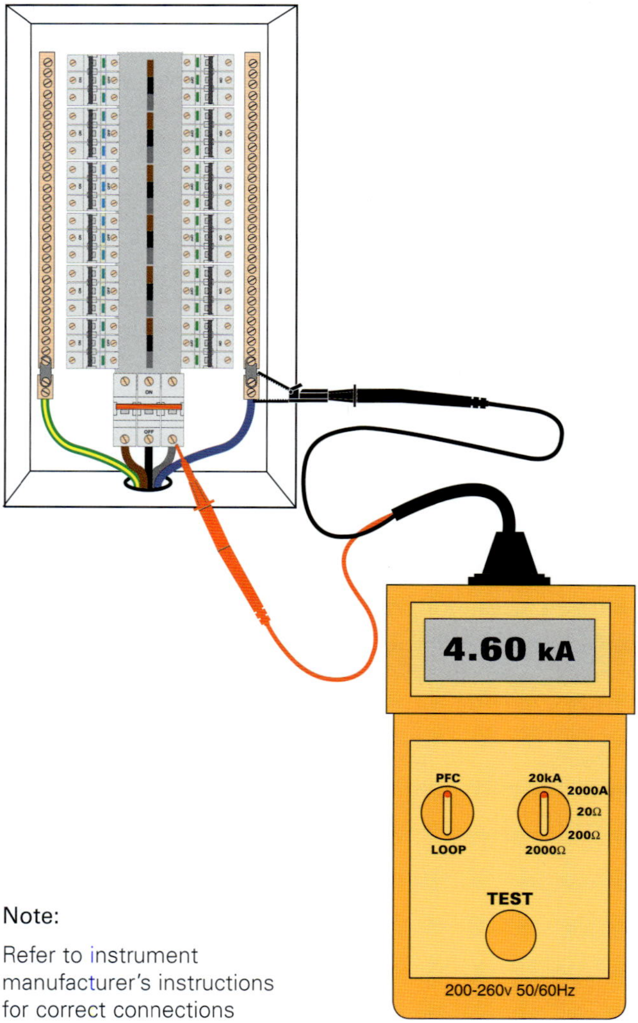

Note:

Refer to instrument manufacturer's instructions for correct connections

MEASUREMENT OF MAXIMUM PROSPECTIVE FAULT CURRENT

The maximum prospective fault current is one of the 'supply characteristics and earthing arrangements' to be recorded on the second page of the Electrical Installation Certificate, second page of the Domestic Electrical Installation Certificate, or the third page of the Electrical Installation Condition Report.

This is the current that would flow in the event of a fault at that location, either between live conductors (maximum prospective short-circuit current) or between live conductors and protective earth (maximum prospective earth fault current), whichever is the greater. The value can only be measured by testing at the origin of the installation, which is at the position where the electrical energy is delivered. The tests should, therefore, be conducted at the main switch or at other switchgear connected directly to the tails from the electricity distributor's metering equipment (or at the main low voltage switchgear connected to the tails from the consumer's sub-station transformer if the supply is delivered at high voltage).

Take particular care during the testing process, as fault conditions are most severe at the origin of an installation, where this test is being performed.

The prospective short-circuit and prospective earth fault current are to be measured (or determined by an alternative method) at the origin and at other relevant points in the installation. Note that a measurement made at a point in the installation such as an item of switchgear fed by a distribution circuit would not be the maximum for the installation.

The earthing conductor, main protective bonding conductors and circuit protective conductors should all be connected during these tests, because the presence of these and any other parallel paths to earth may reduce the impedance of the fault loop and so increase the prospective fault current.

The instrument to be used is an earth fault loop impedance test instrument, with or without a prospective fault current range. A set of test leads is required, having two or three probes to suit the requirements of the particular test instrument.

The figure opposite shows a two-lead test instrument connected across the line and neutral of an incoming supply. Note that for measuring a line to earth value, the instrument must be connected across the line and main earthing terminal.

Measurement of maximum prospective fault current using a three-lead test instrument

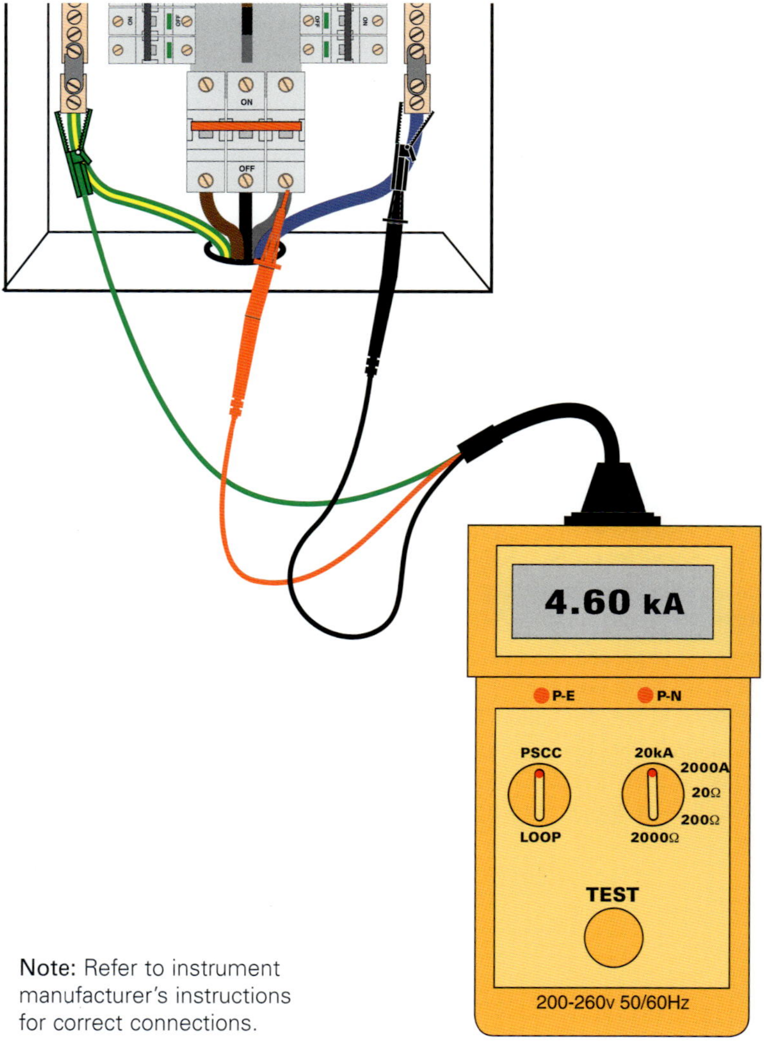

Note: Refer to instrument manufacturer's instructions for correct connections.

The figure opposite shows a three-lead test instrument connected across the line, neutral and earth of an incoming supply. Note that the connections may need to be different for some tests - refer to the instrument manufacturer's instructions.

Procedure:

- Check that the test instrument, leads, probes and crocodile clips (if any) are suitable for the purpose, and in good serviceable condition.
- Select the appropriate range and scale (for example, for a TN system earthing arrangement, prospective fault current 20 kA).
- Observing all precautions for safety, connect the instrument to the incoming energised supply to measure a line to neutral value.
- Check the polarity indicator (if any) on the instrument for correct connection.
- Press the button.
- Record the reading.
- Repeat the above steps, as appropriate, with the instrument connected for measurement of the line to earth value.

If the test instrument does not have a prospective fault current range, the readings given by the above procedure are fault loop impedances (in ohms). To convert each of these readings into a prospective fault current, divide them into the measured value of line to neutral voltage.

For example, if the voltage measured at the time of the test is 230 V, and the measured value of fault loop impedance between line and neutral at the origin is 0.05 Ω:

Maximum prospective short-circuit current (line to neutral) = 230/0.05 = 4600 A (or 4.6 kA)

(This value would have been given directly if the instrument had a prospective fault current range).

The same procedure is now repeated, taking readings between line and earth to determine the maximum prospective earth fault current.

The higher of the two prospective fault currents (line to neutral or line to earth) should be recorded on the certificate or report.

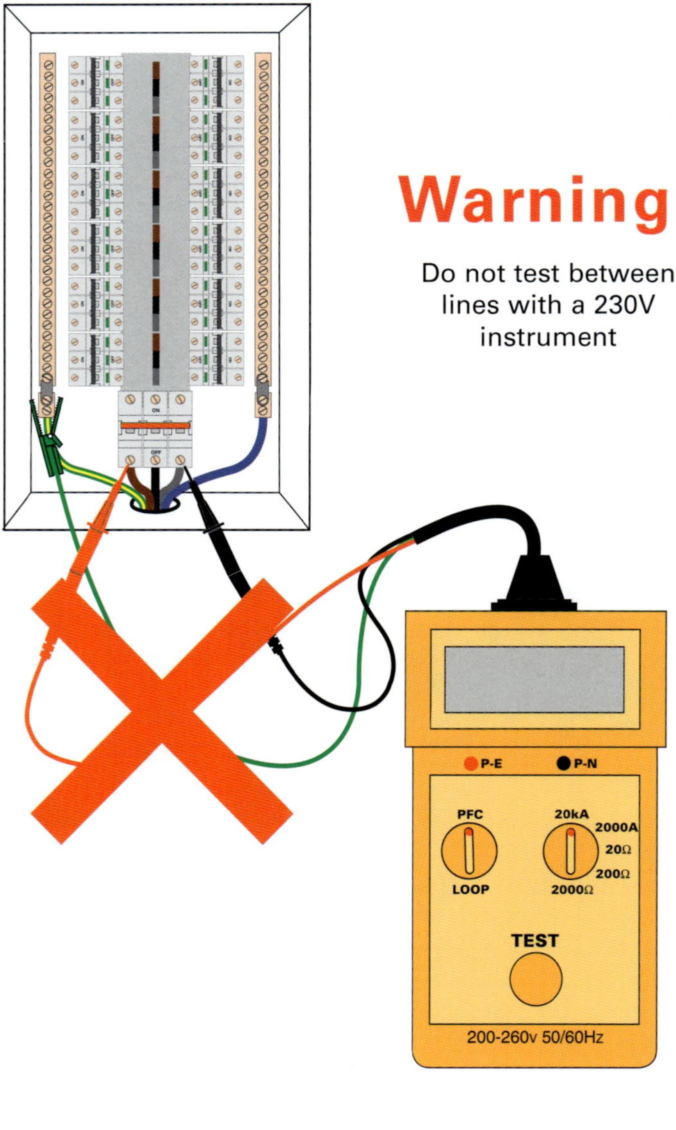

Warning!

Do not test between lines with a 230V instrument

Three-phase supplies

Unless a test instrument designed to operate at 400 V is available, it will be necessary to calculate the prospective fault current between lines.

Where an installation is supplied by two or more phases, the maximum prospective fault current is likely to be between line conductors. If this is found to be the case, then this is the value to be recorded on the certificate or report.

The prospective fault current between lines can be determined by using the measured value of the line to neutral prospective fault current (obtained as described on the preceding pages). There is a complex relationship between the line to neutral and the line to line values of prospective fault current, which is beyond the scope of this book. As a first approximation, which tends to err on the safe side, the prospective fault current line to line can be taken as twice that of the prospective fault current line to neutral.

Using the previous example, line to neutral prospective fault current multiplied by two gives:

$$4.6\ \text{kA} \times 2 = 9.2\ \text{kA}$$

(for the calculated value of prospective fault current between lines).

Why do we have to determine prospective fault current?

A fault current protective device, particularly when fitted close to the supply intake position, must generally be capable of successfully interrupting the current which would flow under conditions of short-circuit or earth fault. Otherwise there may be a serious risk of arcing, damage and fire, particularly for circuits having high prospective fault currents. Accordingly, the short-circuit capacity of a device must be no less than the prospective fault current at the point in the circuit at which it is installed. The only exception to this rule is where a device having a lower short-circuit capacity is installed in conjunction with what is sometimes called 'back-up' protection (for example, the design might require a circuit-breaker to be backed up by an appropriate HBC fuse).

Typical circuit-breaker identification

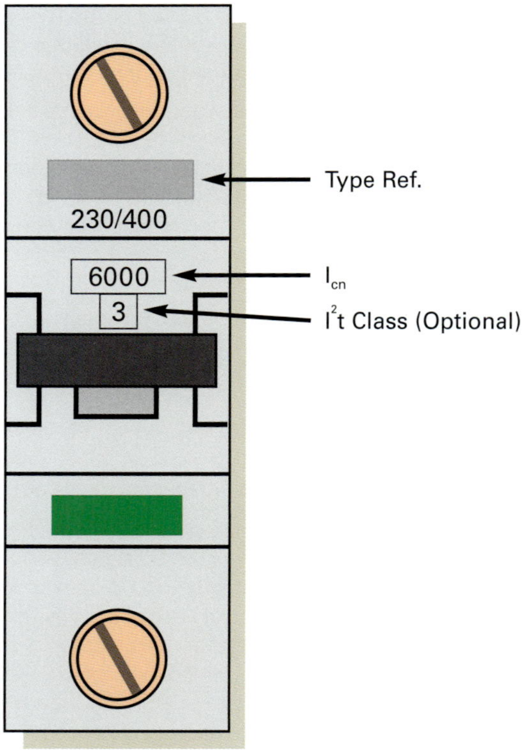

Front view only

The short-circuit capacity of typical devices are as follows:

Circuit-breakers to *BS EN 60898* have a value in a small rectangular box indelibly marked on the device, for example:

6000

This is the 'rated short-circuit capacity' of the device, I_{cn}, assigned by the manufacturer (in amperes, not kA). The value is determined on the basis of type-tests. It is the ultimate short-circuit capacity; and the device may be designed to break a fault of this magnitude only once.

The maximum fault current that the device is designed to break more than once, called the 'service short-circuit capacity', I_{cs}, may be less than the ultimate short-circuit capacity marked on the device, and the manufacturer's data should be consulted for details.

A circuit-breaker to *BS 3871* will have an 'M' number marked on it. This indicates its short-circuit capacity in kA.

For example: M4 denotes 4000 A (4 kA), M9 denotes 9000 A (9 kA).

Fuses are not so straightforward:

Typical values are:

BS 3036 - 1 kA to 4 kA (depending on duty rating)

BS 1361 - 16.5 kA

BS 88-2 - 80 kA (a.c.) 40 kA (d.c.)

BS 88-3 - 16 kA (Type I) 31.5 kA (Type II)

The above values are given only as a guide, and the manufacturer's data or other relevant information for the particular device should be consulted.

NOTE: Overcurrent protective devices having a rated current up to and including 45 A incorporated in a consumer unit conforming to Part 3 of *BS EN 60439: 1991+A2: 2001* (Annex ZA refers) are considered adequate for a prospective fault current of up to 16 kA, provided the consumer unit is fed by a service cut-out having an HBC fuse to *BS 1361* Type II, rated at not more than 100 A, on a single-phase supply of nominal voltage up to 250 V.

Measurement of earth fault loop impedance

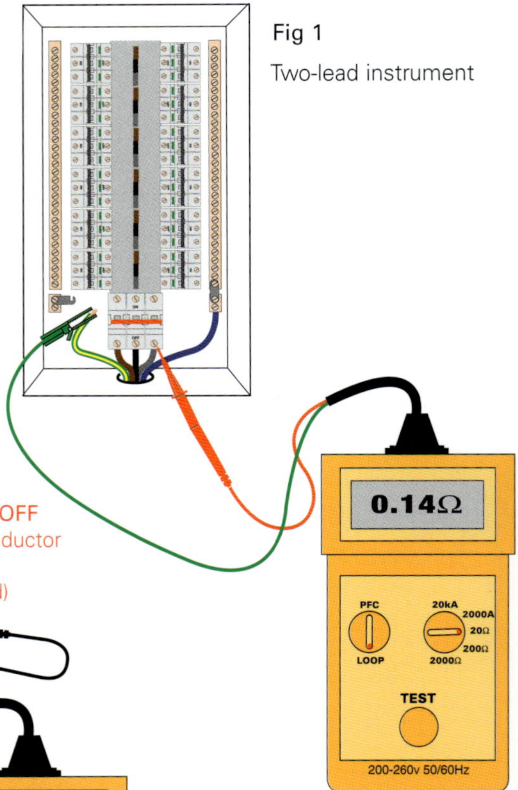

Fig 1

Two-lead instrument

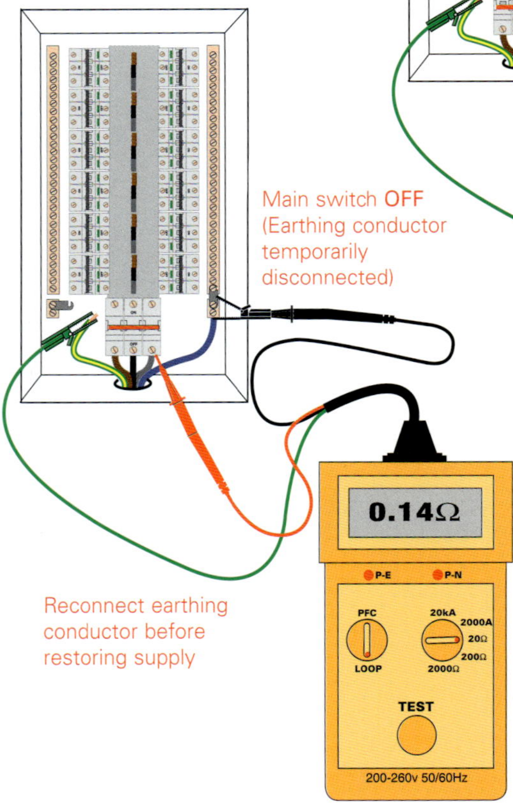

Fig 2

Three-lead instrument

MEASUREMENT OF EXTERNAL EARTH FAULT LOOP IMPEDANCE, (Z_e)

The external earth fault loop impedance, Z_e, is another of the 'supply characteristics and earthing arrangements' values to be recorded on the second page of both the Electrical Installation Certificate and the Domestic Electrical Installation Certificate or the third page of the Electrical Installation Condition Report.

Z_e is the earth fault loop impedance of that part of the system which is external to the installation. Like the maximum prospective fault current, Z_e can only be measured by testing at the origin of the installation.

Before the test, the earthing conductor must be disconnected from the main earthing terminal or otherwise separated from all parallel earth paths such as bonding and circuit protective conductors, as the purpose of the test is to prove that the intended means of earthing is present and of an acceptable ohmic value. Any parallel earth paths present during the test would result in a false reading of Z_e, being obtained and might perhaps conceal the fact that the intended means of earthing is defective, or even non-existent.

For safety reasons, it is essential that the entire installation is isolated from the supply before the earthing conductor (or, if necessary, any other protective conductors) is disconnected from the main earthing terminal, and that the installation is isolated for the duration of the testing.

On completion of testing and before the installation is re-energised, the earthing conductor or other protective conductors that were disconnected to facilitate the measurement of Z_e must be reconnected.

Take particular care during the testing process, as the fault conditions are most severe at the origin of the installation, where this test is being performed.

The instrument to be used is an earth fault loop impedance test instrument complete with a set of test leads, having two or three probes to suit the particular instrument. In the **two-lead** version, connection is made between line and earth of the incoming supply (see Fig 1). In the **three-lead** version it is necessary to make a connection to the neutral of the incoming supply as well as to line and earth (see Fig 2).

If the supply is derived from a three-phase system and there is no neutral present, then the neutral lead of a three-lead test instrument should be connected to the earthing conductor.

Some instruments have a facility for polarity indication. Before proceeding with the test, it is necessary to follow the manufacturer's instructions with regard to correct polarity and test procedure. Do not proceed with the test unless the indications on the instrument show that it is safe to do so.

Where the supply is provided with an earth connection from the electricity distributor's network, such as from a TN-S or TN-C-S system, it is unlikely that Z_e will exceed one ohm, and the lowest range of the instrument will be the most appropriate (usually 0 to 20 Ω).

Typical maximum values of Z_e for single-phase supplies of up to 100A published by electricity distributors are:

TN-S 0.80 Ω
TN-C-S 0.35 Ω

In a TT system, where the means of earthing for the installation is provided by an installation earth electrode, the value of Z_e is likely to fall within a higher range of the test instrument.

Procedure:

- Check that the test instrument, leads, probes and crocodile clips (if any) are suitable for the purpose and in good serviceable condition.
- Open the main switch to disconnect the whole of the installation from the source of supply, and secure the switch in the open position.
- Disconnect the earthing conductor from the main earthing terminal or otherwise separate it from all main bonding conductors and circuit protective conductors.
- Observing all precautions for safety, apply the test probes.
- Check the polarity indicator for correct connection.
- Press the test button.
- Record the result.
- **Reconnect the earthing conductor, main protective bonding conductors and circuit protective conductors immediately after the tests have been completed and before the supply is restored to the installation.**

Why do we have to measure external earth fault loop impedance?

In order to verify compliance with *BS 7671*, knowledge of the earth fault loop impedance is required for each circuit that relies on Automatic Disconnection of Supply (ADS) as the protective measure.

Without a sufficiently low earth fault loop impedance, the magnitude of the earth fault current will not be enough to cause the protective device to automatically disconnect the circuit within the maximum time permitted to provide protection against electric shock or to provide overcurrent protection against earth fault currents. The external earth fault loop impedance of an installation forms part of the earth fault loop impedance of every one of its circuits. Thus *BS 7671* requires that Z_e be determined. Importantly, establishing Z_e by measurement also verifies that the intended means of earthing is present.

INSTALLATION EARTH ELECTRODE RESISTANCE, (R_A)*

A TT system is required to be equipped with an installation earth electrode as its means of earthing. The function of the earth electrode is to make electrical contact with the general mass of earth to provide a suitable path for earth fault current to return to the source (such as via the earth electrode at the distribution transformer). Measurement of the resistance of the installation earth electrode to the general mass of earth provides information necessary for verifying that the earthing arrangement satisfies the requirements of both *BS 7671* and the particular installation design. The method of measurement and the measured resistance value need to be recorded, together with the type of electrode and its location, in the appropriate boxes under the heading of 'particulars of the installation at the origin' on the second page of both the Electrical Installation Certificate and the Domestic Electrical Installation Certificate or the third page of the Electrical Installation Condition Report.

Two methods of measuring the resistance of an earth electrode are as follows:

- Method 1: using a proprietary earth electrode test instrument.
- Method 2: using an earth fault loop impedance test instrument.

Where sufficient and suitable ground area is available, a proprietary earth electrode test instrument may be used. However, where there is insufficient space, or where hard surfaces make the use of such a method impracticable, the use of an earth fault loop impedance test instrument may be appropriate.

For safety reasons, the installation must be isolated from the supply before the means of earthing is disconnected to allow these tests to be performed.

Method 1

Having first isolated the installation, the earth electrode should preferably be disconnected from the earthing conductor which connects it to the main earthing terminal. If this is not possible, the earthing conductor must be disconnected from the main bonding conductors and other protective conductors at the main earthing terminal, to remove any parallel paths to the general mass of Earth. If such parallel paths are not removed before the measurement is made, an unrealistically low reading of the resistance of the electrode to Earth will be obtained.

* R_A is defined in *BS 7671* (411.5.3) as the sum of the resistances of the earth electrode and the protective conductor(s) connecting it to the exposed-conductive-part (in ohms). In most installations the resistance of the protective conductors will be small compared to the resistance of the earth electrode and R_A can be taken as the installation earth electrode resistance.

Measurement of installation earth electrode resistance

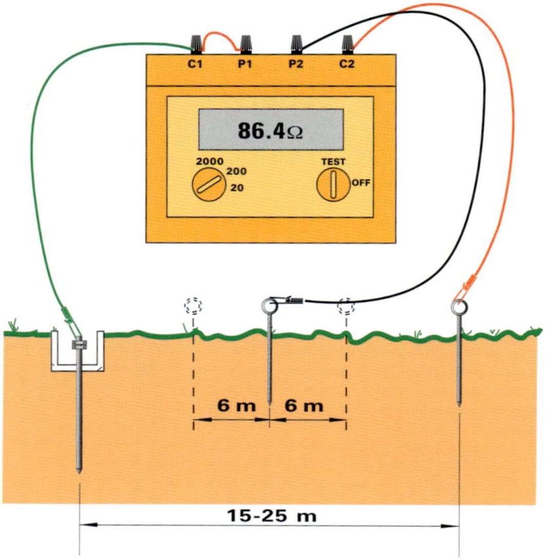

Method 1 (using a four-terminal proprietary earth electrode test instrument)

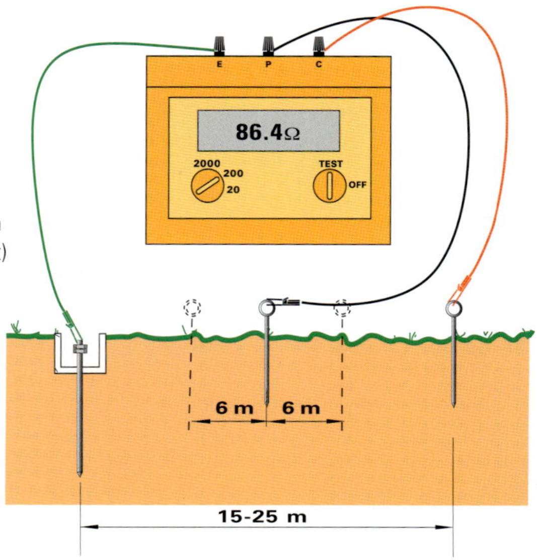

Method 1 (using a three-terminal proprietary earth electrode test instrument)

If the test instrument is a four-terminal device, the terminals marked C1 and P1 are linked together and connected to the electrode under test. The remaining two terminals are connected to temporary electrodes as shown opposite. Where the instrument is a three-terminal device, the corresponding configuration is shown opposite. Many proprietary instruments have a facility for checking the resistance of the temporary electrodes. Where the resistance of a temporary electrode is found to exceed the limit stated in the instrument manufacturer's instructions, the resistance should be reduced to a value within the stated limit.

A sufficient reduction in the resistance of the temporary electrodes may be achieved by driving longer temporary rods into the ground. The ground adjacent to the installation earth electrode must **not** be treated with water or brine, as this would make the resistance measurement invalid for the purpose of verification or reporting.

Where possible, the test instrument should be situated close to the installation earth electrode under test. If the test instrument has to be situated some considerable distance from that electrode, two separate leads should be run out from C1 and P1 to minimise the effect of lead resistance, with the link being formed at the installation earth electrode.

In principle, the instrument passes a current through the ground between the two current terminals C1 and C2. At the same time, the voltage drop between the installation earth electrode and the general mass of earth is determined by means of the voltage (potential difference) at terminals P1 and P2. The instrument then has sufficient information to calculate and display an ohmic value for the resistance of the installation earth electrode under test.

The temporary (current) electrode C2 is placed in the ground some distance away from the installation earth electrode under test. Unless the soil resistivity is very high, a distance of 15-25 metres is usually sufficient for this purpose. The temporary (potential) electrode P2 is placed approximately mid-way between the other two electrodes.

One reading is taken with P2 in the mid-way position, and a further two readings are taken with P2 approximately 6 metres on either side of the mid-way point.

The average of these three resistance readings should then be calculated, and compared with the individual readings. None of the individual readings should differ from the average by more than 5%. If they do, and there is a clear progression in the readings from one position of P2 to the next, it may mean that the resistance area of the installation earth electrode is overlapping that of temporary electrode C2. To overcome this problem, electrode C2 should be moved further away from the installation earth electrode, and the test procedure repeated. When three acceptable resistance readings have been obtained, record the average value on the certificate or report.

Re-connect the earthing conductor and all bonding and protective conductors on completion of the test, before the installation is energised (or re-energised).

Measurement of installation earth electrode resistance

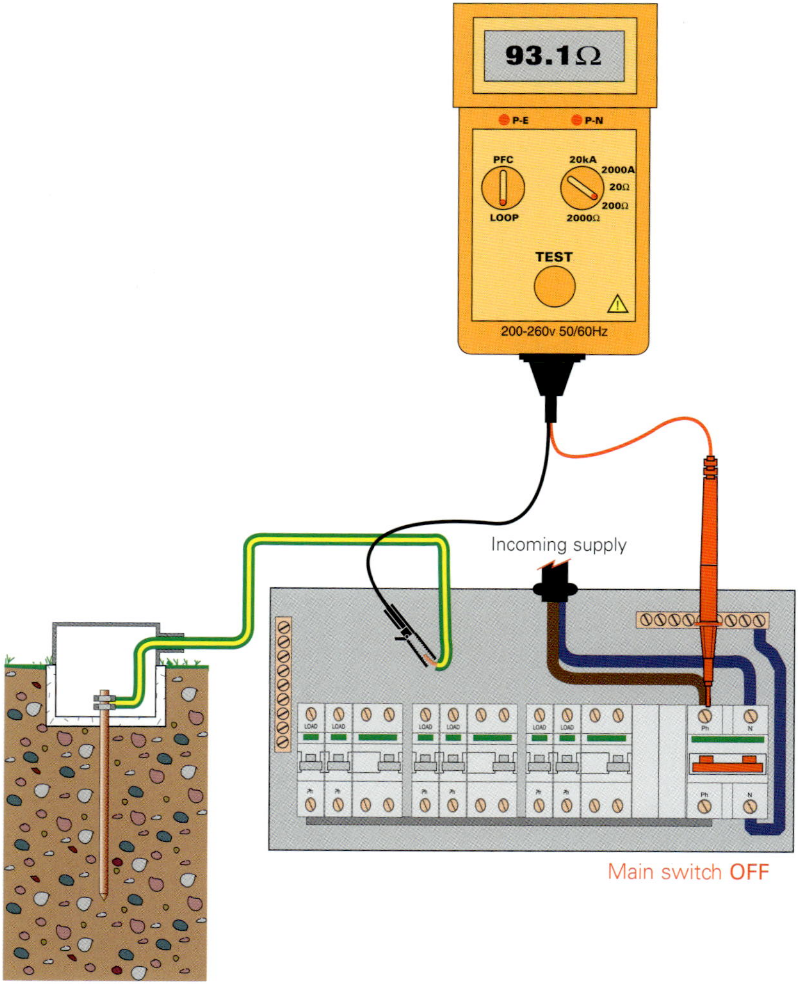

Method 2 (using an earth fault loop impedance test instrument).

Method 2

This method should only be used when the following conditions can be met.

1. Safe isolation can be achieved before accessing the inside of the distribution equipment, and
2. basic protection meets or exceeds the requirements of IP2X, and
3. the terminal insulated covers inside the distribution equipment are unlikely to be displaced.

If any of the three conditions cannot be met then then it is recommended that Method 1 is used.

This method is essentially the same as the method used to measure the external earth fault loop impedance, Z_e. The measured value of Z_e for a TT system may therefore also be used as the approximate value of the resistance of the installation earth electrode.

The test method measures the impedance of the earth fault loop from the earthing conductor via the installation earth electrode, the earth return path, the source earth electrode, the supply distribution transformer, and the supply line conductor back to the line supply terminal at the origin of the installation.

As the impedance of the other parts of the earth fault loop can be expected to be relatively low, the measurement given by the earth fault loop impedance test instrument may be taken as the resistance of the installation earth electrode to Earth. (The measurement, which will include the resistance of the means of earthing at the source distribution transformer, will err on the safe (high) side).

The earthing conductor must be disconnected from the main earthing terminal (MET) for the duration of the test. Disconnection of the earthing conductor is required to remove any parallel paths to the general mass of Earth provided by other protective conductors. If any such parallel paths are not removed before the test is conducted, a misleadingly low reading of the approximate resistance of the electrode to Earth will be obtained.

The earth fault loop impedance test instrument is connected to the supply (energised) side of the main switch, and to the earthing conductor, as indicated in the figure opposite.

Re-connect the earthing conductor and all bonding and protective conductors immediately on completion of the test.

Why do we have to measure the resistance of the installation earth electrode?

Measurement of the earth electrode resistance is required to ensure the resistance is as low as practicable, to aid disconnection time. Generally resistance values less than 200 Ω are desired as values exceeding 200 Ω may not be stable.

BS 7671 recognises the use of the following two types of protective device to provide automatic disconnection of a circuit forming part of a TT system under fault conditions:

a) An RCD.

b) An overcurrent protective device (Regulation 411.5.2).

The former is preferred as the latter may only be used where a suitably low value of earth fault loop impedance (Z_s) is permanently and reliably assured.

Where an RCD is used for earth fault protection, Regulation 411.5.3 requires the following conditions to be fulfilled:

- 0.2 s maximum disconnection time for a.c. final circuits not exceeding 32 A (Regulation 411.3.2.2) **or**
- 1 s maximum disconnection time for distribution circuits and final circuits exceeding 32 A (Regulation 411.3.2.4), **and**
- $R_A \times I_{\Delta n} \leq 50$ V

Where:

R_A is the sum of the resistance of the earth electrode and protective conductor connecting it to the exposed-conductive-parts (in ohms).

$I_{\Delta n}$ is the rated residual operating current of the RCD.

The requirements of Regulation 411.5.3 are met if the Z_s of the final circuit protected by the RCD meets the requirements of Table 41.5 of *BS 7671*.

Where an overcurrent protective device is used, Regulation 411.5.4 requires the following conditions to be fulfilled:

$$Z_s \times I_a \leq U_0 \times C_{min}$$

Where:

Z_s is the impedance in ohms (Ω) of the fault loop comprising:

- the source
- the line conductor up to the point of the fault
- the protective conductor of the exposed-conductive-parts
- the earthing conductor
- the earth electrode of the installation, and
- the earth electrode of the source.

I_a is the current in amperes (A) causing disconnection of the protective device within the time specified in Table 41.1 of Regulation 411.3.2.2 or, as appropriate, Regulation 411.3.2.4.

U_0 is the nominal a.c. rms or d.c. line voltage to Earth in volts (V).

C_{min} is the minimum voltage factor to take account of voltage variations depending on time and place, changing of transformer taps and other considerations.

For a low voltage supply C_{min} is assigned the value of 0.95 (Regulation 411.5.4 refers).

Knowledge of the resistance of the installation earth electrode is therefore essential in order to be able to verify that the installation satisfies these safety requirements.

Note: When this condition is satisfied, it does not indicate that the touch voltages under earth fault conditions will be limited to 50 V.

CONTINUITY OF PROTECTIVE CONDUCTORS

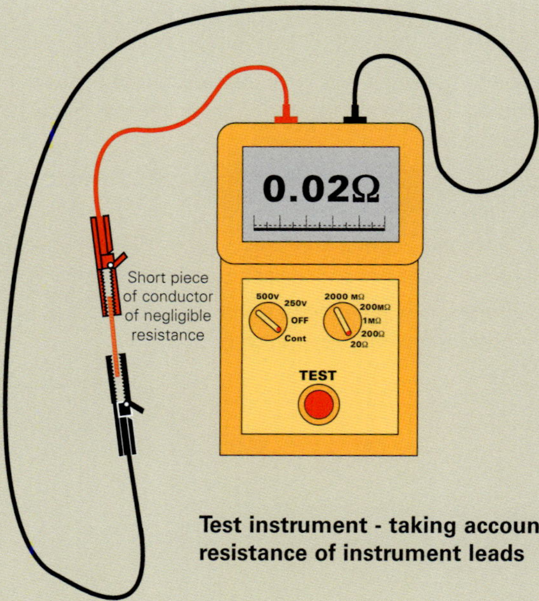

Test instrument - taking account of the resistance of instrument leads

Measuring the resistance of the leads of a continuity test instrument is necessary so that this value can be subtracted from test results for protective conductor continuity. Some test instruments have a built in facility to 'zero out' the lead resistance, making subtraction from test results unnecessary.

CONTINUITY OF PROTECTIVE CONDUCTORS

Errors caused by parallel paths

Before carrying out a test to confirm the continuity, or to measure the resistance, of a protective conductor, care should be taken to locate and disconnect (where practicable) any conductive paths which may be connected in parallel with all or part of it. Such parallel paths could be present due, for example, to a connection from a protective conductor to an electrically continuous system of pipework at one or more points along the protective conductor. Such parallel paths could lead to incorrect test results and may even conceal the fact that a protective conductor is not electrically continuous.

However, it is recognised that in some installations, such as those incorporating metal conduit or metal trunking which is fixed to a metallic structure, or where luminaires are fitted to structural steel, it would be impracticable to attempt to disconnect all parallel paths. In such circumstances, the continuity of a protective conductor may be verified only by inspection in addition to testing, during erection and after completion.

Test instrument

The test instrument to be used is an ohmmeter having a low resistance range, or an insulation and continuity test instrument set to the 'continuity' range. It is recommended that the instrument has a short-circuit output current of not less than 200 mA (a.c. or d.c.) and an open-circuit voltage of between 4 V and 24 V. Continuity test readings of less than 1 Ω are common. Therefore, the resistance of the test leads is significant, and should not be included in any recorded test result. If the particular test instrument does not have provision for correcting for the resistance of the test leads, it will be necessary to measure the resistance of the leads when connected together, and for this measured value to be subtracted from all the test readings. See adjacent illustration.

The (R_1 + R_2) method

This method is applicable to circuit protective conductors and their associated line conductors. It is not applicable to main or supplementary bonding conductors. The (R_1 + R_2) method of testing the continuity of circuit protective conductors has the following advantages:

- The information required to complete the (R_1 + R_2) column of the Schedule of Test Results is obtained directly.
- Polarity is verified as each continuity test is performed.
- The method may be more convenient than the 'wander lead' method (see following section).

Testing continuity of the protective conductor to a lighting point by the ($R_1 + R_2$) method

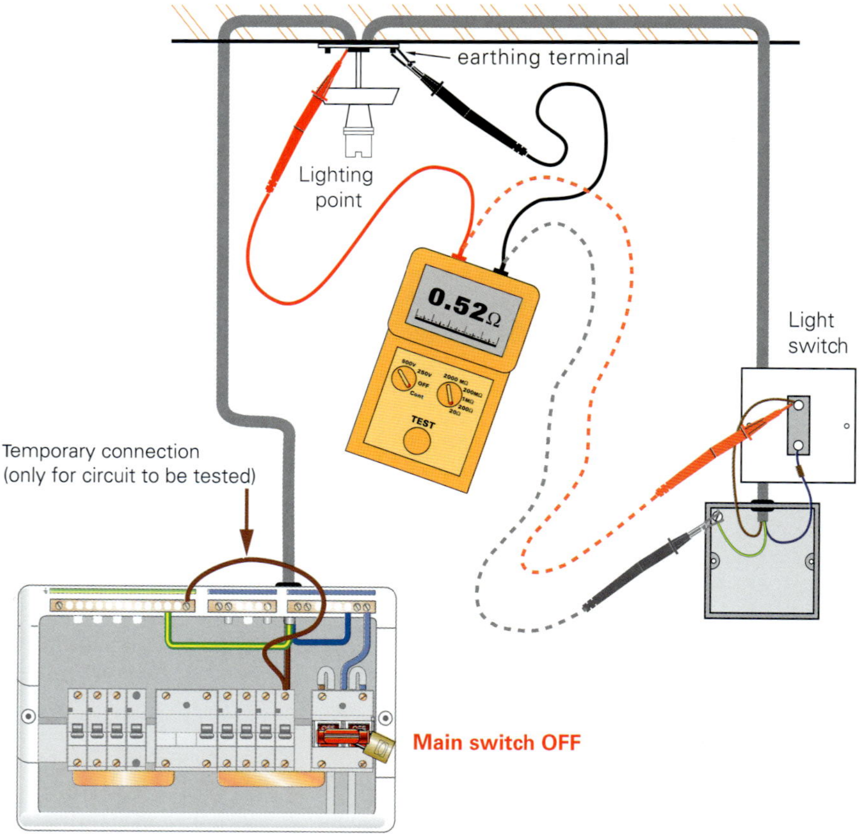

This test procedure also enables correct polarity to be verified.

The test provides a measured value of resistance for the line conductor and the circuit protective conductor of a circuit, in series. The test may be carried out, **having first securely isolated the supply**, by temporarily connecting together the line conductor and circuit protective conductor at the supply end, and then connecting the test instrument to the terminals of the line conductor and the circuit protective conductor at each point and accessory on the circuit in turn.

The value of (R_1 + R_2) measured at the point or accessory electrically most remote from the supply will be the maximum value, and it is this value that should be recorded on the Schedule of Test Results. The test readings at the other points and accessories on the circuit serve to verify that the protective conductor is continuous to each of them, and that the polarity is correct.

Procedure:

- **Securely isolate the supply.**
- Disconnect any bonding connections that could affect the test readings.
- Make a temporary connection, at the supply end of the circuit (for example, at a consumer unit) between the line and cpc of the circuit to be tested.
- Measure the resistance between line and cpc at each point and accessory on the circuit (thereby also confirming correct polarity).
- Record the reading at the electrically most remote* point or accessory (the highest value) of the circuit (and confirm correct polarity for the circuit).
- **Re-connect any bonding conductors disconnected for the test.**
- **Remove the temporary connection.**

Whilst the primary purpose of testing for protective conductor continuity is to ensure that such continuity exists, the result of an (R_1 + R_2) test can be used to determine the earth fault loop impedance at the point or accessory at which the test is applied. This procedure is explained under the subject heading of 'earth fault loop impedance' in this chapter.

* Note: In the simplified diagram shown, polarity should be verified at both the lighting point (as shown) and the switch. However, the electrically most remote point in this particular circuit will be the switch. The (R_1 + R_2) value recorded for this circuit will be that measured at the ceiling outlet between the switch line and cpc.

Testing continuity of the protective conductor at a lighting switch by the wander lead method.

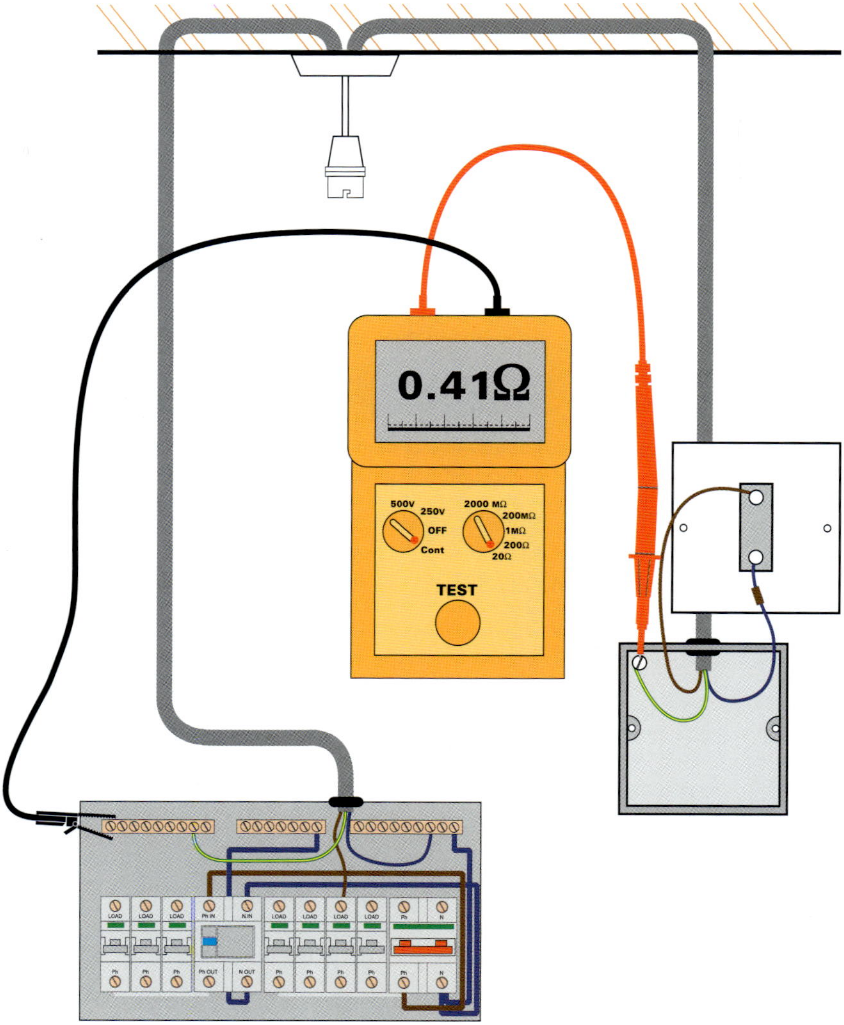

The wander lead method

This method is used principally for testing protective conductors that are connected to the main earthing terminal (main protective bonding conductors, circuit protective conductors and so on). The correct polarity of circuit connections will need to be verified separately.

Where a continuity test involves the opening of enclosures etc, that part of the installation will need to be isolated.

One terminal of the continuity test instrument is connected to the main earthing terminal with a long lead (or 'wander lead') and, with a lead from the other terminal, contact is made with the protective conductor at every position to which it is connected in that circuit, such as at socket-outlets, lighting points, fixed equipment points, switches, exposed-conductive-parts and extraneous-conductive-parts. By this means, provided that no parallel paths are present, the continuity of the protective conductor back to the main earthing terminal can be verified, and its resistance measured.

The wander lead used to carry out this test may be as much as 50 m in length. As such the resistance of the lead will be significant. It is essential therefore that the resistance of the wander lead is either 'nulled' prior to testing or is subtracted from the value obtained from testing.

A main or supplementary bonding conductor can be tested by simply attaching the leads of the test instrument to each end of the conductor, having temporarily disconnected one end of that conductor to remove parallel paths.

Why do we need to test the continuity of protective conductors?

It is essential to ensure that all circuit protective conductors and bonding conductors are continuous. Otherwise, an exposed-conductive-part, an extraneous-conductive-part or the earthing terminal of a point or accessory could be left without an effective connection to Earth, giving no fault protection in the event of an earth fault.

Continuity testing of a ferrous enclosure using the wander lead method

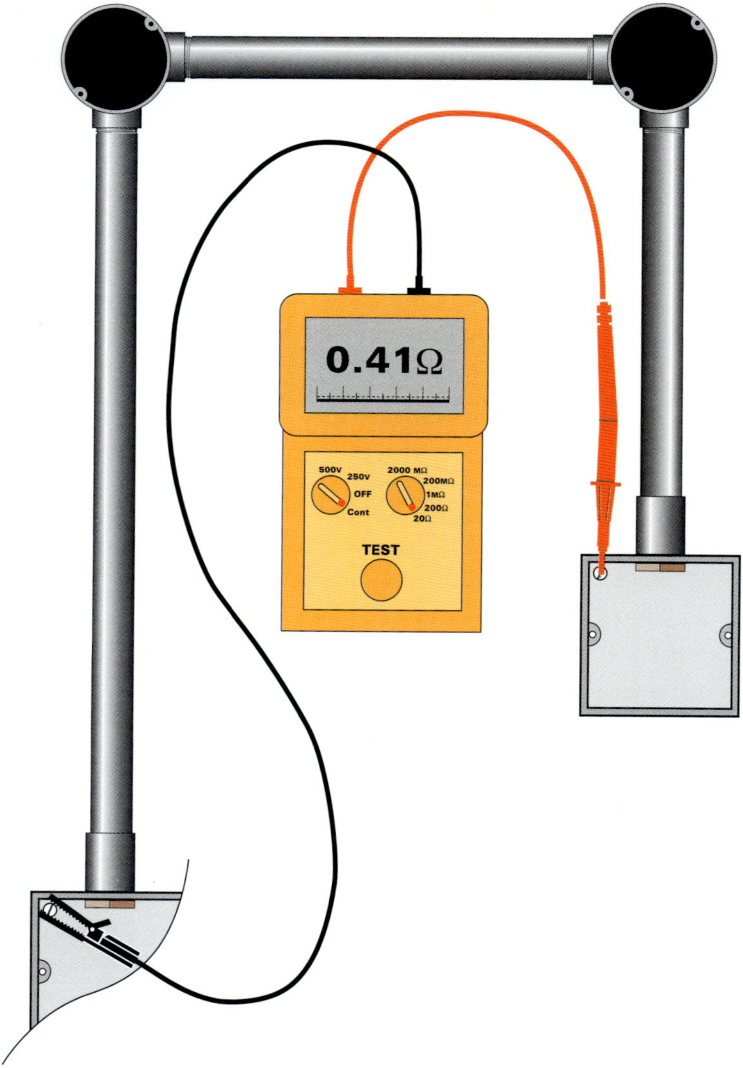

Continuity testing of ferrous enclosures

Where a ferrous enclosure, such as steel conduit or steel trunking is used as a circuit protective conductor, the integrity of the enclosure should be verified for compliance with *BS 7671*, where reasonably practicable by inspection and testing.

Inspection is to confirm the soundness of the enclosure's conductive path; the inspector should identify any deterioration such as excessive corrosion or the ability of any joints to provide durable electrical continuity and adequate mechanical strength.

Where safe to do so, testing of the conduit or trunking can be carried out by the wander lead method. Although this is a 'dead test', this test may require access to enclosures containing live parts, therefore **safe isolation must be carried out** prior to gaining access, to prevent contact with any live parts. Before carrying out the continuity test, confirm that access to the equipment is not restricted, and once the consumer unit cover is removed check that:

- the basic protection inside the consumer unit meets or exceeds the requirements of IP2X or IPXXB, **and**
- the terminal insulated covers are unlikely to be accidentally displaced during testing.

The wander lead method for obtaining R_2 values has been described previously in this chapter.

Ring final circuit continuity steps

Step 1

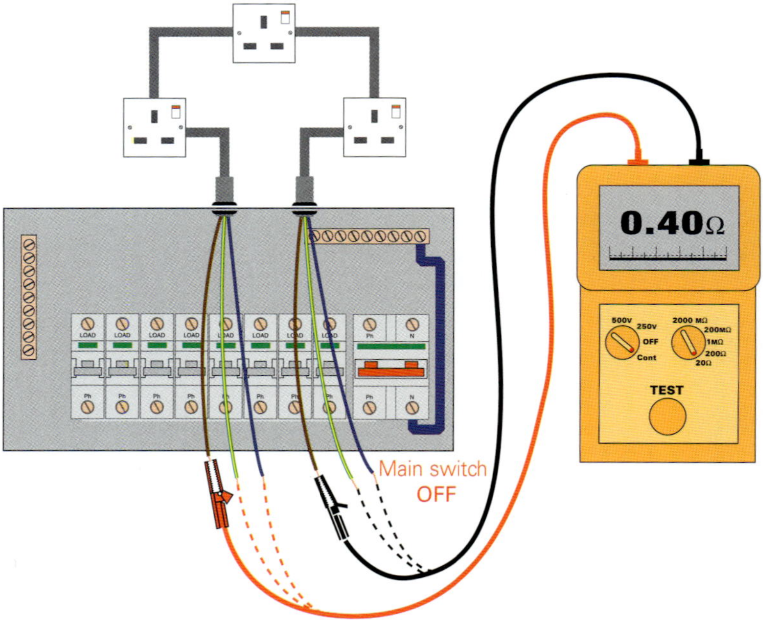

CONTINUITY OF RING FINAL CIRCUIT CONDUCTORS

The cables of a ring final circuit start at the outgoing terminals of a consumer unit or distribution board, connect to all the points in the ring, and return to the same outgoing terminals. The live (line and neutral) conductors must form a complete unbroken loop without interconnections, as must the circuit protective conductor, unless it is formed by a continuous metal covering or enclosure (such as a steel conduit) containing all the live conductors.

The test instrument to be used is one of the types described earlier in this chapter for testing the continuity of protective conductors.

Procedure:

When carrying out this test, remember either to note the resistance of the test leads for subtraction from the overall measured value or to use the 'auto-null' facility of the test instrument so that the test value recorded does not include the resistance of the test leads.

Confirm that the circuit to be tested has been securely isolated. Using a low resistance ohmmeter set on its lowest scale (typically 0-20 Ω or similar), carry out the following three-step test procedure:

Step 1

Measure the end-to-end resistance of the

- line conductor (r_1)
- neutral conductor (r_n)
- cpc (r_2)

The results obtained should be more or less equal (± 0.05 Ω, say) except where the circuit is wired using 'twin and earth' type cables having a cpc of reduced cross-sectional area, where the resistance of the cpc will be higher on account of this.

Ring final circuit continuity steps (continued)

Step 2

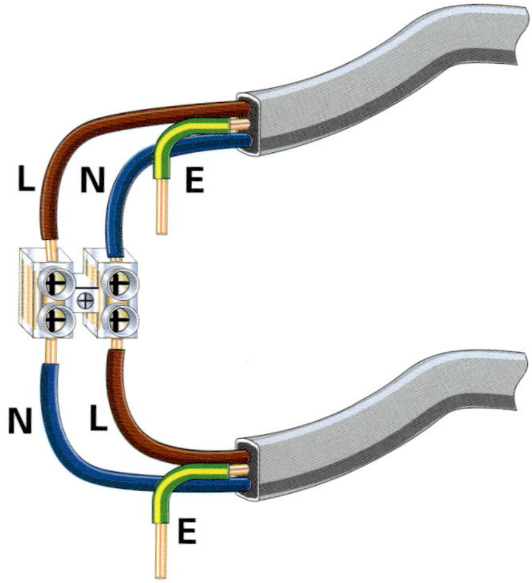

Cross-connection arrangement for Step 2

Step 3

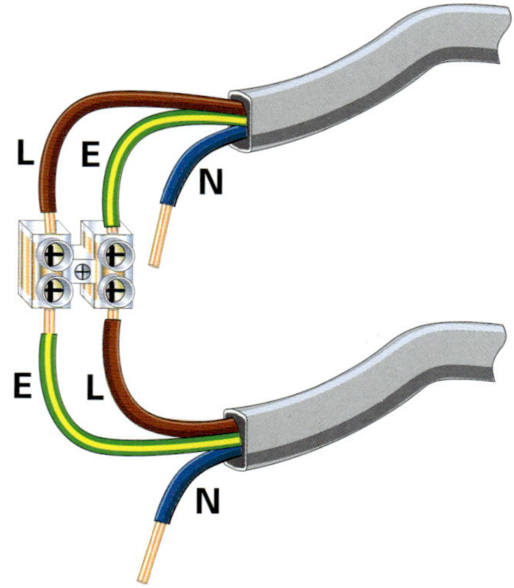

Cross-connection arrangement for Step 3

Step 2

Connect the outgoing line conductor of the circuit to the incoming neutral conductor of the circuit and vice versa at the distribution board or consumer unit, as shown opposite.

Measure the resistance between line and neutral terminals at every socket-outlet connected to the circuit. The results obtained should be substantially the same at each socket-outlet and should be approximately one quarter of the combined resistance of the line loop (r_1) and neutral loop (r_n) – that is, $\frac{r_1 + r_n}{4}$

Any socket-outlets connected as spurs will have a higher resistance value as a result of the resistance of the spur conductors.

Step 3

Now connect the outgoing line conductor of the circuit to the incoming cpc of the circuit and vice versa at the distribution board or consumer unit, as shown opposite.

Measure the resistance between line and cpc terminals at **every** socket-outlet connected to the circuit under test. The results obtained should be substantially the same at each socket-outlet and should be approximately one quarter of the combined resistance of the line loop (r_1) and cpc loop (r_2) – that is, $\frac{r_1 + r_2}{4}$

Any socket-outlets connected as spurs will have a higher resistance value as a result of the resistance of the spur conductors.

The highest value of resistance obtained should be recorded on the *Schedule of Test Results* as the ($R_1 + R_2$) value of the circuit.

Note: If, where single-core cables have been used for the circuit wiring, the resistance readings obtained increase as the distance from the distribution board or consumer unit increases, it is likely that the cross-connections have been made to conductors from the same leg of the circuit (i.e. both incoming or outgoing) and not to opposite legs. If this occurs, correctly cross-connect the circuit and start the testing again.

Socket-outlets wired as spurs will give a slightly higher resistance reading depending on the length of the spur. Where the presence of a spur is identified from such a resistance reading, the inspector should assess whether adequate protection against overload has been afforded for that spur.

On completion of the testing, reconnect the conductors to the correct terminals.

Why do we need to check the continuity of ring final circuit conductors?

Incorrectly connected, or open circuit, conductors in an installed ring final circuit can lead to overloading of the circuit cables. Testing by the above procedure verifies continuity and correct connection, as well as correct polarity.

It also provides confirmation that both legs of the ring final circuit have been connected into the same protective device. The incorrect connection of a ring final circuit across two protective devices would leave the installation in a dangerous condition particularly when safe isolation of a final circuit was required.

INSULATION RESISTANCE

Precautions may be necessary to avoid damage to electronic devices. The presence of any circuit or equipment vulnerable to a typical test should be indicated in the diagram or schedule provided for the installation. For practical reasons it may be necessary or desirable to sub-divide the installation in order to carry out insulation resistance testing.

Before proceeding with this test, the inspector should ensure that for the circuit to be tested:

- All pilot or indicator lamps that are likely to interfere with the test (by providing a path between line and neutral) have been disconnected.
- All items of equipment which are at risk of damage from the test voltage have been disconnected.
- The incoming neutral has been disconnected so that there is no connection with Earth.

The test should be performed using an insulation resistance test instrument capable of supplying the test voltage indicated in Table 61 of *BS 7671* (which is reproduced below), when loaded with 1 mA.

Minimum values of insulation resistance:

Circuit nominal voltage (V)	Test voltage d.c. (V)	Minimum insulation resistance (MΩ)
SELV & PELV	250	0.5
Up to and including 500 V with the exception of the above systems	500	1.0
Above 500 V	1000	1.0

NOTE: Functional extra-low voltage circuits shall meet all the the requirements for low voltage circuits (Regulation 612.3.4).

The insulation resistance is deemed satisfactory by *BS 7671* if the main switchboard and each distribution circuit tested separately with all its final circuits connected, but with current-using equipment disconnected, have an insulation resistance not less than the appropriate value given in Table 61.

The insulation resistance is normally measured between live conductors (line and neutral), and between live conductors and Earth.

The term 'Earth' relates to the protective conductor(s) being connected to the the earthing arrangement (Regulation 612.3.1 refers).

Where it is not reasonably practicable to disconnect equipment which might affect the results obtained and/or which might suffer damage from exposure to the test voltage being applied, (including surge protective devices (SPDs) and in particular, fixed socket-outlets incorporating SPDs) the person carrying out the testing may adopt one of the following approaches:

- Perform the insulation resistance test with the live (line and neutral) conductors connected together and test between the live conductors and Earth (Regulations 612.3.1 and 612.3.3 refer).
- Perform the insulation resistance test between conductors using an applied test voltage of 250 V d.c. Although the test voltage is reduced, the minimum acceptable insulation resistance remains 1 MΩ (see Regulation 612.3.2).

Main switch ON and all circuit-breakers on

Measurement of the insulation resistance between live conductors and Earth for a single-phase distribution board with all its final circuits connected, but with current-using equipment disconnected

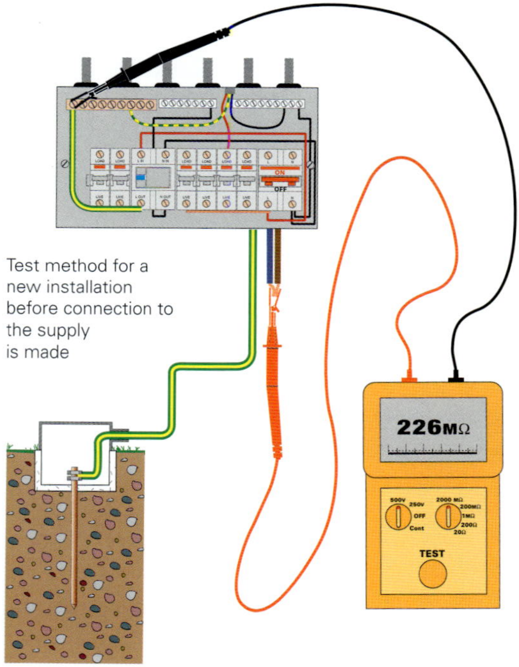

Test method for a new installation before connection to the supply is made

Main switch OFF

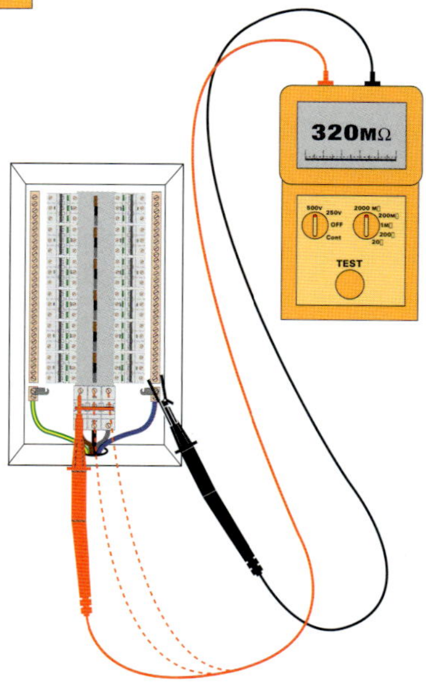

Measurement of the insulation resistance between one of the line conductors and neutral for a three-phase distribution board with its final circuits connected

Insulation resistance testing between live conductors

To test the insulation resistance between live conductors (line and neutral), a voltage is applied to the conductors, in pairs, from the origin of the circuit. Any leakage current from one conductor to the other is indicated in the form of a reduction in insulation resistance. Any short-circuits, due to incorrect connections or damage to cables are indicated by a low reading. Very low values of leakage current will be indicated by a resistance well beyond the range of the instrument, which may be 200 M Ω or more.

Procedure:

- Securely isolate the circuit under test, including the neutral, from the supply.
- Disconnect all current-using equipment including fluorescent and other discharge luminaires. Remove filament lamps and check that all switches are closed (two-way switches should be operated to include all live conductors in the test).
- Disconnect all equipment which is vulnerable to the test voltage.
- Check that the instrument and leads are in sound condition.
- Check the condition of the batteries in the test instrument.
- Select the appropriate test voltage and range.
- Connect the instrument, and record the readings as follows:
  - For a single-phase installation:
    Line to neutral
  - For a three-phase installation:
    Line 1 to Line 2
    Line 2 to Line 3
    Line 3 to Line 1

Then test the line conductors collectively to the neutral.

If the result obtained is unacceptable, it will be necessary to test each line to neutral separately to identify the location of the fault.

Insulation resistance between live conductors and Earth

Procedure:

Having taken the necessary precautions as before, the inspector should:

- Link together all line conductors and neutral.
- Connect the test instrument between the linked conductors and protective Earth.
- Measure and record the result.

As may be seen from Table 61 of *BS 7671*, the minimum acceptable value for a 400/230 V installation may be as low as 1.0 MΩ. However, such a very low value should not be accepted without question. If any test carried out at a distribution board reveals an insulation resistance lower than 2 MΩ, the circuits should be separated and tested individually in order to identify the cause of the low reading so that it can be remedied. The overall low reading may, depending on the particular wiring system, be due to an accumulation of individual circuit readings, and hence be considered acceptable. Alternatively, should the low insulation reading be due to one particular circuit, this would merit further investigation.

Why do we need to test insulation resistance?

The insulation resistance tests give an indication of the condition of the insulation of the conductors. Effective insulation is required to provide basic protection and to prevent short-circuits and earth faults.

Unintended leakage currents due to inadequate insulation can present a risk of electric shock to persons and livestock. They can also cause further deterioration to the insulation and conductors if allowed to persist, when they may present a fire risk. It is therefore important that insulation resistances are tested either to verify the satisfactory condition of new installation work before the supply is connected, or to check the condition of an existing installation.

PROTECTION BY SELV, PELV OR BY ELECTRICAL SEPARATION

Separated extra-low voltage (SELV), protective extra-low voltage (PELV) and electrical separation are protective measures against electric shock. In each of these protective measures, separation of live parts from other circuits and, except for PELV, separation from Earth is required.

There are two protective measures recognised in *BS 7671* for electrical separation.

- Where used to supply an individual item of equipment.
- Where used to supply more than one item of equipment.

Only the first protective measure will be considered here. The second protective measure is applied only where the installation is controlled or under the supervision of skilled or instructed persons.

The source for electrical separation must provide at least simple separation at a voltage not exceeding 500 V (Regulation 413.3.2 refers), with no connection of live parts of the separated circuit to another circuit or to Earth or to a protective conductor (Regulation 413.3.3 refers).

To comply with the requirements of *BS 7671*, verification of the electrical separation conditions for each of the protective measures previously listed must be confirmed by measurement of the insulation resistance. The values obtained must be in accordance with Table 61 of *BS 7671*. Persons who are unfamiliar with the detailed requirements for the protective measures SELV, PELV and electrical separation need to take particular care when testing installations that rely on these protective measures.

The following tests should be performed as applicable using an insulation resistance test instrument.

Test requirements for SELV

Details of test performed	Applied d.c. test voltage	Minimum acceptable insulation resistance (MΩ)
Between a SELV circuit and Earth	250 V	0.5
Between a SELV circuit and a SELV or PELV circuit	250 V	0.5
Between a SELV circuit and a circuit of voltage not exceeding 500 V	500 V	1.0
Between a SELV circuit and a circuit of voltage in excess of 500 V	1000 V	1.0

Test requirements for PELV

The requirements are the same as those described for SELV above, except that it is not necessary to perform a test between PELV circuits and Earth.

Test requirements for electrical separation

Details of test performed	Applied d.c. test voltage	Minimum acceptable insulation resistance (MΩ)
Between the circuit protected by electrical separation and a circuit of voltage not exceeding 500 V	500 V	1.0
Between the circuit protected by electrical separation and a circuit of voltage in excess of 500 V	1000 V	1.0

Sources of supply

For a SELV or PELV system, the source of supply must be selected from one of those listed in Regulation 414.3 of *BS 7671*. This means that it must be derived from a source such as a safety isolating transformer complying with *BS EN 61558-2-6* in which there is no connection between the output winding and the transformer casing or the protective earthing circuit, if any. Alternatively, the source may be one of the other listed types, giving equivalent electrical separation.

Use of the standard test finger

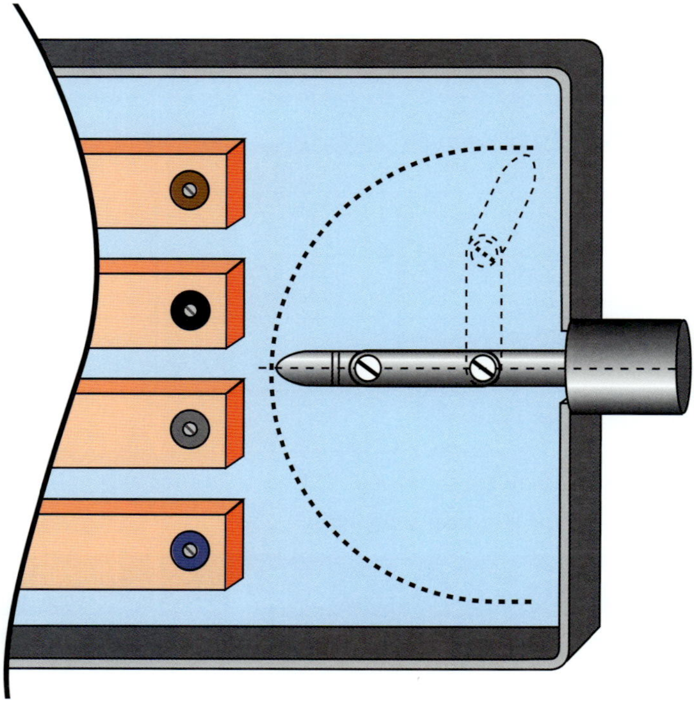

BASIC PROTECTION BY A BARRIER OR ENCLOSURE PROVIDED DURING ERECTION

This is a test to verify that each barrier or enclosure provided during erection gives suitable protection against the risk of electric shock through contact with live parts by fingers and solid conductive objects.

The test also applies to barriers or enclosures which, although provided in factory-built equipment, have been affected by the erection process. For example, if an opening has been formed in an enclosure on site for the entry of cables, but is oversized or unused, the enclosure must be capable of meeting the test criteria in order to comply with the requirements of *BS 7671*. If the enclosure fails to comply when tested, remedial action should be taken (such as reducing the size of the opening).

The degree of protection provided by each barrier or enclosure must not be less than IP2X or IPXXB (see Regulation 416.2.1). For readily accessible top surfaces, the degree of protection must not be less than IP4X or IPXXD (Regulation 416.2.2 refers). IP2X means that the barrier or enclosure provides protection against contact with live parts by a standard test finger to *BS EN 61032* which is 12 mm in diameter, 80 mm long and is capable of bending through 90° twice in the same plane (like a human finger). The test finger is applied with a force not exceeding a specified maximum value, and is used in conjunction with an electric signalling circuit. IPXXB is equivalent to IP2X in this context.

IP4X is protection against the entry of a wire, strip or similar object which is not more than 1 mm thick, or a foreign object which is not greater than 1 mm in diameter. IPXXD is broadly equivalent to IP4X.

The test procedures are more fully described in *BS EN 60529: 1992 Degrees of protection provided by enclosures*. In practice, a visual inspection will usually be sufficient to confirm the compliance or otherwise of barriers and enclosures with the above requirements. If all unused entries are suitably closed, a test may not be necessary.

INSULATION RESISTANCE/IMPEDANCE OF FLOORS AND WALLS

Testing the insulation of non-conducting floors and walls is required where the protective measure is provided by a non-conducting location.

This protective measure although included in *BS 7671*, is not recognised for general application (Regulation 418.1 refers). It should only be applied where the installation is under the supervision of skilled or instructed persons so that unauthorised changes cannot be made (Regulation 410.3.6 refers).

The testing requirements for resistance/impedance of floors and walls for compliance with Regulation 418.1 are outlined in Regulation 612.5, which states *'at least three measurements shall be made in the same location'.* Methods for measuring the insulation resistance/impedance of floors and walls to Earth or the protective conductor system are given in Appendix 13 of *BS 7671*.

POLARITY

Polarity tests are made to verify that any single-pole control devices or single-pole protective devices are connected in the line conductor only. This includes switches, fuses, thermostats etc. All non-reversible plugs and socket-outlets also need to be checked for correct connection. Edison screw and other centre-contact lampholders (except for E14 and E27 lampholders to *BS EN 60238*) should be connected in such a way that the line conductor is connected to the centre contact, and the neutral to the screw thread or the part of the lampholder which makes contact with the lamp cap. A check should also be made to ensure that the polarity of the incoming supply is correct, otherwise the whole installation would have the wrong polarity. (Such situations are not unknown).

The tests should be carried out before the circuit is energised, using a low-reading ohmmeter or continuity test instrument.

Much of the polarity testing can be carried out during the process of testing cpc continuity by using the $(R_1 + R_2)$ test method.

Why do we need to confirm correct polarity?

Incorrect polarity can give rise to danger in a number of ways, including:

- Parts of the installation may remain connected to the line conductor when switched off by a single-pole device but, for all intents and purposes, will appear to be 'dead'.
- In the event of an overload, the circuit-breaker or fuse protecting that part of the installation would disconnect the neutral of the circuit, leaving the load at full line voltage.
- An earth fault current might remain undetected by overcurrent protective devices.

EARTH FAULT LOOP IMPEDANCE, (Z_s)

The measurement of earth fault loop impedance at the origin of the installation (Z_e) is described earlier in this chapter. The guidance below relates to the measurement of earth fault loop impedance other than Z_e. The type of earth fault loop impedance test instrument to be used is the same as that used for measurement of Z_e.

The earth fault loop impedance, Z_s, should be measured for every distribution circuit and final circuit having Automatic Disconnection of Supply (ADS) as its protective measure. The measurement should be made at the point or accessory electrically furthest from the supply to the circuit. During periodic testing, if the continuity of the circuit protective conductor is not tested at each point and accessory, it may be necessary to measure Z_s at each such point and accessory.

Where it is safe to do so, measured values of Z_s can be obtained wholly by means of an earth fault loop impedance test instrument. Alternatively, the (R_1 + R_2) test results obtained during continuity testing may be used, in conjunction with test results obtained by the use of the loop impedance test instrument for other parts of the installation.

The earth fault loop impedance test instrument uses the circuit voltage to pass a test current through the line-earth loop. This type of test can cause the unwanted operation of RCDs or overcurrent devices, such as 6 A Type B circuit-breakers which may be in circuit. In such cases, it may not be possible to obtain a measured value of Z_s. Some instrument makers include features in their earth fault loop impedance test instruments aimed at avoiding some or all of these problems of unwanted tripping. Manufacturers' information should be consulted for details where any doubt exists.

Determination of Z_s using $(R_1 + R_2)$ measured values

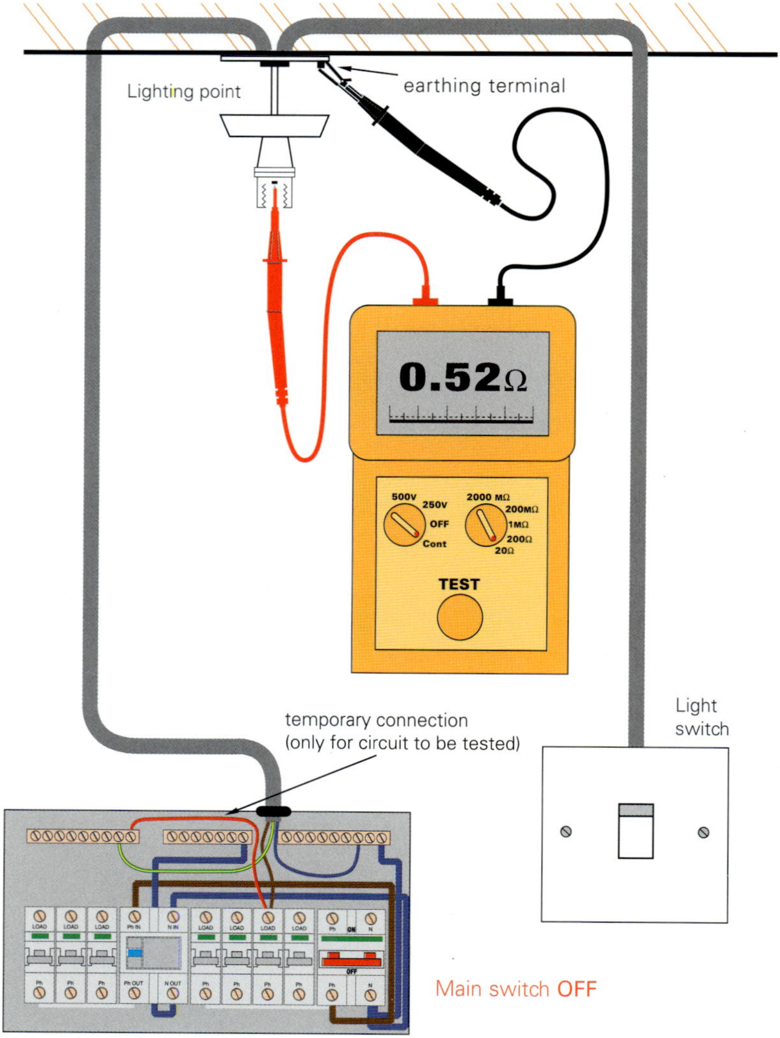

$$Z_s = Z_e \text{ (or } Z_{db}) + (R_1 + R_2)$$

Determination of Z_s using $(R_1 + R_2)$ measured values

As previously indicated, an $(R_1 + R_2)$ test result for a given point in a circuit (generally the point which is electrically furthest from the supply) can be used to determine a value for the earth fault loop impedance, Z_s, at that point. To do this, it is also necessary to know the value of earth fault loop impedance, Z_{db}, at the distribution board or control panel etc directly supplying the circuit, generally from a measurement using an earth fault loop impedance test instrument (upstream of the circuit protective device if this is likely to be operated by the test). The following formula is then used:

$$Z_s = Z_{db} + (R_1 + R_2)$$

or, where the distribution board is at the origin of the installation:

$$Z_s = Z_e + (R_1 + R_2)$$

Strictly speaking, it should not be $(R_1 + R_2)$ that is used in the above equations because this does not take account of the a.c. resistance or the inductive reactance of the line conductor and circuit protective conductor. Instead it should be the impedance $(Z_1 + Z_2)$, which takes these quantities into account. Unfortunately, it is not possible to measure $(Z_1 + Z_2)$ using a d.c. test current, as supplied by most of the commonly available ohmmeters and continuity test instruments. To obtain a value for $(Z_1 + Z_2)$, it is necessary to use an a.c. test current at a frequency of 50 Hz in order to include the a.c. resistance and inductive reactance of the circuit conductors.

Fortunately, for circuits rated up to about 100 A, in which the line and circuit protective conductors are part of the same wiring system or are immediately adjacent to each other and not separated by ferrous material (all as required by *BS 7671*), the a.c. impedance is not significantly greater than the d.c. resistance. In such cases, $(R_1 + R_2)$ is approximately equal to $(Z_1 + Z_2)$, and the use of a test instrument supplying a d.c. test current will generally be sufficient.

For circuits rated at more than 100 A, the use of d.c. test current may lead to a value of Z_s which is optimistically low and may therefore be unacceptable. In such cases, an ohmmeter or continuity test instrument which supplies an a.c. test current at a frequency of 50 Hz should be used. Alternatively, a value of Z_s should be obtained by another method (such as direct measurement by an earth fault loop impedance test instrument).

Measurement of Z_s at a socket-outlet using an earth fault loop impedance test instrument

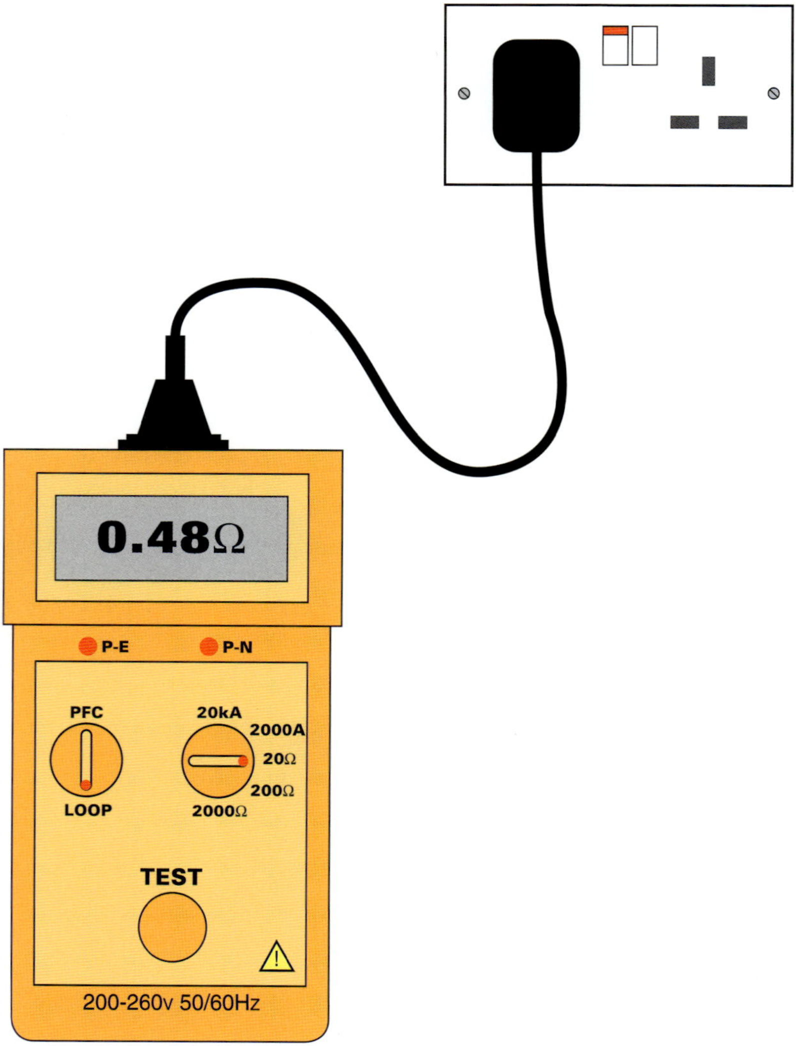

Procedure for measuring Z_s with a loop impedance test instrument

Testing should only be carried out after a thorough inspection and continuity testing have confirmed, so far as is reasonably practicable, that all circuit protective conductors, and main and supplementary bonding conductors, are in place. If this procedure is not observed, there is a possibility that exposed-conductive-parts and extraneous-conductive-parts may become live during the testing process, thus exposing persons and livestock to the risk of electric shock.

Prior to performing the test, check that the test instrument, and its connections including leads, clips and probes, are in good condition.

Before pressing the button on the test instrument, check that the lamps or LEDs on the instrument indicate that it is safe to proceed. If they do not, investigate and resolve the situation before proceeding.

- Remember that this test is conducted with the supply ON. All necessary precautions must therefore be taken to prevent danger.
- Care must be taken to minimise the risk of electric shock and/or burns when working on or near exposed live terminals. Apply appropriate safety measures, correctly connect the instrument, prevent unauthorised access, perform the test and then switch off the supply on completion of the testing.
- For socket-outlets, as a minimum, perform the test on the outlet which is situated electrically furthest from the origin of the circuit. If this is not known, test all socket-outlets in the circuit and record the highest value. A proprietary test lead with a fitted plug should be used.
- For lighting circuits, as a minimum, Z_S at the electrically furthest point or accessory should be determined. This may be at a luminaire, ceiling rose or in some cases the switch.

The value of Z_S for every circuit must, after adjustment to take into account the heating effects of load current, be sufficiently low to allow the overcurrent device to operate within the maximum time permitted by *BS 7671*, or should not exceed a value which might prevent conformity with the requirements of *BS 7671* relating to RCD-protected circuits.

Maximum earth fault loop impedance values for overcurrent protective devices in common use, for fault protection

MAXIMUM EARTH FAULT LOOP IMPEDANCE VALUES FOR OVERCURRENT PROTECTIVE DEVICES IN COMMON USE, FOR FAULT PROTECTION

For fault protection, the limiting values of earth fault loop impedances, Z_s, are given in Tables 41.2, 41.3 and 41.4 of BS 7671, for many commonly-used overcurrent protective devices.

The values given in those tables are the limits that apply under earth fault conditions, when the temperature of the conductors can be expected to be higher than when testing is undertaken (usually under no-load conditions). Consequently, the values of earth fault loop impedance when measured at ambient temperature should be lower than the limits set out in BS 7671.

It is generally accepted that, where the measured earth fault loop impedance of a circuit is not greater than 80% of the relevant limit specified in BS 7671, the impedance can be expected to be sufficiently low under earth fault conditions to meet the relevant limit specified in BS 7671, and for the protective device to automatically disconnect within the time specified.

The following table gives the limiting values of earth fault loop impedance when measured at ambient temperatures up to 20°C. The limits on measured values, corrected for C_{min}, are 80% of the values given in BS 7671, rounded down. The boxes marked 'N/A' (Not Applicable) indicate either that the overcurrent protective device is not commonly available or that, by virtue of its characteristics, the device is not generally appropriate for fault protection.

The impedance values are based on the 'worst case' limits allowed by BS 7671 and, in certain cases, where the manufacturer of the protective device claims closer limits of fault current necessary for operation of the device than allowed for by the Standard, the values may be modified accordingly.

Where the measured value of the earth fault loop impedance exceeds the relevant tabulated value below, further investigation will be necessary to evaluate the particular circumstances to confirm that compliance with BS 7671 has been achieved.

Limiting values of measured earth fault loop impedances for common overcurrent protective devices, for fault protection, operating at 230 V based on 80 % (approx) of the values given in BS 7671

Rated current (A)	Fuses										Circuit-breakers to BS 3871 or BS EN 60898 or RCBOs to BS EN 61009					
	BS 88 (gG) Parts 2 and 6		BS 1361 or BS 1362		BS 3036		BS 88-2 Fuse systems E (bolted) and G (clip in)		BS 88-3 Fuse system C		Type 1	Type 2	Type B	Types 3 and C	Type D	
	0.4 s	5 s	0.4 s	5 s	0.4 s	5 s	0.4 s	5 s	0.4 s	5 s	0.4 s and 5 s				0.4 s	5 s
2	N/A	N/A	N/A	N/A	N/A	N/A	26.48	34.96	N/A	N/A	N/A	N/A	N/A	N/A	N/A	N/A
3	N/A	N/A	12.46	17.63	N/A	N/A	N/A	N/A	N/A	N/A	N/A	N/A	11.64	N/A	N/A	N/A
4	N/A	N/A	N/A	N/A	N/A	N/A	12.48	16.64	N/A	N/A	N/A	N/A	N/A	N/A	N/A	N/A
5	N/A	N/A	7.94	12.48	7.28	13.44	N/A	N/A	7.94	11.64	8.73	4.99	N/A	3.49	1.74	3.49
6	6.47	10.28	N/A	N/A	N/A	N/A	6.24	9.70	N/A	N/A	7.28	4.16	5.82	2.91	1.45	2.91
10	3.88	5.63	N/A	N/A	N/A	N/A	3.71	5.45	3.71	5.45	4.36	2.49	3.49	1.74	0.87	1.74
13	N/A	N/A	1.83	2.90	N/A	N/A	N/A	N/A	N/A	N/A	N/A	N/A	N/A	N/A	N/A	N/A
15	N/A	N/A	2.49	3.80	1.93	4.06	N/A	N/A	N/A	N/A	2.91	1.66	N/A	1.16	0.57	1.16
16	2.05	3.17	N/A	N/A	N/A	N/A	1.93	3.17	1.84	3.12	2.72	1.56	2.18	1.08	0.54	1.08
20	1.34	2.20	1.28	2.12	1.34	2.91	1.34	2.24	1.54	2.56	2.18	1.24	1.74	0.87	0.43	0.87
25	1.08	1.74	N/A	N/A	N/A	N/A	1.02	1.74	N/A	N/A	1.74	0.99	1.39	0.69	0.34	0.69
30	N/A	N/A	0.87	1.39	0.83	2.00	N/A	N/A	N/A	N/A	1.45	0.83	N/A	0.57	0.28	0.57
32	0.79	1.39	N/A	N/A	N/A	N/A	0.79	1.39	0.72	1.24	1.36	0.77	1.08	0.54	0.27	0.54
40	0.62	1.02	N/A	N/A	N/A	N/A	N/A	1.02	N/A	N/A	1.08	0.62	0.87	0.43	0.21	0.43
45	N/A	N/A	0.43	0.72	0.44	1.20	N/A	N/A	N/A	0.79	0.96	0.55	0.77	0.38	0.19	0.38
50	0.45	0.79	N/A	N/A	N/A	N/A	N/A	0.79	N/A	N/A	0.87	0.49	0.69	0.34	0.16	0.34
60	N/A	N/A	0.28	0.52	0.31	0.84	N/A	N/A	N/A	N/A	N/A	N/A	N/A	N/A	N/A	N/A
63	0.34	0.62	N/A	N/A	N/A	N/A	N/A	0.62	N/A	0.54	0.68	0.39	0.55	0.27	0.13	0.27
80	0.23	0.43	0.21	0.37	N/A	N/A	N/A	0.43	N/A	0.40	0.54	0.31	0.43	0.21	0.10	0.21
100	0.17	0.31	0.14	0.27	0.14	0.40	N/A	0.33	N/A	0.29	0.43	0.24	0.34	0.16	0.08	0.16
125	0.12	0.24	N/A	N/A	N/A	N/A	N/A	0.25	N/A	N/A	N/A	N/A	0.27	0.13	0.06	0.13
160	0.09	0.19	N/A	N/A	N/A	N/A	N/A	0.20	N/A	N/A	N/A	N/A	N/A	N/A	N/A	N/A
200	0.07	0.14	N/A	N/A	N/A	N/A	N/A	0.14	N/A	N/A	N/A	N/A	N/A	N/A	N/A	N/A

This table is included with each pad of certificate and report forms published by NICEIC or ELECSA.

Why do we need to test earth fault loop impedance?

Under earth fault conditions, a circuit which relies on the protective measure ADS for fault protection is generally required to be disconnected under fault conditions within the maximum time permitted by *BS 7671* for that type of circuit or location.

Tables 41.2, 41.3 and 41.4 of *BS 7671* give maximum permitted values of Z_s for different types of overcurrent protective devices and different maximum permitted disconnection times.

It should be appreciated that the tabulated values contained in Tables 41.2, 41.3 and 41.4 of *BS 7671* have been determined using the voltage factor C_{min} (0.95).

It is generally necessary to adjust the values obtained by the test before comparing them with the maximum permitted values given in *BS 7671*. This is because the values referred to in *BS 7671* are based on the conductors having been heated up by the passage of load current, which increases their resistance, whilst test results are usually obtained when the conductor temperature is somewhat lower. As a rule of thumb, the measured value of Z_s should not exceed 0.8 times the relevant value given in *BS 7671*, such as in Tables 41.2, 41.3 and 41.4 (see Appendix 14 of *BS 7671*).

The table shown opposite gives the limiting values of measured earth fault loop impedance when measured at ambient temperatures up to 20 °C. These limiting measured values are based on 80% of the values given in *BS 7671* for 0.4 second and 5 second disconnection, as appropriate.

Note that the value to be recorded in the schedule of test results is the measured value.

If the protective device is not of a type whose maximum permitted Z_s value is given in *BS 7671* then, as a rule of thumb, the measured value should not exceed 0.8 times the value given by the formula on the first page of Appendix 3 of *BS 7671*.

ADDITIONAL PROTECTION

The means of additional protection by supplementary bonding and RCDs as discussed in Chapter 7 are required to be verified for their effectiveness by visual inspection and test:

- Supplementary bonding may be tested by continuity methods previously outlined in this chapter
- RCDs are required to be tested to confirm the relevant requirements of Regulation 415.1.1 are met. Suitable methods of testing are outlined later in the chapter.

Supplementary bonding

Continuity testing as previously outlined in this chapter would be a suitable method of testing.

RCDs - conditions required for a satisfactory test result

General purpose RCDs to *BS 4293,* and RCD-protected socket-outlets to *BS 7288*

Test	Instrument test current setting	Satisfactory result
Test 1	100% of rated operating current	Device should trip in less than 200 ms

RCDs to *BS 4293* (incorporating a time delay)

Test	Instrument test current setting	Satisfactory result
Test 1	100% of rated operating current	Device should trip between 200 ms+ 50% of the time delay and 200 ms+ 100% of the time delay

For example, if the trip has a rated time delay of 100 ms, it should operate between 250 ms and 300 ms

General purpose RCDs to *BS EN 61008,* and RCBOs to *BS EN 61009*

Test	Instrument test current setting	Satisfactory result
Test 1	100% of rated operating current	Device should trip in less than 300 ms

RCDs to *BS EN 61008* and *BS EN 61009* Type 'S'

Test	Instrument test current setting	Satisfactory result
Test 1	100% of rated tripping current	Device should trip between 130 ms and 500 ms

RCDs

RCDs should be tested to confirm that the relevant requirements of Chapter 41 of *BS 7671* are met. Suitable methods of testing are outlined later in this chapter.

VERIFICATION OF PHASE SEQUENCE

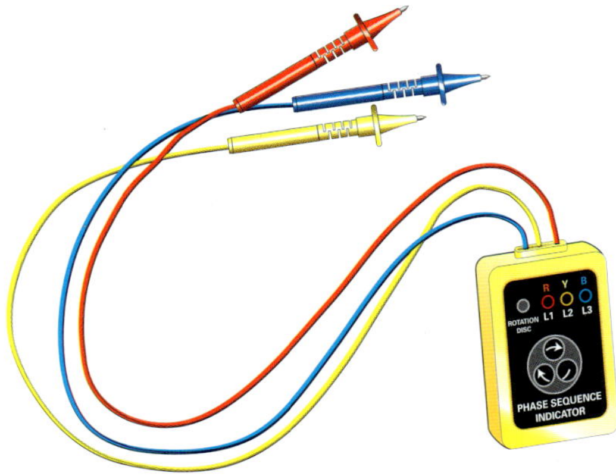

Regulation 612.12 requires a verification that phase sequence has been maintained in polyphase circuits – that is, that the conductor connected to 'L1', 'L2', 'L3 and 'N' at each point throughout the installation is the same as that connected to 'L1', 'L2', 'L3 and 'N' respectively, at the origin of the installation.

The most effective way of achieving this check at the initial verification stage is to carry out a variation of the (R_1 + R_2) continuity of protective conductors test method as described earlier in this chapter, with the instrument set on its lowest range. Before the supply is connected:

- disconnect the conductors at both ends
- temporarily connect the 'L1' conductor to one end to the protective conductor of the circuit under test
- connect one lead of a low resistance ohmmeter to the other end of the 'L1' conductor, and the other lead of the ohmmeter to the protective conductor of the circuit
- a 'low' reading – that is, close to the zero end of the scale, will indicate continuity
- where necessary, identify both ends of the conductor in accordance with Table 51 of *BS 7671*
- terminate the cable into the corresponding terminals at both ends

The above procedure should be repeated for each live conductor of the circuit in turn.

The procedure described above should be carried out for all distribution circuits throughout the installation.

Testing of an RCD

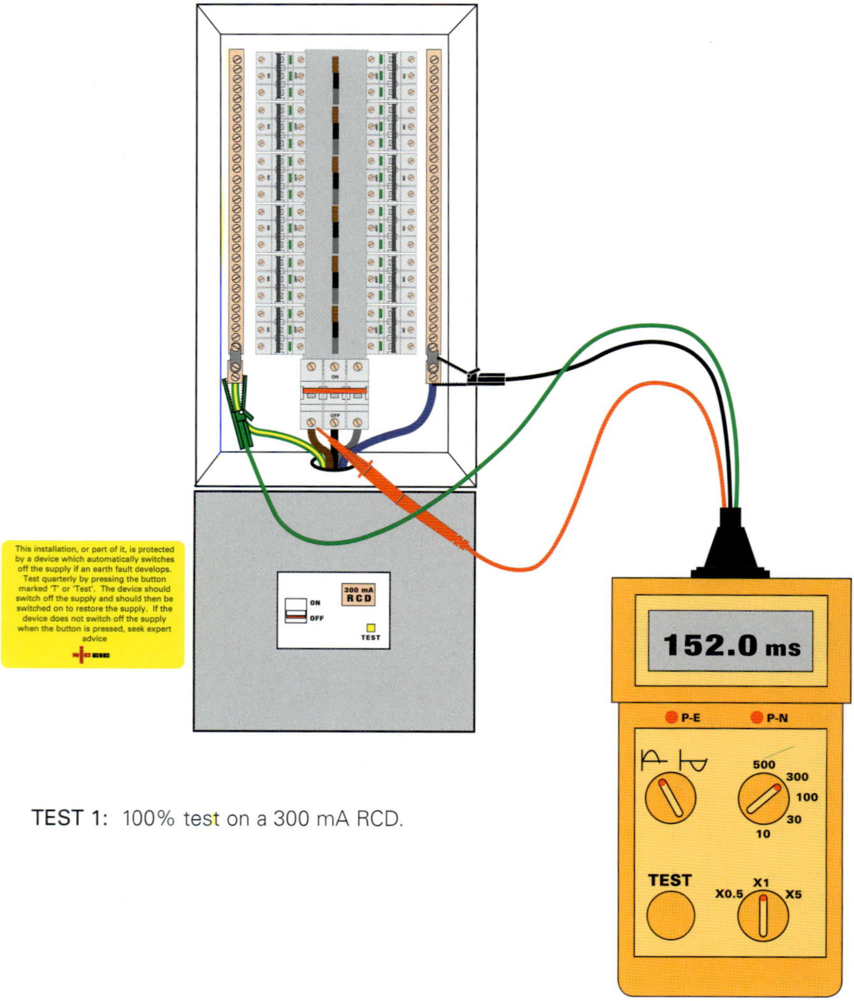

TEST 1: 100% test on a 300 mA RCD.

PHASE ROTATION

A phase rotation instrument utilising either a rotating disc or indicator lamps (or both) can be used to confirm that three-phase equipment, including rotating machines, is connected in the correct sequence or, in the case of motors, rotates in the intended direction.

OPERATION OF RESIDUAL CURRENT DEVICES

Each residual current device must be functionally tested to verify its effectiveness. The procedure comprises two basic parts, namely:

- Simulating an appropriate fault condition using an RCD test instrument.
- Testing the operation of the device by means of the integral test button.

Note: **The test button on the RCD should not be operated until the electrical tests with the RCD test instrument have been completed, as this may influence the electrical test results.**

Test instrument

The RCD test instrument should be capable of applying the full range of currents required to test the RCD in question, and of displaying the time, in milliseconds (ms), taken for the device to operate. For reasons of safety, the test instrument will normally automatically limit the duration of the test to a maximum of 2 seconds.

Testing of an RCD which incorporates an intentional time delay will only be possible if the test instrument is capable of providing a test duration which exceeds the permitted maximum operating time of the RCD. Owing to the variability of time delay, it is not possible to specify a maximum test duration, but 2 seconds should normally be found sufficient in practice.

Test procedure

- The RCD test instrument should not be used unless it has first been established that the earth fault loop impedance of the circuit is sufficiently low to satisfy the requirements of *BS 7671* for the RCD to be tested. That is to say, the loop impedance in ohms, when multiplied by the rated residual operating current of the device in amperes, must in general not exceed 50 V.
- Contact by persons or livestock with exposed-conductive-parts or extraneous-conductive-parts of the installation must be prevented during the test. This is because potentially dangerous voltages may appear on these parts during the testing procedure.

Testing of an RCD

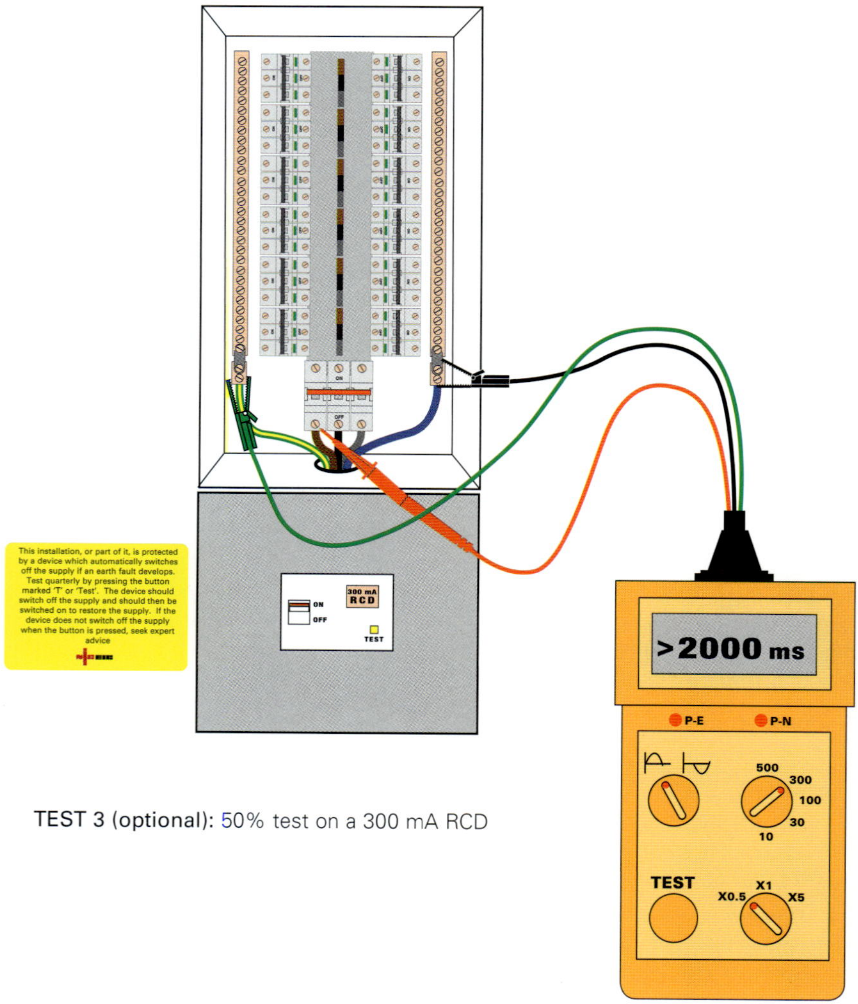

TEST 3 (optional): 50% test on a 300 mA RCD

- The test instrument is connected to the line, neutral and earth on the load side of the RCD, with the load disconnected. The connection can be made at any convenient point in the circuit, such as a socket-outlet or, using a split 3-lead connection incorporating probes, at the outgoing terminals of the device. If the supply is 2 or 3-phase with no neutral connection available, the earth and neutral probes should both be connected to the protective earth. If the test instrument has a facility to indicate whether or not polarity is correct, testing should proceed only where correct polarity is being indicated.
- Many RCD test instruments have a facility whereby tests can be carried out during the positive or negative half-cycles of the supply waveform in turn. For tests 1 and 2 below, the operating time to be noted is the longer of those measured during the positive and negative half cycle tests.

Test 1

Adjust the current setting to 100% of the rated operating (tripping) current of the device, push the button on the test instrument and note the time taken for the RCD to operate (See illustration on page 278).

> This installation, or part of it, is protected by a device which automatically switches off the supply if an earth fault develops. Test quarterly by pressing the button marked 'T' or 'Test'. The device should switch off the supply and should then be switched on to restore the supply. If the device does not switch off the supply when the button is pressed, seek expert advice

The measured operating time(s) should be compared with the appropriate value(s) in the tables shown earlier in this Chapter, which relate to the type-tests carried out under specified conditions by RCD manufacturers in accordance with the relevant product standards.

Despite manufacturers' recommendations and the presence of the notice required by *BS 7671*, RCDs may not have been operated by the users at quarterly intervals, by means of the 'test' button on the RCD. If, during a periodic inspection, a device does not trip within the expected time (including failing to trip at all) when first subjected to a test current equal to the rated operating (tripping) current, but operates satisfactorily when subjected to such a test subsequently (perhaps after manual switching), an appropriate observation and recommendation should be made on the report.

If the inspector considers that the result of the subsequent test is satisfactory and indicates the operating characteristic had the device been operated at quarterly intervals as intended, it would be in order to record the result of the subsequent test, subject to the related observation and recommendation. In particular, the attention of the recipient of the report should be drawn to the safety implications of not operating the device at quarterly intervals.

Test 2

An RCD provided for additional protection should have a rated residual operating (tripping) current $I_{\Delta n}$ not exceeding 30 mA. Regulation 415.1.1 requires that, when type-tested under specified conditions in accordance with the relevant product standards, such RCDs must operate in a time not exceeding 40 ms at a residual current of 5 $I_{\Delta n}$.

When testing an installed RCD of this type using an RCD test instrument, the RCD should normally not be considered to be in a satisfactory condition unless it operates in a time not exceeding 40 ms when subjected to a residual (test) current of 5 $I_{\Delta n}$.

It should be noted, however, that some RCDs intended to provide additional protection are designed such that they operate under type-test conditions in a time only marginally less than 40 ms at a residual operating current of 5 $I_{\Delta n}$. Such RCDs may operate under installed conditions in a time marginally exceeding 40 ms at 5 $I_{\Delta n}$. If in doubt about the acceptability of measured RCD operating times, the inspector should consult the manufacturer to help determine whether the RCD(s) should be replaced.

Test 3 (optional)

- Adjust the current setting on the test instrument to 50% of the rated operating (tripping) current of the device. (See illustration on page 280).
- Push the button on the test instrument and wait.
- The RCD should not operate.

Note: Where there is no neutral connection available, and the neutral probe of the test instrument is connected to protective earth as previously described, there is a consequent increase in the residual current, which may cause the RCD to operate during **Test 3**. If this occurs, the manufacturer of the RCD should be consulted about the operating parameters of the device in order to establish whether it is or is not faulty.

The test button

Following the electrical test procedure described above, each RCD should be operated by means of its integral test facility. This confirms that the device is responding to its design level of sensitivity and that all the mechanical parts are functioning. The users of installations are advised (by means of a notice at or near the origin of the installations - see Regulation 514.12.2) to carry out this simple test at quarterly intervals, but it is not a substitute for the electrical test procedure as described.

VERIFICATION OF VOLTAGE DROP

Verification of voltage drop is not normally required during the initial verification of either a new installation or an alteration or addition to an existing installation. This is because the designer of the electrical work should have sized the circuit conductors so that the voltage drop requirements of Section 525 of *BS 7671* are met, having regard to the circuit lengths and design currents.

However, in the case of the periodic inspection and testing of an existing installation, the inspector may judge it necessary to verify the voltage drop for a particular circuit (or circuits), if he or she has doubts that the voltage drop requirements of Section 525 are met for the circuit (Regulation 612.14 refers). This may be the case, for example, where there is evidence that a circuit has been extended or that additional load has been connected to it.

A detailed explanation of the voltage drop requirements of Section 525 is beyond the scope of this book. However, as given in Regulation 525.202, the requirements of Section 525 are deemed to be met if the voltage drop between the origin of the installation (usually the supply terminals) and a socket-outlet or the terminals of fixed current-using equipment does not exceed that stated in Section 6.4 of Appendix 4 of *BS 7671*. For a low voltage installation supplied directly from a public low voltage distribution system, Section 6.4 of Appendix 4 gives maximum voltage drops of 3 % for lighting circuits and 5 % for other circuits. Greater voltage drops than given in Section 6.4 may be accepted for a motor during starting periods and for other equipment with high in-rush currents provided it is verified that it is acceptable for the equipment (Regulation 525.203 refers).

Regulation 612.14 lists the following two ways to verify the voltage drop for a circuit.

- Evaluate the voltage drop by measuring the circuit impedance
- Evaluate the voltage drop using calculations

Evaluation of voltage drop by measuring circuit impedance (worked example)

Suppose that it is desired to verify that the voltage drop does not exceed 5 % in an existing single-phase 230 V, 50 Hz radial circuit supplying a 20 A heating load connected at the end of the circuit. The circuit is supplied directly from a distribution board at the origin of the installation. The line and neutral conductors of the circuit have thermoplastic (pvc) insulation and their resistance (R_1+R_n) is 0.3 Ω when measured at ambient temperature (say 20 °C).

As the circuit rating does not exceed 100 A and the supply frequency is 50 Hz, (R_1+R_n) may be taken to be the circuit impedance (that is, inductive reactance may be ignored).

To evaluate the voltage drop, the measured value of (R_1+R_n) should be increased on the basis of the increase in conductor temperature due to load current, and then multiplied by the design current of the circuit (I_b). In the absence of better information, a correction factor of 1.2 should be used to increase the conductor resistance in this case. This assumes an increase in conductor temperature from 20 °C (ambient) to 70 °C (the maximum permitted operating temperature for thermoplastic insulated conductors).

The voltage drop (V_D) for the single-phase circuit in this example is therefore given by:

V_D = measured value of $(R_1+R_n) \times 1.2 \times I_b$

Therefore $V_D = 0.3\ \Omega \times 1.2 \times 20\ A = 7.2\ V$.

A voltage drop of 7.2 V is equivalent to 3.13 % (given by 100 % x 7.2 V ÷ 230 V). It has therefore been verified that, in the case of this example, the voltage drop in the circuit does not exceed 5 %.

Evaluation of voltage drop using calculations (worked example)

The calculation method mentioned in Regulation 612.14, as an example, is to use diagrams or graphs showing maximum cable length versus load current for different conductor sizes with different percentage voltage drops for specific nominal voltages, conductor temperatures and wiring systems.

In the absence of such diagrams or charts, the voltage drop for a circuit may be calculated by using the tabulated values of voltage drop given in Appendix 4 of *BS 7671*, in accordance with the instructions given in Section 6 of that appendix. To do this, it will be necessary to ascertain the type and size of cable by inspection, and to estimate the length of run for the circuit.

FUNCTIONAL TESTING OF ASSEMBLIES

All equipment should be checked to ensure that it functions as intended, and has been properly mounted, adjusted and installed in accordance with the relevant requirements of *BS 7671*.

Switching and controlling devices and systems should be checked for correct operation. Motors, motor drives and starters should be checked, along with lamps, luminaires and all equipment that forms part of the electrical installation. The inspector should not sign the Electrical Installation Certificate, the Domestic Electrical Installation Certificate, the Minor Electrical Installation Works Certificate, the Electrical Installation Condition Report or the Domestic Electrical Installation Condition Report, until it has been established that all equipment has been properly mounted, adjusted and tested for satisfactory operation.

Where there is any doubt as to the intended method of controlling any part of an installation (such as a control system), the inspector should consult the designer of the installation or, for an existing installation, the user, if appropriate.